Capital and Labour
Redefined

Capital and Labour Redefined

India and the Third World

Amiya Kumar Bagchi

Anthem Press
London

Anthem Press is an imprint of
Wimbledon Publishing Company
PO Box 9779
London SW19 7QA

This edition first published by Wimbledon Publishing Company 2002

© Amiya Kumar Bagchi

First published by Tulika, India (hardback) 2002

All rights reserved. No part of this publication may be reproduced, stored in a retrieval system, or transmitted, in any form or by any means, without the prior permission in writing of Wimbledon Publishing Company, or as expressly permitted by law, or under terms agreed with the appropriate reprographics rights organization.

British Library Cataloguing in Publication Data
Data available

ISBN
1 84331 068 6 (hbk)
1 84331 069 4 (pbk)

1 3 5 7 9 10 8 6 4 2

Printed by Newton Printing Ltd, London, UK.   www.newtonprinting.com

Contents

Acknowledgement	vii
Capital and Labour at the Dawn of the Twenty-first Century	ix

History and Nature of the Indian Bourgeoisie

The Economics of Business and the Business of Economics	3
Merchants and Colonialism	17
Reflections on the Nature of the Indian Bourgeoisie	71
Colonialism and the Nature of 'Capitalist' Enterprise in India	91

Labour in the Toils of Colonial and Global Capital

The Ambiguity of Progress: Indian Society in Transition	139
Wealth and Work in Calcutta: 1860–1921	156
Working-Class Consciousness	176
Dualism and Dialectics in the Historiography of Labour	201
Neo-liberal Economic Reforms and Workers of the Third World: At the End of the Second Millennium of the Christian Era	241

Multiculturalism, Communalism and the Bourgeoisie

Predatory Commercialization and
Communalism in India   263

Multiculturalism, Governance and the
Indian Bourgeoisie   292

Index   321

Acknowledgement

The idea that this collection of essays should be put together originated with Tulika, especially its moving spirit (fortunately in a wonderfully corporeal form), Indira Chandrasekhar. The friendship of many other persons in India and abroad was necessary for me to write these papers in the first place, and their enthusiasm for seeing them re-published in an easily accessible form induced me to put them together. I thank all those friends for their encouragement. But the readers should not blame them if the outcome shows their enthusiasm to have been misplaced.

Capital and Labour at the Dawn of the Twenty-first Century

The Threat to Life and Liberty Posed by *Bungalow–Chawl–Haveli* Capitalism

As I write the introduction to this selection of my essays, one barbarism based on an unbounded faith in the supremacy of capital and the white race is fighting, with weapons of mass destruction, another barbarism based on an unbounded faith in a backward-looking interpretation of a great world religion. The barbarism of the Talibans was sedulously fostered by the same cowboys of the west, as suitably led and represented by President George W. Bush, in order to defeat the most systematic challenge capital ever faced—the challenge of a power that professed to base its policies on the theories of Marx, Engels and Lenin. The most fearsome war machines of history wielded by the US imperialists are pounding the caves and hovels of perhaps the poorest country in the world. In the name of restoring human civilization, they are pitilessly killing infants, mothers, and the old and the sick, in their rubbles of homes and their rudimentary hospitals. All this is being done under the Swiftian code name, Operation Enduring Freedom.

As the operation is launched in its full fury, the Nobel Committee awards its prize for peace to Koffi Annan, the Secretary General of the United Nations, who acts as a not-so-mute witness to the US-led aggression against Afghanistan. The attack was launched from the soil of a dictator-ruled Pakistan. The Pakistani government has had to severely repress domestic public opinion in order to allow the US government to launch its genocidal attack. In yet another land in Asia, Israeli soldiers are daily destroying homes, hospitals and schools, and killing innocents, in support of forcible occupation of the lands of the rightful dwellers, and in revenge for the killing of a few of the guilty murderers. This is happening in a state that was supposedly born of a revulsion against Nazism and Teutonic racism. The major media of the world are cheering this brutal genocide. The protesters are not given any newspaper or television coverage in most countries. The central government in India has formed part of the entourage of cheerleaders, thus conniving at the criminal immorality of punishing the innocent without being able to catch hold of the guilty. But the rulers and their supporters in India also seem to be unaware of the fact that the same war machines can be turned against the citizens of India when the racist rulers of the USA and Britain decide that it is the Indians who have now to pay the price for some injury for which they are unable to fix the responsibility.

Such is the state to which globally triumphant capitalism has reduced the world, and such is the state of political and moral impotence that characterizes the current rulers of a country that is marked by a malformed capitalism carrying the diseases of feudal, colonial and tribal social relations and power structures within its body-politic.

The relations between labour and capital, between peasants and landlords, between transnational corporations and producers enclosed in gleaming battery-factories or toiling in slums and pestiferous workshops, and murdering, racist rulers in the White House or Downing Street or scheming communalists in New Delhi, Mumbai or Lucknow acting as watchdogs of capital, are all part of a global order of unequal interdependence. This global order, however, is not seamless, however much the media barons might proclaim that a buyer of Coca Cola in the shanty-towns of Bogota or Mumbai is the equal of an American presidential candidate patriotically quaffing from the same symbol of US monopoly capital. For the latter Coca Cola is a symbol of Yankee power over the world; for the slum-dweller it is an expression of denial of consumer choice by the sovereignty of transnational capital.

My effort has always been directed at uncovering the seams in the facade of capital, and finding out where the facade may be fractured or crumbling, if not now, in a decade or a generation. For, without some sense that the global order is all the time threatened by internal contradictions and has to be mended continually by its beneficiaries, it would seem to be hopeless to try to tear it apart, so as to lessen the injustice that is continually being heaped on the majority of human beings.

In their *Communist Manifesto* (1848) Karl Marx and Friedrich Engels had predicted that capitalism would dissolve all 'natural', human relations. That prediction has come true everywhere. But capitalism has also transformed some of those relations and subordinated them to its use, such as patriarchy in virtually all the family structures inherited down to the twentieth century. Capitalism has also made the amorphous, rudimentary racialism of earlier civilizations into a leading principle of differentiation and government.

I have elsewhere characterized the social formation in India as *bungalow–chawl–haveli* capitalism, or BCH capitalism (Bagchi 1999a). I now think that this is not an inappropriate epithet for global capitalism. Let me try to explain the structure of this social formation, and then I will specify some of the causal relations linking them. The *bungalow* was the favoured type of residence of British officials and merchants in colonial India. It was adapted from a typical *atchala* of Bengal, but it was very clearly differentiated from the original in terms of the materials used and the furnishings inside. This was the locus of control of foreign capital spreading into all the remote districts of India. This can now be taken as the locus of control of transnational capital everywhere, whether it operates out of downtown New York, the gleaming glass-cages of the City of London, or the enormously expensive offices of the overcrowded metropolis of Mumbai. Foreignness and necessary adaptation to the local environment continue to characterize the management styles of transnational capital and its clones among the aspiring *nouveau riche* of third-world countries (For a description of the spread of transnational capital in the different regions of India as of the early 1990s, see Banerjee-Guha 1997.)

The *chawls* of Mumbai and their counterparts in cities, towns, shanty-towns, squatter-settlements, or Dalit or 'black' or 'native' quarters all over the world, shelter the proletariat, without whom capitalism would wither and disappear. Spokesmen of capitalism have harboured an ambiguous attitude towards the life and freedom of the proletariat from the time the European incarnation of capitalism with its armed competition spread out to conquer and penetrate the rest of the world. On the one hand, capital wanted labour to be free of its traditional bondages such as serfdom, debt peonage and custom-bound slavery and bondage. Such freedom and the expropriation of the means of production of the producers by capital and the capital-friendly state would deliver up the proletariat for unlimited exploitation by capital. On the other hand, whenever the exploitable mass of the proletariat has been considered insufficient by capital, it has never hesitated to enslave them at the location, or abduct them forcibly and reduce them to the status of slaves, or indenture them and subject them to slavery in all but name. Thus arose systems of indentured labour transported from Europe, the grotesquely massive flows of Africans enslaved and transported across the Atlantic in the age of the European Enlightenment, and the scarcely less oppressive system of indentured labour transported from India and China in the age of the triumph of liberalism in Europe. Of course, from the late eighteenth century, 'free' workers were subjected to the discipline of mines, workshops and factories, and their lives were regulated almost to the minutest detail as Taylorism and Fordism came to be the organizing instruments wielded by management. The real civil and political freedom had to be fought for by the working class from well before the rise of the factory system (Linebaugh and Rediker 2000). That struggle continues with scarcely less abated intensity today even if management seems to have the upper hand in this phase of rich man's globalization.

Many third-world countries are ruled by democratic systems, although the majority still have only either a straightforward dictatorship, as in the sheikhdoms of West Asia, or a semi-democratic system in which elections are rigged or in which only one party or one coalition is effectively allowed to contest the elections, as in Peru, Paraguay or Zimbabwe. But even in systems in which rulers are chosen through regularly held elections, workers—especially in the so-called informal sector—do not enjoy even basic civil rights, such as easy access to the legal system, and freedom from harassment or torture by the police or the strongmen of the village or the urban slum. (cf. O'Donnell 2001 on the Latin American situation; many novels or stories of Mahasveta Devi, Anita Agnihotri and other littérateurs have depicted the situation more vividly than the dry prose

Introduction

of a social scientist can). The workers enjoy few 'social rights', such as the right to a decent subsistence, security from starvation, or protection against illness or disability, whether in youth or old age. The deprivation in these directions has become more glaring with the onward march of liberalization. The relative size of the formal sector in which workers enjoyed some of these social rights has been shrinking, and even within the formal sector many of these rights are being abridged in the name of labour market reforms. Thus, the right to vote has been stripped of a real access of democracy in workers' lives in most countries of the third world and, increasingly, of the first world as well.

If capital has shown its double-dealing nature in the case of workers' freedom, its duplicity and ambiguity with regard to their physical well-being and survival have been equally pronounced during the five centuries that capital has sought to re-arrange the world to suit its own needs. Francis Bacon, that loyal if blatantly corrupt official of the Tudor kings of England, and the justly celebrated theorist of empirically-oriented scientific investigation, advocated genocide for 'the many-headed Hydra'—meaning the rebellious proletariat—when the latter would appear to threaten the sacred order of propertied power (Linebaugh and Rediker 2000: 36–40). At the same time, of course, a plentiful and cheap supply of labour has been a potent instrument of competition wielded by capital. Bernard Mandeville, a fierce advocate of private vices (such as greed for ever-increasing quantities and varieties of consumer goods and luxuries) as a means of promoting public virtue, wanted wages to be low and labour to remain uneducated so that its docility would be ensured (Mandeville 1724/1989). In one of his many incarnations, Daniel Defoe, the archetypal journalist, author and informer, strongly opposed the idea that the poor should be given relief when they were without work, for they would not put in an honest day's work if they could subsist without work (*Giving Alms not Charity and Employing the Poor Grievance to the Nation* [1704], as quoted by Polanyi 1944/1957:108–09). But in later writings, when he was trying to proclaim the supremacy of English woollen textiles in intra-European trade, he argued against a policy of depressing wages as an instrument of competition, for this would tend to lower the morale and the productivity of the true-born Englishman. As it turned out, real wages remained depressed in England throughout the period of the rise of the factory system, and began their secular rise only from the middle of the nineteenth century.

Not only have wages been depressed through competition and state policy under the sway of capital, often going below the level at which a family could be reproduced on the wages of the adult earners of the family (so that children had to assist in the struggle for subsistence)—life itself has been weighed in the capitalists' balance against profits and has been found wanting. Thomas Robert Malthus was neither the first writer nor the only one to proclaim that the poor and the less-than-civilized peoples of the world bred too much for the rich man's comfort. Even those spokesmen of a hierarchical order of society who may be unaware of the Malthusian doctrine of population share the Malthusian prejudice, namely, that if the poor are given decent wages they will squander them all through procreation, thereby reducing their own breed to the same level of penury as before, and in the process burdening the state, society and nature itself with the problem of feeding that multitude and keeping it in order so that the civilized can lead a decent life.

The Venetian monk Giammaria Ortes, writing in 1777, and the English parson Joseph Townsend, writing in 1786, both saw hunger as the great disciplinarian, keeping the poor subservient to the hierarchical social order (for the relevant citations, see Marx 1886/1965: 646–47). The current proponents of 'flexible wages' with no protection for wages, job security or conditions of work of the workers are following the trampling treads of Mandeville, Ortes, Townsend and Malthus.

It is not accidental that all these predecessors lived in a Europe in which the feudal culture was very much alive, even if the oligarchy of Venice grew out of merchant princes and the English landlords embraced mercantile transactions as a way of furthering their interest. For, the third of the triad I have mentioned, viz., the *haveli*, is not only easily recognizable in India, but a new *avatar* of the *haveli* is now seeking to bring the whole world under its domination. The characteristic of an Indian *haveli* is that its denizens know the use of the bank (or the *gaddi*) and the marketplace but do not want either of them to be freely accessible to everybody. The use of

Introduction

non-market coercion and the regulation of market competition in the interest of the *haveli*-dwellers is a practice hallowed and renewed under the semi-feudal democracy India inherited. In the current order of global capitalism, transnational corporations have emerged as the regulators of lives everywhere.

Commentators as different in their political orientation as Noam Chomsky, the great linguist, and Sir John Sulston, a major figure in the decoding of the human genome and a former director of the Sanger Centre of Cambridge, have characterized it as 'corporate feudalism' (Chomsky 1998, 2001; *Statesman* 2001). In a number of his writings, Chomsky has pointed out that corporations do not like competition and try to thwart it in every way possible. The so-called property rights that international law and most written constitutions of the world and court decisions seek to protect, as he has also pointed out, are the rights of people with property. A very large part of the property of the rich was not obtained through competition in the marketplace but through the forcible usurpation of the land and other possessions of the ordinary people (witness, for example, the property in land of the whites in South Africa or Zimbabwe). Moreover, corporations have pressurized the international bodies to create private property in objects which were earlier free for everybody to use: 'intellectual property rights' are a leading example of such corporate usurpation. Sulston, no raving radical himself, was protesting against the monopolization of the use of the human genome or its parts by private corporations, a process that seriously hampers research and use of scientific knowledge for human welfare. So, old-style feudalism now co-exists with corporate feudalism. The USA has emerged as the chief *kotwal* or policeman for preserving and extending the power of that feudalism. The fortress of the *haveli* now threatens the whole world: its henchmen can kill or maim people in their thousands—with immunity—in Nicaragua, Sudan, Iraq, Afghanistan, or Bhopal, for that matter. The so-called National Missile Defence that is being constructed by the USA despite the opposition of some of its own allies has the potential of finishing off the career of the whole human race on earth.

Indian capital may have embraced liberalization (or 'economic reforms') in the fond hope that it will compete in the global marketplace, and will be strengthened by the inflow of foreign funds into its domestic turf. The controllers of the global order of corporate feudalism knew otherwise, and decreed accordingly. They faced little resistance from the Indian rulers because the society they presided over remained steeped in illiteracy and ill-health, and oppressed by landlordism, usurious capital and patriarchy. More than fifty years after Independence, literacy rates in India remain far lower than in any country of East and Southeast Asia and all the major nations of Latin America, not to speak of the affluent capitalist nations. The average longevity of Indians, though much higher than at the time of Independence, fell short of the average longevity in Japan, North America, western Europe, or such countries as Cuba or Sri Lanka, by between ten and eighteen years. Access to public health and education facilities were denied to the poor, and especially to women, in virtually all the north Indian states that had earlier been ruled by the Congress and have now come under the domination of the Bharatiya Janata Party. Uttar Pradesh is the most populous (accounting for a sixth of the Indian population) and politically the most important state, since it has produced all the Indian Prime Ministers, barring one, who ruled for at least one full term. But it ranked below the all-India average in respect of education, health, women's status in society and industrialization.

Such an environment in a continent-scale country is an unlikely candidate for producing a dynamic capitalism—with or without liberalization. Most of the 'business maharajas' that some enthusiasts tried to talk up into glory became like the Maharajas in the so-called 'native states' of British India. They occupied their gaudy *masnads* on sufferance of big capital, but the latter steadily encroached on their domain. In 1991, as a result of six years of almost deliberate mismanagement of fiscal policy by its rulers, India got into a balance-of-payments crisis. Then, with the eager cooperation of the mandarins of the Ministry of Finance, the International Monetary Fund extended a loan to the government of India with the usual conditionalities. The industrial licensing system was abolished—a measure that could have stimulated competition among Indian firms and accelerated industrial growth. But this measure was accompanied by a red-carpet treatment of foreign capital. Within a period of five years or so, practically all the restrictions on portfolio or direct foreign investment were lifted, and the government encouraged the growth of a market for corporate control. The rupee depreciated rapidly against all hard currencies, and the domestic rate of interest remained far above the rates prevailing in international markets. Naturally, foreign firms enjoyed a large advantage in terms of financing costs over Indian firms. They, of course, also enjoyed the enormous advantage of control of frontier technologies and an R & D apparatus capable of churning out new technologies. Indian private concerns, on the other hand, had invested little in R & D, and most of them remained abjectly dependent on foreign suppliers of foreign technology. One result was the collapse of many Indian industrial firms and the take-over of a host of local firms and joint ventures by foreign companies. In the period 1994–98, in fifteen major product groups accounting for virtually the whole organized industrial sector under private ownership, while foreign firms or companies controlled by non-resident Indians accounted for 237 acquisitions of Indian firms, only in sixteen cases did Indian firms acquire any foreign or joint-venture firms operating in India (Dasgupta 1999: Table 3.3).

The 'reformers' in India have never put on their agenda some of the basic conditions for stimulating economic development on a sustained basis, let alone the development of the human capabilities of every Indian, which must, after all, be the *raison d'etre* of pursuit of a strategy of economic growth. These basic conditions include thoroughgoing, pro-peasant land reforms, abolition of most of the grosser forms of discrimination based on caste or religious affiliation, according of equal rights to men and women in respect of civil rights, property rights and access to public services, and implementation of a programme for universal literacy and steady improvement in the standard of education acquired by the majority (for a discussion of these requirements, see Bagchi 1987, 1993, 1998).

It is, of course, implausible that in the vast countryside or small towns of India, social change is entirely dependent on the intentions of the upholders of the status quo or on the agenda of conscious political or social activists. A very large part of the turmoil caused by the acceptance of or resistance to the recommendations of the Mandal Commission that provided for extensive reservation of public employment for the so-called Other Backward Castes was, for example, itself precipitated by the emergence of some of these castes as important players in the economy and politics of Uttar Pradesh, Bihar and other parts of north India. (It is often forgotten that such reservations had been operative in southern India and Maharashtra for more than a half-century before the Mandal Commission-related agitations in 1990–91). To take another instance, the fixing of the price of rice at Rs 2 a kilogram—much lower than the ruling market price—by N.T. Rama Rao's government in Andhra Pradesh may have raised the real earnings and hence the bargaining power of agricultural labourers and marginal farmers vis-à-vis the 'big men' of the villages in that state. Contrariwise, the 'prosperity effect' of the enrichment of land-holding groups by the green revolution may have strengthened patriarchy in states like Haryana and Gujarat (Chowdhury 1994; Agnihotri 2000). As we shall see, social change by means other than principled egalitarianism has imposed enormous costs in terms of serious failures of governance, starting from the villages or forest settlements of the Adivasis up to the central ruling apparatus in New Delhi.

The liberalizers in India have not attempted to carry out the necessary tasks of social transformation, except in a very half-hearted way in some cases. They have not tried either to bring about necessary legal and institutional reforms that closely affect the operation of capitalist enterprises. Take, for example, the operation of the stock exchange. When the office of the Controller of Capital Issues who regulated public offerings in the stock exchange was abolished, the government did not empower the Securities and Exchange Board of India (SEBI) with the necessary authority to regulate the operations of brokers, promoters and other firms involved in transactions in bonds and equities. I had predicted in June 1991 in an article published in the *Business and Political Observer* that since the government had not assumed the necessary regulatory powers and since Indian stock-brokers are not celebrated for possessing clean hands, there would be mayhem in the share market. Before my words were one-month old, a boom erupted in the stock market—a boom that collapsed in May 1992 as the Harshad Mehta scam came to light. The then Indian Finance Minister, when questioned about the expanding bubble in the stock markets, declared that he will not lose his sleep just because the stock market was booming. In fact, when the boom collapsed, thousands of small

Introduction

investors lost their hard-earned savings, and Rs 6,000 crore (60 billion) worth of money lent by banks vanished without any trace. Among the biggest losers were the public sector banks, including the State Bank of India and the National Housing Bank. The chairman of the latter, a trusted advisor of the central government and chairman of a body to look into the modalities of new stock exchanges, died under mysterious circumstances. The stock market went through a boom between 1992–93 and 1995–96, but the primary market for equities virtually disappeared after 1997 (Bagchi 2000: 132). There was another mini-boom sparked by information technology company shares between 2000 and 2001, but it ended again with the Ketan Parekh-UTI (Unit Trust of India) scam in 2001. The scam again showed up the ineffectiveness of SEBI as a monitoring organization. But more sinisterly, it was suspected that the Finance Ministry had egged the UTI (a government-controlled mutual fund—the oldest and the biggest in India) to invest in hundreds of companies that were not even listed on the stock exchange. This was done as a ploy for boosting confidence just before the central budget of 2001–02 and, in the process, also lining the pockets of the cronies of the ruling politicians. The profits of the UTI were badly eroded by these goings-on, and holders of its flagship scheme US-64 were denied redemption. However, big corporate houses had inside knowledge of the impending crisis and sold their holdings to the UTI at the inflated prices. This further aggravated the liquidity crisis of the mutual fund.

Under the regime that has prevailed since Independence, the major part of finance for both working capital and fixed investment of non-bank firms has been provided by banks. One of the aims of the liberalizers was to bring down the proportion of bank finance in the total liabilities of firms and to raise that of equity finance. The feebleness of the primary market in shares has defeated that objective. At the same time, the laxness of supervision of the Banking Department of the Ministry of Finance and the Reserve Bank of India for decades together has led to the accumulation of a mountain of non-performing assets by nationalized banks. The culpability of the supervisory authorities is compounded by the complexities of the *Mitakshara* variety of Hindu personal law, and the laws relating to religious trusts. These laws allow debtors to escape liability by showing their assets as property of kin or a particular deity or religious foundation. The combination of complex personal and property laws, the company law and income tax legislation, and the use of *benami* (anonymous or proxy) transactions have been exploited by the major wealth-holders to cheat the government of its due taxes, to cheat the banks of their dues on loans, to deprive the workers of their hard-won provident fund or other retirement benefits, and even their wages. The major public sector banks are saddled with huge burdens of non-performing assets, and the central government has sought to bolster them by infusing new capital into their balance-sheets. However, the government has weakened its own fiscal capacity by making indulgent concessions to the rich and refusing to punish the big tax-evaders. Hence its capacity to recapitalize the banks has been badly eroded. Moreover, when the global economy and the Indian economy have entered into a period of recession, the collaterals pledged to the banks have depreciated in value, and good projects have often turned into sticky loans. The advocates of financial liberalization have never grasped that merging of all money and capital markets, and securitization of all assets and liabilities, lead to an enormous increase in systemic risk, although even the General Manager of the Bank for International Settlement has tried to hammer this point home (Crockett 2001).

At the end of the 1990s, as a fall-out of the so-called economic reforms, the Indian capitalist class has become almost as subservient to global capital as during the colonial period. The eminent Marxist historian D.D. Kosambi had reviewed Jawaharlal Nehru's *Discovery of India* (1946) under the heading, 'The bourgeoisie comes of age in India' (Kosambi 1946). The policies adopted by the government of the newly-independent country, especially those of increasing public investment in various infrastructural and production sectors and simultaneously promoting domestic private industry, appeared to strengthen the Indian bourgeoisie. However, the contradictions of a virtually unreformed social structure and a political process largely dominated by landlords, upper castes and capitalists soon corrupted the planning process and increasingly incapacitated Indian capital for competing in the arena of global capitalism, except in the fields of drugs and pharmaceuticals and some narrow areas of capital goods and transport industries. Hence, unfortunately, the adulthood proclaimed by Kosambi has proved ultimately to be the prolongation of a stunted adolescence, and the Indian people are paying a heavy price for being under the heel of such a dependent ruling class.

Indian Capital in the Embrace of Liberalization

From the 1930s, peasant movements in colonial India had been directed against the rule of landlords in the countryside. The communists and the left-leaning sections of the Indian National Congress had agitated in favour of giving land to the tiller, and improving the share and the security of tenure of sharecroppers, where the land was tilled by the latter. The J.C. Kumarappa Committee, appointed by the Congress Party at the time of Independence, had recommended the abolition of revenue-farming (that was embodied in the *zamindari* and *taluqdari* settlements) and allowing only actual cultivators to own and operate land. But due to the opposition of landlords in Bihar, Uttar Pradesh and other states, and court decisions in their favour, the ruling party confined itself to abolition of revenue-farming and virtually jettisoned the 'land-to-the tiller' part of the agrarian reforms agenda (Thorner 1976; Ghose 1983).

The decision to retain landlordism by other names impeded the growth of market-oriented production under the control of the actual cultivators, and hence stymied necessary changes in crop patterns and technology except in areas in which actual cultivators were already in control. It also had a deleterious effect on governance and legality in independent India. The entrenched land-holders and the upper castes to which they belonged had been allowed by the British administration to effectively police the countryside in their own interest, so long as they did not threaten the Raj itself. After Independence, as the agenda of the state was broadened, the lineages of caste leaders, landlords and patrons also extended their reach. When the abolition of revenue-farming led to the vesting of part of the *zamindari* land and forests in the state, the new power-brokers effectively brought much of that public land under their private control. Since this could not be done through strictly legal means, laws were violated all the way, and electoral means were sometimes used to retrospectively sanction those violations. The misuse of the properties accruing to the state, through the break-up of the rich *zamindari* estates of northern Bihar by the governing elites, is a tragic illustration of this process. But similar processes can be observed in the case of the properties of most 'native states' and big *zamindars* in erstwhile British India.

The dominant caste or landlord lineages not only took over public property in the name of the state—by virtue of their vested position, their members came up as recognized representatives of rural society. Thus, for example, members of the Maravar caste emerged as village headmen in Tamil Nadu, and managed to appropriate the major returns yielded by irrigation works carried out by the state (Mosse 2000). In Punjab and Haryana, however, the dominant cultivating castes were also the major land-holders, and they acted as lobbies to persuade the state in independent India to undertake extensive irrigation works and construct other infrastructural facilities for their benefit.

The take-over of the benefits of the developmental work or the properties theoretically owned by the post-colonial state was facilitated by the entry of dominant castes and landlord lineages in ever greater numbers into the bureaucratic establishment of that state. However, much of the take-over was accomplished by violating or bending the laws in unprincipled ways. The most extensive evasion of irrigation or electricity dues or bank loans extended to rich farmers occurred in the green revolution belt of Punjab, Haryana, western Uttar Pradesh and other parts of India which witnessed the emergence of a rich farmer class. Violation of legality became built into the governance pattern of those states of India—and those were the vast majority—which came to be ruled by upper-caste or dominant caste lineages.

Those analysts who have tried to attribute all corruption and major deviations from the stated objectives of development plans in post-colonial India to 'restricted trade regimes' or 'licence and control raj', and have attributed power to a disembodied or socially disembedded class of bureaucrats (cf Bhagwati and Desai 1970; Bardhan 1984) have been almost totally blind to the major forces promoting corruption and illegality in the fastnesses of rural India and their extensions into government offices and legislative assemblies. This dominance of the forces I have sketched above also meant a fragmentation of authority and weakness of the state. Such a state

Introduction

was characterized by Myrdal (1968) as the 'soft state' without, however, an understanding of the origins of the softness; Joel Migdal (1988) has argued that where societies are strong the state tends to be weak and regionally fragmented, and this is the fate of most third-world countries. A society can, of course, be strong when it is egalitarian rather than hierarchical, and is suffused with democratic and civic virtues (Putnam 1993). But that is not the sense in which society is strong in most parts of rural India: it is strong only in the sense that groups at the top of the social and political structure can resist the legitimate demands of governance, such as respect for laws and due democratic processes.

Economic and political change brought about a crisis in governance in northern, western and most parts of southern India. The green revolution, combined with the logic of electoral democracy, led to the precipitation of the so-called Other Backward Castes and some dominant castes not so characterized (such as the Jats of Haryana and western Uttar Pradesh), to the upper echelons of the power structure. Where the Other Backward Castes had already obtained various privileges under the system of reservations for public employment and admissions to government-funded educational institutions, as in most states of southern India, legality was not blatantly violated in the process of displacement of the old upper-caste elites. But such violations were rampant in states in which the older elite caste groups were slow to accommodate the demands of the newly dominant groups. Paradoxically enough, an economic change of an opposite kind since the end of the 1970s—so cataclysmic in its effects—also allowed the formation of alliances seeking to monopolize public resources and use the state apparatus in an illegitimate fashion. This cataclysmic event is the collapse of the traditional cotton textile mills, which were the largest employers of labour in the organized sector in western India and isolated industrial centres such as Delhi and Kanpur in northern India. Since these states accounted for the majority of the voters in India, the whole ruling apparatus has been infected by a crisis of legitimacy—a crisis which it is trying to overcome by using slogans of communalism and jingoism.

We will have to situate the structure of the Indian capitalist class—especially that portion of it which is constituted by the big business houses—against this background of an unreformed social arrangement, incomplete legality, attempts to manipulate the state apparatus for particularist interests, and a defensive strategy of accommodation with foreign capital (for analysis of some of these issues in detail, see Degnbol-Martinussen 2001; Mukherjee Reed 2001; and Tyabji 2000). Indian, especially Hindu, business families, utilized the *Mitakshara* law and the opacity of Company Law— and the virtual immunity with which they could evade taxes and the legal dues of their employees when their firms got into difficulty— to preserve their wealth and even increase it while the economy was less than dynamic. Among them, those groups prospered which could build up and manipulate their political connections to use those types of government regulations that favoured them and at the same time exploit new technologies or necessary economies of scale (Chandrasekhar 1999).

The economic liberalization starting in the 1990s has posed a challenge to the family-based business groups which were the dominant form of business organization among big business groups. The protection that they enjoyed against the competition of transnational corporations because of their political connection has been eroded by the steady incursion of transnational corporations into their economic space. The former had been able to bargain for technology with foreign enterprises on favourable terms because of their better knowledge and control over the domestic terrain. With liberalization and with the intellectual property rights regime inscribed in the treaty leading to the setting up of the World Trade Organization, they lost that bargaining advantage. In this situation, the cohesion of the business groups was threatened, and different members of the family tried to chalk out different strategies of collaboration and accommodation with foreign enterprises (see, in this connection, Bhargava 1993, as paraphrased by Tyabji 2000: 10–11). But this accommodation has often taken the form of surrender: most of the firms that started as joint ventures between India and foreign enterprises have been taken over by the latter. Many business houses have either broken up or retreated from their manufacturing interests and confined themselves to dealing in real estate, finance or various service firms.

The only new development in the 1990s has been the rise

of a dynamic information technology sector. It is not accidental that the best-performing firms have come up in southern India, with about the most literate populations in the country. However, the significance of the information technology (IT) sector and the so-called 'new economy' has been exaggerated, not only in India, but even in the USA, the Mecca of IT professionals (see, in this connection, the collection of articles in *Monthly Review*, 52 (11), April 2001). The value-added from software in India is probably no more than 1 per cent of national income even in 2001, and the percentage of national employment generated by it is even lower than that. The IT sector was responsible for much of the global boom in stock markets in 2000, and the collapse of NASDAQ has been associated with a prolonged slump in world stock markets which communicated itself to, and exaggerated, the slump in Indian stock markets, the roots of which have already been sketched above.

However weakened the Indian business class at the top may have been through foreign competition, that class, along with wheeler-dealers for foreign enterprises, and politicians and corrupt bureaucrats seeking to make a fast buck for themselves or their friends, have succeeded in effecting a virtual capture of the commanding heights of the state. The unprincipled and headlong rush to privatize valuable state enterprises (the privatization of Bharat Aluminium Company being only a *cause celebre* because it was resisted by the workers of the company and the people of Chhattisgarh) and hand over vast tracts of the country to transnational enterprises in the name of encouraging the development of new technology or agro-processing industries, is a naked manifestation of such capture. Economic liberalization has led not to a broadening of democratic choice but to its severe constriction.

The Real Life of Indian Workers

The history of capital and labour still remains an under-researched area in India. The gaps in labour history have been to some extent filled by a number of recent books (see, for example, Breman and Das 2000; Ghosh 2000; Nair 1998; and Sen 1999) and by a number of studies by social scientists published in the *Economic and Political Weekly*, the *Indian Journal of Labour Economics* and *Social Scientist*. This is not the place to summarize the findings of the work of these scholars. I will here mention some of the more important issues that have been analysed in these studies.

The studies have brought out the enormous degree of heterogeneity within the Indian working class. This heterogeneity originated partly in the way the working class was constituted in the first place. The workers came from different backgrounds: some were artisans displaced from their earlier occupations; some were peasants who had lost their land or peasants whose families had to work in factories as a way of supplementing their incomes; some were women who followed their kin, or were recruited by labour contractors (very often with false promises), or women who could not survive without looking for work. But the heterogeneity was also caused by the trajectory of capitalist enterprise in India and by strategies deliberately adopted by managements. As workers came from different regions or communities they were often 'housed' (if their hovels and slums can be so designated) in separate localities, and men and women were assigned different types of work with a differential in wages and status in favour of men built into the system. Workers used their memories and their links through castes, communities or regional origins to forge alliances and new communities. All 'primordial' loyalties were reshaped and transformed through their struggle to make a living in the new surroundings, and through occasional strikes or other movements of resistance against the oppressive system.

Various styles of discrimination were built in not only in labour processes in the workplace but also in the way life is lived outside the workplace. Women were assigned generally low-skilled, low-paid jobs at the workplace; at home too they served as household drudges, working many more hours than their menfolk—husbands, sons or other kin living in the same family. Most Dalits and Adivasis were slotted into low-skilled, insecure jobs by their employers. Such assignment was rationalized by their general lack of education. Their poverty and lack of access to educational facilities condemned them to these semi-permanent niches.

However, public action had an impact even in this story of what appears to be a ceaselessly unequal struggle of labour against capital. The proportion of women employed in the public sector including industry, administration and other services, especially in decision-making positions, is far higher than in the organized private sector. One of the effects of liberalization the world over has been the enhanced casualization of labour, and women have entered increasingly into that casualized workplace (Bagchi 1999).

More important for changing the conditions of living of the workers were struggles launched by the workers and political movements supporting them. Trade union movements have been traditionally directed at factory or office workers. However, movements have also come up among workers in the so-called unorganized or informal sector. The most successful movements of this type have occurred in Kerala as part of the movement of left forces in general. But in other parts of India also, in West Bengal, the mining belt of Bihar (today's Jharkhand state), in the forest and mining regions of Madhya Pradesh (predominantly in the region which has been separated out as Chhattisgarh state), movements have developed among agricultural labourers, rickshaw-pullers, porters, forest workers and mine workers and have sometimes covered the whole working population of a region. Women workers have been separately organized in a pioneering movement in Gujarat.

These movements, supported in many cases by rising the productivity in agriculture and other related sectors, have helped in raising the real wages of labour even in a situation of rising unemployment. Higher degrees of awareness of their civil and political rights have also stiffened the workers' resistance against retrenchment, slashing of nominal wages or curtailment of rights in other ways.

However, the agents of capital have mounted counter-attacks in the form of murder of trade unionists and leaders of left movements, whipping up communalism or casteism, abridgement of civil rights, corrupt electoral practices which deprive ordinary people of their right to choose their rulers, and illegal use of the state machinery to repress people's movements. After the collapse of the Soviet Union, neoliberal economic reforms and unabashed use of force by the USA and its allies against any threat to the power of capital, as represented by the multi-billion dollar transnational companies, have threatened freedom and democracy in every third world country, including India. The US Federal Bureau of Investigation has now opened an office in India. Needless to say, our police establishment does not enjoy a reciprocal privilege in the USA. The struggle of labour against capital rampant is merging into people's struggles for real national liberation in every country from Mexico to South Korea.

As I have indicated in several of the essays included in this volume, labour history was not bereft of intellectual excellence before some of the postmodernist writers had the arrogance to suggest that they were the first historians to write the real history of workers and that they 'represented' the workers and spoke for them. Although this was not made clear in their writings, they 'represented' them to privileged academic audiences in western countries or their overseas offshoots, rather than to the people of India or the third world.

Of course, there were many areas of workers' lives which did not become part of an academic discourse until recently. Such was, for example, the sanitary environment and records of mortality of workers which have been analysed by Ghosh (2000). The gender dimensions of the existence of workers and the struggles of women workers against the oppression heaped by a patriarchal, caste-ridden social structure in a colonial society have been brilliantly illuminated by Nair (1998) and Sen (1999). The local context of workers' daily struggle to survive and with dignity has been brought out by the work of Vinay Bahl, Rajnarayan Chandavarkar and Dilip Simeon, which I have used in some essays in the book. The contribution of trade union movements to living conditions in Kerala has been brought out by the work of Kannan and others. The way workers' struggles have been distorted by forces of communalism or casteism and how even socialists have often failed to grasp the real structures of oppression feeding such forces have also formed part of some recent work. The increased burden of work on women in the phase of a greater degree of commercialization of agriculture followed by economic liberalization has been analysed with sympathetic acumen by Swaminathan (1997), Jeyaranjan and Swaminathan (1999) and Ramamurthy (2000), among others. Connected with patriarchal oppression of women, there continues to be severe discrimination against the very survival of girl children (Agnihotri 2000).

All these existential conditions are reflected in, and refracted through, workers' conciousness, and the latter in turn helps change

Introduction

their own conditions of living and work. It is not accidental that Kerala, the state with the longest history of social movements, a powerful left movement and a high rate of literacy, is about the only state where female foeticide is not changing the ratio between females and males in an adverse direction (Agnihotri 2001).

My aim during all these years has been to understand the complex of relations between capital and labour. Since I found, at the beginning of my academic career, that the behaviour of the Indian capitalist class was relatively under-researched, perhaps that aspect has received the greater share of my research effort. But I hope that the papers will show that the existential conditions of capital and labour and the states of consciousness of workers and capitalists and their changes can be handled within the same historicized, dialectical framework of analysis.

References

Agnihotri, S.B., 2000, *Sex Ratio Patterns in the Indian Population: a fresh exploration*, Sage, New Delhi.

———, 2001, 'Declining child and infant mortality in India: How do girl children fare?, *Economic and Political Weekly*, Vol. 36, 20 January, pp. 228–33.

Bagchi, A.K., 1987, 'East Asian capitalism: an introduction', *Political Economy: Studies in the Surplus Approach*, 3 (2), pp. 115–32.

———, 1993, '"Rent-seeking", new political economy and the negation of politics', *Economic and Political Weekly*, 28 (34), 21 August, pp. 1729–36.

———, 1998, 'Local and global monopolies and the prospects of global democracy', in D. Nayyar (ed.), *Economics as Ideology and Experience: Essays in Honour of Ashok Mitra*, Frank Cass, London, pp. 96–124.

——— (ed.), 1999, *Economy and Organization: Indian Institutions under the Neoliberal Regime*, Sage, New Delhi.

———, 1999a, 'Indian economic organizations in a comparative perspective', in Bagchi, 1999, pp. 19–82.

———, 1999b, 'Economic reforms and employment in India', in Oshikawa Fumiko (ed.), *South Asia under the Economic Reforms*, Japan Centre for Asian Studies, National Museum of Ethnology, Osaka, pp. 15–64.

———, 2000, 'Globalizing India: a critique of an agenda for financiers and speculators', in J.D. Schmidt and J. Hersh (eds), *Globalization and Social Change*, Routledge, London, pp. 121–42.

Banerjee-Guha, S., 1997, *Spatial Dynamics of International Capital: a study of multinational corporations in India*, Orient Longman, Hyderabad.

Bardhan, P., 1984. The Political Economy of Development in India, Oxford University Press, Delhi.

Bhagwati, J. and P. Desai, 1970, *India: Planning for Industrialization*, Oxford University Press for the OECD, Delhi.

Bhargava, S., 1993, 'Indian business houses in the 1990s', *Economic Times*, 17 June.
Breman, J. and A.N. Das, 2000, *Down and Out: Labouring under Global Capitalism*, Oxford University Press, Delhi.
Chandrasekhar, C.P., 1999, 'Firms, markets and the state: an analysis of Indian oligopoly', in Bagchi, 1999, pp. 230–66.
Chomsky, N., 1998, *Class Warfare: Interviews with David Barsamian*, Oxford University Press, Delhi.
———, 2001, 'Microsoft: One World Operating System; a Corporate Watch interview with Noam Chomsky' (URL: http://www.corpwatch.org).
Chowdhury, Prem, 1994, *The Veiled Woman: Shifting Gender Equations in Rural Haryana, 1880–1990*, Oxford University Press, Delhi.
Dasgupta, Nandita, 1999, *A Study of the Corporate Restructuring of Indian Industries in the Post NIP-Regime: The Issue of Amalgamations/Mergers*, unpublished Ph.D. thesis, University of Calcutta.
Degnbol-Martinussen, J., 2001, *Policies, Institutions and Industrial Development: Coping with liberalization and international competition in India*, Sage, New Delhi.
Ghose, A.K. (ed.), 1983, *Agrarian Reform in Developing Countries*, Croom Helm, London.
Ghosh, P., 2000, *Colonialism, Class and a History of the Calcutta Jute Millhands 1880–1930*, Orient Longman, Hyderabad.
Jeyaranjan, J. and P. Swaminathan, 1999, 'Resilience of gender inequities: Women and employment in Chennai', *Economic and Political Weekly*, Vol. 34, 17 April, WS-2–WS-11.
Kosambi, D.D., 1946, 'The bourgeoisie comes of age in India', *Science and Society*, Vol. 10, pp. 392–98.
Mandeville, B., 1724/1989, *The Fable of the Bees*, 4th edn, London; rpt, Penguin Books, Harmondsworth, Middlesex.
Marx, K., 1886/1965, *Capital*, Vol. 1, translated from the German by S. Moore and E. Aveling and edited by F. Engels; rpt, Foreign Languages Publishing House, Moscow.
Migdal, J.S., 1988, *Strong Societies and Weak States: State–Society Relations and State Capabilities in the Third World*, Princeton University Press, Princeton, N.J.
Mosse, D., 2000, 'Irrigation and Statecraft in Zamindari South India', in C.J. Fuller and Veronique Bénéï (eds), *The Everyday State and Society in Modern India*, Social Science Press, New Delhi, pp. 163–93.
Mukherjee Reed, Ananya, 2001, *Perspectives on the Indian Corporate Economy: The paradox of profits*, Palgrave, New York.
Nair, Janaki, 1998, *Miners and Millhands : Work, Culture and Politics in Princely Mysore*, Sage, New Delhi.
O'Donnell, G., 2001, 'Reflections on contemporary South American democracies', *Journal of Latin American Studies*, 33 (3), August, pp. 599–609.
Putnam, R., 1993, *Making Democracy Work: civic traditions in modern Italy*, Princeton University Press, Princeton.
Ramamurthy, Priti, 2000, 'The cotton commodity chain, women, work and agency in India and Japan: the case for feminist agro-food systems research', *World Development*, 28 (3), pp. 551–78.

Sen, Samita, 1999, *Women and Labour in Late Colonial India: The Bengal Jute Industry*, Cambridge University Press, Cambridge.

Statesman, 2001, 'Genome for the people' [reprinted from *The Times*, London: a report of Sir John Sulston's Chatham, Trinity College, Oxford], 29 October.

Swaminathan, Padmini, 1997, 'Work and reproductive health: A Hobson's choice for Indian women?', *Economic and Political Weekly*, Vol. 32, 25 October, WS-53–WS-61.

Tyabji, N., 2000, *Industrialization and Innovation: The Indian Experience*, Sage, New Delhi.

History and Nature
of the Indian Bourgeoisie

The Economics of Business and the Business of Economics

I

The birth of economics as a discipline can be traced to the rise of capitalism as a system. In his *Politics* Aristotle distinguished between the uses of a good in exchange and for production or consumption. But he was concerned mainly with management of the material needs of a slave-owning family typical of the 'free' citizens of the Greek states of his time. Kautilya's *Arthashastra* also occupies itself more with state-craft than with the economic relations prevailing between different constituents of a state or society. It was between the seventeenth and eighteenth centuries that political economy, which analyses the economic relations between subjects and classes of people living in a modern state, took shape. And then came a long interlude between the late nineteenth century and modern times when, in orthodox 'Groves of Academe', (title of a novel by Mary McCarthy), a pure economics was concocted, which eschewed not only mention of classes but also any discussion of the rationale and the inner workings of modern commercial and industrial enterprise, although the latter had provided the nourishment for economics as a subject when it was young. A rather specialized, hybrid branch of the discipline, calling itself 'managerial economics', was tolerated by the high priests and was accorded the same status, intellectually speaking, as shorthand-writing and book-keeping. However, the need for understanding the working of a fast-changing landscape of enterprise has provided fresh stimulus for preparing new alloys out of

Text of the Sir Purshotamdas Thakurdas Memorial Lecture, delivered on 29 December 1984.

the theory of organization, transaction costs, bounded rationality and traditional micro-economics. On the other side, the recognition that socialism as a system has come to stay and provides a beacon for political activists all over the world, has injected new blood into the old body of political economy which refuses to recognize a strict division between the subjects of politics, economics and sociology, and combines elements from each discipline in its own corpus. I mean in this chapter to pass back and forth between the new economics of business and the old discipline of political economy without offering any further apology.

When we think of modern business, competition between large conglomerate enterprises at once springs to mind. And few such businesses can entirely dissociate themselves from the huge arms expenditures of a modern state. However, in medieval Europe, as in ancient India, commerce and war were often considered to be poles apart. Even when businessmen were caught up in the wars of the princes, the vocation of the former was supposed to consist in keeping their word.

Indeed, trust and confidence are the basis of successful trade. Trust in business associates is the foundation of the multifold transactions that have formed the stuff of commerce since the mythical days of triangular barters. Confidence about the future is necessary in order to plan for future business transactions. The time-horizon for which a businessman had to plan has tended to become longer as investment has become more capital-intensive, and as innovations have become a regular feature, changing products, processes, market frontiers and modes of finance.

A discourse about trust and confidence is no longer the exclusive province of moralists and philosophers, if it ever was. Trust is part of the institutional framework governing business decisions, and economists from Adam Smith down to Kenneth Arrow have theorized about the actual institutions governing economic decisions and about the design of better institutions to induce better decisions.

In the realm of commodities, economists and lawyers have long distinguished between private and public goods. Private goods are those that can be appropriated exclusively by an individual or a group of individuals. They possess the property that it is possible to exclude others from their use, and that the more somebody uses a particular good the less there is for somebody else to use. Public goods are at the other extreme: it is normally not possible to reserve their use for a particular individual, nor is it the case that the more somebody uses them the less there is for somebody else to use. There are very few pure public goods, with overcrowding and congestion spoiling the enjoyment of such public goods as air, public roads or open seas. But one could say that in many situations one of the aims of a sane public policy is to restore the publicness of public goods.

Trust has been characterized by Kenneth Arrow as a public good. But it is unlike air in the sense that it is not just there, it has somehow to be brought about, though many of us who implicitly trust our colleagues and friends and hope that the feeling is reciprocated are not aware of this fact. Nor is it something like a railway across the Bhoreghat pass or a satellite in space which can be created by imperial *diktat* or the decision of the chief executive of a sovereign state. Trust is the result of cooperation among many individuals over a longish period of time, and it is a fragile good in the sense that a conscious betrayal or even an unconscious departure from the norms of good behaviour can dent it irreparably.

In the modern world we all know that in order to do well in business you have to win in the competitive race. As the victories of the North and South Koreans in the Asian Games, and as the triumphs of the Americans, the Soviet teams, the Japanese and the newly-entering Chinese in the Olympic Games demonstrated, winning in track races and gymnastics is no longer a matter of individual genius but a result of meticulous preparation at the national level. In exactly the same way, a considerable amount of organization built on finely-tuned monitoring devices and on trust at different levels of control and between different divisions at the same level of control is needed to sustain a large volume of business and, even more, to increase its dimension and spread.

How well have Indian businessmen performed in building up networks sustained by trust? In the sixteenth and seventeenth centuries, when European traders and travellers appeared on the shores of India, most of them were impressed by the astuteness and trustworthiness of the Indian traders and bankers they dealt with. During the nineteenth century, eminent Indian bankers and merchants were often exempted from appearing in the courts or taking oaths when they appeared, because their word was considered to be absolute truth.

This network of trust, however, was confined primarily to the group that was supposed to belong to those who deserved trust. This would often be a caste group of a particular locality, but in many towns and commercial centres this would comprise of other traders and bankers of eminence, and their valued customers. It is not known how far this kind of consideration was extended to *hoi polloi*, or exactly when it was thought that a person had ceased to be trustworthy and could be treated shabbily.

Under the Mughals and in the successor-states which rose on the ruins of the Mughal empire after Aurangzeb, great merchants handled the revenues of the state. The franchise of the mint was also generally held by trusted financiers. When Murshid Quli Khan was the *subahdar* of Bengal, the house of Manik Chand and Fateh Chand, which acquired the honorific title of Jagatseth, rose to a position of eminence unrivalled by any mercantile house of the time. The two senior partners of this house, Jagatseth Mahtab Rai and Maharaja Swarup Chand, were still the custodians of the Nawab's finances when Siraj-ud-Daula succeeded Alivardi Khan as the Nawab of Bengal. They decided to conspire with the British against Siraj-ud-Daula, and thereby not only betrayed their country but also their own narrow self-interest. For, the higher echelons of Indian businessmen were more or less decimated with the assumption of supreme power by the British in Bengal. The decision to break the older ties of trust could not have been taken by Indian merchant princes at a less opportune moment and with a more misinformed set of assumptions about the adversary they were inviting into their *haveli*.

When traders moved into modern industry, with a few exceptions, the control of business remained vested in kinship or family groups. British and Indian managing agency houses resembled one another in many respects: their time-horizons were equally short, their portfolios almost equally diversified, their attachment to trading as the sheet-anchor of their fortunes equally strongly rooted. But in the recruitment of managerial cadres they parted company. While there were exceptions, such as Bird and Co., where control remained vested within the same family group for close to a century, in most British managing agency houses control rarely remained with the founder's family for more than a generation or two. By contrast, Indian business families and communities retained a tenacious grip on the businesses they controlled. This, of course, necessitated both an untrammelled flow of trust within the family and an active element of distrust with respect to members outside the kinship group.

Even in British days, Indian traders of lower ranks or Indian moneylenders ceased to enjoy much reputation for trustworthiness. The deliberate adulteration of cotton or the deliberate mixing of superior with inferior varieties of jute were a constant irritant to the exporters of these commodities. Let us look at the reasons for the apparent failure of British laws, chambers of commerce and important exporting houses to entirely stop these practices.

First, start with the situation where Indian cotton enjoys (if that is the word) a reputation for bad quality, given the staple length and other easily recognizable characteristics. Then, even if one particular trader brings in better quality cotton, he is unlikely to get a better price than the average. A close inspection to establish the quality may be costly for the wholesale trader and he may not consider it worthwhile to ascertain the exact quality of the cotton tendered by a particular supplier. Let us now look at the next level, namely, the producer from whom the *pykar* or trader in the *mandi* purchases the cotton or the jute. The trader knows that he is unlikely to be sufficiently rewarded if he buys the better quality cotton at a higher price. The producer in his turn will be discouraged by such indifference. In fact, if the producer is a poor peasant he will not only have little incentive to improve his product quality, but he may not be able to afford it in the first place unless he receives an advance or promise of a large price from the buyer. It is the joint presence of two phenomena that guarantees the continuance of the situation: the existence of numerous poor producers who have been driven to the lowest level at which they can go on producing, and a group of large traders who have no effective channel for keeping any long-term links with a small sub-section of the producers, and who have themselves suffered from a kind of statistical or probabilistic discrimination because of race and the fact of political dependence.

It is interesting to note that the staple length of Indian cotton began to increase and complaints about quality became more muted when an indigenous cotton industry grew and emerged as the biggest customer of Indian cotton. Indian mills could organize their cotton supplies for a longer term and build up stable customer–supplier relationships with the chief traders. Where the traders themselves became the major shareholders of the cotton mill companies, they had to calculate the relative profits to be made as between lowering the quality of the cotton and improving the quality of the goods to be produced by the mills. Not all suppliers could resist the temptation to short-change the mills they controlled, with disastrous effects for the health of the industry all over India.

Apart from what one might call the professionally conditioned short-sightedness of many of the traders, three other factors interfered badly with the growing closeness of suppliers and consumers of inputs in manufacturing industry. First, while the British businessmen still controlled the jute industry, there was a recognized racial distance between the mill-owners and the producers, and there was no question of an adventurer from the land of the kirk recognizing a Bengali Muslim or Hindu peasant as his brother. Unfortunately, when the control of the industry passed into Indian hands, a linguistic, and often a religious, difference still maintained an impassable barrier between the grower of the raw material and the mill-owner.

Secondly, with the onset of a trade depression, the big traders and mill-owners could never resist the temptation to pass the costs on to the workers supplying the labour and the peasants supplying the raw materials. In the case of jute, for example, standards were arbitrarily raised every time there was a glut of jute in the market, but they were rarely lowered in times of prosperity. There was also a collusive arrangement between British officials and jute mill-owners to systematically mislead the jute grower about the existing stocks of jute and probable prices—variables that entered critically into his sowing decision for the next season. Policies with respect to wages followed the same trend. This attitude also prevented the emergence of the kind of principal–sub-contractor relationships that have been cited as one of the main strengths of Japanese industry.

Finally, I want to stress that the level of desperate poverty at which the majority of the workers and peasants live in most parts of the country is both the result and the cause of the predator–prey relationship in which businessmen and primary producers are caught, to the detriment of both groups. And, in the case of a predator–prey relationship there is no question of mutual trust. What is often overlooked is that, with the possible exception of wolf-packs and packs of wild dogs, most predators also hunt alone, or in small groups, so that the network of trust, which is as much a foundation of business prosperity as mutual competition, is rent asunder again and again.

It is a commonplace that few Indian business groups have really believed in the economy of high wages. Ahmedabad in the inter-war period may have provided an exception, but elsewhere workers have had to engage in bitter struggles to obtain a living wage. This has meant that few businesses have been able to call on their workers' loyalty when the need arose and, conversely, that few businesses have cared to invest in the training of their workers. There are few business groups in which any kind of internal labour market operates. Thus, as in the case of the fly-by-night pedlar and the gullible buyer, a large number of businessmen treat their customers and workers, for all practical purposes, as if it was a once-for-all contract terminable at a moment's notice on either side. But as organization theorists have found out recently and successful business houses have known all the time, the logic of organizing a business firm with employment of workers other than the owners is precisely that the firm replaces the transient contacts of the *bazaar* with a long-term relationship from which everybody hopes to gain.

II

We now turn to the other aspect of business success, namely, confidence in the future. One of the essential ingredients of economic dynamism is a high rate of investment in productive sectors. There can be differences of opinion about the relative contributions of investment in capital, education and research to economic growth, but there can be little doubt that economic growth does not occur without a high rate of investment. For most of its history since Independence, the Indian economy has not performed very well in terms of industrial growth or investment. The rate of investment has gone up since about the middle of the 1970s, but by not as much as is officially claimed, nor has it resulted in a perceptible quickening of industrial growth. Even if the rate of investment has gone up, it is not enough to give Indian exporters the competitive edge they need in international markets. For, competitors with a higher rate of investment and a greater share of capital stock embodied in superior technology can outsell Indian producers in both the international and the domestic markets.

While investment is crucial for economic growth, explaining investment has remained a Sisyphean task for the professional economist. John Maynard Keynes, the economist who brought in the rate of investment as the crucial variable explaining deficiencies of aggregate demand and unemployment in a capitalist economy, did not have much more to offer than an unconvincing schedule of marginal efficiency of capital and 'animal spirits' of investors as explanations for the level of investment and its movements. Perhaps 'animal spirits' does provide a clue to the kind of enquiry we should conduct, while recognizing that man is a rather peculiar animal, capable of much more devious and much more strategic behaviour than any cunning beast or bird. Why have Japanese capitalists out-performed most other capitalists in the field of long-term investment? What is it that makes the Japanese economy behave much more like a supply-constrained socialist economy than a demand-constrained private enterprise economy? In trying to answer such questions we have to reckon with the enormous variations in social structures and mores within the general system of capitalism itself.

Fortunately for the scribe but unfortunately for all ordinary citizens, there is no enigma about the nature of the constraints binding the Indian economy. I recall the days in the late 1960s and early 1970s when somebody like me was distinctly unpopular for saying that a couple of good agricultural harvests are not enough to put sufficient purchasing power in the hands of the common people, or to stimulate private capitalists to invest heavily in industry, or to release public investment from the tyranny of deficit budgets and foreign exchange shortages. There have been shortages of producer goods and infrastructure from time to time in India, but they can mostly be traced to past failures in public and private investment. Top policy-makers in the government have now woken up to the endemic problem of demand failures and investment lapses, but so far they have seemed to put their faith in better management methods to get us out of the wood. Better management in business, however, very much involves the problem of building up a durable relationship between workers and owners or supervisory personnel. Barring

The Economics of Business

some few hundred plants spread over India, in most other cases, management–labour relations have remained mired in mutual distrust. In most cases, the management has been content with resorting to coercion to enforce obedience, and has naturally been met with rebelliousness whenever the environment has changed for the worse.

Moreover, better management in a micro-economic sense is hardly enough to get us out of the self-fulfilling cycle of low investment in expectation of low profitability being succeeded by deficient demand leading to a low level of investment, and so on. Private as well as public investment did pick up in India in the years of the Second and the Third Five-Year Plans, but the rate of growth was not really spectacular when compared with the achievements of the Japanese, Chinese or South Korean economies in recent years. And then private investment sagged after the middle of the 1960s, and despite numerous transfusions of blood in the form of government subsidies, tax concessions, a *damad's* treatment for non-resident Indians, the patient still seems to be only taking his constitutional walk rather than running to catch up with the leaders in the Asian capitalist track meet.

Not only has investment not been enough in volume; it has also often involved long lags in gestation and fruition, and it has been embodied in the wrong shapes. Indian capitalists have often followed a policy akin to slash-and-burn cultivation with respect to particular regions and sectors. When a sector has become unprofitable with old product-mixes or with old technologies, instead of investing in changing the product-mix or changing the technology, they have too often simply mined the plant, off-loaded it on to a complaisant government and moved on in search of fresh plots for *jhoom*ing. When a region has become plagued with industrial sickness, instead of trying to restore its health with a better infrastructure and investment in promising new products, they have siphoned off funds to other regions—including foreign countries. No large industrial house, let alone the middle-level groups, can be absolved of the charge of deliberately slaughtering ailing firms or abandoning them on the church-steps of Our Father, the government.

The more dynamic business groups have been very active in searching for modern technology and have engaged in massive imports of technology from abroad. But Indian enterprises have not been very adept at the absorption of new technology. As the experience of such countries as Japan and South Korea and the examples of exceptional enterprises in Argentina and India indicate, successful absorption of borrowed technology requires a considerable amount of in-house expenditure on R&D and adaptive engineering. But despite lavish fiscal concessions by the government, private R&D expenditures in India have been low by any respectable international standards.

A number of economists believing in the efficacy of private enterprise have held up South Korea as a model to emulate. However, the South Korean 'miracle' is as much a triumph of *dirigisme* as of carefully fostered private enterprise. There are so many systemic differences between the Indian and South Korean economies that it is not possible to make India resemble South Korea by minor tinkering, even if it were politically and socially desirable to do so. The critics who point their finger to the government for interfering too much in the Indian economy, thereby spoiling its chances of growing nearly as fast as South Korea, fail to mention the enormous difference between the dynamism of private enterprise in South Korea and India. In 1982, South Korea had a population which was only one-eighteenth that of India's. But she had an industrial output exceeding US$29 billion, as against an Indian industrial output measuring about $47.5 billion. When such a formidable difference in per capita industrial output is built up over a span of only about two decades, everybody has to sit up and try and find the reasons for the difference. From the point of view of growth-inducing investment in the future, it is interesting to note that while the R&D expenditures by the private sector in 1981 and 1982 amounted to $138.5 million and $166.3 million respectively in India (counting the US dollar as equal to Rs 9), private funds for R&D expenditure came to $236.3 million and $383.9 million respectively in the relevant years in South Korea. Thus, with a lower industrial output South Korean private businessmen outspent their Indian counterparts by more than 100 per cent in 1982 (assuming that the funds for private R&D expenditures in India all came from private coffers—which may not be true).

Thus, not only have holes and tears in the private network of trust in India impeded business performance; business confidence, which we take to be confidence in the future, has also been a rather unsteady skiff in Indian waters. What is often forgotten is that the confidence of men in business also depends to a large extent on other people's behaviour. Thus faith in the future becomes linked up with confidence in men and doubles back on trust as a public good.

We seem to have arrived at an impasse. If both trust and confidence are lacking in the first place, how does one set about building it up? In answer to such a query, social scientists have taken a cue from game theory and modelled the typical situation of two operators whose interests are not necessarily in consonance. The most celebrated of such games is that of the Prisoners' Dilemma. In this game, there are two prisoners who are not in communication with each other. If neither of them confesses to the crime, they both get away with a light sentence, because the police have some minor charges against each of them anyway. If both confess to the crime, they receive a considerably heavier sentence. But if one confesses and the other does not, then the former is released forthwith and the latter has the book thrown at him. If there is no prior agreement between the prisoners which can be made to stick (say, through the threat of a mafia-style punishment for the squealer), then it turns out that the safest thing for the two crooks to do is to confess. Then, of course, they both end up worse off than if they had preserved the proverbial honour between thieves.

It is depressing to find how many situations involving cooperation and conflict of interest between people can be modelled on the Prisoners' Dilemma. For example, the same game would fit the situation of a mountain tribe which leaves its saleable goods at the bottom of the hill in the expectation that the shopkeeper from the valley will pick up the goods and leave behind an equivalent amount of goods desired by the tribe. It is even more disconcerting to find that however many times the game is played (so long as it is played a finite number of times), there is always an incentive for one of the players to rat on the other and thus plunge both of them in an unprofitable situation of mutual non-cooperation.

However, a more hopeful outcome seems to have been found by an American political scientist, Robert Axelrod, who pitted not one player against another but a large number of players against one another, each with his own strategy, in a computer tournament. It turned out that the strategy with the best chance of winning was one that was a nice and forgiving one. That is, the player with the 'nice' strategy never ratted first. Secondly, he punished the squealer or the rat by ratting just once, and then went back to being nice as soon as the other responded with a cooperative move. The reason why the nice strategy won was that it did not set up a chain reaction of mutual non-cooperation among all the players against which the strategy was played, whereas the more cunning and aggressive strategies did precisely that.

To go back then to the Indian business scene, the problem still remains as to how businessmen could set up a healthy chain reaction of nice strategies and—to change the metaphor slightly—how they could start upward by investing in mutually and socially profitable ventures in a mood of mutual reassurance. The Assurance Game can be helpful here. It is a variation on the game of the Battle of the Sexes, and has been analysed by Amartya Sen. In adapting this game to an investment situation, one could take two groups of investors, one planning to invest in integrated circuits and the other in micro-processor technologies using those circuits. If both groups invest in right amounts, they can utilize economies of scale and hope to be competitive in international terms. If, however, the prospective investors in integrated circuits fail to invest an adequate amount, the builders of micro-processor technologies will go without a domestic supply of inputs and it may be costly to import them from abroad. On the other side, if the prospective investors in micro-processor technologies postpone or curtail their investment, the producers of integrated circuits will be in trouble. Without adequate trust in one another and without confidence in the future, all the investors may end up by investing too little and thus inviting more trouble both for themselves and for the economy than if they had not invested at all, or if they had invested sufficiently large sums in integrated circuits and in micro-processor technologies.

What complicates the outcome of this game and many such similar games is that behind the two players and essential to their success stands the great Indian public (or the great Brazilian public, for that matter). For a successful outcome of the game, the general mass of ordinary people must have adequate purchasing power and sufficient confidence in their future. When we bring in such considerations, we have to move out of the format of a game, however intriguing it may appear to an addict of logical puzzles.

To go back to our main theme, one standard alibi of Indian businessmen for their failure to invest and grow has been government interference. Some people would dismiss such a complaint by alleging that by and large the government serves the businessmen's interests in India. Without taking sides on such an issue, it may be safely asserted that if government decisions influence business, businessmen also influence government decisions, both in detail and in their general outline. If there have been import and quota restrictions in numerous fields, there has been intensive lobbying by particular sections for retaining those restrictions or imposing them when their interests are threatened. In the area of industrial licensing, there are any number of instances of businessmen trying to raise barriers to entry into certain fields by taking out licences and implementing them only partially, and using the potential or actual excess capacity as a threat against prospective competitors. The exporting record of Indian business has not been very glorious either. While China bargains toughly to have her textile and other quotas for import into the USA increased every year, our merchants have failed repeatedly to fill their quota of exports to the EEC and the USA. This has happened despite large subsidies being given by the government to the exporters in various forms. Internally, the sugar industry has time and again behaved more like a combine of speculative traders than a group of competing industrialists. The environment of mutually reinforcing restrictive practices is as much a contribution of business culture as of fussy interference by the government.

More generally, the callousness and opportunism of businessmen have been as instrumental in sabotaging most anti-poverty programmes as landlord intransigence. Thereby businessmen have also undermined any prospect of demand growth and productivity improvement through a better-educated and better-fed working class. I am not suggesting that any national group of capitalists deliberately set out to improve the condition of workers without first encountering a strong challenge from the latter. But the dynamism of a business community confident about the future in most advanced capitalist countries leads to a tighter labour market, and through mutual cooperation and competition between different industrialists, to progressively rising real wages and a gradient of steady productivity growth. This has not happened in India. As I argued in the first part of the essay, Indian capitalists find it opportune to play on the utter poverty of their workers and most of their customers, and keep them degraded. The latter then find no other language than that of class struggle with which to confront them. Whether the present system would allow the workers and the capitalists to get out of this trap remains a moot question.

I have confined my analysis primarily to the behaviour of the private sector in India. But the observations made on movements of investment would apply almost equally to both private and public enterprises. Moreover, when one talks about confidence one must distinguish it from mere braggadocio. Too often, the claims of our top decision-makers are tainted by bragging. Despite, for example, the dismally poor performance of Indian nuclear power plants after the lavishing of hundreds of crores of rupees on atomic energy, the top technocrats concerned continue to declaim the virtues of our effort. Confidence must grow out of performance, whether in plant operation, process innovation or in the great task of eradication of poverty. It is needless to say that hollow claims can be as damaging to confidence as mutual distrust.

In discussing the economics and sociology of successful business, one has inevitably crossed the usual boundaries of managerial economics, and taken up questions involving inter-systemic comparisons. This is one of the reasons, as was indicated at the beginning of the essay, why economics cannot be confined merely to matters which can be somehow related to the measuring-rod of money, but has to venture into the terrains of culture and politics.

Merchants and Colonialism

Merchant Capital and Pre-capitalist Social Formations

Merchants form a component of the capitalist class in a developed capitalist economy (that is, in an economy in which the owners of means of production and the workers form distinct classes, and in which the dominant production relations are those of the sellers of labour power to the owners of means of production). But merchants exist in societies which are not all capitalist and are not in the process of undergoing a transition to capitalism. They may even perform vital functions in such pre-capitalist societies. In general, the behaviour of merchants in pre-capitalist societies is widely different from that of capitalists in developed capitalist societies. In developed capitalist societies, capitalists, generally with state support, play a very important part in modifying techniques of production and seeking ways of expanding their markets. By contrast, the pace of modification of techniques of production is generally much slower in pre-capitalist societies, and owners of capital need not play a significant role in such modification.

Karl Marx recognized both the facts of integration of merchants in pre-capitalist social structures in general, and their innovative role in developed capitalist societies. The canonical discussion of the role of merchants in pre-capitalist societies occurs in *Capital*, Vol. III (Marx 1996: Chapter XX, 'Historical Facts about Merchant's Capital). The discussion of the innovative role of capitalists occurs in *Theories of Surplus Value* (Marx 1971: 288–89). In this latter passage, Marx describes the function of capitalists in inventing new methods of production of old substances, new uses for old substances, new substances, and diversifying the product-mix in general. But he associates such behaviour clearly with a developed capitalist economy in which most of the population have been converted into wage-earners, the tenant farmers have become agrarian or industrial capitalists, and all property has assumed the form of easily negotiable capital.

Thus, in Marx's analysis, it is not the subjective volition of individual merchants or capitalists, or even of groups of merchants or capitalists, but the nature of the societies in which they function that plays the predominant role in conditioning their behaviour. Of course, there is no impenetrable barrier separating pre-capitalist from capitalist societies, nor is there an implication that the behaviour of the merchants or capitalists cannot influence the evolution of societies. In fact, it is the contradiction of the drives of an emerging capitalist class with a predominantly feudal society that is seen to constitute a major force for transition to capitalism. However, that contradiction must be coupled with other contradictions, such as those of free peasants and feudal lords, or of yeoman farmers with landless labourers, in order for the transition to actually occur.

Our aim here will be to analyse some of the ways in which merchants adjusted to British paramountcy. This will necessarily involve some discussion of the ways in which the merchants interacted with pre-British socio-economic formations. The interaction would take the form of adjustment punctuated by incidents of conflict. The adjustment to British paramountcy would also take the form of both collaboration and conflict. But the nature of collaboration or conflict in the two epochs would generally differ.

Most analysts would agree in characterizing pre-British social formations in India as pre-capitalist formations. However, there are a hundred-and-one ways in which a mode of production or social formation can differ from capitalism. All the hundred-and-one ways are not viable and only some clusters might be actually observed. An even smaller number might have survival value in the sense of characterizing a recognizable social structure over a certain length of time. But these different clusters would provide their own environment for the formation of an identifiable and separate group of merchants and their survival as a separate group. When British colonialism brought the Indian economy under its sway, the pattern of interaction of mercantile capital with the rest of the society would change and, correspondingly, some changes would also take place in the internal organization of merchant communities and groups. One of the tasks of a historian of Indian society is to look at these processes of selection of capitalists, and the further processes of survival and growth or extinction of particular mercantile groups. The current essay advances certain hypotheses that might help order the seemingly endless parade of mercantile groups across the pages of Mughal and British Indian history.

Some Salient Characteristics of Mercantile Groups in India in the Seventeenth and Eighteenth Centuries

Pre-British mercantile groups in India were enormously variegated in terms of ethnic and religious affiliation, connection with internal or external trade, the degree of diversification of functions, the scale of their operations, their connection with the actual processes of production, and their propensity to collaborate with the British. There has been a considerable amount of work by economic and social historians in recent decades bearing on the fortunes of particular business communities in India. But practically the only works that look at the organization and behaviour of business communities across the whole of India in the British period and immediately before it are D.R. Gadgil's *Origins of the Modern Indian Business Class: An Interim Report* (1959)[1] and V.I. Pavlov's *Indian Capitalist Class* (1964). Gadgil's book, although shorter and less informative in many ways than Pavlov's, achieves a greater depth of analysis, mainly because he is far more aware than Pavlov of the extremely vulnerable agrarian structure that provided the backdrop for the operations of Indian merchants in pre-British times. By vulnerability of the agrarian structure, we mean (i) the high degree of susceptibility of crop output to fluctuations in weather conditions, (ii) the near-subsistence level of living to which vast numbers of peasants, dependent labourers (including artisans) and wage-labourers had been depressed, and (iii) the huge drain of resources from agriculture to the urban areas. This vulnerability also provided opportunities for usury capital and speculative trading or banking capital by producing large fluctuations in harvest prices as between

---

[1] M.V. Nemjoshi assisted Gadgil in writing this book.

seasons, years and regions.[2] Pavlov's advantage lies in the use of an explicitly Marxist framework, but his grasp of the material he handles is much less sure-footed than Gadgil's.[3]

The issues discussed in this essay are not central to Gadgil's pioneering study. Moreover, in some respects, I have benefited from the work of economic historians which was not available when Gadgil wrote his monograph. The major differences in our emphasis compared with his work may be summarized as follows. First, while Gadgil emphasizes the high degree of exploitation of cultivators and the largely one-way flow of surplus from rural areas to towns under the Mughal (and post-Mughal) dispensations, he does not point out that this also provided an opportunity for making profits to the big bankers who supported the revenue-raising operations with advances for subsistence to ordinary cultivators.[4] Second, as a corollary, Gadgil rather exaggerates the role of urbanization in the growth of business communities of India. Third, Gadgil pays little attention to the variety of ways in which merchants or bankers interacted with rulers in different parts of India. He underplays both the importance of political patronage (and correspondingly, the opportunities available to *individual* merchants or particular business groups for acquiring political influence) for mercantile fortunes, and the conflicts between merchants and rulers that broke out from time

---

[2] Irfan Habib, in an authoritative article (Habib 1971), gives a lucid account of the dominant mode of appropriation under the Mughal dispensation, and of the importance of merchant capital in Mughal India. But he does not draw the inference that the mode of appropriation that thwarted the expansion of the agrarian economy through real capital formation and technical change also paradoxically strengthened merchant capital. He also attaches too much importance to the alleged dislocations of the eighteenth century in curbing the growth of incipient capitalistic modes of organization of production.

[3] There are two other books by Soviet scholars, viz., A.I. Chicherov's *India: Economic Development in the 16th–18th Centuries: Outline History of Crafts and Trade,* and A.I. Levkovsky's *Capitalism in India: Basic Trends in Its Development.* Although quite useful for discussion of particular issues, Chicherov's book suffers from a rather mechanical view of the evolution of socio-economic formations in India, and Levkovsky's from an uncritical attitude towards the data he gathers from a variety of sources. In any case, neither of the books is primarily focussed on the functioning or organization of business groups.

[4] This aspect is referred to by Pavlov (1964), in Chapter 2.

to time. Fourth, Gadgil fully accepts Van Leur's formulation that the distinction between 'pedlars' and 'merchant gentlemen' which was valid in the case of western Europe, say, in the sixteenth or seventeenth century, did not apply to Asian traders. If this was just a question of a convenient classification of the activities and status of particular mercantile groups, an empirical refutation would suffice.[5] But this is also connected with Gadgil's implicit view that only individually large accumulations of capital devoted to specialized production matter for economic growth.[6] Fifth, Gadgil tends to put more emphasis on formal guilds and associations of merchants and artisans and less emphasis on their informal modes of organization than the evidence about the power or influence of such guilds to withstand external pressure warrants. The power of sudden strikes or collective action on particular issues by the merchants or artisans of a particular locality was probably as great or as little as that of organized associations in getting the rulers—indigenous or foreign— to change their policies or regulations. Finally, the strength of Gadgil's account—its lack of commitment to any rigid frame of analysis—is also a source of weakness. He fails to delineate how changes in the general structure of polity and society constrained or stimulated the activities of particular groups of merchants and traders.

[5] See Van Leur (1955). His views have been reiterated by Niels Steenagaard and criticized, among others, by K.N. Chaudhuri and Ashin Das Gupta. It may be worth pointing out that Van Leur's distinction did not have much validity in the city-states of Renaissance Italy either (see Luzzato 1953). The enormous fluctuations in commodity prices dictated a high degree of diversification as a hedging device; and the uncertainty of political fortunes and, connected with that, the uncertainty of fortunes of even big merchants, dictated that a high proportion of resources be kept regionally liquid. The latter demanded a pyramidal structure of control and resort to petty trade and moneylending in the local context.

[6] See, for example, his statement (Gadgil 1959: Section 5): 'Accumulation of capital, innovation, etc., were much more possible and were likely to be more evidenced among the trading and financing classes than among the large number of scattered tradition-bound and relatively poor artisans.' There is no evidence that the traders and financiers were any less tradition-bound than artisans in India, or that they pioneered any more innovations than these artisans. They definitely accumulated more capital, but that capital was mostly used to perpetuate a mode of exploitation and control which severely inhibited innovations in production methods.

We shall pay a good deal of attention to the ways in which Indian merchants adapted their behaviour in the face of British colonialism. In order to assess what constituted adaptive behaviour and what was simply a continuation of patterns evolved in pre-British times, it is necessary to have some idea of the typical pattern of behaviour in the earlier period. We have already posited that since the pre-British social formations were a good deal variegated, we would expect an enormous degree of variation in the organization, behaviour and modes of interaction of mercantile communities. However, at the risk of being accused of perpetrating extreme oversimplification, we shall pick out certain specific features of these three aspects, viz., the organization, behaviour and modes of interaction (with the rulers as well as with the peasants and artisans) of important mercantile groups in pre-British times.

Merchants were organized in identifiable communities in most parts of India. There were big merchants, ship-owners or financiers such as Virjee Vora, Abdul Ghafur or Fateh Singh Jagat Seth in Gujarat or Bengal. They were wealthy merchants on their own but they were identified as belonging to particular communities. There was considerable cross-communal cooperation in matters of business and other matters of common interest, and the governments often recognized the heads of particular families (such as the family of Shantidas at Ahmedabad) or the leaders of particular communities as spokesmen for the business community, the city, or particular sections of the business community or particular localities of the city. Of course, there were business rivalries among prominent merchants, and sometimes these rivalries were given a specific communal colouring (for an example, see Khan 1965: Chapter 156). But there were many cases where business rivalries cut across any obvious communal lines or where different business groups cooperated in the face of a common threat (see Das Gupta 1970; Mehta 1981).

In some towns and cities, particularly in Gujarat, both merchants and artisans were organized in various associations or guilds (Gadgil 1959: Section 7; Pearson 1972; Bhadra 1976; Bayly 1978). The *mahajans* of merchants or the *panches* of artisans regulated commercial matters. Sometimes a caste *panchayat* and the mercantile or artisan *panchayat* were one and the same body, but this did not necessarily follow. Moreover, in some cities, particularly Ahmedabad, the Nagarseth represented the city in crucial negotiations with rulers or invaders. Although these institutions were most prevalent and formally organized in Gujarat, *mahajan panchayats* and looser commercial associations, often cutting across caste barriers, have also been found in cities as widely dispersed as Poona, Murshidabad and Benaras. The institutions of Nagarseths and *panchayats* of merchants were widely prevalent in Rajasthan (Tod 1829: 119–20, 553).

There were, of course, different levels among the merchants and financiers. This is easiest to see in the case of the financiers. Some 'bankers' lent to the Mughal *subedars* or their successors—the local *nawabs* or *rajas* who grew up in different parts of India—some lent to the big landlords, and some mere 'moneylenders' lent to peasants and artisans and the smaller landlords. Similarly, the big merchants trading across the seas operated side by side with wholesale traders transporting goods from one region of the country to another, petty traders acting as procurement agents of the bigger merchants and, of course, shopkeepers and pedlars.

Since we are speaking about a rather ill-defined period stretching roughly from the beginning of the seventeenth to the end of the eighteenth century, and since the information on any sub-period is rather fragmentary, it is not possible to make any generalization about the relative importance of seagoing merchants, big merchants of the interior, other wholesale merchants, and the vast numbers of petty traders who were engaged in mainly local trade. But it is important to emphasize the diversity of the organizational patterns and the continued survival of vast numbers of independent, small and not-so-small traders in various parts of the country. There were seagoing merchants owning a number of ships and dealing in millions of rupees, there were *banjaras* transporting vast quantities of grain and other produce from one part of the country to another, and there were *pykars* or *byaparis* owning a number of pack animals or bullock-drawn carts transporting goods from one mart to another. The Armenians seem to have played a special role in linking different parts of India and the rest of middle and west Asia with India.[7] The

---

[7] On the role of the Armenians in Indian and Asian trade, see Seth (1937: Chapters 21–34); Ferrier (1973); S. Chaudhuri (1975). On the importance of petty traders in the economy of Mughal India, see Bhadra (1980).

Gujarati ship-owning merchants, particularly the Muslims among them, seem to have played a similar role in linking Bengal and Gujarat. The acquisition of political power by the (British) East India Company led to a drastic decline in the fortunes of the Armenians and of the Gujarati merchants in Bengal.

When the Europeans came to trade in India, they adopted many of the features of the agency or *dalali* system, and the system of procurement through advances (*dadan*) that were practised by the Indian merchants. But whenever they could, they cut out the intermediaries and procured directly from the producers, or from the small traders who acted as their agents. Many Indian intermediaries acting as collaborators of the foreigners were in fact ruined in the process. We shall deal with this issue a little later.

Most of the big Indian merchants dealt in a variety of commodities and often engaged in the retail trade (this might include local moneylending by big bankers). Most of the European companies also tried to procure a variety of goods for sale in Europe and for intra-Asian trade. As has been pointed out already, this was a rational policy in view of the enormous fluctuations and uncertainties of the markets in goods as well as in credit.

We come now to the behaviour of the merchants and their interaction with the rest of the society and polity. The two themes are inextricably linked and we shall deal with them together.

The relations of bankers with ruling politicians are perhaps the simplest to describe. The bankers often acted as keepers of the state treasury and were often given the task of regulating the currency of the state.[8] They advanced money to the rulers when revenues fell short, or when the rulers (whether they were Mughal *subedars* or Maratha chieftains) needed money to finance their campaigns. In many cases, particularly in Rajasthan, the bankers also acted as tax farmers. The rulers sometimes relied on the bankers and the merchants for supply of essential commodities such as grain in times of scarcity, and for regulating prices in normal times.[9] Customs duties and other transit duties in ports were often collected by the rulers

---

[8] For a description of the activities of the House of Jagatseth in relation to the *subedars* and *nawabs* of Bengal, see Little (1967).

[9] For a summary of the evidence relating to such activities, see Pavlov (1964: Chapter 2).

Merchants and Colonialism

with the cooperation of leading merchants. Such reliance on Indian merchants or bankers apparently also extended to the Portuguese dependencies on Indian soil.[10]

While it was not entirely unknown for the nobles or high officials of the Mughals to engage in commerce, anything more than a temporary interest was frowned upon. Thus Azim us-Shan, grandson of Aurangzeb, was removed from the *subedari* of Bengal because he indulged excessively in private trade (Karim 1964: 16). If it was unusual for nobles to become full-time merchants, it was also unusual for merchants to become nobles, particularly when their functions included military duties. (Mir Jumla, of course, was an outstanding exception.) Big bankers and merchants could, and did, become ministers of kings and *nawabs* but, on the whole, it was understood that they would not aspire to membership of the class or group which ruled by sword and by hereditary right. There are stories of kings and rulers confiscating the property of merchants or bankers, but they are mostly exaggerated. Sequestration of property on the death of a wealthy man seems to have been carried out mainly in the case of royal servants who were suspected of improper gain.[11]

Some of the big Muslim merchants (particularly in Gujarat) seem not to have obeyed the unwritten code of mutual forbearance between merchants and rulers, but they seem correspondingly to have suffered much more drastically than their Hindu counterparts when political fortunes changed.[12]

This code of mutual forbearance also applied to the relations between bankers or moneylenders and *zamindars* or owner-cultivators. There were occasions when *zamindari* rights changed

---

[10] Pearson (1972). Port dues at Surat or customs duties (on salt) at the inland mart of Palli (in Rajasthan) could amount to a substantial fraction of total state revenues.

[11] There were specific instructions against indiscriminate sequestration. See, for example, Khan (1965: Chapter 109), 'Copy of a memorandum of court events in respect of confiscation of mansabdars' property'.

[12] See, for some examples of the vicissitudes of fortune of Muslim merchant princes, the cases of Mulla Muhammad Ali and Ahmed Challaby, in Khan (1965: Chapters 208, 216, 219). Hindu merchants also suffered because of personal quarrels with rulers or other merchants who had the ear of the rulers, but their families often survived as members of the 'peaceable' community.

hands because of indebtedness, but the transfers were probably limited within the circle who traditionally claimed rights of lordship. The transfer of ownership of land cultivated for indebtedness was rare: generally such transfers required the consent of village *patels*, *patidars* or local *zamindars*. Evidence is accumulating, however, of more frequent transfers of land in the eighteenth century in Bengal and Rajasthan (for Rajasthan, see Singh 1973). However, in Bengal, the *subarnabaniks*, the traditional goldsmith caste, are supposed to have desisted from purchases of land, and it is only the rising *telis* or *gandhabaniks*, with interests in intra-village or intra-regional rather than inter-regional or riverine or coastal trade, that were supposed to have deviated from the earlier mercantile code (Sanyal, 1975: 87–88).

These modes of interaction also went with typical modes of protest. The Charans or Bhats, who acted as the carriers of Rajasthan (and later on, as *banjaras*, foremost transporters of northern and western India from Rajasthan to Mysore on one side, and the borders of Bihar on the other), had a colourful mode of protest: they would threaten to commit suicide if their demands were not met (Tod 1978: 554–56). Other merchants or artisans would resort to *hartals*; in extreme cases, merchants would threaten to desert a place *en masse* (see, in this connection, Bhadra 1980: 75–76). These protests were often quite effective because the purses of the rulers would be directly hit, and because they could not easily organize an alternative method of meeting the supply or credit requirements of people in their seats of power. Artisans and workers of various kinds as well as merchants could sometimes use their freedom to migrate, to break contracts and use their collective organizations to make effective protests against extreme exploitation (for some examples, see Das Gupta 1979: 36–42). One of the distinguishing marks of British dominion in India was the relative ineffectiveness of such protests with rulers who were also merchants.

How did the merchants interact with the artisans? The typical modes seem to have been the following. (i) The artisans often worked on their own, buying their own raw materials, working them up themselves, and selling them either to the nearby marts or to wholesale merchants (or their agents) who traded with other regions. (ii) The artisan would be given an advance in money by the merchant. The former would buy the raw materials and deliver the product to the merchant at an agreed price. (iii) The merchant would advance the raw materials to the artisan, who would then deliver the finished or semi-finished product and be paid at a piece-rate. In this case the artisan would essentially be reduced to the position of a wage-labourer. (iv) There were also many factories in which a number of workers were brought together under one roof under the control of a merchant or merchants. But they were generally rare, for the reason that household-based industry allowed the merchant to expropriate the products of labour of all the members of the family, and no significant economies of scale seemed to operate in handicraft production. There were royal *karkhanas*[13] but they did not have to obey the dictates of the market.

In later sections we shall refer back to some of these modes of interaction of merchants with the rest of the society in pre-colonial India and, in the process, also elaborate on some of these modes.

Influence of European Traders on Indian Merchants and Artisans before the Establishment of British Supremacy

Under the governorship of Afonso de Albuquerque, the Portuguese established themselves as the most powerful maritime power in the Arabian Sea and also in the eastern seas up to the Indonesian archipelago. They proceeded to utilize their position partly to monopolize the sea route to Europe round the Cape of Good Hope, and partly to exact tributes from other sea-going merchants for 'protection' afforded to them. The Gujarati merchants initially offered stiff resistance against the depredations of the Portuguese, but after the 1530s, they generally accepted Portuguese control of the sealands and took out *cartazes* and paid duties to the Portuguese at Diu.[14] The Portuguese control over trade on the mainland was,

---

[13] See Gadgil (1959: Sections 6–10) and Habib (1971: Section III). Habib seems to overestimate the importance of the royal *karkhanas* as potentially capitalistic organizations. In a situation in which the wages of artisans were extremely low, and owners of production had little incentive to adopt more capital-intensive techniques, royal *karkhanas* could hardly lead to a systematic development of large-scale production or production techniques.

[14] On Portuguese conquests and operations in the Arabian Sea, Bay of Bengal and the Indian Ocean, see Boxer (1973: Chapter 2); and on

however, extremely limited: they were fully occupied defending Goa and other mainland enclaves they had established.

With the coming of the Dutch in the seventeenth century, a new record was reached in the ruthlessness and determination to monopolize trade. The attention of the Dutch East India Company came to be concentrated mainly on Indonesia and Ceylon. However, although their presence in India was limited to only a few settlements, they tried to control the channels of trade flowing out from, or flowing into, those points. For example, they tried to monopolize the trade between Hugli in Bengal and Ceylon (Om Prakash 1964).

The Dutch were followed soon by the French and the English, and the ultimate tussle for supremacy in India and the surrounding seas lay between the French and the English. So long as the Mughal power in India was intact, neither of these trading companies could make much headway in territorial conquests, but that was not for want of trying. The English were apt pupils of the Dutch who drove a hard trade with the aid of armed ships and armies where needed. The English came armed with the notion that it was only with force and the exercise of at least local sovereignty that they could establish bases for trade, and that it was only by inspiring fear among the Asians they could overcome the obduracy of the local rulers (K.N. Chaudhuri 1978: Chapter 6; Watson 1980).

How far did the operations of the European companies and private traders (including 'interlopers') lead to the enrichment of Indian merchants and artisans? The enrichment could come about through an expansion of the output of Indian fields and cottages, because of the stimulus provided by expanding trade, through a rise in the share obtained by the merchants and artisans of a constant retained value of the articles exported or through an increase in the values of the articles exported in comparison with those of imported articles. The evidence on all these aspects is as yet fragmentary. It has sometimes been claimed, mainly on the basis of the records of the European trading companies, that the total exports of India increased significantly in the seventeenth and eighteenth centuries. Even the records of the trading companies do not show an unambi-

---

Gujarati merchants' adaptation to the Portuguese presence, see Pearson (1976: Chapter IV).

guous trend. For example, the total imports from Asia into Britain on account of the English East India Company reached a value of £802,527 in 1684 and remained well below that figure until 1741; it is doubtful whether any increasing trend in the figures could be established between 1684 and 1760, when the figure of imports was £711,340 (K.N. Chaudhuri 1978: 508–10).

It is possible that increasing exports to other regions of India by the European companies could have been the dynamic element in the export trade. But on that score also the evidence is not unambiguous; a part, probably a major part, of the increase attained by the European companies was at the cost of the Asian merchants, and there were significant diversions of trade as between Asia and Europe and as between different Asian regions. The evidence regarding the terms of exchange between imports and exports as a whole remains equally ambiguous.

But what is not ambiguous is that the European companies meant to engross the major part of the gains that accrued from intra-Asian maritime trade and from trade between India and Europe. Their control of the sea-lanes to Europe and the total exclusion of Indian merchants from access to markets in Europe, or to sources of supply of the few commodities (including bullion) that were brought from west of Arabia to India, gave the European companies a decisive advantage over the Indian merchants.[15]

Of course, the Europeans were not content with domination of the sea-lanes, or the markets in Europe. They also wanted to exercise monopolistic control over supplies of the exportables in India. Where their political presence was feeble their ability to subordinate Indian merchants was of a low order, but they had a good try nevertheless, and many merchants were ruined in the process of trading with them.[16] In a situation of widely fluctuating markets and large cash requirements for working capital and for advances to suppliers, small merchants were often ruined in the course of

---

[15] This is the crux of the problem of trade between 'unequal partners' that was pointed out by me in my critique of K.N. Chaudhuri (1969). See Bagchi (1969).

[16] Thus many traders dealing with the House of Jagatseth were supposed to have been ruined in the process: see N.K. Sinha's 'Introduction' to Little (1967).

dealing with big bankers and merchants.[17] But the European companies were often in the position of borrowers in relation to the Indian merchants. It was essentially the political power wielded by the European companies that enabled them to subordinate their Indian suppliers—both merchants and artisans—and drive many Indian merchants out of business in the process, or ruin or impoverish them financially. Thus, for example, the English East India Company was much more effective in organizing 'joint stocks' of supplying merchants subordinate to them in Madras at a time when their attempts to do so in Bengal were as yet unsuccessful, because they exercised more complete local sovereignty at Fort St George than at Calcutta before the Battle of Plassey.[18]

Finally, there is no evidence whatever that artisans obtained a larger share of the value of their produce when they supplied the goods produced (either directly or through intermediaries) to the European trading companies.

The Fate of Independent Merchants and Artisans in the Areas of Colonial Control

The direct imposition of colonial control blocked certain avenues of development of both mercantile groups and artisanal work in the eighteenth and nineteenth centuries. In the context of Europe, Marx noted that there was a three-fold transition from merchant capital or artisanal industry to industrial capital:

> First, the merchant becomes directly an industrial capitalist. This is true in crafts based on trade, especially crafts producing luxuries

---

[17] For some examples of resistance by Indian merchants to the systematic attempt at the exercise of monopoly control by the English East India Company in the period 1670–1720, and the ruin of some of the big Indian merchants in the process, see S. Chaudhuri (1975: Chapter 4). The way the historian's language is influenced by the kind of source material he uses (East India Company records, in this case) is illustrated by this chapter. Indian merchants are seen as trying to organize 'rings' or dealing with 'interlopers', whereas the constant attempt of the Company to exercise monopoly control is played down.

[18] K.N. Chaudhuri (1978: Chapter 12), and S. Chaudhuri (1975: Chapters 4–5). See also my review of the first in *The Times of India*, 2 September 1979. Indrani Ray (1980) has elaborated on the theme of subordination of Indian collaborators by various European trading companies.

and imported by merchants together with the raw materials and labourers from foreign lands, as in Italy from Constantinople in the 15th century. Second, the merchant turns the small masters into his middlemen, or buys directly from the independent producer, leaving him nominally independent and his mode of production unchanged. Third, the industrialist becomes merchant and produces directly for the wholesale market. (Marx 1966: 325)

In the same chapter, he characterized the third path of transition as 'the really revolutionizing way'. Whether Marx's statement can be applied in the same way to Germany, Russia or Japan, as to Britain, France or the USA—and whether any distinctions in this regard pick out the countries undergoing a bourgeois-democratic revolution from those in which such revolutions had to await their defeat by foreign countries or were rendered unnecessary by a socialist revolution—are questions we will not debate in this essay. What is obvious is that the last two modes of transition were practically never observed in India or in other third world countries. Modern industrialists arose from the ranks of merchants who initially imported the needed techniques and methods of organization from abroad, with some local adaptations.

One of the reasons for the failure of the third or even the second mode of transition in India was that the operation of colonialism initially decimated the ranks of independent artisans or merchants who had close links with the production of craft industries. The change brought about by colonialism in this respect can be easily seen by comparing the situation of independent merchants and artisans at the end of the eighteenth century in Bengal and in Tipu Sultan's Mysore soon after the British had conquered that state. Information about the latter state is available from the reports of Francis Buchanan, who was sent by the East India Company to survey the resources of the conquered territories (Buchanan 1807).

If we look at the situation of merchants and artisans in eighteenth-century British Bengal, then several patterns of life-cycles of merchants can be observed: they could be traders on their own, middlemen between artisans and European chartered companies or private traders, putters-out, employers of wage-labour and of artisans as independent producers, artisans acting as production agents of merchants or European companies, artisans as wage-labourers in their own crafts, and artisans turning into landless agricultural or general labourers. A typical sequence was as follows: the East India Company buys cotton or silk goods from middlemen; after a few seasons it puts pressure on the middlemen to cut down prices either by rejecting the goods supplied as sub-standard or by refusing payment to them for the full quota; the middlemen are ruined or retreat from the market, the Company moves in to give advances to the artisans directly or through *dalals*, and binds the artisans not to sell their goods to competitors; the artisans are effectively reduced to mere wage-earners or worse, since peons are posted on them for collection of the finished goods and they are arrested and molested in other ways if they fail to comply with the legal or illegal demands of the Company's servants. Then the external market for the goods purchased by the Company collapses, the latter refuses to buy goods in former volumes, the artisans are in turn ruined and either hang on precariously to their earlier occupations or become general labourers looking for any employment (since few of the artisans owned land).

The developments in the various spheres of production up to the beginning of the 1780s, and the fate of the Indian merchants and producers connected with them, were brilliantly summed up in Burke's *Ninth Report*.[19] The trade in cotton cloth formed the major staple of the Company's investments, and here the heavy-handed coercion of the Company and its servants was felt perhaps by the largest number of direct producers. The *dalal* merchants or agents of the Company suffered in their turn as the Company changed its policy. The merchants or agents, of course, tried to transmit the pressure down to the weavers, generally successfully.

Trade in salt, over which the pre-British rulers had exercised only a loose kind of monopoly, was brought under a rigorous monopoly by Clive's Society of Trade. When this monopoly was abolished, and production and trade were thrown open to other traders—subject to the payment of a duty—the Company's servants managed to corner most of the trade (Barui 1979: Chapter II). There were various

---

[19] S.K. Sen (1969). The usefulness of this edition is impaired by unexplained excisions and lack of the full apparatus of citation.

turnabouts in the policy regarding salt, but the Company always retained monopoly rights in its trade. Salt production had been organized earlier by Indian merchants and *zamindars*, and produced by a class of producers called *molungees*. Under the dispensation of the Company, the supervision (and profits) of production devolved either on the Company's servants or salt farmers who were often *benamis* of those servants. The oppression of the *molungees* probably increased as the Company sought to fix the prices as well as quantities of salt to be delivered by the *molungees*.

In the case of silk production, one of the earliest moves of the Company was to discourage the production of finished silk goods, often by using force, since it was found to be more profitable to export silk yarn. In an attempt to improve the spinning and reeling methods of silk, the Company promoted the introduction of Italian silk filatures.[20] Many Indian merchants (including substantial ryots) set up filatures on their own. Filatures were also set up by *pykars* who acted as the middlemen between the *chassars* (cocoon-rearers) and the East India Company or other buyers of raw silk.

However, in order to prevent silk yarn from being sold to rival European companies or traders or Indian merchants trading with other parts of India, the EIC (from now on, EIC will denote the English East India Company) tried to compulsorily rent or buy up the filatures belonging to *pykars* or independent Indian producers. These measures naturally led to conflicts. However, from the end of the 1820s, a decisive decline in the demand for silk yarn and silk goods set in, and many independent producers gave up the production of yarn and voluntarily turned into agents for procurement of the Company's cocoons or raw silk.

Similar stories can be told of the suppliers of most of the other items of 'investment', such as opium or saltpetre, in which the EIC was interested. Against the relentless pressure of the EIC to monopolize the trade in all the items it was interested in, the Indian merchants and middlemen had three types of escape routes. The first was the opportunity for trading with other European Companies or traders (Sinha 1965: Chapters II-IV and IX; Mitra 1978). Apart

---

[20] The following account is based on Bhadra, *The Role of Pykars in the Silk Industry of Bengal*.

from the French and Danish Companies, there were the private European traders who operated legally or illegally within the EIC's territory, and who provided some competition against the EIC. The Company's servants also traded on the side and connived with their Indian collaborators in evading some of the regulations of the EIC. But the Napoleonic wars saw the disappearance of French competition, although they at the same time stimulated 'smuggling' and 'interloping'.

The second escape route available to both the Indian merchants and artisans was sale to the home market. However, the scope for such sales became more restricted as the EIC took increasingly effective measures to eliminate the competition of the Armenian and other merchants trading with the other parts of India, and as the incomes of Indian consumers and the demand for both luxury goods and necessities declined as a result of policies adopted by the Company. The tariff policy of the Company, of course, compounded the problem.[21] Smuggling of salt and of opium could also be treated as exploitation of the Indian home market by the Indian merchants (sometimes in collusion with the Company's servants) in a situation where the Company left no room for the legitimate activities of the independent merchants (Barui 1975; Barui 1979: Chapters V, VI).

The third escape route for the Indian merchants and middlemen was to pass the pressure down to the producers. This took the form of binding the producers by giving them advances (*pykars* and salt farmers resorted to this extensively), using actual physical force or the threat of physical coercion, and invoking the authority of the Company to browbeat the producers. Debt bondage was an extremely effective device because of the inexorable revenue demands of the Company—a demand that was rarely abated for famines, floods, droughts or other natural calamities.[22] Thus the EIC in effect imposed a mutually reinforcing policy of exploitation for grinding the primary producers—artisans and cultivators alike—down to subsistence level.

The direct producers, naturally, had much fewer escape

---

[21] On the continued sale of coarse goods outside the controlling authority of the Company, see Sinha (1970: 10).

[22] On the details of the revenue settlements made by the EIC, see Sinha (1968); Sinha (1970); Islam (1979: Chapters I–III); Ray (1979: Chapters II, IV).

routes. So long as the custom of rival traders was available, they could try to elude the control of the Company. The producers of handloom cloth would produce for the local market, but once the EIC consolidated its rule, the producers of luxury goods or exportables did not have much of a home market to fall back on.

In the face of all these pressures, there were naturally protests and collective resistance. The handloom weavers of Santipore in Bengal put up a determined resistance against the constant attempt at price-cutting by the Company (Sinha 1965: 169–70). Salt merchants combined with local *zamindars* to frustrate the attempts of salt farmers to control the trade as authorized by the Company, and carried on a thriving trade in contraband salt. Such resistance was, of course, sought to be put down by the Company with the use of force. But where there was an internal market for the commodity new 'smugglers' grew to take the place of older merchants.

Sometimes, the protest by the artisans took the form of giving up the calling altogether, as happened with the makers of *tanjeebs* at Teetabadly in Dacca district (Sinha 1965: 168–69). Increasingly, of course, as the forces of de-industrialization released by the Company's industries and the advent of machine-made goods from Europe overwhelmed the country, more and more merchants and producers lost their capital or their means of livelihood and were pushed back to the land as cultivators or as landless agricultural workers. *Pykars*, or independent merchants of silk, who had earlier advanced money to the Company or other buyers of their goods, now had to seek advances from the Company in order to meet their revenue and other cash obligations (Bhadra, *The Role of Pykars*, Section VI). Many artisans who had earlier worked on their own became dependent on moneylenders for financing their requirements of raw materials and subsistence. In northern India, handloom weavers rose in violent rebellion again and again as the forces of de-industrialization swept over them. For example, at Mubarakpur in the Azamgarh district of Uttar Pradesh, between 1813 and 1842, *julahas* broke out in violent riots in several cases, the major target of their wrath being the moneylenders (Pandey 1981: 33). Throughout the nineteenth century, there were many movements of artisans as well as peasants, in which moneylenders were singled out as targets of attack.

Even in post-Plassey Bengal, some Indian merchants prospered, but few of them prospered as independent merchants. Most of them owed their position directly or indirectly to the protection of powerful servants of the EIC, such as Clive, Hastings, Vansittart, Verelst, or, later on, to their collaboration with European business houses such as Palmer and Co., Alexander and Co., or Mackintosh and Co. They might be called *banias, sarkars,* or *dewans.* We shall use the generic name *banian* for all of them.[23] The servants of the EIC needed them as fronts for their illegal trading operations, as go-betweens for collecting information or bribes, as their channels of information on the Indian environment, and often as the initial providers of capital.

But the need of the Europeans for the services of these Indian collaborators diminished as the EIC gave up its trading monopoly so that private European capitalists could trade on their own in an unrestricted fashion, and as the Europeans acquired a better grip over the local money market through the floating of banks such as the Bank of Bengal, Union Bank and the Agra and United Services Bank. Furthermore, as European capital was directed towards indigo and sugar plantations and to the importing of manufactures rather than to the export of products of the Indian craft industry, and as British control over the hinterland intensified, the dependence of the Europeans on their Indian partners diminished greatly.

In order to understand what happened to the fabulously wealthy Bengali *banians* or *dewans* of the EIC's servants or its various departments (for example, Dwarkanath Tagore was *dewan* of the Salt Department) (Kling 1976: 19), it may be useful to divide this class of people into two broad groups: those who had made their money before 1800 or so, and those who made it afterwards. Most of the *banians* who made their money before 1800 as associates of the servants of the Company had easy opportunities of investing it in landed property. For example, Gokul Ghosal, the *banian* of Verelst, and the founder of the Bhukailas Raj family, was a big trader and a farmer of revenues. He and his nephew, Joynarayan Ghosal, acquired

---

[23] On the use of the term *banian* or *banyan*, see Yule and Burnell (1886: 63–64). The word *banian* was an Anglo-Indian coinage used to denote the servants or partners of European firms in Calcutta and eastern India.

landed property, and the family joined the ranks of the leading *zamindars* of Bengal (Sinha 1965: 104–06; Sinha 1968: 223; Islam 1979: 20). The same thing happened with the senior (Pathuriaghata) branch of the Tagore family.

The families which remained closely connected with the leading European agency houses or tried to compete with them in the usual export trades were less lucky. The Burrals, who were *banians* of Alexander and Co. for at least two generations, went down when that firm closed its doors in 1832. The collapse of the handloom exports of Bengal and the crisis in the indigo trade in the late 1820s and the 1830s brought down not only the leading agency houses and their close associates, but also such leading Indian firms as Mathooramohun Sein and Co. Only those Indians whose fortunes could not be forfeited as belonging to nominal partners of European agency houses, and who managed to create some substantial property in land or real estate, escaped the holocaust of the 1830s. The fall of the Union Bank only marked the end of a process which had begun much earlier: the defaulting European merchants decamped with the money or passed practically unscathed through the portals of the courts as insolvent debtors, while their Indian *banians* and partners were sold up for the debts of the firms. It is symptomatic that it was only Dwarkanath's knowledge of the law and his foresight in putting his *zamindaris* in trust for his sons that saved his *zamindari* property from the debtors while his business was wound up on his death (Kling 1976: Chapter X).

The question as to why the Parsi or Gujarati collaborators of the Europeans in Bombay survived as businessmen has been raised and answered in different ways. No satisfactory answer can be given until we have as much scholarly work available on the trade and economy of the Bombay Presidency in the early part of the nineteenth century as we have on Bengal. I have argued elsewhere that a major part of the explanation probably lies in the earlier and more complete domination of the hinterland of Calcutta by the British (Bagchi 1972: Chapter 6; Bagchi 1976). In elaboration of that argument, I would add that since the Maratha Confederacy was not finally defeated until 1818, and the EIC lost its trading monopoly between Europe and India in 1813, the merchants and artisans of western India escaped the worst excesses of the coercive monopoly imposed by the EIC and its servants. The British often needed the help of the Parsis in their wars against the Marathas, and the Parsis were eager to follow the British in establishing trading connections, particularly in China and East Africa. At least until the British had acquired unchallenged political supremacy in that part of India, these factors enabled the Parsis to secure more of a semblance of equality with their European partners.

The type of products exported from western India in the early part of the nineteenth century also offered certain advantages to the Indian merchants. Both cotton and opium came from deep inside the hinterland, often from areas that were within the native states and which were relatively inaccessible until the advent of the railways. The British never succeeded in completely controlling the production and trade in Malwa opium, in contrast to their monopolization of opium production and trade in eastern India. The same was true of trade in cotton, which was produced by millions of peasants. It would appear that in the first half of the nineteenth century (at least until 1813 or so), most of the internal trade in cotton in western India had passed from the hands of the Europeans, who probably found it more profitable to concentrate on external trade (Benjamin 1973). Moreover, the export trade in neither of these crops experienced a crisis of the magnitude that occurred in the case of exports of cotton cloth, silk goods or indigo in eastern India.[24]

On the negative side, collaborators of British officials never had the opportunity of acquiring revenue farming rights that the new *babus* and *rajas* of Bengal enjoyed in the later part of the eighteenth century and the early part of the nineteenth century.

However, the survival of Indian merchants with a toehold in big-time export trade in the early nineteenth century did not necessarily guarantee that they would be the first group of Indians to invest on a large scale in modern manufacturing industry. The Indian merchants in western India obtained a new lease of life from the cotton boom of 1862–65, and then the enormous profitability of the pioneer cotton mills in Bombay showed them the way to the

---

[24] For the general background of trade and exchange in Bombay in the nineteenth century, see Douglas (1900); Sullivan (1937); Nightingale (1970); Guha (1972); Dobbin (1972: Chapter I).

future.²⁵ Many Indian merchants were eliminated in the financial crisis of 1865–67. However, the holocaust was less severe than that which overtook the merchants of Calcutta in the aftermath of the agency house collapses of 1830–34, for three reasons. (i) The majority of Indian mercantile houses in Bombay were by then trading on their own, and they did not have to pay the debts of their British counterparts. (ii) An insolvency law passed obligingly by the Bombay government made it very difficult for creditors to get hold of the property of the insolvent debtors. (iii) Since most Bombay merchants were governed by the *Mitakshara* system of inheritance laws, it made it difficult for creditors to sell up the property of the defaulting debtors.

Even apart from the financial crisis of 1865–67, the Indian mercantile community of Bombay was exposed to other forces tending to undermine their position vis-à-vis European houses. First, the extension of railway communications into the interior enabled European export houses, such as Ralli Bros., Volkart Bros., etc., to penetrate directly into the cotton districts and eliminate the smaller Indian merchants. The acquisition of the cotton-rich Berar districts by the British government from the Nizam in the 1850s, gave the British firms a far easier access to those districts. Furthermore, the large-scale operations of the big European export houses enabled them to reap the advantages of technology that was complementary

---

[25] The prospectus for the Anglo-Indian Spinning and Manufacturing Company, floated in Manchester in 1874 for operating in Bombay, estimated that Indian mill-made cotton goods consumed in India enjoyed a cost advantage of 30 per cent compared with similar goods exported from England to India. It quoted one Lancashire man managing a mill in India as saying that an efficiently managed mill there ought to return its cost in three years. The appeal to prospective shareholders in India on behalf of the mill (one-third of the shares were reserved for subscription in India) quoted the following figures of the latest dividend rates declared by Bombay mills (figures in per cent):

Mill	Rate	Mill	Rate
Alliance	32	Great Eastern	24
Bombay Royal	19	Alexandra	24
Manockjee Petit	15	Albert	20
Oriental	30	Morarjee Goculdass	20
Bombay United	20	Jivraj Baloo	23

These attractive figures were well below the *profit* rates realized by the pioneer cotton mills.

to railway carriage. At first, the cotton crop was sent in loosely packed *dokras*, or rough sacks; their bulk made it impossible for the Great Indian Peninsula Railway to carry them off to the ports promptly. Then presses and half presses were set up for packing cotton into fully pressed and half-pressed bales. The railways conferred an advantage on the owners of full presses by charging a higher freight rate on half-pressed bales (Lyall 1870: Chapter XII). Naturally, the big European export houses controlling large numbers of presses in the cotton districts came to enjoy an enormous advantage over the majority of Indian cotton exporters.

The spread of European-dominated financial institutions also tended to favour the big merchants with Presidency-wide connections in relation to the smaller merchants, and European merchants in relation to the Indians. When the (old) Bank of Bombay opened a branch at Broach, it favoured the Europeans and Eurasians at the expense of the Indian dealers, so that the Bombay *Gazetteer* recorded in 1877 that the greater part of the cotton trade was by then 'carried on by Europeans and Eurasians, only about one-eighth remaining in the hands of the local capitalists' (*Gazetteer of the Bombay Presidency* 1877: 446). Similarly, in the district of Khandesh, it was reported in 1880 that with improved communications local moneylenders and traders had been worsted by Marwari merchants and Bhatias from Bombay (the latter were said to be 'masters of the new system of trade by rail and wire'), and the trade at Jalgaon was mostly in the hands of nineteen firms, two of them European—the Mofussil and the New Berar Companies (*Gazetteer of the Bombay Presidency* 1880: Chapter V, 191–93).

The upshot of all this was that the Europeans apparently managed to acquire a much larger share of the cotton trade in 1875 compared with 1851.[26] However, in spite of these changes, Indians did manage to retain a significant share in cotton exports. The British government were also not able to bring the export of 'Malwa' opium entirely under their control, and Indian traders had a freer hand in

---

[26] Vicziany (1979). The degree of decline of Indian share in cotton exports has probably been overestimated in this paper, for, according to some contemporary evidence, a considerable amount of Indian-owned cotton was exported under the umbrella of European names. Cf. also Benjamin (1973).

the native states from where this opium came than the British territory. However, what really saved the Indian mercantile community in western India was the growth of cotton mills in Bombay and Ahmedabad. Most of the merchants setting up these mills continued to have a large stake in trade as well as industry, and the pattern has continued till today.

The Absolutism of Tipu versus Capitalist Colonialism

Our comparison between Indian merchants in eastern India and in Bombay or Gujarat has at best been incomplete. In particular, we have said little about the fate of artisans in Bombay proper, mainly because I am not familiar with the material available on the subject. But incomplete as it is, we have seen that it is possible to discuss the fates of the *babu* collaborators of Calcutta and the *saheb* collaborators of Bombay without postulating *ab initio* that it was the difference in their values or even their lifestyles that led to the difference in their fates. There were definite differences in the aspirations of the Parsi *sahebs* and the Bengali *babus*: the former wanted to be esquires, knights and baronets, the latter were satisfied with the titles of *rajas* and *maharajas*.[27] The Bengali *babus* were probably more inward-looking than the Parsis, for the simple reason that the latter belonged to a small community which had prospered with migration from Surat to Bombay, and had therefore no larger

---

[27] The literature on the Bengali *babu* culture is enormous. A reference to the anthologies compiled by Brajendranath Bandyopadhyay and Benoy Ghose and to their own books will provide enough documentation. The Parsi craze for imitating the lifestyles of the British is well-known. In 1834, the Governor of Bombay issued a minute directing that the following persons should be addressed as 'Esquire': Juggonath Sunkersett, Bomanjee Hormusjee, Framjee Cowasjee, Nowrojee Jamsetjee, Jamsetjee Jejeebhoy, Dadabhai Pestonjee, Dhakjee Dadajee, Cursetjee Cowasjee, Cursetjee Cowasjee Dady, Mohamed Ali Rogay, Cursetjee Rustomjee, Mohamed Ibrahim Mocha, Hormasjee Bhicajee Chinoy (Maclean 1880: 37). Of the thirteen honorary esquires, at least nine were Parsis. This was a much higher proportion than that of Parsis to the Indian population of Bombay city or of the number of Parsi merchants to the total number of Indian merchants in the city. It is also interesting that the only baronets to be created by the British from among their Indian or Asian subjects in India in the nineteenth century seem to have been three Parsis (Jamsetjee Jeejeebhoy, Cowasjee Jehangir and Dinshaw Manokjee Petit) and one Baghdadi Jew settled in Bombay (Albert David Sassoon).

community to seek approbation from. But the difference can be exaggerated. An enlightened *babu* such as Dwarkanath Tagore might endow the Calcutta Medical College or start steamship companies, and might yet spend an enormous sum on alms to *brahmans* on the death of his adoptive mother. On the other side of India, Ardeseer Cursetjee Wadia, the first Indian to be elected a Fellow of the Royal Society, even when travelling to England with the object of improving his skills as a mechanical engineer, would refuse to eat cooked food if it had not been prepared by a Parsi (Kling 1976: Chapters I, II, VII; Wadia 1957: Chapter XVIII). In respect of expenditure for entertaining the Europeans, there was probably not much to choose between the two groups of collaborators. The Bengali *babus* almost certainly wasted more money on ceremonies, without getting any financial return. But such wasteful expenditure was at least partly a result of the blocking of their investment channels. Most of the differences in the fortunes of the two communities can be explained by the greater degree of independence from individual Europeans acquired by Parsi merchants such as Jamsetji Jeejeebhoy, Framjee Cowasjee, etc., and by the easier access they enjoyed to external trade. The study of differences in such objective factors caused by the differential impact of colonialism has to go much further before we need to bring in differences in world outlook to explain the differences in the fates of Bengali *banians* and Parsi guarantee brokers.

We have already seen, by comparing Mughal and British India, that the political power acquired by the EIC had a significant impact on the fortunes and position of Indian merchants and artisans. Interestingly enough, colonialism can be seen to have had a decisive impact even compared with the kind of absolutist state Tipu Sultan sought to set up in Mysore. Tipu's government had a monopoly of trade in sandalwood, black pepper and cardamom. It engaged in foreign trade on a large scale and sought to engross some sectors of the wholesale trade.[28] Some measures of Tipu's government, such as prohibition of trade with British-controlled territories, were almost certainly dictated by his inimical relations with the EIC's government

---

[28] For a description of Tipu's policies in regard to trade, see Gopal (1971: Chapter II).

and by the continual tendency of the merchants to evade some of the regulations.

These measures of Tipu may have alienated some of the bigger merchants. But many artisans, employers of wage labour and smaller merchants seem to have prospered under his reign. Production by artisans on the basis of advances made by merchants was also very widespread in his kingdom. Francis Buchanan bears ample testimony to this. These iron-smelting enterprises in Mysore generally were operated by artisans employed as wage-labourers by proprietors. Buchanan found the apparent profit remaining to the proprietor to be rather small (this was true of iron-smelting in the districts of Madhu-giri, Chin-narayan-durga, Hagalawadi and Devarayadurga). He concluded that the proprietor in general got the money from the merchant, and that 'his only claim for reward was some trouble in settling the accounts and the risk of some of the people running away with the advances made to them' (Buchanan 1807: 33).

At Satimangalam (on the way from Kaveri-pura Ghat to Coimbatore) Buchanan found weavers taking advances from Indian merchants as well as from the Commercial Resident of the EIC at Saliem (Salem) (Buchanan 1807: 239–40). His view was that the Indian merchants kept the weavers always in debt: so long as the weaver was indebted to a merchant, he must always work for him at a low wage; and if a merchant wanted to take a new weaver in employ, he must repay the latter's debt to his former master. But in the same district, Buchanan found weavers rich enough to make the cloth on their own account, and sell it to the best advantage.

At Coimbatore, which had earlier been within Tipu's kingdom, Buchanan found weavers either taking advances from Indian merchants or producing cloth with their own capital:

> Each of the different classes of weavers here forming, as it were, a kind of family, the richer assist the poor; so that those who work for country use are either able to make the cloth on their own account, or at least are not obliged to take advances from a native merchant for more than one piece at a time. Those who once get into the debt of a native merchant are ever afterwards little better than slaves, and must work for him at a low rate.

Even under Tipu, thus, handicraftsmen could not entirely

avoid the fate of debt-slavery to merchants (Buchanan 1807: 264). Moreover, Tipu's kingdom was, after 1792, a beleaguered fortress, constantly under threat of British occupation. Also, in spite of his attempts to shut out the evil influence of the British traders, the artisans and merchants were subjected to the pull of their export-oriented business connections. Subject to all these limitations, artisans and merchants retained a considerable degree of independence in Mysore, particularly when they catered to the home market: Tipu's policies were at least not designed to contract the size of that market. In fact, some of his policies went further in diffusing new skills—such as those of metalwork and gun-making, and stimulating local production. British policies and the influence of the international capitalist network could only thwart artisanal production and mercantile independence. At Satimangalam, for example, Buchanan found that many weavers had given up working, in protest against a stamp-duty on the amount of cloth produced which had replaced a tax on looms that Tipu had levied (the latter would, *ceteris paribus*, stimulate output) (see Gopal 1971: 15–16).

Over the course of the nineteenth century, the handloom industry remained far more intact in south India than in most other parts of India. The relative inaccessibility of much of the terrain, the consumption habits of the people, the access to local supplies of cotton, the desperately low standard of living of the handicraftsmen—may all have contributed to this outcome. But it is worth asking how much Tipu's desperate stand against the British till the very end of the eighteenth century was responsible for this outcome. While Tipu's government tried to monopolize trade in certain articles, most internal trade was left free, and encouragement was also offered to specific (generally non-British) groups of merchants or individuals for trading with his kingdom. Further, in the trading corporation set up by Tipu's state, ordinary subjects could take a share (Kareem 1973: 168). Thus, Tipu's monopoly was of a very different kind from the one imposed by the EIC and private European merchants in Bengal between 1757 and 1813. Moreover, the encouragement of production of new types of goods, including armaments and metal products, mainly for internal use, also provided stimulus to both artisanal and mercantile activity. Some of the mercantile groups which thrived under Tipu's dispensation somehow survived in the truncated state of Mysore, and helped slow down the process of deindustrialization and the European monopolization of mercantile activity in the interior of south India. But these suppositions need to be substantiated by intensive work on the transition between Tipu's kingdom and the native state of Mysore under British protection.

Artisans as well as merchants were all the time at risk when faced with the deliberate weapons and the impersonal forces released by colonialism. But there were some areas less at risk than others. A greater degree of organization among merchants and artisans probably did increase their power of resistance against colonial depredations. Gujarati merchants, as we shall see, made a better showing in this respect than most other mercantile communities. Gujarati artisans seem also to have shared some of this relative immunity. Even as late as the latter part of the nineteenth century, we have accounts of artisans in Gujarat who were themselves men of some capital. For example, among the Bhavsars—calico-printers and dyers by profession—there were men of capital who owned from Rs 5,000 to Rs 20,000, and prepared articles on their own account. But the majority seem to have been employed by traders and 'other men of capital', and were paid according to the number of robes or *sarees* they printed (*Gazetteer of Bombay Presidency* 1899: 178).

In order that merchants should be able to control production and accumulate capital on that basis, the craft organization of production itself must survive, and must prove a profitable avenue for employment of capital. For master craftsmen to become industrial capitalists, the same condition must apply and, in addition, the craftsmen must be prosperous enough to accumulate capital for investment in increasingly capital-intensive enterprises.[29] In colonial India,

[29] For an earlier discussion, on similar lines, of the obstacles against craftsmen becoming industrial capitalists in British India, see Buchanan (1934, rpt 1966: 145–46 and 343). Buchanan distinguished between the putting-out system and 'the finance and order' system which, according to him, characterized the relationship of the Indian artisan and the merchant. Under the latter system, the producer continues to superintend the work and the merchant can exploit the labour of the whole family of the craftsman (ibid.: 110–11). However, by the beginning of the twentieth century, in many parts of India, employers were putting several workers together under one shed for producing silk and cotton cloth. Furthermore, under the putting-out system also, the labour of the whole family was often at the disposal of the putter-out.

it was the merchants who emerged as industrial capitalists because the artisans were too poor, and because many of them had been thrown out of craft employment through processes of de-industrialization. But in the rare cases where craft production survived, it provided a reservoir of skills for some branches of modern industry. Thus, in Gujarat, the craft skills of bleaching and dyeing proved useful for mill production of cotton cloth (Bagchi 1976: 264). In England, skills of wood-working were often transferable to the fabrication of the early vintages of machines with wooden as well as metal parts (Musson 1972).

The survival of clusters of merchants and artisans moving jointly into the machine age was practically ruled out in most parts of British India. Even Gujarat provides only a partial exception. The only link between the craft skills and machine industry was often provided by the *julahas* or *tantis* manning the weaving departments of jute mills and cotton mills: this generally meant only a transition from semi-servile wage-earners in craft industry to semi-servile wage-labourers in mill barracks.

Conditions for Survival of Mercantile Communities in Nineteenth-Century India

While independent artisans practically disappeared from the face of the Indian earth, some mercantile communities survived to provide the controllers of large business houses in twentieth-century India. Given the fact that, after 1818, no major part of India was outside British political hegemony, what were the conditions for survival of the mercantile communities? Without presuming to provide an exhaustive answer to such a question, the following four sets of factors may be singled out for special attention. First, the relationship of merchants to land was crucial in determining whether merchants would simply become landlords, or whether they would be wiped out in a major depression when they were not backed by the security of land, or whether they would find a mode of survival as merchants by diversifying into the control of the usufruct of land while remaining merchants. Second, and connected with the first set of factors, the continued existence of numerous native principalities provided a limited sanctuary to some groups of bankers against the worst blows of British rule. Third, the laws relating to inheritance seem to have been very important in preserving or destroying mercantile property. Paradoxically enough, the communities under the more 'progressive' (because more individualistic) system of property laws were wiped out, whereas those who survived were all under some variant of the 'less progressive' system of *Mitakshara* law. Fourth, only those mercantile communities survived which managed to retain an intra-communal cohesiveness as merchants. In a sense, the community must be semi-open and dense in terms of organizational network. It should be capable of digesting intelligence regarding changes in the patterns of trade and reacting to it appropriately; at the same time, it must have claims on communication and trade which cannot be disrupted by competitors from outside.

Land and the Indian Mercantile Community

In pre-British India, by and large, private property in land was hedged around by various restrictions imposed by the superior political authority or by local communities. Superior rights to the produce of the land in the form of a right to share in the rent went with claims to a position within the political hierarchy (Neale 1979). Right to cultivate the land, on the other hand, belonged to the peasants or ryots, whose movement was sought to be limited by various devices. Merchants did not fit into either of these categories. In Gujarat the Hindu merchants shared with the common (non-Rajput) peasantry the characteristic of being unarmed (*Gazetteer of the Bombay Presidency* 1901: 25)—and with the ruling princes or mercenary soldiers, that of having no special restrictions on mobility. But they had to seek the protection of controllers of land, be they Mughal princes or *subahdars*, Rajput or Maratha kings or chieftains, or autochthonous tribes.[30] The inability of the merchants to fight

---

[30] This situation prevailed also in other parts of India. A curious example can be found among the Komati traders of south India. They were related to the Madigas (the leather workers of the 'Telugu country') by an interesting custom. The former had to invite the latter to any marriage ceremony and obtain the Madiga's consent. If a Madiga was not satisfied, he could 'effectually put a stop to a marriage by coming to the house at which it was to be celebrated, chopping away the plantain trunks and carrying them off'. According to Thurston and Rangachari (1909: 327), this custom was a recognition of the lordship exercised by these depressed castes in bygone days.

oppression politically, which has been commented on, has something to do with this enforced disarmament of the mercantile community—particularly among the Hindus.[31]

The introduction by the British of generalized private property in land and the effective separation of land-ownership from the right to share in the political decision-making process (Ray 1979: Chapters II and IV) changed all this. But the change was by no means complete nor of a uniform character in all parts of India.

When the British laws, aimed at making land a vendible commodity and abolishing most of the traditional restrictions on the alienation of land for debt, were introduced, certainly more merchants and moneylenders began to acquire land than they had ever done before. But in most parts of India, merchants or moneylenders did not corner the major fraction of the land that changed hands, nor did they rush in to buy land or revenue-farming rights wherever an opportunity presented itself.[32]

There were certain obstacles against merchants turning landlords in British India. First, the purchase of land renders capital illiquid so that the merchant is not able to take advantage of more profitable opportunities of investing it, should they be available in future. The more localized and the more imperfect the market in land or in superior rights to land is, the greater is the illiquidity or immobility of capital invested in land-ownership or revenue-farming. The difficulty of communication between different parts of the country before the spread of the railways all over India, and the existence of overlapping rights in the same piece of land held by several persons, meant that land was both an imperfect and, from a financial (and not just physical) point of view, an immobile asset.[33]

---

[31] In refutation of this point, it may be said that the *banjaras*, the leading overland transporters in eighteenth-century India, were armed. However, their failure to observe the code of mutual forbearance prevailing between merchants and landlords or cultivators contributed to their dissolution as a mercantile group. They became marauding bands or nomadic tribes, and were hounded by the British as their conquests covered the land.

[32] For a careful study of the pattern of change in superior land rights in the Benaras region, and the reasons for purchase of land by men who had made money as government officials or merchants, see B.S. Cohn (1979: 78–79).

[33] One symptom of the lack of mobility of property in land or superior revenue-farming rights was that no specialized estate agents or surveyors

The second obstacle in the way of merchants becoming landholders was that the British did not really convert land into a fully vendible commodity. For political reasons, they had to recognize, at least in the region outside Bengal, that there were several layers of claims to the same piece of land, so that an unambiguous property in land could not be created. Moreover, no land could be held by a proprietor absolutely except in Assam or other plantation areas, where the British introduced the right of holding land under a 'fee simple' for the benefit of European planters. The regular payment of rent or tax to the government was the condition for holding any piece of land, and the governmental claim in this respect over-rode the claims of all other creditors. In the Permanently Settled areas of Bengal, the British government perhaps came closest to ignoring the rights of the inferior right-holders and peasants, and it is not surprising that many wealthy merchants bought *zamindari* rights there. However, even in Bengal it would be wrong to say that merchants became *zamindars* and therefore ceased to be merchants. It would be more appropriate to say that with the drying up of investment opportunities and the extreme vulnerability of exports of traditional commodities, prudence dictated that a substantial part of the wealth, however acquired, should be invested in *zamindari*, urban real estate, or government securities. In fact, many wealthy merchant families, by and large, avoided *zamindari* (the management of which was not within the range of skills expected of a traditional merchant) and invested their wealth in the other two kinds of assets.[34]

The third obstacle against merchants turning into landowners was the existence of strong *zamindars* (persons recognized from pre-British days as possessing the right to pay government revenue), or *taluqdars*, or their equivalents on the land, and their resistance against the attempt of an outsider or a local new man to exercise superior rights in land.

In the *ryotwari* areas, these difficulties were compounded

---

of the type made familiar by the novels of George Eliot relating to the English countryside ever grew up in colonial India. Nor could somebody simply decide, following Bingley of Jane Austen's *Pride and Prejudice*, to buy an estate neighbouring that of a friend.

[34] Cf., for example, the inventory of assets of Ramdulal De, in Sinha (1978: 79–80).

by another factor. The cost of managing a large number of scattered holdings could be quite high, so that a really big merchant or banker would not find it profitable to lock a substantial part of his capital in land. Moreover, the government probably appropriated a much larger fraction of the surplus produced by *ryotwari* land, so that the attractiveness of revenue-farming was lower than in the Permanently Settled areas. Moreover, in the Permanent Settlement, the surplus accruing to the *zamindar*, or the holders of intermediary rights, tended to go up with population growth, growth of output and increase in the proportion marketed to total output. The *ryotwari* areas, on the other hand, probably enjoyed a higher rate of growth of agricultural productivity (cf. Bagchi 1976: Sections IV, V) after their vulnerability was reduced through better irrigation. The merchant could often extract a higher surplus from the peasant there by keeping him in debt bondage and sequestering part of his produce every year, than by taking the land away from him.

The factors mentioned above would go a long way to explain why many important mercantile groups remained merchants and did not become landed magnates. There are even cases recorded of merchants who wanted to retain an 'image of the "*accommodating saraf*"' by lending money to *zamindars* at high rates of interest, but without acquiring a permanent title to land (Kolff: 1979: 61–62). Of course, when opportunity beckoned, merchants were not backward in acquiring *zamindari* rights cheaply, particularly if the firm was big enough to consider such purchases as just a way of spreading risks as between different assets in its portfolio. Thus, several large Marwari firms, which had been generally reluctant to hold illiquid assets, became big *zamindars* in Uttar Pradesh, owning scores of villages each (Timberg 1972: Chapter V). Moreover, for the sake of prestige (which might not be without its commercial value), a branch of the family might become landlords, or describe themselves as *zamindars*.[35] However, too close an involvement in land-ownership and management generally meant the doom of the family as merchants.

---

[35] G.D. Birla, for example, was described as 'mill-owner, merchant and zamindar', in the *Indian Year-Book: 1939–40*. In the same volume, R.K. Dalmia is included in the ranks of 'Indian nobles'.

Because of peasant resistance and fear of ruin of old *zamindar* and *taluqdar* families, the British government, from the 1870s onwards, interposed legal obstacles against the acquisition of land or *zamindari* rights by Punjab. This did not, of course, stop transfers of land to merchants or bankers under various pretexts or disguises, nor did it stop the so-called 'agriculturists' themselves turning into usurers vis-à-vis declining or extravagant *zamindars* and seasonally or chronically starving peasants. Hence, in order to analyse the peculiar amalgam of methods of exploitation through usury, landlordism and monopoly in trade, we have to study the phenomenon of the landlord acting as usurer and trader as closely as that of the merchant or banker turning into a landlord. Even where the landlord was the main exploiter, the merchant was often a crucial servicing agent to the mechanism of exploitation. He supplied funds to the *zamindar* regularly or in emergencies,[36] he helped market the produce retained by the *zamindar* or sold in distress by the peasants, and lent money to the peasantry and kept them in thraldom, often acting as an agent of the *zamindar*. There were many conflicts between the *zamindar* and the merchant, but such conflicts did nothing to change the mechanism of exploitation.

What I have said underscores the fact that many old mercantile houses in the interior of India must have seen their role, even under British rule, as a continuation of their earlier function of servicing the landed magnates rather than supplanting them. At least, this must have been true in the first half of the nineteenth century in those areas where the rights of the so-called village *zamindars* or village proprietors could not be swept away by the British. In the post-1857 period, even in such areas, many merchants encroached on the sectors of traditional dominance by the landlords, but that is, properly speaking, a story of the final consolidation of the semi-feudal modes of exploitation and the further development of their internal contradictions.

---

[36] When Awadh *talukdars* borrowed from the Bank of Bengal in the 1870s, local *sahukars* were often guarantors of the loans. See Bagchi (1987).

Native States as Sanctuaries of Indian Merchants

During the troubled years of the eighteenth century, in various parts of India, great bankers used to lend large sums of money to warring chieftains, who included members of the Maratha Confederacy as well as the *nawabs* and *subedars* who had divided the remnants of the Mughal empire. The lending by bankers on the guarantee of state finances continued in the native states even in the nineteenth century. (British adventurers had participated on an enormous scale in the spoliation of the Nawab of Arcot, the Nizam of Hyderabad and the Nawab of Awadh, but that is yet another story.) In 1805, for example, when Colonel Walker, as the agent of the East India Company, was trying to reform the finances of the Gaikwad of Baroda, he 'consolidated the demands of certain shroffs which with interest amounted to Rs 6,00,286' (*Gazetteer of the Bombay Presidency* 1883). This sum did not include the debts owed to the great state bankers of Baroda, Hari Bhakti and Narsu.

In spite of Colonel Walker's reforms, the Baroda state retained the so-called *potedari* system, under which the state did not maintain any treasury of its own but instead drew on a handful of state bankers called *potedars*, for such sums as it required. 'It did not at any time lodge money with the banker, but it granted him a *varat* or letter of credit on some *izaradar*, or farmer, of the state revenues in one of the *mahals*, who honoured the *varat* at the time of paying in the rent of his farm' (*Gazetteer of the Bombay Presidency* 1883: 396). So Sayajirao II entered into a partnership with the *potedars*, often becoming their rival in lending to his own state. The system of farming revenues to *izaradars* and of using the state banks and the *potedars* as the state treasury continued until Sir T. Madhava Rao was appointed by the British treasury as the Dewan of Baroda.[37] Naturally, under the earlier system, the state bankers possessed enormous funds, some part of which was also employed outside the state. Thus, even in 1883, eight years after the reforms of Madhava Rao, the houses of Hari Bhakti and Gopalrao Mairal, the two biggest state bankers of Baroda, were said to possess a capital of Rs 75,00,000 each (ibid.: 125).

---

[37] For a description of the history of farming and *potedari* systems, see *Gazetteer of the Bombay Presidency* (1883: 392–420).

In Hyderabad, Indian bankers acted as treasurers of the Nizam's government until they were virtually supplanted by the firm of William Palmer and Co., which held the whole of the Nizam's territory to ransom. Although determined opposition by Charles Metcalfe, the then Resident at Hyderabad and later, Governor-General of India, compelled Palmer and Co. to disgorge some of the gains, the influence of that firm and, later on, that of a financier called Dighton, continued.[38] The system of taking loans from the Arabs (who controlled the mercenary forces and became big landlords), the *amils* and the *sahukars* continued. The *sahukars* were often in league with those Europeans who were supposed to have an influence with the Residency and the Nizam's government. In spite of a degree of stabilization achieved by Salar Jang, the most famous minister of the Nizam in the nineteenth century, the Nizam's government continued to borrow money from the *sahukars*, as well as from the Bank of Bengal when the latter established a branch there. Thus, in 1883, for example, the Nizam's government borrowed money from the following *sahukars* at 6 per cent per annum in lieu of *hundis* on the district treasuries:

Sahukar	Amount of loan (Hallec sicca Rs)
Seolal Motilal	5,00,000
Bansilal Abirchand	3,25,000
Motilal Ramanna Govindass	2,00,000

The Nizam's government proposed to borrow additional amounts in 1889 at 9 per cent per annum from three other *sahukars* as 'an exceptional favour'.[39] Bansilal Abirchand was a very big firm which had acted in the 1870s as the *khazanchee* of the Bank of Bengal at places as distant as Amritsar and Bombay, and had been a serious contender also for the *khazanchee*-ship in Hyderabad. This access to the revenues of native states provided many of the *sahukar*

---

[38] For summary accounts of the affairs of William Palmer and Co., see Kaye (1858: 31–94) and Thompson (1937: Chapter XIII).

[39] Andhra Pradesh State Archives, Instl. 22, List 2, S. No. 34, file on 'Loans and Advances', 1889. Interesting newspaper reports of loans from *sahukars* are given in Syed Mehdi Ali (1884).

firms with the opportunity for investing their funds on a large scale, and correspondingly enabled them to mobilize large amounts of capital when required.[40]

The single most important region which served both as the source and as the base of the biggest mercantile community in India, viz., the Marwaris, was Rajasthan. The petty and not-so-petty principalities of Rajputana served as the organizational bases of various sections of Marwari traders. Since the *banias* in these states often served as ministers, state treasurers and tax farmers, they also accumulated some capital from these operations.[41]

The native states provided the merchants also with opportunities for speculation. Not only Hyderabad and Baroda but also a small state such as Jaisalmer, with only a lakh of rupees as revenue in a normal year (around 1908), had its own currency, *akhai shai*, whose value fluctuated widely in relation to the British Indian rupee (*The Imperial Gazetteer of India* 1908: Vol. XIV: 8). Indian merchants played these exchanges, made money and retained their skills in exchange speculation when the foreign exchange transactions between India and the rest of the world were monopolized by British-controlled exchange banks and agency houses.

The native states which provided the initial bases for mercantile firms were not necessarily the major beneficiaries of the industrial ventures which these firms started. It was Baroda and Gwalior rather than Jaipur and Bikaner which succeeded in attracting mercantile firms promoting industrial ventures. But that shows that while the native states might have provided a sustaining medium for Indian mercantile houses, they could not stimulate industrial growth in the absence of several other facilitating conditions. But that broad statement is true of British Indian territory as well as the native states.

---

[40] For further information on the firm of Bansilal Abirchand, see Timberg (1972: 136–37.)

[41] On the origins of the Marwari mercantile communities, see Gadgil (1959: Section 6), and R.V. Russell and Hira Lal (1916, rpt 1975: 116–18). On their position in the Rajput states, see ibid. (118–19) and Timberg (1972: Chapter V).

A Pre-bourgeois Law of Inheritance for Preserving Mercantile Wealth

Raja Rammohun Roy, in an essay entitled 'On the right of Hindus over ancestral property' (reprinted in Nag and Burman 1945), had defended the right of the Bengalis to be governed by the system of law of inheritance known as *Dayabhaga*, rather than by the system known as *Mitakshara*. Rammohun listed the major points of distinction between the two systems of law; of the list, the fifth and sixth are worth quoting:

> Fifth. A man having a share of undivided real property is not authorized to make a sale or gift of it without the consent of the rest of his partners according to the *Mitakshara* but according to the *Dayabhaga* he can dispose of it at his own free will.
>
> Sixth. A man in possession of ancestral real property, though not under any tenure limiting it to the successive generations of his family, is not authorized to dispose of it, by sake of gift, without the consent of his sons and grandsons, according to the *Mitakshara*, while according to the *Dayabhaga*, he has the power to alienate his property at his own free will.

According to Rammohun, under the *Dayabhaga* dispensation, 'Anyone possessed of landed property, whether self-acquired or ancestral, has been able, under the long-established law of the land, to procure easily, on the credit of that property, loans of money to lay out on the improvement of his estate, in trade or manufactures, whereby he enriches himself and his family and benefits the country' (ibid.: para 12). Rammohun protested against a reported proposal to replace the *Dayabhaga* with the *Mitakshara* system which governed the Hindus in practically the whole of India outside Bengal. He also protested against the upsetting of the long-established precedent that a father could not only dispose of any self-acquired property but also of ancestral property without the consent of his sons or grandsons (even though it might be shown that this precedent was due to Raghunandana, rather than to Jimutavahana, the author of the *Dayabhaga* principles).

A standard text on Hindu law puts the essential distinction between the *Dayabhaga* and the *Mitakshara* systems as follows:

The *Mitakshara* recognizes two modes of devolution of property, namely, survivorship and succession. The rule of survivorship applies to joint family property; the rules of succession apply to property held in absolute severalty by the last owner.

The *Dayabhaga* recognizes only one mode of devolution, namely, succession. It does not recognize the rule of survivorship even in the case of joint family property. The reason is that while every member of a *Mitakashara* joint family has only an *undivided* interest in the joint property, a member of a *Dayabhaga* joint family holds his share in *quasi-severalty*, so that it passes on his death to his heirs as it was absolutely seized thereof, and not to the surviving coparceners as under the *Mitakshara* law. (Desai 1978: 85–86)

The *Dayabhaga* is a far more individualistic system of law than the *Mitakshara*, and the notion of private property embodied in the discourse of Jimutavahana fits the requirement of mobility of capital demanded by a full-fledged capitalist economy far better than the *Mitakshara* does. Ironically, however, as with many other principles upheld by the leaders of the Anglophile Bengali intelligentsia of the nineteenth century, the *Dayabhaga* system proved quite subversive of the foundations of Indian property in Bengal. The undisputed disposers of property were quickly separated from their patrimony as they became embroiled in insolvency suits as partners of defaulting (and often decamping) Europeans, and designing creditors found it easy to mulct young heirs when their propensity to squander their inherited wealth could not be curbed by family authority. In contrast, those whose property was held jointly with other coparceners found it easier to protect it because of the legal uncertainty. The Hindu joint family system of property-holding also aided tax avoidance and evasion in the post-Independence period, but that belongs to a different phase of the history of the Indian mercantile community. Along with the relative invulnerability of the jointly held mercantile properties, the uncodified and customary nature of much of Hindu law made the seizure of debtors' property rather difficult, particularly within the jurisdiction of the native states. The *Mitakshara* system was appropriate to the legal facade for the continuation of the familial basis of the Indian merchants' business.

The Survival Value of Inter-group and Intra-group Cohesion among Merchants

The merchants of colonial India inherited an India-wide network of commercial and financial relations. The *hundis* of great bankers were honoured throughout most of India;[42] insurance was available for commodities and bullion transported from one region of the country to others, and the rates of insurance were remarkably low. As late as 1873, the Bank of Bengal agent at Hyderabad was instructed to send specie via *shroffs'* insurance, rather than by any other means of remittance. There were *jakhmi hundis* which combined the characteristics of an insurance policy and an exchange bill. Although deposit banking had not developed on a systematic basis all over the country, there were many bankers who received deposits.

We have seen earlier that there were many commercial associations and civic organizations that cut across caste and community lines. Some of these organizations survived into colonial times. However, the British rulers, unlike their predecessors, gave only a token recognition or none at all, to Nagarseths, leaders of *mahajans, panchayats,* or *chaudharis* of market-places.[43]

However, in spite of official indifference or hostility, many of the inter-caste and inter-community links among mercantile communities in British India survived (see, in this connection, Bayly 1978). And most of the important pre-British mercantile communities of the interior survived as well.

For the early part of the nineteenth century, we have numerous accounts of the high level of inter-regional organization maintained by the Indian mercantile communities as well as by individual business houses. For example, James Douglas gave a list of twentyone 'conspicuous' *shroffs* established in Bombay in 1845, some of whom, such as Jivraj Balloo, were established before the nineteenth century opened (Douglas 1900). According to him, 'you might have gone to almost any of them, and if you wished a draft on any place from

---

[42] For an account of the organization of indigenous banking in India, see Jain (1929: Chapters II and III).

[43] The institution of *chaudhuris* is described in detail by Buchanan Hamilton in his report on Bhagalpur. See Montgomery Martin (1838, rpt 1976: 282–83); and the reasons for the decline of the 'chiefs of trades' are given by F. Buchanan (n.d.: 700).

Peshawar to Travancore, you would get it.' Some of the most remarkable examples of the resistance of mercantile communities against the ill effects of colonial rule relate to their ability, in particular areas and particular periods, to overcome the monetary stringency caused by the continuous drain of silver from India. Thus, in Gujarat, the merchants used *ant* (the fictitious currency for settling accounts without the actual transfer of coin) extensively when the British temporarily closed the mint and when British policies caused a shortage of medium of exchange. This system prevailed up till 1846 in Dhollera for settling all mercantile transactions, and in Ahmedabad for carrying out all banking transactions, at least up to the end of the 1870s (see *Gazetteer of the Bombay Presidency* 1884: 212; and vol. VIII, p. 212). This may have partly insulated Gujarati merchants against the long depression which affected most parts of India between 1826–27 and 1852–53 or so. At Mirzapur and nearby towns, *toras* of Farruckabad coins bearing the names and guarantees of important merchants were used as the medium of exchange. The Farruckabad rupees had a lower bullion value than the British Indian rupee, but the *toras* might even circulate at a premium from time to time. The pressure to invest the money and thereby keep the *toras* in circulation kept interest rates low at Mirzapur—sometimes they were lower than in Calcutta or London.[44]

Coming to particular communities, Colonel Wade reported for the 1830s, that the only people who dealt regularly in European commodities in the 'countries beyond the Indus and Sutlej' were the *banias* of Jodhpur and Shekhavati. In order to illustrate the scale of Marwari connections, he gave the example of ten sons and grandsons of Bugotee Ram, who was the treasurer or *photedar* of the then Nawab of Fatehpur. These ten descendants of Bugotee Ram, who were themselves called *photedars* (or Poddars), had *gomostahs* or agents at the following places (besides their houses at Ramgarh in Shekhavati and Choroo in Bikaner): Bombay, Surat, Baonagar,

[44] See the note of the Treasury Officer of Mirzapur enclosed by J.M. Erskine, officiating Deputy Auditor and Accountant General, United Provinces, in his letter dated 22 December 1962 to the Secretary to the Financial Department, Government of India, in National Archives of India, Financial Department Proceedings, 1864, No. 28. For further details see Bagchi (1987).

Merchants and Colonialism

Muscat, Pali, Jodhpur, Nagore, Jaisalmer, Shikarpur, Ajmer, Bikaner, Jullundur, Amritsar, Lahore, Ludhiana, Patiala, Nabha, Jagadhari, Hissar, Hansi, Bhiwani, Rohtak, Delhi, Jaipur, Kotah, Amraoti, Ujjain, Indore, Nagpur, Hyderabad, Poona, Hathras, Chandausi, Farruckabad, Mathura, Agra, Mirzapur, Benaras, Murshidabad, Patna, Calcutta and Goalpara. The *gomostahs* were all from Bikaner or Shekhavati.[45]

Colonel Wade stressed the economies enjoyed by a house with such far-ranging connections:

> They are able to carry on trade with smaller profits and this combined with their extensive connections and the good understanding they have with one another, have given them a decided commercial ascendancy in upper India. They are the general insurers for other people, but the superior facilities they enjoy and the extensive nature of their transactions render insurance unnecessary in their own case.

While the Marwaris became the biggest single business community of modern India, Banjaras, originating from the same region, either became cultivators or were reduced to the status of scheduled tribes or gypsies. What accounts for this difference in fate? In general, three sets of factors, viz., the internal organization of a mercantile community, its specific position in the economic and social structure, and its success or failure in adapting to new circumstances, together determined whether it would prosper or not. It is difficult to verify these hypotheses within the compass of this essay; all I can do is to proffer some corroborative evidence from the histories of the Banjaras, the Lohanas and the Marwaris.

The Charans or Bhats of Rajasthan were supposed to be the ancestors of the Banjaras. Their sacred character gave them protection in their native lands, and they turned to the business of carrying messages and goods (Tod 1829, rpt 1978: 554). In the late seventeenth and eighteenth centuries, they emerged as the suppliers of goods to the warring Mughal and other armies, as well as to the

---

[45] An extract from the report is given in the *Report of the Bombay Chamber of Commerce for the Fourth Quarter: 1839–40*, Appendix. This is the house whose further fortunes as the firm of Tarachand Ghanshyamdas have been traced by Timberg (1972: 137–45).

civilian population of practically the whole region from the Punjab to Mysore, and from Maharashtra to Bihar. As more and more of the sub-continent passed under British sway, and as the new rulers organized their own system of military supplies, the importance of Banjaras as army suppliers declined. As armed bands, they also came into conflict with local rulers and the general populace in many regions. They were to be found as carriers of goods in the Central Provinces and Hyderabad even as late as the 1860s (see Temple 1882; Saunders 1884: 276). The decline of the Banjaras as merchants was completed by their inability to establish any permanent trading stations. In parts of Uttar Pradesh, they took to the profession of breeding and dealing in cattle or horses (Crooke 1896, rpt 1974: 164; *Gazetteer of the Rampur State* 1911: 15). In other areas they were described as dacoits. They took an important part in the Great Indian Revolt of 1857 (Stokes 1978). In many parts of the country, they became pedlars, leading a life very similar to that of the gypsies.

Another community which resembled the Banjaras in many ways was that of Dasnami Gossains. They became traders and financiers on a large scale in the eighteenth century. But their *maths* served as permanent stations for them, and although their trade declined, in some areas such as Benaras and Tarakeswar in Bengal, they seem to have accumulated a considerable amount of landed property (Wilson 1828, rpt 1980: 38–42; Sarkar, n.d.: Chapter X; Cohn 1964).

The Lohanas of Cutch apparently owed their pre-eminence in the seventeenth century to royal favour. In the eighteenth century, they were persecuted by the local rulers and declined in importance. By 1880, the *Gazetteer* of Cutch reported that few of them were men of much wealth and position within the limits of Cutch.[46] In their most important base, Shikarpur, they were still an important trading community, although the *Imperial Gazetteer* considered it necessary to differentiate between Amils and other Lohanas, and classed the Amils as clerks and government servants as well as traders (*Imperial Gazetteer of India* 1908: 276–77 ['Shikarpur Town'] and 407–08 ['Sind']). The Amils emerged as important financiers in

---

[46] *Gazetteer of the Bombay Presidency* (1880: 55). Both in Cutch and in Kathiawar, it was stated that the poorer people among the Lohanas were cultivators, masons, labourers, vegetable-sellers: *Gazetteer of the Bombay Presidency* (1884: 149).

Hyderabad and Multani *shroffs* were to be found all over India, but many of them were Marwaris rather than Lohanas. The general drying up of opportunities for trade and finance in Sind with the incursion of Europeans into trans-frontier trade seems to have taken a toll on a major section of the Lohanas in their role as merchants.[47] In the case of the Lohanas it was more the imperfect adjustment to rapidly changing opportunities for trade and finance than any lack of internal cohesion that seems to have accounted for their relative retardation as a mercantile community (compared with the Bhatias or the Marwaris).

All successful mercantile communities seem to have been marked by a high degree of formalization of the rules of training, recruitment and general intra-community relations. This can be seen in the case of the Komatis or Chettiars of the south as well as the Marwaris and the Gujarati *banias*. The Gujarati *banias* and the Komatis both possessed elaborate arithmetical tables with fractions and multiples of rupees, annas, which both sharpened the powers of quick calculation required of a trader or banker and facilitated the keeping of accounts. Both the communities seem also to have possessed a special language, including a set of signs, for striking bargains among themselves (a special set of signs or sounds for bargaining and keeping trade secrets seems to have been characteristic of many other closely knit trading groups: see *Gazetteer of the Bombay Presidency* 1899: 80; Thurston and Rangachari 1909, Vol. III: 308–09)). The training of young merchants generally took place within the mercantile establishment itself. As late as 1909, most Nattukottai Chettis apparently regarded English education as rather impractical, preferring the long apprenticeship to which young Chettis were subjected traditionally (Thurston and Rangachari 1909, Vol. V: 252).

---

[47] With a general decline of handicrafts and establishment of European control over major arteries of trade and communications, many mercantile communities simply became agriculturists. For example, *banajigas*, who were a big trading caste of Karnataka at the time Buchanan conducted his survey of the region, were reported in 1926 to be mainly agriculturists, 'only a sixteenth part of the caste' being engaged in trade. See Rao (1927: 213); and also Thurston and Rangachari (1909, Vol. IV: 232–36).

The Marwari traders generally operated within a well-regulated community framework: any newcomer to a region found help from his caste fellows, or from other traders from the same region. The Marwari settlers in a group of villages usually chose some leading men to form a council or *panchayat*, for arbitrating in 'social disputes, arranging for the support of their temple and its worship, and for the management of the provident fund' (*Gazetteer of the Bombay Presidency* 1899: 104–05). Similarly, the Komatis settled in each place had a leader, called a Pedda Setti, and the Kalinga Komatis, in addition, had a headman styled Kularaja or Vaisyaraje, for several villages. It was these leaders who settled important questions relating to the caste, by fine, excommunication, etc. 'Komatis [had] recourse to the established courts of justice only as a last resort. They (were) consulted by other castes for the settlement of their disputes' (Thurston and Rangachari 1909, Vol. III 309–10).

The Nattukottai Chettiars from the Ramnad district of Madras had an elaborate system of training and recruitment of members of the community. A boy of ten or twelve was expected to apply himself to business, learn accounts and attend the shop of his father. After his marriage, all his expenses were debited to him, and he was expected to save as much as he could out of the allowance or initial capital granted to him. Every rupee earned was laid out at as high a rate of interest as possible.[48]

The Chettiars travelled far outside their district to all parts of south India and set themselves up as traders and moneylenders in Sri Lanka, Malaysia, Burma, Indo-China and Indonesia. There was an elaborate system of recruitment of agents (belonging to the same community as the owners of the home firm) for these places, which was described thus in 1907:

> People of moderate means usually elect to go to distant places as agents of the different firms that have their head offices either at Madura or in the *zamindaris* of Ramnad and Sivaganga. The

---

[48] Thurston and Rangachari (1909, Vol. V: 253). A very similar account of the sharing of financial responsibility within the family and of the training of a young trader of the Meshri *bania* community of Gujarat is given in *Gazetteer of the Bombay Presidency* (1899: 79–88). Keeping of account books was a sophisticated task, and demanded long apprenticeship.

pay of a local agent varies directly with the distance of the place to which he is posted. If he is kept at Madura, he gets Rs 100 per mensem; if sent to Burma, he gets three times as much, and, if to Natal, about twice the latter sum. If an agent proves himself to be an industrious and energetic man, he is usually given a percentage on the profits. The tenure of office is for three years, six months before the expiry of which the next agent is sent over to work conjointly with the existing one, and study the local conditions. On relief, the agent returns directly to his head office, and delivers over his papers, and then goes on to his own village. With this, his connection with his firm practically ceases. He enjoys his well-earned rest of three years, at the end of which he seeks re-employment either under his old firm, or under any other. The former he is bound to do, if he has taken a percentage on the profits during his previous tenure of office. If the old firm rejects him when he so offers himself, then he is at liberty to enter service under others (Hayavadana Rao, *Indian Review*, 1907, quoted in Thurston and Rangachari 1909, Vol. V: 257).

The Nattukottai Chettis were permitted by custom to partition the property among the brothers but voluntarily decided to adopt a joint family system for purposes of management, although individual members were encouraged to keep a part under their own control for purposes of business (Thurston and Rangachari 1909, Vol. V, article on 'Nattukottai Chettia'; Ito 1966). This organizational pattern was a sophisticated combination of community code of mutual trust and confidence and encouragement of individual initiative, and made abundant sense in a world of uncertainty (cf. Arrow 1971). Many members of the society outside the group of males belonging to the caste, such as poor peasants, and a sizeable section within the community, like the women, bore the brunt of this system of community risk-sharing here. While the family was the basic unit of control in the business organizations of the Chettiars, the Marwaris or the Gujarati *banias*, the employment of members of other castes as important links in the organizational set-up was not unknown. For example, the Meshri *banias* sometimes employed Brahmins (and Parsis) as clerks and managers (*Gazetteer of the Bombay Presidency*, 1880: 79); and some Marwari firms also employed Brahmins as clerks (Timberg 1972: 134). But employment of men from the same caste or community was more common.

While Indian industrialists are generally accused of being rather unadventurous, Indian merchants were often accused of a great fondness for speculation. The role of speculation in rationalizing capitalist activities in general is as yet unexplored. But there seems to be evidence that certain forms of speculation or gambling were institutionalized among Gujarati *banias* as well as the Marwaris. In Ahmedabad, for example, time bargains or forward trading in *ant* was widely prevalent[49] and time bargains (called *vaida*) in opium and other commercially important commodities 'except perhaps grain' were rife in 1849 as well as 1879 (*Gazetteer of the Bombay Presidency* 1880: 66–67). Time bargains in shares boomed during the period 1864–66, and were a major factor in bringing down the (old) Bank of Bombay and many other financial institutions and real estate companies. The custom of gambling seems to have been built into the religious ritual of *banias* of Gujarat and Central Provinces. In both the regions, Diwali was an extremely important festival for the *banias*, and apparently continues to be so.

> The *banias* close their accounts on this day. '*Diwali-baki*' or loans outstanding on *Diwali* are not liked by merchants who try their best to repay their loans and recover their bills in the days preceding *Diwali*.... Merchants transact business of new varieties of goods and give some cash to one another to enter the account of sale and purchase in the new books as a token of goodwill. They also send some items of their merchandise to their permanent customers as *bani* or the auspicious first deal and enter their names in the new book (Trivedi 1965: 65).

Describing very similar customs prevailing among the *banias* of the Central Provinces, Russell and Hira Lal added: 'The Banias and Hindus generally think it requisite to gamble at Diwali in order to bring good luck during the coming year; all classes indulge in a little speculation in this season' (Russell and Hira Lal 1916: 126).

---

[49] This was the reason for Mohtarim Khan banning the use of *ant* in 1715, for the rise in the value of *ant* had brought all trade virtually to a standstill. See Khan (1965: 363).

The Indore state derived a regular income from *satta* (or forward exchange combined with gambling) transactions in opium (*Imperial Gazetteer of India* 1908, Vol. XIII: 346). Thus, a state run on pre-capitalist principles could accommodate a system which the British administrators often regarded as anathema. Successful merchants seem to have regarded it essential for maintaining their profession, that they should have their speculative activities to counter or take advantage of the instability caused by harvest fluctuations in an economy dominated by agriculture.

Epilogue

A detailed account of the way in which successful mercantile groups collaborated with or dissociated themselves from the European-dominated export–import transactions or European-style financial and industrial firms is a separate theme and we shall not pursue it here. Most of the successful merchants in most of the regions collaborated with the British, both commercially and politically.[50] During the Great Indian Revolt of 1857, merchants and moneylenders were often subjects of attack by the revolting Indians, and merchants generally collaborated with the British (Stokes 1978: 159–74; Metcalf 1979: Chapter 6). However, there were exceptions, although they were few in number. For example, Ramji Dass, of the Gurwala banking firm of Delhi, lent large sums to Emperor Bahadur Shah II during 1857–58, and was hanged by the British for his sins (Joshi 1975: 42–43). More typical was the case of Chunnamal Saligh Ram, who had made a fortune out of supplying shawls, brocades and piece-goods to the emperor's *toshakhana* but simply deserted his cause and lay low until the storm blew over, to wax prosperous again under British rule. Yet a third pattern was provided by Budri Dass, the great grandfather of Lala Shri Ram, who amassed a fortune as the treasurer of the British cantonment at Karnal, as *kotwal* at

---

[50] Captain T. Macan, deposing before the Select Committee on the affairs of the East India Company (1831–32) and Colonel Sleeman, writing in 1844, both singled out Indian merchants as being specially interested in the maintenance and stability of British rule. See Macan's evidence in Irish Universities Press reprints of *British Parliamentary Papers* (1831–32, Vol. 6: 156); and also W.H. Sleeman (1844: 142–43).

the British cantonments of Ferozepore and Delhi, and as a loyal collaborator of the British during the Revolt of 1857.[51]

However, the degree or pattern of collaboration or involvement of Indian traders and financiers with Europeans merchants was by no means constant over time. Many Parsi merchants achieved a degree of autonomy vis-à-vis foreign merchants over the course of the nineteenth century. Many Marwaris who had kept a distance between the Europeans and themselves became collaborators of British firms. In the twentieth century, the mutual relations between foreign capital and different mercantile groups changed again.

Moreover, at the lower levels, among *baladia* (cattle-owning) travelling merchants or smaller traders, there are numerous examples of resistance against British rule. An intelligible account of the variations in merchants' behaviour must take into account both political and economic constraints on their freedom of action and relate the evolution of such constraints to larger movements of Indian society. A beginning in this direction is yet to be made, at least for an analysis of mercantile behaviour in the nineteenth century.

References

Ali, S.M., 1884, *Hyderabad Affairs,* Vol. II, Hyderabad.

Arrow, K.J., 1971, 'Control in large organizations', in K.J. Arrow, *Essays in the Theory of Risk-bearing,* Markham, Chicago.

Bagchi, A.K., 1969, 'Comments on "Some Trends in India's foreign trade in the 17th Century"', *Indian Economic and Social History Review,* Vol. VI, No. 1, March.

———, 1972, *Private Investment in India: 1900–1939,* Cambridge University Press, Cambridge.

———, 1976, 'Reflections on patterns of regional growth in India under British Rule', *Bengal Past and Present,* January–June.

———, 1979, 'Review' of K.N. Chaudhuri's *The Trading World of Asia, The Times of India,* 2 September.

———, 1987, *History of the State Bank of India,* Vol. I, Oxford University Press, Bombay.

Ballhatchet, K., 1980, *Race, Sex and Class under the Raj,* Weidenfeld and Nicolson, London.

---

[51] Budri Dass had amassed so much property at Ferozepore, that the British could not make his son a *kotwal* in succession to him although they wanted to do so (Joshi 1975: 41). Among the duties of a *kotwal* at a British cantonment in the 1830s and 1840s was the regulated supply of female camp followers. See Ballhatchet (1980: Chapter 1).

Barui, B.C., 1975, 'The Smuggling Trade of Opium in the Bengal Presidency: 1793–1817, *Bengal Past and Present,* July–December.

———, 1979, 'The Salt Industry of Bengal: The Relations of Production in the Industry and Trade in Salt, 1757–1830', unpublished Ph.D. thesis, Calcutta University, Calcutta.

Bayly, C.A., 1978, 'Indian merchants in a "traditional" setting: Benaras, 1780–1830', in C. Dewey and A.G. Hopkins (eds), *The Imperial Impact: Studies in the Economic History of Africa and India,* Athlone Press, London.

Benjamin, N., 1973, 'Raw Cotton of Western India: a comment', *Indian Economic and Social History Review,* Vol. X, No. 1.

Bhadra, G., 1976, 'Social groups and social relations in the town of Murshidabad', *Indian Historical Review,* Vol. II, No. 2, January.

———, 1980, 'Mughal Jugey Bharatiya Banik' (in Bengali), *Ekshan,* Autumn.

———, 'The Role of Pykars in the Silk Industry of Bengal: c. 1765–1830' (Typescript).

British Parliamentary Papers, Vol. VI, 1831–32, Irish Universities Press reprint.

Boxer, C.R., 1973, *The Portuguese Sea-borne Empire: 1415–1825,* Penguin, Harmondsworth.

Buchanan, D.H., 1934, *The Development of Capitalistic Enterprises in India;* rpt, Frank Cass, London, 1966.

Buchanan, F., 1807, *A Journey from Madras through the Countries of Mysore, Canara and Malabar,* Vols I–III, London.

———, (n.d.), *An Account of the Districts of Bihar and Patna in 1811–12,* Vol. II, Bihar and Orissa Research Society, Patna.

Chaudhuri, K.N., 1969, 'Towards an "Inter-continental Model": Some Trends in Indo-European Trade in the Seventeenth Century', *Indian Economic and Social History Review,* Vol. VI, No. 1, March.

———, 1978, *The Trading World of Asia and the English East India Company: 1660–1760,* Cambridge University Press, Cambridge.

Chaudhuri, S., 1975, *Trade and Commercial Organization in Bengal: 1650–1720,* Firma K.L.M., Calcutta.

Chicherov, A.I., 1971, *India: Economic Development in the 16th to 18th Centuries: Outline History of Crafts and Trade,* Nauka Publishing House, Moscow.

Cohn, B.S., 1964, 'The role of the gossains in the economy of the eighteenth and nineteenth century upper India', *Indian Economic and Social History Review,* Vol. I, No. 4, April–June.

———, 1979, 'Structural change in Indian rural society', in R.E. Frykenberg (ed.), *Land Control and Social Structure in Indian History,* University of Wisconsin Press, Madison.

Crooke, W., 1896, *The Tribes and Castes of North-Western India,* Vol. I; rpt, Cosmo Publications, Delhi, 1974.

Das Gupta, A., 1970, 'The Merchants of Surat, c. 1700–1750', in E. Leach and S.N. Mukherjee (eds), *Elites in South Asia,* Cambridge University Press, Cambridge.

———, *Indian Merchants and the Decline of Surat, c. 1700–1750,* Franz Steiner Verlag, Wiesbaden.

Desai, S.D., 1978, *Mulla's Principles of Hindu Law,* N.M. Tripathi, Bombay.

Dobbin, C., 1972, *Urban Leadership in Western India,* Oxford University Press, London.

Douglas, J., 1900, *Glimpses of Bombay and Western India,* London.
Ferrier, R.W., 1973, 'The Armenians and the East India Company in Persia in the 17th and Early 18th Centuries', *Economic History Review,* second series, Vol. 26.
Gadgil, D.R., 1959, *Origins of the Modern Indian Business Class: An Interim Report,* Institute of Pacific Relations, New York.
Gazetteer of the Bombay Presidency, 1877, Vol. II: *Surat and Broach,* Government Central Press, Bombay.
———, Vol. IV, Government Central Press, Bombay.
———, 1880, Vol. V: *Cutch, Palanpur and Mahi Kantha,* Government Central Press, Bombay.
———, 1880, Vol. XII: *Khandesh,* Government Central Press, Bombay.
———, 1883, Vol. VII: *Baroda,* Government Central Press, Bombay.
———, 1884, Vol. VIII: *Kathiawar,* Government Central Press, Bombay.
———, 1899, Vol. IX, Part 1: *Gujarat Population, Hindus,* Government Central Press, Bombay.
———, 1899, Vol. IX, Part 2: *Gujarat Population, Mussalmans and Parsis,* Government Central Press, Bombay.
Gazetteer of the Rampur State, 1911, Government Press, Allahabad.
Gopal, M.H., 1971, *Tipu Sultan's Mysore,* Popular Prakashan, Bombay.
Guha, A., 1972, 'Raw Cotton of Western India: Output, transportation and marketing', *Indian Economic and Social History Review,* Vol. IX, No. 1.
Habib, Irfan, 1971, 'Potentialities of Capitalistic Development in the Economy of Mughal India', *Enquiry,* Winter.
Imperial Gazetteer of India, 1908, Vol. XIII: *Gyaraspur to Jais,* Clarendon Press, Oxford.
———, 1908, Vol. XXII: *Samadhiala to Singhana,* Clarendon Press, London.
———, 1908, Vol. XIV: *Jaisalmer to Kaira,* Clarendon Press, Oxford.
Islam, S., 1979, *The Permanent Settlement of Bengal: A Study of its Operation, 1790–1819,* Bangla Academy, Dacca.
Ito, S., 1966, 'Business combines in India—with special reference to Nattukottai Chettiars', *Developing Economies.*
Jain, L.C., 1929, *Indigenous Banking in India,* Macmillan, London.
Joshi, A., 1975, *Lala Shri Ram,* Orient Longman, New Delhi.
Kareem, C.K., 1973, *Kerala under Haidar Ali and Tipu Sultan,* Paico Publishing House, Ernakulam.
Karim, A., 1964, *Dacca: The Mughal Capital,* Asiatic Society, Dacca.
Kaye, J.W., 1858, *The Life and Correspondence of Charles, Lord Metcalfe,* Vol. II, London.
Khan, Ali Muhammad, 1965, *Mirat-I-Ahmedi,* translated by M.F. Lokhandwalla, Oriental Institute, Baroda.
Kling, B.B., 1976, *Partner in Empire,* University of California Press, Berkeley.
Kolff, D.H.A., 1979, 'A Study of Land Transfers in Mau Tehsil, Jhansi', in Chaudhuri and Dewey (eds), *Economy and Society,* Oxford University Press, New Delhi.
Levkovsky, A.I., 1972, *Capitalism in India: Basic Trends in its Development,* People's Publishing House, New Delhi.
Little, J.H., 1967, *The House of Jagatseth,* Calcutta Historical Society, Calcutta.
Luzzato, G., 1953, 'Small and great merchants in the Italian Cities of the Renais-

sance', in F.C. Lane and J.C. Riemersma (eds), *Enterprise and Secular Change*, Allen and Unwin, London.

Lyal, A.C., 1870, *Gazetteer for the Hyderabad Assigned Districts Commonly Called Berar*, Bombay.

Maclean, J.M., 1880, *A Guide to Bombay*, 5th edn, Bombay.

Martin, M., 1838, *The History, Antiquities, Topography and Statistics of Eastern India*, Vol. II; rpt, Cosmo Publications, Delhi, 1976.

Marx, Karl, 1966, *Capital*, Vol. III, Progress Pubishers, Moscow.

———, 1971, *Theories of Surplus Value*, part III, Progress Publishers, Moscow.

Mehta, M.J., 1981, 'Business Environment: Urbanization and Economic Change in India: A Case Study of Ahmedabad in the Nineteenth Century', *Vidya* (The Journal of Gujarat University), January.

Metcalf, T.R., 1979, *Land, Landlords and the British Raj*, Oxford University Press, Delhi.

Mitra, D.B., 1978, *The Cotton Weavers of Bengal: 1757–1833*, Firma K.L.M., Calcutta.

Musson, A.E., 1972, 'Introduction' and 'The Diffusion of Technology in Great Britain during the Industrial Revolution', in Musson (ed.), *Science, Technology and Economic Growth in the Nineteenth Century*, Methuen, London.

Nag, K. and D. Burman (eds), 1945, *The English Works of Raja Rammohan Roy*, Part 1, Sadharan Brahmo Samaj, Calcutta.

Neale, W.C., 'Land is to rule', in R.E. Frykenberg (ed.), *Land Control and Social Structure in Indian History*, University of Wisconsin Press, Madison.

Nightingale, P., 1970, *Trade and Empire in Western India 1784–1800*, Cambridge University Press, Cambridge.

Pandey, G., 1981, 'Economic Dislocation in Nineteenth Century Eastern U.P.: Some Implications of the Decline of Artisanal Industry in Colonial India', Occasional Paper No. 37, Centre for Studies in Social Sciences, Calcutta, May.

Pavlov, V.I., 1964, *The Indian Capitalist Class*, People's Publishing House, New Delhi.

Pearson, M.N., 1972, 'Indigenous dominance in a colonial economy: The Goa Rendas, 1600–1670', in *Mare Luso-Indicum*, Tome II, Geneva.

———, 1972a, 'Political Participation in Mughal India', *Indian Economic and Social History Review*, Vol. IX, No. 4, December.

———, 1976, *Merchants and Rulers in Gujarat: The Response to the Portuguese in the Sixteenth Century*, University of California Press, Berkeley.

Prakash, O., 1964 'The European trading companies and the merchants of Bengal: 1650–1725', *Indian Economic and Social History Review*, Vol. I, No. 3, January–March.

Rao, C.H., 1927, *Mysore Gazetteer*, Vol. I: *Descriptive*, Government Press, Bangalore.

Rao, Hayavadana, 1907, Indian Review.

Ray, I., 1980, 'Multiple Faces of the Early 18th Century Indian Merchants', Occasional Paper No. 29, Centre for Studies in Social Sciences, Calcutta, August.

Ray, R., 1979, *Change in Bengal Agrarian Society*, Manohar, Delhi.

Report of the Bombay Chamber of Commerce for the Fourth Quarter 1839–40, Appendix.

Russell, R.V. and H. Lal, 1916, *The Tribes and Castes of the Central Provinces of India,* Vol. II; rpt, Cosmo Publications, Delhi, 1975.

Sanyal, H., 1975, 'Social mobility in Bengal: Its sources and constraints', *Indian Historical Review,* Vol. II, No. 1, July.

Sarkar, J., (n.d.), *A History of Dasnami Naga Sanyasis,* Panchayati Akhara Mahanirvani, Allahabad.

Saunders, C.B., *Administration Report for Hyderabad for 1869–70;* reprinted in S.M. Ali, *Hyderabad Affairs,* Vol. V, 1884.

Sen, S.K. (ed.), 1969, *Edmund Burke on Indian Economy,* Progressive Publishers, Calcutta.

Seth, M.J., 1937, *Armenians in India,* Calcutta.

Singh, D., 1973, 'The role of Mahajans in the rural economy in eastern Rajasthan during the Eighteenth Century', paper presented at the Indian History Congress, Chandigarh.

Sinha, N.K., 1965, *The Economic History of Bengal,* Vol. I, Firma K.L.M., Calcutta.

———, 1968, *The Economic History of Bengal,* Vol. II, Firma K.L.M., Calcutta.

———, 1970, *The Economic History of Bengal,* Vol. III, Firma K.L.M., Calcutta.

Sinha, P., 1978, *Calcutta in Urban History,* Firma K.L.M., Calcutta.

Sleeman, W.H., 1844, *Rambles and Recollections of an Indian Official,* Vol. II, London.

Stokes, E., 1978, 'Rural Revolt in the Great Rebellion of 1857 in India: A Study of the Saharanpur and Muzaffarnagar Districts', in E. Stokes, *Peasants and the Raj,* Cambridge University Press, Cambridge.

Sullivan, R.J.F., 1937, *One Hundred Years of Bombay: History of the Bombay Chamber of Commerce, 1836–1936,* Times of India Press, Bombay.

Temple, R., 1882, *Men and Events of My Time in India,* John Murray, London.

Thompson, E., 1937, *The Life of Charles, Lord Metcalfe,* Faber and Faber, London.

Thurston, E. and K. Rangachari (eds), 1909, *Castes and Tribes of Southern India,* Vol. III and V, Government Press, Madras.

Timberg, 1972, *Rise of the Marwari Merchants as Industrial Entrepreneurs,* Ph.D. thesis, Harvard University, Cambridge, Mass.

Tod, J., 1829, *Annals and Antiquities of Rajasthan,* Vol. I; rpt, N.B.D. Publishers, New Delhi, 1978.

Trivedi, P.K., 1965, *Fairs and Festivals (Census of India, 1961,* Vol. V, Gujarat, Part VII-B), Government of India Publications, Delhi.

Van Leur, J.C., 1955, *Indonesian Trade and Society,* W. Van Hoeve, The Hague.

Vicziany, M., 1979, 'Bombay Merchants and Structural Changes in the Export Community: 1850 to 1880', in K.N. Chaudhuri and C.J. Dewey (eds), *Economy and Society: Essays in Indian Economic and Social History,* Oxford University Press, New Delhi.

Wadia, R.A., 1957, *The Bombay Dockyard and the Wadia Master-builders,* Bombay.

Watson, I.B., 1980, 'Fortifications and the Idea of Force in Early East India Company's Relations with India', *Past and Present,* No. 88, August.

Wilson, H.H., 1828, 'A sketch of the religious sects of the Hindus', *Asiatic Researches,* Vol. XVI; rpt, Cosmo Publications, Delhi, 1980.

Yule, H. and A.C. Burnell (eds), 1886, *Hobson–Jobson;* rpt, Munshiram Manoharlal, New Delhi, 1968.

Reflections on the Nature of the Indian Bourgeoisie

In recent times there has been a considerable amount of work on the ideology of the working class and on its behaviour. Some of the young social scientists and historians have found the working class very deficient in some respects. They have been found to be not sufficiently class-conscious. They have been found to be communal in some contexts (Chakrabarty 1989; for a critique, see Bagchi 1990), and far too attached to their own regions and linguistic and ethnic identities. But the same kind of attention has not been paid by many social scientists to the exploiters of those workers. If the workers have been communal, what has happened to the capitalists? Have they inherited all those secular values which their superior education, their superior property position and their overwhelming advantages in life give them access to? In understanding the growth of capitalism in India, of the kind of capitalism that we have in India, I do think that understanding the behaviour of the capitalist class is extremely important. Even if we cannot always settle why they behave the way they behave, it is important to know how they behave in certain particular contexts, and what kind of ideologies, in a very broad sense, seem to motivate them. What I am going to discuss here is to some extent complementary to the First V.P. Chintan Memorial Lecture given by B.T. Ranadive. There he talked about the growth of a scientific ideology in India. Here I talk about the persistence and even growth of 'unscientific' but locally advantageous ideologies amongst some of the masters of our destiny.

This is the text of the Third V.P. Chintan Memorial Lecture delivered at the Indian School of Social Sciences, Madras, on 19 October 1989.

Capitalism as a term has come into general use only after the Marxists used it to characterize and critically analyse the modern societies of western Europe and the USA. Marx and Engels spent their life constructing a theoretical model of capitalism, unravelling its inherent contradictions and suggesting the means of overcoming those contradictions. They indicated a social agency, namely, the working class, which in its own collective interest would overcome those contradictions and give birth to a new order of society, namely, a socialist society—an order that would be superior to the capitalist system that had been overthrown. However, neither Marx nor Engels ever thought that there was a pure capitalism on earth. They took the British economy and society as their primary object of study. I have to discuss these things because sometimes both the lovers of capitalism and its opponents talk as if somewhere there is pure capitalism—as if all those free market forces really act freely and as if all individuals are free-floating atoms. We have always to understand that they are all the time bounded by various kinds of social forces conditioning the nature of markets and circumscribing freedom.

Marx and Engels took the British economy and society as their primary object of study mainly because it had in their time progressed farthest in the direction of unfolding capitalist relations. Even in the case of Britain, as Marx's and Engels' extensive comments on the British political scene demonstrate, the aristocratic ideologies and interests of powerful landlords were often mixed up with the pursuit of capitalist goals and diffusion of ideologies more directly associated with capitalism. And not only in their time: we can still see how religion played havoc with the society of northern Ireland, which was one of the earliest colonies of the new British capitalist empire. Neither colonialism nor religious wars have gone away because of the flowering of capitalism. If pure capitalism did not exist even in Britain of the 1850s and 1860s, it certainly did not exist in any other country of Europe or in the United States at that time.

Some people take capitalism to be the final flowering of a free social system and this free social system, they think, was just born (like Venus) in Europe and in the United States in the eighteenth and nineteenth centuries. Nothing like that happened. Capitalism was given a more explicit constitutional form in France and in the US than in England. The hegemony of capitalists or bourgeois ideologies had also been recognized more explicitly in those countries than in Britain. In England the parliament was dominated by the class of landlords until 1832 and down to the 1840s. In France, after the French Revolution, the bourgeoisie definitely came to be the dominant force but the monarchy remained. The Americans had to fight a bloody Civil War in the 1860s in order to establish the dominance of industrial capitalism over a slave-holding landlord group. In France, after the revolution of 1789 there were four monarchies and two major civil wars before the claims of capitalism and its most advanced form of governance, viz. parliamentary democracy, could be firmly established.

By the end of the nineteenth century, Germany had become the most powerful European country, economically speaking. There, the ruling group was a combination of feudalized bureaucrats, military men and businessmen in combination with a set of aristocrats directing the state apparatus for the goal of maximizing the economic and military power of Germany. Germany also had the largest Social Democratic Party professing a Marxist ideology. Explicit codes restricted the political activities of the socialists. A parliamentary set-up existed but with a final veto power wielded by the Kaiser. Germany also contained a capitalist class whose leaders exercised paternalistic control over the workers and the employees. It was not, again, a society of free capitalists. Landlords and landlords' values, and monarchical values were intermingled in it. We have thus the sorry spectacle of the largest Marxist Social Democratic Party supporting the First World War—a party which was therefore designated by Lenin as a social imperialist party. We can see that just because something grows for the first time in a country, it does not necessarily triumph. Neither pure capitalism nor a pure working class hegemony could triumph in Germany in 1914.

The point about this sketchy reference to the development of capitalism elsewhere is that while with the work of Marx, Engels, Lenin and other Marxists we have a large body of literature dissecting the anatomy of capitalism, we must remember that the development of that system has not followed any pure line in any country. Nor did the leaders of the Marxist tradition expect any such purity in the development they analysed. Lenin's work on the development of capitalism in Russia can be read as a delineation of the peculiarities of capitalism as well as a demonstration that the system could grow on that social matrix in spite of, and sometimes because of, those peculiarities.

Hence, when we turn to a study of Indian capitalism, there is no use looking for an ideal type. An ideal type can be used to understand some particular structure at a moment of history, or to explain better the evolution of one slice of reality—but not to capture the complexities of the Indian society, or any other society, as it evolved. The theory and history of capitalism in the North Atlantic seaboard, in the Mediterranean countries and in Japan have been studied far more intensively than in India or, for that matter, in any third world country. In order to gain a comparative perspective, we will have to glance at some European, Japanese and American analogies from time to time. But we must not take the pattern of development in any country as an ideal or norm. For, the serpentine history of capitalism does not permit the illusion that its destructiveness could be eliminated by some optimal social arrangement or development sequence. There is no such entity as optimal capitalism. Capitalism has always been a horrible system full of very peculiar social formations. And capitalism as it has existed on earth has to be seen as full of these contradictions.

Before capitalism came in as a system anywhere, there were capitalists. The first group of capitalists were the merchants. And there have been merchants in India for a very long time. There have been pockets of wage labour in India at least since the late eighteenth century, where capitalists controlling the means of production employed wage labour for producing surplus value. But, as we know, this did not produce capitalism in India at that time. Pre-capitalist relations have not fully triumphed over capitalist production relations in most parts of India even today. Labour, especially agricultural labour, and much of labour working in the so-called informal, unorganized or basically low-wage occupations, remains bound to employers not only by the cash nexus but also by relations of non-market coercion and dependence. There still exist bonded labourers, whose numbers are given from time to time in Government of India documents. Every year we hear of bonded labourers who are still being freed through political activity in different parts of India. Capitalists have also not succeeded in transforming the structure of the economy decisively. Nor have they succeeded in evolving an ideology that has a hegemonic presence in the whole society. In fact, Indian capitalists continue to harbour ideologies that are largely derived from pre-capitalist social formations. In many other countries, such as Japan or Taiwan, capitalism has successfully used pre-capitalist ideologies to consolidate its power. This has in fact made the exploitation of the working class more intense in those countries. An extreme form of repression was practised on the Japanese working class, especially before the Second World War, and is still practised on the working class in countries like Taiwan and South Korea, but workers have fought back against that repression.

In India, the prevailing mixture of pre-capitalist and capitalist production relations and ideologies has made the exploitation of workers and peasants no less intense. In many areas, wage-labourers are still treated like slaves. However, the particular kinds of mixture of modes of exploitation that have dominated the country have made the economic and social space so fragmented and so permeable to the dominance of international capital as to almost cripple the transforming power of capitalism. In Western Europe and in the United States, capitalism did transform the society ultimately in most cases. In India, it is yet to do that in any basic way. The prevailing amalgams of social relations and their messiness have their roots in the history of India as a colonial country, with pre-existing capitalist relations in isolated pockets and newly consolidated pre-capitalist relations in others, and in the contradictory logic of capitalism itself.

We shall briefly look at some parts of the logic of capitalism, especially of industrial capitalism, which tends to create problems for capitalist growth everywhere except in some core countries. In most of the advanced capitalist countries, a putting-out system grew to replace simple commodity production. Before that, artisans used to work in their homes with their own means of production. Then, artisans worked with advances from merchants. The artisans were given raw materials and part of the equipment by the merchants, and this was how the putting-out system was born. And then, finally, artisans were brought together as wage-labourers into factories and the modern factory system arose. Once capitalism has developed out of this whole complex process, it begins to evolve more and more complicated systems of organization of production. These latter go hand-in-hand with the development of machinery which serves at one and the same time as instruments for raising the productivity of labour and strengthening the control of owners of means of production. Once machinery comes in, it becomes masters of men.

The continued evolution of machine-based techniques of production is in many ways dependent on the production units being located in particular regions. Workers and technicians have to go on experimenting with these methods of production at a particular location. They have to try out new tools and new materials and new designs. They have often to reorganize the production process. They cannot do this well if they are moving about all over the place. Even when techniques of production are evolved or adapted in scientific or technological laboratories attached to educational institutions or research institutions, rather than industrial establishments, these laboratories need to be within easy distance of the factories. Moreover, one of the major forces driving productivity-raising innovations is the rise in the cost of labour in general, or at least of critical types of skilled labour. This means that for such forces to be effective, the supply of labour to capitalists has to become scarce from time to time. The capitalists should not have access to unlimited supplies of labour forever if they have to be impelled to introduce labour-saving innovations. Delimitation of the operation of capitalist classes within the definite boundaries of national states provided the location-boundedness needed for accumulation of learning and technical development, and operated as a strong incentive for continually replenishing the reserve army of labour. Because labour became more and more expensive within a given location, capitalists had to find new ways of economizing labour. Periodic crises led to unemployment of many workers so that they did not have too much bargaining power. However, while this pool of labour was renewed cyclically, in the long run in the regions where capitalist growth really got going, the proportion of the surplus labour or the reserve army to the total labour force tended to decline.

From the very beginning, capitalism was involved in a major contradiction while augmenting labour productivity through economies of agglomeration. By its logic of growth, capital would seek areas of employment which promised the highest rate of profit—not the highest level of labour productivity. The capitalist does not care whether labour produces more or less. What he bothers about is whether the use of labour produces enough profit for him. This means that the surplus value produced by labour at one location would migrate under the direction of capital and create employment or raise productivity elsewhere if that other location promises more profit. David Ricardo, whom Marx had acknowledged as his master in political economy, knew this. He assumed that capital was not mobile between different countries. And he *recommended* that it should not be so mobile. But this goes against the logic of capitalism itself. So what happened was that capital migrated from one place to another in search of profit. As profit rates declined in one location, capitalists, in their drive to maximize profit, sought out new locations. In spite of this mobility of capital, in European countries in the nineteenth century a considerable amount of growth took place. The surplus invested in these countries was extracted not only from the European countries, including Britain, but also from the colonial countries under European domination. This capital was invested within their own homeland *and* in the settlements overseas where the white workers settled, such as the United States, Canada and Australia. So in European countries and in white settler colonies, mobility of capital was consistent with growth of productivity. However, this did not happen in the colonial countries. There the surplus was sucked out and very little new capital was invested in these countries. On the other side, the labour force in these non-white colonies continued to grow and remain cheap. It was cheapened not only by the growth of the labour force but also because of the kind of repression to which labour was subjected in all these countries. In the Assamese tea plantations, for example, a practically servile labour process was installed in the nineteenth century. When labour was taken out from India to be employed in Mauritius, Trinidad or Ceylon, again they were treated practically as slaves. And, of course, in South Africa, Asians and black workers are still being treated as second-class citizens.

In considering the growth of capitalism in India, it has to be borne in mind that bringing about capitalist production relations was not an integral part of the design of capitalist colonialism. The British were themselves capitalists. But they were interested in introducing capitalist relations into India only in so far as they would increase the revenue and profit that would be gathered by the British tributary state and by the British or the European capitalist class in general. The British rulers and capitalists had not come to do any missionary work here. This is sometimes overlooked not only by liberal, but also by Marxist historians. They tend to assume that because the British were capitalists, they were about to transform India into a capitalist country. They had no such intention. In fact most of the Christian missionary activities had been stopped by the British in the very beginning when they found that this was interfering with their major goal, which was maximizing the total amount of revenue that they would extract from this country. If the peasant–*zamindar* or peasant–*mirasidar* relations were altered in some cases so that they resembled capitalist relations, in other respects such alterations strengthened the grip of revenue farmers rather than peasant proprietors. In some cases, as in the areas of the Patwardhan lordship in the Maratha territory, the new revenue laws led to the curbing, if not decimation, of an emerging capitalist–landlord stratum. The British, in fact, effectively hampered the growth of capitalism in many parts of India in the early nineteenth century. It was not only in agriculture that production relations were changed in a way that hindered, rather than helped, the growth of capitalism and capitalist farmers for much of this period of British rule. In handicrafts industry and trade also, British rule led to a decline of merchants associated with those occupations and, even more importantly, of substantial artisans whose counterparts were often emerging as industrialists in Europe.

Marx has talked somewhere about two paths to industrial growth. One is the conventional path, that is, where merchants become industrialists, and the other is a more revolutionary path, where the producers themselves, the artisans, accumulate enough capital to become the new industrial capitalists. In India there were, in places like Gujarat, quite prosperous artisans, such as the Bhavsars, for example. But their occupations were destroyed by the policies that were followed under British rule. Thus, not only the merchants who were associated with handicrafts but also some of the more prosperous artisans lost their chance of ever evolving into industrial capitalists. This part of our argument can be summarized by saying that India under British rule by and large experienced the short end of the contradictions of capitalism and colonialism—effects which can be described as 'backwash effects' in the terminology of Gunnar

Myrdal. This was reflected in the condition of the exploited peasantry, artisanate and the ever-expanding mass of the proletariat, and also in the conditions of survival and growth of the indigenous capitalist strata.

The nature of capitalist classes or the extent of their growth is not, of course, synonymous with the nature of capitalism. In order to understand capitalism, we have to understand the other classes also—including the way those classes interact with one another and the way those classes interact with the state apparatus. It is not possible to tackle all the complexities of those interactions here. What I will do here is primarily discuss the behaviour of the Indian capitalist classes, all the time remembering that the behaviour of the capitalist system as a whole—or whatever we call the social system that we have in India—will need an analysis of the behaviour of the workers, the peasants, the landlords and the working of the whole state apparatus.

In Asia and Europe, class society had its origins in distant antiquity. However the class society originated, defining the upper classes required rules of closure. A member of the class of feudal lords in Europe generally required a sign of noble parentage and a recognition from his peers and superiors that he, indeed, possessed the qualities needed to be designated as a nobleman. In India, where a Hindu king ruled, he generally acquired the status of Kshatriya, often being formally anointed as such by a Brahmin. We know the story of Shivaji's anointment as a Kshatriya king as a member of the Kshatriya caste, even though his origins might have been very different. Now, although capitalism is supposed to provide equal opportunities for everybody, capitalists everywhere have tried to form exclusive associations. They have had their own rules of closure and these are the rules that I shall now concentrate on.

In Europe there were guilds or associations of merchants at least from the time of the Italian city-states of the thirteenth and fourteenth centuries. Many of these guilds and associations acquired considerable political power and thereby impeded the growth of other capitalist groups and of capitalist production relations. The breakdown of feudalism in Europe was generally associated with the breakdown of such exclusive guilds or associations. But again with the further growth of capitalism, other exclusive clubs grew with formal or informal rules of membership, and these associations often exercised considerable political power. The Manchester Chamber of Commerce, for example, exercised a notorious degree of influence on British–Indian relationships in the nineteenth century. In India too merchants have their own rules of closure. The first rule is, of course, the possession of property. Without some money you cannot be a merchant. But that is not the only rule. The most basic requirement in most Indian cases of successful entrepreneurship was membership of particular castes. Even with a change of religion, such castes endured. The Memons and Bohras, for example, who were converted to Islam from Hindu trading castes, form very distinct groups among Muslims and many of the successful Muslim merchants belong to these two communities. I came across references to some very powerful Memon merchants in Madras in the late nineteenth century (Bagchi 1989: 51). Of course, not all Memons and Bohras were merchants, just as not all Marwaris or Nattukottai Chettiars are merchants. It was also not true that only persons belonging to the so-called mercantile castes could be merchants. There were Brahmins or Kshatriyas or people belonging to non-Vaishya castes who were merchants. The Nadars of Tamil Nadu illustrate the rise of a caste, through the utilization of new opportunities, to the status of wealthy merchants. But generally speaking, throughout India, you can identify mercantile groups with specific castes or sub-castes. There were also mercantile associations that cut across caste and community. In Ahmedabad and Surat, for example, there were many associations which straddled castes and communities. But despite all this, by and large, over the centuries we find a surprising degree of persistence of some particular castes as merchants.

When capitalists from Europe invaded other lands and sought to dominate and rule them, they evolved new rules of closure for themselves. The most blatant of these was derived from a racialist ideology. Racialism and, to a lesser extent, religion, were used to differentiate the conquered from the conquerors, the blacks from the whites, and to keep the former in a socially, economically and politically inferior position. When the rulers belonged to a capitalist nation, as the British did, for example, and introduced bourgeois laws with formal equality of treatment before law, they had to frame special rules to guard the privileges of the rulers, such as for example, that only European juries could try Europeans. But apart from passing such laws, the ruling capitalist groups organized themselves in formal or informal associations or clubs to which only whites would be admitted. The Madras Chamber of Commerce, throughout the nineteenth century, had hardly any Indian members. In India, this discriminatory treatment operated in different ways in different regions, because of the differences in the circumstances under which the capitalists from Britain or other European countries operated, and the differences in the competitive power of the Indian capitalist groups. For example, in the first half of the nineteenth century, Bengali capitalists in Bengal and Parsi capitalists in Bombay were in a subordinate position. But they collaborated with the British and, of course, competed with them in many mercantile activities. By contrast, in the early part of the nineteenth century, there were practically no big capitalists in Madras who were either collaborating or competing with the British.

This situation changed over the nineteenth century. At the end of that century Bombay still presented the most cosmopolitan picture so far as large-scale trade and the emerging cotton mill industry were concerned; there we find Europeans and Indians represented in the direction of many companies. Bengali capitalists had disappeared practically from all large-scale trade. In eastern India, the Marwaris had not yet appeared as big traders. And in Madras a new group of Indian merchants were thrusting forward. When Arbuthnot and Co., for example, collapsed in 1906, most of the gains in market shares were made not by the British groups there but by new Indian mercantile groups. This is where the differences in the social or production relations as between different regions come into the picture. We cannot analyse the effect of the behaviour of capitalists without analysing the social relations which surround them. If we take the development of modern industry in south India and contrast it with that in Bengal, we find that British rule initially had a disastrous effect on every section of south Indian society (unlike in Bengal, where some collaborating groups seem to have prospered at first). Demographic disasters struck Madras at the end of the eighteenth century and continued to operate down to the 1870s. There is work by Ronald Lardinois which shows that Madras was experiencing depopulation in the early part of nineteenth century. In the 1830s famines wiped out one-third of the population of the district of Guntur, for example. This kind of situation continued till the 1870s, when southern India experienced one of the worst famines in Indian history. After this period, southern India seems to have recovered demographically and even prospered, in so far as it makes sense to talk about prosperity of any but the top 5 per cent of the population in those days. When we talk about of the rich we are really talking about some of the merchants, some big peasants, and so on.

The factors that made this kind of recovery possible had to do with the internal social structure of Madras. The British, in their greed to extract as much revenue as possible, introduced the *ryotwari* system in most parts of Madras Presidency. That gave them a lot of revenue—more revenue than in Bengal as a proportion of total agricultural output. But in the process *zamindars* and *mirasidars* disappeared from most parts of Madras. That released the forces of capitalism to a greater extent than in Bengal where the *zamindars* continued to dominate the countryside. An external factor was added to this development. South Indian merchants went out to Sri Lanka, Malaysia, Indo-China and Burma and made profits there which were invested in India. These developments led, in the twentieth century, to the growth of modern industry in places like Coimbatore, and later on in other parts of Madras Presidency. Such a burst of indigenous capitalist growth did not occur in eastern India. In Bengal and Bihar, the British continued to dominate practically all large-scale industry and trade, and the new types of industry that came up were controlled by them. They took out most of the surplus from these enterprises and re-invested very little locally; the political power of the British in that region had to be removed before Indian capitalists could come in. The Marwaris did not really take over from the British as the biggest capitalist group in eastern India until the end of the Second World War. Here we can see a complex of international factors and internal factors acting to differentiate the rates of growth of Indian capitalists in two different regions of India under British rule.

In colonial India a large number of factors operated against the growth of capitalist relations in society. The British themselves had preserved revenue farming in many parts of India and did not allow capitalist farming to grow fast. They extracted a major part of the surplus out of India and invested it elsewhere. The growth of the

Indian home market, as a result, was continually hampered. A policy of 'one-way free trade' (to borrow R.P. Dutt's phrase) was followed. All these factors led to the underdevelopment of productive forces in the country, and of the capitalist classes as well. If Indian capitalists could garner only a small proportion of the surplus how could they fatten themselves?

With the removal of British rule many of these circumstances changed—but not all of them. The grosser forms of revenue farming were abolished everywhere in independent India. The *zamindari* system was abolished in Bengal, Uttar Pradesh and in those parts of Madras Presidency—such as Pudukottai and Ramnad—where there was a formal *zamindari* system. The home market was protected for all capitalists operating within the borders of the country. Large public work programmes in irrigation, power supply and transport networks were undertaken in order to provide the infrastructure needed for economic growth. However, as countless analysts have pointed out, the socio-economic transformation was halted by vested class and factional interests before it really got going. Peasant proprietorship of land remains a dream and not even a proximate goal in most states of India. With the exception of Jammu and Kashmir, West Bengal, Tripura, Kerala, and perhaps Karnataka, Punjab and Haryana, landlordism stalks the Indian countryside. The mass of the population remains illiterate.

One point that I have to stress again and again is that no country in the world has as yet experienced a high rate of industrial growth without abolishing illiteracy. Our leaders have grandiosely talked about 'hi-tech' and the twenty-first century. But an illiterate population is not a base on which a thriving industrial future can be built. Infant technologies and design expertise developed in public research laboratories and public sector enterprises and consultancy firms are throttled by the unprincipled import of foreign expertise and the deliberate fostering of dominance of transnational capital. Trade unions remain fragmented and ineffective over vast areas of economic activity, leading to an erosion of the bargaining strength of the working class. This also erodes the thrust for profit through improving productivity. Rising wages would have induced capitalists acting in their own interests to try to upgrade the technologies used by the workers. Indian capitalists by and large continue to use workers in sweat-shops where they have very little equipment to work with. One major reason for this state of affairs is that the levels of wages, outside a few enclaves of organized industry and finance, remain extremely low. I would like to stress that the behaviour of the Indian capitalist class is an important factor impeding Indian economic and social development. Of course, as pointed out earlier, capitalist groups are not fully autonomous, free to act as they like. Their behaviour is shaped by their perception of the environment, but that behaviour is a very important part of the environment itself, whether they perceive it that way or not.

Let me take up some aspects of capitalist behaviour in India for a more critical look. First of all, most Indian capitalist groups have not got out of the swaddling clothes and the associated behaviour that attended their infancy. Shaped by rules of closure of caste, they remain wedded to casteist and communal ideologies. What protected them and distinguished them from the rest of Indian society at one stage still makes them erect barriers against the entry of competitors into their cherished preserves. Unless the Vaishyas had their special rules, they would have been swamped under the pre-independence autocratic regimes. They would have been swamped also by the metropolitan capitalists: they could not have competed with the British, even on the unequal basis that they did in many areas. But those rules of closure now protect them against the entry of new groups which could have quickened the growth of capitalism in India.

Secondly, their behaviour is shaped by racism in very complicated ways. I have argued earlier (and I have developed this argument in much more detail in earlier writings: Bagchi 1972: Chapter 6; Bagchi 1982: Chapters 2–4) that racism was part of the formative ideology of capitalist colonialism. And it operated in a colonial dependency such as India not only to differentiate the rulers from the ruled but also, more particularly, the capitalist groups from Europe and North America, from Indian or Asian capitalists in general. It led to very anomalous, even funny, situations. The *Times of India Directory and Almanac* of the nineteenth century provided lists of Indian and European firms. And so, take one year at random: in the *Directory of the Times of India of 1882–83*, the Sassoon firms or the Jewish firms in general are categorized as European firms. These Sassoons, or most other Jews so categorized, came from West Asia and they were just a generation old. Elias David Sassoon was still alive in the 1860s and 1870s, when the firms controlled by his sons and other relations began to be characterized as European firms. This happened because these Jews had connections in Europe and therefore by ascription were regarded as Europeans. So you have this funny situation of people of Asian origin being characterized as Europeans, through and through. This kind of racial differentiation was very prevalent in all commercial dealings in India. Such differentia-tion had real implications because the Sassoons very soon took most of their capital out of India. They were one of the first groups origi-nating in India to organize an international bank—the Eastern Bank —which began to operate as a foreign bank on Indian soil. The Sassoons were truly the predecessors of the non-resident Indians (NRIs) today. NRIs go out of India and when they come back and operate in India, they behave like foreign firms.

Most Indian upper-class groups continued unquestioningly to accept the superiority of the whites even after independence, as far as commercial, military and technical power was concerned. It is only by such supposition that one can explain the continued tolerance of many ill-educated Europeans in supervisory positions of firms that had by then been acquired by Indians. For example, in the Indian Iron and Steel Co., which went sick, a bunch of rather incompetent Europeans were in charge throughout the 1960s. At that time everybody, except the directors of the company, knew what was happening—or rather, what was not happening—in that firm. Such examples can be given from many jute companies and mining companies in eastern India. Then, let us look at the number of foreign collaboration agreements that India signed with Britain. By the end of the 1950s, Britain had become technologically backward as compared to other OECD countries. But even in the 1960s, when Japan and West Germany—let alone the United States—were far ahead of Britain in most of the production technologies, the largest number of collaboration agreements entered into by Indian firms was with British firms. And this was again due, at least partly, to a sense of colonial inferiority from which many Indian capitalists suffered. This feeling was not confined to capitalists. It was shared by many of our top bureaucrats, some of whom were much more deferential to the white men than even our capitalists who after all counted their money and had to have some degree of accuracy in their calculations. The continued distrust of home-grown experts and technologists on the part of Indian firms also had partly a similar origin.

When we look around we find that, especially in Africa, members of the Indian upper class generally adopted a racist attitude towards blacks of other countries. The troubles faced by Indian businessmen in East Africa were partly due to this attitude. That the new political regimes often opposed Indian exclusiveness with their own chauvinism and revanchism did not justify the unthinking racism of the immigrant communities.

The exclusivist attitude of Indian capitalist groups had some positive aspects as far as Indian development was concerned. Most of them continued to regard India as their home. So there was not much flight of capital from India, say, in the 1950s and early 1960s. Some of the profits of Indian enterprise abroad were also remitted to India. However, as Indian private capital grew in strength and, paradoxically enough, at the same time failed to mould the Indian environment to suit the needs of long-term capitalist growth, they began to look overseas for investment of capital. As the Indian capitalists grew in number and strength overseas, they looked less and less upon India as their home. They continued to be excluded from the top clubs of European, American and Japanese capitalists, but they could organize their own ghettos and operate from there. This 'internationalized domestic capital' (to borrow a phrase from Latin America) could now play it both ways. In foreign deals capitalists belonging to that group could act as intermediaries for the political bosses and top capitalists in India. They could also act as intermediaries for foreign firms without a strong presence in India when the latter wanted to set up a base of operations in this country. So the exclusivist Indian capitalists turned collaborationists and acted as major agents for transfer of capital from India to other countries. These non-resident Indian capitalists acted also as a major pressure group forcing India into an unplanned liberalization programme and thus threatening to embroil the country in a debt trap. (For an analysis of the policies which international capital and internationalized domestic capital has sought to foist on third world countries, see Bagchi 1990a.) By now (1989) India has run up somewhere around 60 billion dollars of foreign debt, which comes to about 96,000 crores of rupees. Most of that debt was contracted during the preceding four years—during the period of so-called liberalization and opening up of the economy—and in all these deals not only transnational banks but our own home-grown Indian capitalists, both officially non-resident and officially resident, have played a very important role.

Throughout all these changes Indian capital did not turn secular or embrace democratic values. The ideologies they profess are mostly backward-looking. Sometimes they ape the most reactionary ideologies emanating from the advanced capitalist countries. Many of them do not understand that these cannot be applied to India even for fostering the growth of capitalism. Some of them are aware of the inappositeness of the message of free trade to the Indian situation and, to protect their own narrow self-interest, will oppose any thoroughgoing move for free trade. But free trade is a good slogan with which to counter the struggles for genuine freedom waged by ordinary Indians. Capitalist groups and the media under their control cynically exploit that slogan in order to deflect the attention of the struggling people from the real issues. The acolytes of Milton Friedman, for example, have been entertained frequently by some Indian chamber of commerce or other. They are invited to give lectures to the Indian public, as if they have a message to give to our politicians.

Sheltering under the undemocratic power wielded by landlordism, many fractions of capital remain casteist and communalist to the core. I will cite two recent (this was written in 1989) examples from Calcutta. It was a group of north Indian traders who wanted to celebrate the anniversary of the burning of Roop Kunwar in Deorala in the Sati temple maintained by them. Again, very recently, the first puja of *Ramshila* for the infamous project of erecting a temple at the mythical site of Ram Janmabhoomi (and the actual site of Babri Masjid) was performed in a temple maintained by the same group of north Indian traders. The support given by traders and many capitalists in north India to the murderously communalist politics of the BJP and the VHP (Vishwa Hindu Parishad) became far more blatant in 1990. Even big capitalist groups, such as the Birlas, have extended financial and moral support to these elements. For example, schools under the control of the Birla group in Calcutta gave a special reception to L.K. Advani.

More than a hundred years ago, Marx had written, in reference to merchant capital, that its existence and development to a certain level are historical premises for the development of capitalist production. He cautioned, however, that its development is by itself incapable of promoting genuine capitalism and explaining the transition from feudalism to capitalism. This formulation still remains valid today but it has to be interpreted in the light of our particular circumstances. The Indian ruling classes, in their urge for self-preservation at any cost, have erected formidable obstacles against the development of industrial capitalism in India. Indian agriculture in many parts of the country remains locked in semi-feudal relations. Outside a few enclaves of organized industry and finance, Indian labour faces extreme repression whenever it tries to set up effective unions. (For an analysis of the attitudes of capitalists to workers and the treatment received by the latter in the industrially booming state of Gujarat, see Bremen 1990: 446–608.) Indian technologists see their efforts being continually subverted by touts of foreign enterprises. Indian civil law remains fragmented into myriad divisions of religious injunction.

Some years back, in the controversy over the Shah Bano case, the Congress (I) government at the centre instituted a particularly retrograde variant of Muslim personal law against the opposition of many sections of Muslim opinion and of all politically active women. In one blow it made the position of Muslim women in India inferior to that of Muslim men. At that time I found many of the Hindu communalists very enthusiastic in their opposition to the enactment of the Muslim personal law because they thought that if this was Muslim law, they could show how Muslim law as such was inimical to the welfare of ordinary people. What nobody talks about is that Hindu law remains tied to the apron-strings of religion and is extremely divided, varying in different parts of the country. It is with the help of the *Mitakshara* law that many of the Indian capitalist groups and property owners protect their property in legal and semi-legal ways. And these laws go against most of the rules of bourgeois logic. As yet, among all these enthusiasts who fought for bringing back Muslim personal law into the general arena of civil law, there is no move to bring all Hindus under the umbrella of a non-religious civil law meant for all Indians. To my sorrow and surprise, most of my radical friends too have not yet really voiced this demand as strongly as they should have done.

Big Indian capitalists by and large remain casteist, communalist, collaborationist, authoritarian, and thrive by corruptly utilizing governmental machinery. They behave like short-sighted merchants even when they control large factories. The few who try to behave as industrial capitalists and exploit the home market for increasing output and making productivity gains, are all the time hobbled by myopic governmental policies favouring collaboration with foreign capital on unequal terms. There is plenty of evidence from eastern India in areas such as drugs and pharmaceuticals, engineering, ceramics and metallurgy, that the more progressive and more nationally oriented forms of industrial capital have been again and again overwhelmed by the less progressive and more collaborationist forms (Ghosh 1983; Ghosh 1984; Chaudhuri 1988; Bagchi 1990b: 212–23). This situation applies to many other parts of India. The fostering of a reactionary ideology has all the time been accompanied by the reproduction of social relations that has made this possible. The government has now allowed the development of a highly speculative capital market which can be manipulated by unscrupulous wheeler-dealers to the detriment of real industrial progress (Barua and Raghunathan 1990: 2559–62). An attack on the degraded society built by merchant capital, the newly-emerging finance capital and landlords in India, requires a frontal assault on the whole ideology of casteism, communalism and collaborationism spread by them, and cannot be confined simply to bargaining for higher wages in a few sectors of the economy.

References

Bagchi, A.K., 1972, *Private Investment in India 1900–39*, Cambridge University Press, Cambridge.

———, 1982, *The Political Economy of Underdevelopment*, Cambridge University Press, Cambridge.

———, 1989, *The Presidency Banks and the Indian Economy 1876–1914*, Oxford University Press, Calcutta.

———, 1990, 'Working Class Consciousness', *Economic and Political Weekly*, Vol. 25, No. 3, 28 July, 'Review of Political Economy', PE–54 to PE–60. (Also included in this volume.)

———, 1990a, 'The IMF view of international economic policy and the relevance of Sraffa's critique of economic theory', in K. Bharadwaj and B. Schefold (eds), *Essays on Piero Sraffa*, Unwin Hyman, London.

———, 1990b, 'Wealth and Work in Calcutta, 1860–1921', in S. Chaudhuri (ed.), *Calcutta: The Living City*, Vol. I, Oxford University Press, Calcutta. (Also included in this volume.)

Barua, S.K. and V. Raghunathan, 1990, 'Soaring stock prices defying fundamentals', *Economic and Political Weekly*, Vol. 25, No. 46, 17 November.

Breman, J., 1990, 'Even Dogs Are Better Off: The Ongoing Battle between Capital and Labour in the Cane Fields of Gujarat', *Journal of Peasant Studies*, Vol. 17, No. 4, July, pp. 446–608.

Chakrabarty, Dipesh, 1989, *Rethinking Working Class History: West Bengal 1890–1940*, Princeton University Press, Princeton.

Chaudhuri, Sudip, 1988, *Bengal Chemical 1892–1977: Growth and Decline of an Indigenous Enterprise* (mimeo.), paper presented at the National Workshop on Sick Industries Syndrome in India, Gandhian Labour Institute, Ahmedabad.

Ghosh, Siddhartha, 1983, 'Jantrarasik H. Bose' (in Bengali), *Ekkhan*, Shorash Barsha, Sankhya 3–4, Sharadiya 1390 BS.

———, 1984, 'Upendra Kishore: Shilpi o Karigar' (in Bengali), *Ekkhan*, Shorash Barsha, Sankhya 6, Sharadiya 1391 BS.

Colonialism and the Nature of 'Capitalist' Enterprise in India

Colonialism in the sense of exploitation and rule over the people of one country by the ruling class of another, produces a distinct gap between the forces of production and relations of production in the dependent country. Such a gap leads to a straightforward confrontation between the controllers of the means of production and of coercion, and the classes or groups to which the control and the coercive mechanism is applied. However, in a capitalist colonial situation, such a confrontation does not lead immediately to a change in the relations of production so as to be consistent with the superior development of the global forces of production. For, some of the basic transmission mechanisms for the implantation of the superior means of production continue to be controlled by the metropolitan power. The political and social system sustained by colonialism acts as a particular mode of regulation of economic activities, and favours certain processes of transmission of information, capital, labour and technology, and either rules out or discourages other modes of transmission of these inputs. The continual tension produced by the irruption of new knowledge, technology and new modes of organization, very often through the instrumentality of competing imperialist powers, is sought to be resolved by ruling groups of the metropolitan power through coercive control of the relations of production so as to make them consistent with the repressed forces of production. This is one reason why coercion plays such an important role in metropolitan–colonial relationships.

This essay was first published in Ghanshyam Shah (ed.), *Capitalist Development: Critical Essays*, Popular Prakashan, Bombay, 1990. A slightly modified version with the same title was published in *Economic and Political Weekly*, 30 July 1998.

Thus, colonialism almost inevitably results in the retardation of the forces of production by inhibiting technical change, routinizing coercive and brutalizing (and not just dehumanizing) labour processes, and sustaining a social system that requires the regular waste of a considerable amount of human and non-human resources. The system requires a 'slack' at several different levels,[1] and the maintenance of a great social distance between the rulers and the ruled. By the existence of 'slack' is meant here the ability of the rulers to generate a surplus, over the disposal of which they have a considerable degree of discretion. Thus, they can use it to extend the territorial frontier, to subsidize the operation of firms from the metropolitan country, or to keep the subordinate or collaborating strata happy.

It is not a straightforward conflict between the forces of production and relations of production that provides the motive power behind the movement against colonialism. It normally takes the wider form of political struggle against the colonial power. But the social forces that sustain the waste of colonialism generally survive after its formal abolition. This constitutes an added reason for trying to understand better the numerous ways in which colonialism promotes slack and retardation in society.

On the other side, the slack permitted to the metropolitan country because of the existence of a substantial surplus extracted from the colonies, can lead to a slowing down of technical change and structural transformation in that country. The relative slowness of change in British industry in the period 1870–1914 may at least partly be attributed to the existence of relatively closed colonial markets. Britain could sell not only cotton manufactures even after these manufactures had ceased to be globally competitive, but also relatively backward capital goods, such as mule spindles.[2] But in

---

[1] For the concept of 'slack' in social organization, see Hirschman (1981: 11–13).

[2] The survival in Britain of older types of labour processes—characteristic of craft unions or of a stage where physical strength was a requirement for operating machines—has been explained on the one hand by invoking labour resistance, and on the other by citing the requirements of hierarchy in management and the inability of any small group of firms to achieve dominance. (See Friedman 1977; Rubery 1978; Lazonick 1979; Zeitlin 1979.) However, the role of the existence of colonies in allowing relatively

Colonialism and 'Capitalist' Enterprise

this essay the reaction of the forces of production of the metropolitan country to the continued existence of profitable colonies is not the central theme: we concentrate on the experience of one colonized country, namely, India.

In the literature on the development of so-called capitalist enterprises in colonial countries, including India, the dominating influence of mercantile capital has been long recognized. But there is little in the literature about what sort of 'capitalist' enterprises these were. The nature of labour processes used within the enterprise, the means of control exercised over the workers, or the political relations of the owners and managers with the state apparatus are rarely brought into the 'economic analysis' of their characteristics and their evolution. What I want to do here is to focus on these questions, but the treatment is illustrative rather than exhaustive.

Most colonial enterprises were established by merchants from metropolitan countries or by the few indigenous merchant groups that survived the onslaught of foreign conquest or which managed to carve out a niche for themselves as collaborators of the metropolitan power. (See, for example, Guha 1970; Bagchi 1982: Chapter 4; Bagchi 1985a; Bayly 1983.) Merchants in the colonial countries had to adapt to the social and political environment created by colonial rule. Indigenous merchants had to reckon with the operation of landlords—often a group favoured by colonial authorities because of their role as collectors of tribute and as representatives of the colonial power in the villages—and undergo various kinds of discrimination at the hands of colonial authorities, and suffer from poverty of access to information about external trade and technical

---

archaic forms of managerial control and the reciprocal influence of such methods on enterprises established in the colonies by metropolitan entrepreneurs have not been adequately studied so far. One of the most widely acclaimed books on the relative decline of industrial capitalism (Wiener 1981) makes its case from a culturalist standpoint. But Wiener completely ignores the fact that one of the most essential aspects of the education of an English gentleman was the training of a ruler of the working classes at home and of colonies abroad. Benjamin Jowett's pupils training for the ICS expected to get several times the average income of their priestly peers. The left and the right (with a few honourable exceptions) seemed to be equally determined to ignore or slur over the fact of empire.

change in the advanced colonial countries. Their investment in industry was often conditional on their being able to realize at least as high a rate of profit in industry as in trade.[3] But in some cases, as for example, in the case of Indian merchants in Bombay in the latter half of the nineteenth century, they were pushed into manufacture because metropolitan capital was taking over much of their trade. In some other cases, Indians were forced to take over much of their trade because foreign capital had monopolized the more certain and more profitable avenues of trade and manufacture. The Indian glass industry before the First World War is illustrative of this kind of adventurousness on the part of Indian entrepreneurs.

The general social and political environment conditioned the behaviour of metropolitan capitalists in a colony as well as that of indigenous merchants and financiers, in the sense that the former's portfolio choices were also biased in favour of trade and speculative activities. In those cases where a close connection with external markets conferred an advantage, metropolitan capitalists were found preferentially to enter industrial activities whose markets lay abroad. But such activities were normally confined to a crude processing of cheap raw materials produced in the colonies. They would also be found perhaps as pioneers in industries requiring more modern technology, but not when they involved a high degree of risk.

Colonialism biased the choices of both metropolitan and indigenous capitalists towards activities where the gestation and fruition lags were relatively short. Furthermore, it acted as a kind of screen between both metropolitan and indigenous capitalists ope-

---

[3] The exact conditions determining the point at which the trader behaves as if he were indifferent to marginal re-allocations of funds as between trade and industrial investment are yet to be worked out. The time profiles of returns and costs in the two cases are by no means the same. Investment in trading capital has generally a much shorter pay-off period than industrial investment. There are other major differences, especially where traders operate against a general background of poverty of the mass of people and the control of people's lives by landlords through their control of the most important means of production, namely, land. Traders can try and raise prices of essential goods from time and time, and thus raise their profit: this is not just profit on alienation or redistribution of surplus value among a group of capitalists, for, this can and does lead to the transfer of purchasing power from poor peasants or workers to the

rating in India and the moving frontier of technology in the advanced capitalist countries. The privileged position of the metropolitan capitalists rendered them rather sluggish in responding to technical change. And since, in many cases, the indigenous capitalists derived their lead from the metropolitan capitalists or from the metropolitan country, any technological lag from which the metropolitan capitalists in the colony or the metropolitan country itself suffered transmitted itself to the indigenous capitalists in the colony.

Generally speaking, the lack of encouragement of sophisticated industrial activity in the colony by the alien government, the general prevalence of privileged niches carved out by the metropolitan products and by metropolitan capitalists, the influence of coercive modes of social organization, and the lack of literacy either among the common people or among the elite groups, led to stagnation of endogenous technical development in the colony. Even in those cases where trial-and-error methods in specific areas of production led to improvements in productivity (as in the case of tea in India or sugar in Indonesia) the methods could not be generalized or diffused to other areas of economic and social activity.[4] One reason for this was that the colonial planters or manufactures enjoyed both first-mover advantages and economies of scale through privileged access to resources throughout the colonial period. There is indeed little evidence to support the claim that British or Dutch-style colonialism in any way promoted the general growth of productive forces along capitalist lines, and even less to sustain the further claim that

---

traders. When commodities are subject to great speculative activity, it is not necessarily the average return on trading capital but the highest rate of return that a successful speculator can aspire to that governs the expected profit on industrial investment. Where the landlord is also a trader, it is the rate of return to the joint, complementary activities of landlord and trader, that industrial investment has to match. The only offsetting possibility is provided by the fact that industrial investment can be a way of raising profit from trade through local monopolization or creating temporary shortages (as, for example, in the case of sugar mills in India). But then that kind of industrial investment will be found to have a sharply declining marginal efficiency of investment schedule.

[4] On the improvement of land productivity in tea plantations in India and coffee plantations in Ceylon, primarily through trial-and-error methods adopted by the planters, see Misra (1985: Chapter 5); Barron (1987).

long-term productivity growth could be sustained in a colony through an indigenous development process.[5]

The macro-economic and macro-social roots of retardation of colonial productive forces were closely linked to the mechanism and extent of extraction and transfer of surpluses from colonial to metropolitan countries or to colonies of white settlement, and they have been analysed elsewhere (Baran 1962; Bagchi 1982). What I will try to do here is to present some specific cases of retardation of productive forces and, relatedly, the embedding of regressive labour processes, through the working of colonialism.

Dissatisfaction with superficial generalizations perpetrated by 'radical' social scientists, such as many (though not all) members of the world-system school, and members of the neo-imperialist neo-Marxist school associated with the names of Geoffrey Kay (1975) and the late Bill Warren (1980),[6] has impelled other social scientists, such as Lipietz (1986), to call for the analysis of concrete historical situations. But they find it very difficult to get away from a Eurocentric, ivory-tower view in which the hundreds of millions of people in the third world appear to serve new gods (or old gods with new names) such as 'peripheral fordism' or 'modes of capitalist regulation'. Neither the analysis of internal social structures, nor the delineation of international networks of domination, nor the depiction of processes or transmission of essential elements that make up the structure of capitalism, find a place in such radical generalizations. The aim of this essay, again, is to carry forward the analysis of

---

[5] The claims of the 'Marxist' new-colonialist school spearheaded by the late Bill Warren (1980) and Geoffrey Kay (1975) can be entertained seriously only by academics whose claim to scholarship extends no further than their access to some so-called radical journals and publishing houses located in the metropolitan countries. In their world, polemics becomes a substitute for analysis or inductive generalization. The convergence between this brand of Marxism and neo-colonialist ideology is perhaps not hard to understand.

[6] How the neo-Marxist neo-colonialist virus affects social scientists who should know better is demonstrated by the entry on Lenin in the *New Palgrave Dictionary of Economics*, penned by Meghnad Desai (1987). He cites Warren (1980) as an effective critic of Lenin without mentioning how the experience of a vast majority of the nations of the third world belies Warren's optimism about the progressive nature of colonialism and imperialism.

actual developments in a specific country within a broadly Marxist framework (cf. Bagchi 1972, 1976 and 1982, for some earlier efforts). History does not have to be a series of tales told by an idiot, or an eternal spinning of dreams by a raconteur who is content to tell others what they ought to be while he relaxes and pontificates in his ivory tower.

Indigo Production as 'Capitalist' Enterprise

In his *Development of Capitalistic Enterprise in India* (1934), D.H. Buchanan devoted practically a whole chapter to indigo as an example of European enterprise. He was careful to point out how peculiar a capitalistic enterprise this was. The materials for appreciating the peculiarity involved had been available from the *Report of the Indigo Commission* (1861), the evidence collected by the Indigo Commission, the official proceedings of the British government in India since the very inception of cultivation and manufacture of indigo under European supervision, and, of course, the literature of protest against the habitual oppression practised by the indigo planters.[7]

The development of capitalist enterprise in India has been discussed elsewhere almost as if what happened with the indigo industry was very much an exception and could be relegated to the dim past, since it has had no discernible influence on later developments. In fact, indigo cultivation and manufacture epitomized the peculiarly colonial character of British exploitation of India. The European indigo planters were adventurers in search of profit. But the means by which they sought to make profit was the creation of 'local indigo seigniories', in the apt phrase used by John Peter Grant, Lieutenant Governor of Bengal during the period of the so-called *Neel Bidroha* or Indigo Revolt.[8] Moreover, indigo cultivation for

---

[7] The *Report of the Indigo Commission* and the evidence are part of the UK Parliamentary Papers (1861, Vols XLV and XLIV). For other relevant evidence, see Buckland (1901); Buchanan (1934); and Chowdhury (1964).

[8] Buckland (1901: 241). Thus, Chowdhury's detailed exposition of how indigo planters tried to create 'local monopolies' (1964: 143–47) misspecifies the nature of the social and political environment that the indigo planters tried to establish.

the benefit of European enterprise involved a significant section of the peasantry of northern and eastern India.

From the beginning the European indigo planters in Bengal and Bihar proved to be a law unto themselves, and the East India Company's government had to promulgate orders time and again to bar them from certain areas or to restrict their operations. The indigo planters operated a system which used both the land and labour of the peasants, whether cultivating or non-cultivating, in a coercive manner. The planters treated the peasants not as the other party in a commercial transaction but as subjects (*praja*), vassals or conquered peoples, for whom the norms of ordinary commercial discourse could be suspended. It may be said that in this the indigo planters were merely following the custom of the land where every petty *zamindar* was a *malik* or even a *raja* in the eyes of his tenants. However, the planters additionally brought with them the mystique of the all-powerful *sahib* with the superordinate force of the *company bahadur* to back it up where necessary. The Indigo Commission of 1861 recognized that indigo cultivation was not profitable for peasants in Bengal proper. It is indeed doubtful whether indigo cultivation produced anything but a loss for the vast majority of cultivators either in Bengal or Bihar. This is why compulsion was necessary in order to get the peasants to use their labour and land to grow indigo.

The planters generally enjoyed the explicit or implicit support of the British government or their local representatives who turned a blind eye to their operations. For a number of years after the collapse of handicraft exports from Bengal, indigo became one of the major export crops and a principal means of remitting the tribute and earnings of individual European officials and traders to England. Hence, the Government of India by and large could not go against the interests of the indigo planters, however much individual collectors or judges might loathe a system that replaced the public law of the government with the private law of the planters, often in collusion with the *zamindars* (especially in such districts as Muzaffarpur, Champaran, Saran and Purnea).

This implicit support sometimes took an explicit form. For example, in 1830, a special law (Regulation V) was passed, which converted a civil offence, viz. breach of contract by the peasants and parties abetting or instigating them, into a criminal one and made them liable to imprisonment for this offence. As was pointed out by the British administrators, this was also a blatant case of class legislation, since planters were not made liable to penal consequences for the breach of the same contract. This regulation was abolished in 1835 on explicit instruction from the Court of Directors of the East India Company (Grant's Minute in Buckland 1901; Chowdhury 1964: 147–65; Banerjee 1984, Vol. 2: 104–05). However, the planters and their assistants continued to subject the peasants to physical punishment and imprisonment whenever the latter refused to plant indigo under the planters' direction, or proved to be otherwise recalcitrant.

The planters not only wanted the peasants' land for cultivation of indigo, they wanted their labour, their bullocks and their carts, very often at times when the peasants' need for the implements and for their own labour for cultivating and marketing grain or other subsistence crops or more profitable cash crops was the most pressing (Fisher 1978).

The labour process employed in the indigo industry was primitive, not only on the fields of the *ryots* but also on the planters' so-called *nij* or *zerat* cultivation, in the rare instances when the planters actually cultivated the crop by hiring labour and using other inputs on land owned or leased in by them. The manufacturing process also involved hard labour under highly uncongenial conditions. Planters tried to recruit labour from tribal or other relatively uncommercialized areas at cheap rates and settle them on land leased in or owned by them, so as to get a labour supply that was cheaper and even more bonded than that of the peasantry among whom they set up operations. Even such devices failed in many cases and the planters then resorted to naked force to get their way.[9]

[9] *Minute by the Lieutenant-Governor of Bengal on the Report of the Indigo Commission* (henceforth Grant's Minute), reprinted in Buckland 1901, Vol. I: 228. For an account of the position of planters vis-à-vis civil authorities in Champaran around 1866, see Beames (1961: Chapter XIII). See Beames (1961: 174), for the record of a case where Baldwin, an indigo planter of Champaran, 'dragged out three ryots ("his subjects" as he called them) and sent them off to the out-factory where they were kept as prisoners until the pressing (of indigo pulp into cakes) was finished.'

It was recognized that planters would almost never be able to cultivate the crop profitably if they paid market prices for the inputs. For many *ryots,* even when the crop was grown with family labour or other labour for which full imputation of market wage was not provided for, its cultivation was both relatively and absolutely unprofitable almost from the beginning.[10] The rise of prices in the 1840s and 1850s, the emergence of jute as an alternative cash crop and the gradual exhaustion of the *char* land, led to major peasant uprisings in Bengal proper and virtual cessation of indigo cultivation in many districts of Bengal (Palit 1975). The survival and even growth of indigo plantations in Bihar and some Uttar Pradesh districts does not, however, prove that indigo cultivation remained profitable for the Bihar *ryots;*[11] even less does it prove that the Bihar planters who extended their *zerat* cultivation actually or nominally in their so-called *dehat* lands (which were more akin to feudal territorial usurpation than to land which planters could be said to own) succeeded in making *zerat* cultivation commercially profitable. One reason why indigo cultivation was carried on by tenants and *zamindars* in Uttar Pradesh is that the advances made by the indigo manufacturers were given exactly at the time when the *kists* of the tenant to the *malik* and of the *malik* to the government fell due (see, in this connection, Whitcombe 1972: 172–74).

When peasant and *zamindar* resistance made it more difficult for indigo planters to carry on in Bengal proper, they shifted their operations to Bihar. Among the main reasons for this shift was the possibility the planters had of leasing in large areas from the great *zamindars* of Bihar, such as the Darbhanga *raj,* or the Bettiah

---

[10] In his minute, Grant pointed out that a system in which some planters could use bonded labour and underpriced land and other inputs, effectively discriminated against those who tried to cultivate the crop commercially (Buckland 1901: 247). By extension, it can be argued that the existence of coercive, feudal or semi-feudal methods of indigo manufacture thwarted the incentive for improving the methods of cultivation of the plant and manufacture of the dye.

[11] See, for example, Hunter (1877b: 102–03 and 269). Many of the *zamindars* themselves were indebted to moneylenders. One way in which the planters acquired leases from them for compelling peasants to grow indigo was to meet the dues of the *zamindars* to the moneylenders and the government (Mitra 1985: Chapter 5).

raj, on *thika* and *mukarrai* tenure (Buchanan 1934: 42–47; Mishra 1978: 97–109). Once the planters had obtained the leases from the *zamindars,* they arrogated to themselves all the legal and illegal powers of the latter. Since indigo cultivation was often in conflict with the cultivation of opium, whose growers were treated as *sarkari* tenants, it might be supposed that the British government would provide some kind of protection for those tenants. In actual fact, however the government itself kept the price of opium paid to the cultivator low and left the traditional or the upstart *zamindars* alone, so long as their actions did not lead to widespread agrarian disturbance. Nor did the operations of the planters keep the peasants from the clutches of the moneylenders, as was sometimes claimed. The planters simply wanted their exaction to be the first charge on the peasants' labour and land, and the moneylenders would be coerced into the position of subordinate exploiters.[12]

Nor did the factories run by the indigo planters raise wages in the locality. They generally paid lower wages to the persons operating the vats than obtained in the area (Mishra 1978: 106). We have already noted that the workers had to be coerced in various ways to induce them to work in indigo factories.

Thus the indigo plantations and factories, which were some of the earliest examples of European capitalist enterprise in British India, worked under a jointly coercive system, in which the British government, the *zamindars,* planters and moneylenders, all played their part. The relative roles of ideology, clan systems and naked force in maintaining the power of the *zamindars,* and of racialism and the threat of the superordinate force of the *sahibs* in sustaining the coercion of the planters, have yet to be properly investigated. There is little doubt that the jointly coercive system and the

---

[12] In fact, the planters themselves were often greatly indebted to Indian *mahajans,* and depended on the latter to control the peasants nearby through their moneylending and, sometimes, *zamindari* operations. In 1873, for example, the Bank of Bengal opened a branch at Muzaffarpur in the hope that the planters of Tirhut could become their constituents. However, it was found that the planters would not leave the Indian *mahajans* to whom they 'were under many obligations', although the *mahajans* might take advantage of the relatively low rates charged by the Bank of Bengal (Bagchi 1987, Vol. II: 183–85).

destruction of alternative employment opportunities through the working of capitalist colonialism had a depressive effect on the forces of production[13] and on the reserve price of labour. The fact that Bihar provided a large catchment area for the recruitment of low-paid labour in the factories, mines and tea plantations of eastern India had as much to do with this jointly coercive system of exploitation as with any putative ecological conditions.

The activities of the indigo planters, *zamindars* and moneylenders were repeatedly opposed by peasant uprisings in Bengal and Bihar. The strength of these uprisings and their effectiveness must have been influenced not only by the pattern of consciousness of the peasantry but also by the strength of the *zamindars* vis-à-vis the planters, the coercive power of the *zamindars* vis-à-vis the peasants, and the degree of hegemony exercised by the *zamindar's* ideology. It would appear that throughout northern and central Bihar and a major part of modern Uttar Pradesh, individual Rajputs and Bhumihars, often with the help of their kinsmen, established themselves as superior right-holders over the original inhabitants who were generally degraded to lower-caste status. (Many of the original inhabitants were of tribal origin and were outside the caste hierarchy.) Sometimes a ruler from outside the caste hierarchy or low in status in that hierarchy would assume upper-caste status and ideology in order to legitimize his rule. (See, in this connection, Hunter 1877a: 208–14 and 368–70; Cohn 1987a; Cohn 1987b.) In every case, of course, the ideology had to be backed by physical force when the authority was challenged. Was the racialist ideology of the white men opposed by the ideology of the Rajputs and Brahmins? Was the latter then subordinated to the former? A full explication of the conditions of existence of the kind of capitalist enterprise created by the Europeans not only in the densely settled rural areas but also in the factory enclaves, mines and tea plantations,

---

[13] The indigo planters' efforts at research were generally too meagre and came too late to save their dye from total destruction within about fifteen to twenty years of the marketing of synthetic dyes by the German chemical industry.

would require an exploration of the consciousness of the workers employed in the latter.[14]

Sugar Manufacture

Our *resumé* of European enterprise in indigo manufacture showed how this enterprise not only did not promote anything like a free market in labour, land or other inputs, but, on the contrary, was predicated upon the reduction of a nominally free peasantry to a condition of abject dependence on *zamindars* and European planters. Where the Indian *zamindars* themselves turned planters, the situation differed only to the extent that the European planters could not arrogate to themselves the special privileges of the members of the occupying race. Indigo manufacture ended before Indians could take over as the major entrepreneurs from the Europeans.

We now turn to sugar manufacture. Small-scale sugar manufacture had long pre-dated European intervention, and refined sugar had long formed an item of long-distance internal and overseas trade; unrefined sugar (*gur*) had been a peasant produce and had circulated locally and over middle distances even more actively. In the nineteenth century, refined sugar went through several cycles as an item of trade in European hands, and as an item of European

---

[14] For exploration of some aspects of the consciousness of workers in the jute mills of Bengal, see Chakrabarty (1983). One argument that was often given by European enterprises for exclusively employing white men in managerial positions was that the workers would not accept Indians in such positions of authority. Since the workers were often recruited from areas where they could see the power of the Europeans directly, and since the reality and symbols of white men's power were all around them, it was not difficult for the Europeans to argue that this is how the workers really thought. Since in eastern India there was hardly any large capitalist enterprise with Indians in managerial authority, this self-reflexive and self-justifying view of the workers' consciousness could not be challenged with any counter-examples. For the same reason, until we have convincing direct records of workers' consciousness in their daily lives, the reconstruction of that consciousness through the reports of violent incidents and the evidence of the white men and their minions will remain problematic. The '*ma-bap*' relationship proudly documented by the colonial rulers may have been nothing more than a ruling-class construct. Or it may have been used deliberately by the workers and peasants to satisfy the craving of the rulers for a display of loyalty.

manufacture.[15] The manufacture of crystalline sugar very often was only the finishing stage of a process, and it was only at the finishing stage that many of the European enterprises were involved. Moreover, the raw sugar (*gur, raab,* etc.) could be obtained from either sugarcane, palm or date-palm. In the case of the latter, the production and generally also the refining remained with the Indians.[16] But the crushing of sugarcane in a centralized sugar factory and the refining of the juice by the centrifugal process were carried out in factories under European control in the nineteenth century (Bagchi 1972: Chapter 12).

The Chart illustrates the structure of the sugar industry, starting from the growing of sugarcane. The different parts of the sugar industry had different rhythms, and these rhythms varied in character from district to district. There was no unilinear progression during the nineteenth century from peasant production to large-scale plantations, or from production of *gur* to the production of white sugar, or from the production of *gur* or sugar by artisanal methods or in small refineries to the refining of sugar in large factories with associated production of molasses, rum or other spirits. The evidence suggests that when, for its own reasons, the East India Company took a keen interest in the export of sugar from India, it tended to encourage European planters to set up plantations and refineries for producing crystalline sugar. Such export drives also had a stimulating effect on peasant production of sugarcane and on refining activities by Indians (Amin 1984: Chapter 12). But peasant production survived primarily on the basis of demand for *gur* for self-consumption and for sale within India.

In many parts of Bihar and Uttar Pradesh, planters shifted back and forth between indigo and sugar plantations, as they experi-

---

[15] For an account of the fluctuations of export of sugar to England and to Europe in general, and the consequent fluctuations in the manufacture of sugar under European and Indian control, see Watt (1893, Vol. VI, Part II: 88–121).

[16] See Watt 1893, Vol. VI, Part I, entry on 'Phoenix Sylvestris', for the structure of the sugar industry and trade based on the production of date-palm in the district of Jessore in Bengal; and Watt (1893, Vol. VI, Part II: 270–77), for details of the refining and trading methods used in the date-palm sugar industry. See also *Bengal District Gazetteer: Jessore,* (1912: 89–101).

Colonialism and 'Capitalist' Enterprise

CHART *Structure of the Sugar Industry*

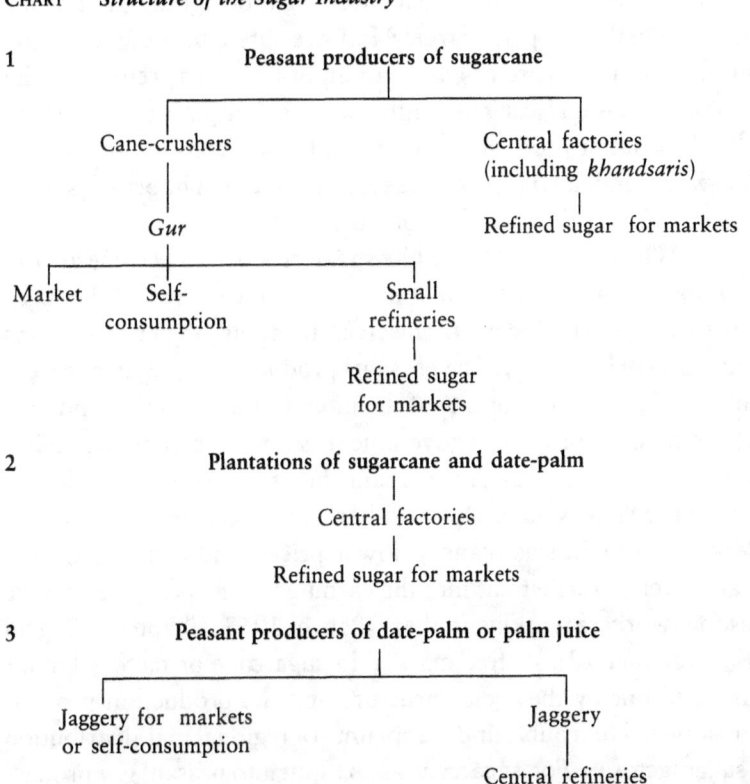

enced unfavourable markets in one or the other product, or faced peasant resistance to coerced production (Watt 1893, Vol. 6, Part 2: 94). As in the case of cultivation of tea, so also in the case of cultivation of sugarcane, the British Indian government gave land to European planters on specially favourable terms. However, many of those grants passed out of European hands or were converted into European *zamindaris*, and cultivation of sugarcane reverted mostly to the peasants: there were, of course, many areas where European planters did not penetrate at all.

While the production of white sugar was influenced by the ebb and flow of international trade, and by the development of the railway network, which made it cheaper to export the Indian product or import foreign sugar, the production of *gur* or jaggery from sugarcane, date-palm or palm largely followed its own course: at the margin, and in the case of *gur* as an input into sugar refineries, the price of white sugar certainly influenced the output of *gur*. But the bulk of the latter product was destined for self-consumption or for trade within India. *Gur* and white sugar were at best imperfect substitutes in consumption, production and trade.

When, in the 1930s, white sugar production became greatly profitable because of the high import duties, the owners of the sugar factories chose to locate themselves in areas of dense peasant production of sugarcane. The peasants producing the sugarcane were usually subject to the control of the moneylender and the landlord. Even though the provincial governments soon stepped in to fix minimum prices of sugarcane, the peasants had to accept various deductions at the factory gate. On the other side, *khandsari* owners were allowed to obtain sugarcane at lower prices, and often used their local power to further cut into the earnings of the peasants and the seasonal workers working in them (Bagchi 1963: Chapter 6; Bagchi 1972: Chapter 12). A 'free market' in sugarcane or factory labour was ruled out by the social structure and the production process. This soon led to trouble and complaints of regional mal-distribution of sugar factories. For, sugarcane as an input into peasant *gur* production had a largely different rationale in terms of costs and benefits, from sugarcane as an input into centralized sugar factories (see, in this connection, Bagchi 1972: Chapter 12). In the 1930s the costs of production in Bihar and Uttar Pradesh—with the existing state of repression of peasant costs through the market and non-market power exercised by landlords, mill-owners and moneylenders—were lower than in other provinces (Bagchi 1972: section 12.6). But the central sugar factories in those states had no way of reaping full economies of scale once their 'catchment areas' for gathering sugarcane were saturated through the location of other central sugar factories and *khandsaris*, and the competition from peasant-produced *gur*. Governmental policy and inertia allowed many of the inefficient sugar factories to survive. But there was a tendency for sugar production to be shifted towards Maharashtra, Andhra Pradesh and other southern provinces. (Some of these problems have been touched upon in Bagchi 1963: Chapter 6.)

Sugar mills, which were used to rigging the market in sugarcane and factory labour, also tried to rig the market in sugar (which was already protected against foreign competition) to feather their nests further. Indian sugar mills tried to organize a cartel as soon as there was a threat of a glut of white sugar in the internal market (Bagchi 1963: section 6.4; Bagchi 1972: 381). The government, which had recognized the Indian sugar syndicate as a representative body with powers to allot quotas of output to individual factories, had to step in and withdraw recognition from the syndicate when the latter used its powers to restrict sales and raise prices (Bagchi 1972: section 12.5). This was one of the occasions when it became clear that an atmosphere of competitiveness could not be ensured by uncontrolled private action if there were conditions favouring the organization of a cartel.

There had been some innovations in the crushing of sugarcane by peasants, such as the introduction of the Behea iron mill by Thomson and Mylne, or the experiments in the small-scale refining of sugar conducted by S.M. Hadi and others in Uttar Pradesh; there were also attempts by Begg, Sutherland and Co. to improve the manufacturing process. However, the major innovation that affected the sugar industry was the introduction of superior varieties of sugarcane which raised outputs per acre from the late 1920s. But this rise in productivity had ceased by the end of the 1930s. By and large, the techniques of refining had also become static by this time. Peasant production of the raw material, coercion of many of the peasants by planters, landlords and moneylenders, and the working of a process of competition in which the primary qualification for entering the sugar industry was possession of a stock of capital, rather than technical knowledge of any part of the process of manufacture or cultivation of the raw material, kept the industry rather stagnant, except when it was stimulated by external forces. Peasants proved to be better adapted to take advantage of innovation than the so-called capitalist entrepreneurs.

Manufacture of Cotton Textiles

The production of sugar was influenced by peasant activities in cultivating sugarcane, palm and date-palm, and the activities of traders or substantial farmers and landlords in running refineries alongside the 'modern' sugar factories. The production of cotton textiles in mills was even more influenced by peasant production of raw cotton, the conditions of credit and marketing governing the growing of cotton, and the activities of artisans and merchants at the stage where the cotton was spun into yarn or woven into cloth. The repression of artisans and master-weavers to the point where they became virtual serfs of the East India Company, and the elimination of Indian middlemen between the weavers and the East India Company (so long as the latter remained the dominant exporter of cotton textiles from India), are well known, and need not be recapitulated here (Hossain 1979). So is the story of the disastrous decline of handloom exports and the loss of livelihood of hundreds of thousands of weavers in most parts of India between the 1820s and at least the 1860s.

The growth of the Indian cotton mill industry in the initial phases, paradoxically enough, owed more to the remnants of the handloom weavers in India and in China than to the home market in mill cloth that had been conquered by the British cotton mills. For, Indian mills at first catered mainly to the demand for yarn—especially yarn of lower counts—emanating from the handloom weavers. Both the Indian cotton mills and Indian handlooms had to make their way against competition from Lancashire cloth.

The progress of the cotton mill industry was halting between the time James Landon and Cowasjee Davar set up their mills at Broach and Bombay respectively, and the time the First World War disrupted the supply of Lancashire cloth. This can be adequately explained by the dominance the latter had achieved in most Indian cloth marts and by the resistance put up by a handloom sector benefiting from a widening cost advantage as against the British produce in the coarser varieties of cloth. The failure of the handloom industry to adopt the flyshuttle loom until the beginning of the twentieth century and the slow progress made by it among the weavers can be explained by the weavers' poverty and the relative costliness of the flyshuttle loom, on the one hand, and the apathy displayed by the government to the task of raising the productivity of the weavers, on the other. In these matters colonialism can be seen to play its part with its policy of 'one-way free trade' and its attendant consequence in the impoverishment of the weavers. Ironically, the poverty of the typical consumer of coarse handloom products explains the survival of the latter. However, there is another direction in which colonialism seems to have played a more insidious role. The adoption in the first place by the Indian mills of many techniques and practices which were considered to be obsolete in most other advanced centres of textile production, and the falling behind of Indian mills in technical change, globally speaking, may both be laid at the door of the distortions of perception and supply channels produced by colonialism, and the associated phenomenon of domination of the countryside by landlords and moneylenders (Bagchi 1972: Chapter 7; Kiyokawa 1983; Chandavarkar 1985).

The influence of colonialism was felt in a complex manner. It started with the nexus between the trader and the cultivator. Up to the beginning of this century a large fraction of the cotton crop was exported. The Indian trader was only the first in a chain of middlemen, and he was unwilling to pay the cultivators more than the absolute minimum, for he could not be sure that he would get a better price for better cotton. During the years of the American Civil War, Indian cotton acquired a bad name abroad, since almost anything resembling cotton was shipped at high price. The traders at different stages (and also many producers) added water and dirt to the cotton in order to increase the weight. The buyers also tended to judge the quality of cotton by the ratio of ginned cotton to the total weight of cotton, including seeds. This led to the practice of mixing different types of cotton in order to get a better result at the time of ginning and pressing (Todd 1924: 30).

Once Indian cotton acquired a reputation for poor quality, a completely decentralized system of production and collection for export failed to provide any incentive to the good trader and the good producer, who were subjected to what has been called 'probabilistic discrimination' (Schatz 1972; also, Akerlof 1970; Bagchi 1982: 189–90). However much the British government and the European traders decried the practice, the former were unable to suppress it through legislation and the latter found it unprofitable to stop such practices through collective action.[17] A Cotton Frauds

---

[17] Sulivan (1937: 78–79, 88). On the question of quality of Indian cotton and a description of the different varieties exported from India, see Watt

Act was passed in 1863 by the Legislative Council of Bombay to penalize the adulteration of cotton, and this was followed up by another Act in 1869 which proposed to apply funds obtained from the tax levied under the first Act to the improvement of cotton cultivation. However, as a result of agitation by the merchants of Bombay (including the Bombay Chamber of Commerce), all legislation relating to cotton frauds was abolished in 1882. A new effort for improving the quality of Indian cotton at the stage of ginning and pressing was made by the (native) state of Hyderabad, which required a licence for setting up ginning and pressing factories, and rendered the licence cancellable on the ground of malpractice (Pearse 1930: 32–34). It was only with the setting up of the Indian Central Cotton Committee in 1921 that a systematic effort was made under British official auspices to improve the quality of Indian cotton.

One reason why measures to improve the quality of cotton failed was the refusal of the government to spend any substantial sum on either research or extension.[18] While exotic varieties were introduced from time to time, or individual administrators tried to introduce improved varieties from other parts of India, there were few government farms and practically no extension services for propagating the better varieties. The mixed cotton with short staple was good enough for spinning the lower counts of yarn and weaving the coarser varieties of cloth that were the products of most Indian mills. So long as Indian cotton producers and mills abroad were separated by a long chain of traders, there was no way the latter could make their demands felt to the producers; this was particularly so when the mills in the UK or on the European continent could get long-staple cotton from the US or Egypt by paying only a relatively small premium.

It may be asked why the British government achieved better success in encouraging the long-staple cotton in Egypt than in India

---

(1890: 52–152). The question of mixing of different varieties of Indian cotton and legislation to check adulteration are dealt with in pages 72–78, and by Todd (1924: Chapter IV).

[18] For an idea of the niggardliness displayed by the Government of India and a provincial government such as that of Madras Presidency towards expenditure on improvement of cotton even at the height of the cotton scarcity in the 1860s, see Bagchi (1987, Part II: 60–62).

Colonialism and 'Capitalist' Enterprise

in the nineteenth century. One answer is that the assured irrigation in the Nile delta provided better conditions for growing long-staple cotton until the major irrigation works of Punjab and Sind were completed. The second reason seems to be that export of cotton was the major vehicle of imperial tribute transfer from Egypt, whereas in India there were a number of other products whose export performed the same function,[19] so that the colonial government did not have to make as much effort for improving the Indian fibre.

At least two conditions were necessary for raising the quality of Indian cotton. One was the provision of a controlled supply of water through public, and complementary private, irrigation facilities. (Many of the small-scale public and private facilities for irrigation had been badly damaged by the change effected by the British in the system of land revenue and rural administration and justice.) Thus, in Punjab and Sind, the move of the growers from short to long-staple cotton had to wait for the construction of large-scale irrigation works (which had to pass the British Indian government's test of being 'productive', that is, financially profitable). Where irrigation facilities were not a major bottleneck, it required the interest of local mills (generally reflected in higher prices paid to the traders and producers for better varieties of cotton) for the producers to raise the quality of cotton.[20] The Indian mills could afford to pay better prices for better quality cotton only when they were shifting their product-mix towards the finer counts of yarn and better

---

[19] The British operated an empire at a relatively low cost to themselves, partly because it was so vast. With a much smaller empire, the Japanese seemed to have put much more effort in developing its exploitable resources. For example, taking the case of cotton, the Japanese displayed more energy into putting in organizational, research and extension inputs in developing the cotton crop of Korea than the British did in the case of Indian cotton (Todd 1924: 59–61). The study of the relative efficiency of different styles of colonial rule is still in its infancy, but for understanding the development of most of the ex-colonies such a study is essential.

[20] 'The best quality of Indian cottons are generally kept in the country for consumption of the Indian mills, as they can afford to pay higher prices than the European mills. Seeing that they have no sea freight to pay; these better kinds of Indian cottons serve to the Indian mills the same purpose as imported American cottons, and on these the freight is high. Several Indian mills have their own ginning factories in the districts which

varieties of cloth. In fact, there is some evidence that Indian mills were paying better prices for local cotton in upper India than exporters as early as 1889 (RTB, 1890: 17).

The somewhat belated growth of the southern Indian cotton mill industry and its pioneering by British producers can be used to illustrate the following propositions: (a) the existence and growth of a home market for yarn or cloth played a privileged role in allowing a cotton mill industry to develop and to transmit some growth-inducing effects on the cotton crop and its quality; (b) the freedom of the metropolitan capitalists operating in India was circumscribed by colonial conditions almost (but not quite) to the same extent as that of the Indian capitalists. In southern India, the handloom industry catering to the local market seems to have survived to a greater extent than in most other parts of India. Supplying yarn to these handloom producers beckoned as a profitable prospect to Indian as well as European capitalists. But for various reasons that had to do with their better, and racially privileged, command over capital and easier access to external markets, including the China market for yarn, it was the European mills under the control of Binnys, Harveys and Stanes, that succeeded better until the First World War. Only two or three Indian mills came up as poor relations (Bhogendranath 1957: 9–19; Baker 1984: 339–42).

On the other side, one reason why large British trading firms went into the cotton textile industry in a big way in south India was probably their relative lack of the alternative investment outlets such as mines and plantations, in contrast to the European (mostly British) firms operating from Calcutta as their headquarters. A kind of informal division of territory was put in operation by large India-based European firms in the different parts of India. While UK-based transnational banks, shipping companies and even the odd transnational conglomerate, such as James Finlay and Co., regarded the whole of

---

produce the qualities most suitable for their purpose and others have their own buying agents scouting round for the best lots. Probably those European spinners who use large quantities of Indian cotton may find it to their interest to emulate the example of the Indian mills, and often it will be necessary to buy a whole season's requirements of special kinds of cotton early in the season, in order to make sure of the quality (Pearse 1930: 48).

India as their bailiwick, the Anglo-Indian firms—those that had grown up on the spoils of trade and government monopolies in India—were mostly confined in their actual operations to their respective territories (Bagchi 1972: Chapter 6). The carving out of government-backed apex banking in India between the Banks of Bengal, Bombay and Madras both symbolized and formalized this territorial division, and in 1867 a battle royal was fought on this issue between the Bank of Bengal on the one hand and the Bank of Madras and the shareholders of the moribund Bank of Bombay (to be reincarnated soon as the New Bank of Bombay) on the other; the latter emerged as clear winners, and the control of particular groups of large European firms on their respective Presidency Banks was confirmed officially (Bagchi 1987: Chapters 27 and 30.) This territorial division went hand-in-hand with the exercise of local monopoly power by the leading firms in each of the main centres.

The south Indian textile firms provided an expanding local market for the better varieties of local cotton, and the rapid growth of the so-called Cambodia cottons owed much to that growth in demand. The influences of expanding local mill demand for better varieties of cotton on the quality of cotton grown in other parts of India was less discernible before the First World War. But when protection and the decline of Lancashire dominance in the supply of cotton cloth provided a more assured market for locally produced cloth, the quality of cotton began to improve and its average staple length increased in most parts of the country (Bagchi 1972: 108–11).

The influence of colonialism and landlordism was also felt in the labour control methods, the behaviour of labour, choice of techniques, and the speed of adoption and diffusion of technical change. We have already referred to the coercive methods of labour control used in the indigo industry. When workers went to work in textile mills, especially those that were located in such centres as Calcutta, Kanpur or Madras, the coercive apparatus of landlordism was evident in the labour control methods. Chandavarkar and others are right in emphasizing the role of labour resistance (which often took a passive form) in slowing down the adoption of sophisticated labour-saving techniques such as automatic looms (Chandavarkar 1985: 659–69). However, the very methods of labour control—

physical coercion, intermediation by jobbers, and the ascription of superior powers in every way to the colour of the skin—militated against many needed changes, such as the induction of technically qualified Indians in supervisory positions (cf. Kiyokawa 1983: 129–30).

Caste hierarchies probably also interfered with upgradation of skills and techniques in many industries (cf. Joshi 1985). But practices associated with caste or community distinctions survived because the rate of industrial growth remained sluggish compared with the growth in the reserve army of labour, and because the chances of workers being rewarded with promotion to superior grades was practically nil in European-controlled firms. The extreme poverty of Indian workers and their lack of education stood in the way of their assuming the role workers played in, say, Japanese factories. When Arno Pearse compared the performance of Japanese and Indian labour in cotton mills unfavourably, he put the 'frail constitution of operatives', 'unsound feeding' and 'living under insanitary conditions', and lack of welfare norms and education, among the important causes of the differences in performance (Pearse 1930: 11).

Kiyokawa has provided a valuable analysis of the influence of British mill managers and British suppliers of machinery in retarding technical change in the cotton textile industry. He has pointed out that the relatively slow growth of the cotton mill industry, after an initial spurt, inhibited technical change in the older mills. The sluggishness in competition permitted, if not actively induced, mills in new locations under the management of traders, who did not have a local cotton textile machinery industry to depend upon, to install second-hand machinery and hold on to obsolete equipment. One major plank of Kiyokawa's argument is that Indian mills followed Lancashire mills in continuing to install mule spindles long after they had been superseded by ring spindles in major centres of textile production, such as the US, continental Europe and Japan. India produced mainly yarn of lower counts, and for such work ring spindles were distinctly superior in terms of productivity per operator (Sandberg 1969). However, ring spindles cost much more in the UK than in the US, one reason being that the UK produced so few of them. Since the UK was the major source of textile machinery for India, in order to overcome this difficulty permanently as Japan did, Indian textile machinery makers, along with other producers of capital and consumer gods, would have needed considerable state patronage: this is where colonialism again obtruded as a structural rather than a perceptual barrier.

There could be two other reasons for Bombay-based Indian firms deciding to stick to mule spindles. Mules were apparently better for spinning short-staple Indian cotton. Yarn spun on ring spindles was much more expensive to transport since it was wound on heavy wooden bobbins (which had to be returned), unlike mule-spun yarn which was wound on paper tubes or on bare spindles. Since a large fraction of the yarn spun by most Bombay-based mills was destined for export to the China market, this could have been a factor working against ring spindles. In fact, Greaves, Cotton and Co., who were among the biggest exporters of cotton yarn, installed mostly ring spindles in their mills, and yet fared badly in the China market in the years immediately preceding the First World War and had to withdraw entirely from the production of cotton yarn. (I would expect combined spinning and weaving mills to adopt ring spindles on a wider scale, but this is something that has to be tested.)

Japanese mills in this respect enjoyed a distinct locational advantage and would find it advantageous to adopt rings for yarn destined for the China market, and they could overcome their other disadvantages through their closer knowledge of the Chinese market and better access to it because of both linguistic and cultural affinity and privileges obtained by imperialist pressures.

Kiyokawa's analysis needs to be supplemented by further emphasizing the contrast in the macro-economic and macro-social conditions prevailing in the British colony of India and in the burgeoning capitalism under the control of an expanding Japanese imperialism. The Japanese were in a position not only to adopt technical innovations independently of the influence of mill managers or technical personnel emanating from a foreign country; they could also extend protection to the domestic industry informally and formally, organize the supply of cotton on a collective basis, market the products in a coordinated manner, educate their workers and imbue them with an ideology of extreme nationalism.[21] (Bagchi 1972: Chapter 7). Even the Japanese drive to export and hence to remain competitive by adopting ring spindles, and then automatic looms, on a more extensive scale than either India or the lagging imperialist country of Britain, can be traced to the imperial ambitions of the Japanese ruling classes. On the other hand, we have still to find out how much the confinement of the Indian mill industry for a long time to the lower-value segment of the yarn and cloth markets in India in a regime of one-way free trade, and the associated lack of improvement of the quality or staple length of cotton, had to do with the slow adoption of ring spindles and, later on, of automatic looms.

The structures and attitudes spawned by colonialism did not end with the end of colonial rule. Our investigation of the reasons for India's slow progress needs to be deepened by a better appreciation of the legal processes, social hierarchies and labour control methods in factories, openness to and absorption of usable foreign technologies, and adoption of rational management methods. A more thoroughgoing enquiry into the nature of the so-called capitalist enterprises set up by Europeans and Indians in colonial India is a necessary preliminary exercise.

Colonialism, Capital Accumulation, Ideology and Society

Karl Polanyi put forward the proposition that under capitalism, the economy is for the first time disembedded from society. In Polanyi's words, 'man's economy, as a rule, is submerged in his social relationships and the economic system is run on non-economic motives' (Polanyi 1957: 46). It is only under the 'market pattern' that society is run as 'an adjunct to the market. Instead of the economy being embedded in social relations, social relations, social relations are embedded in the economic system' (ibid.: 57). This has generally been taken as a reformulation of the Marxian proposition that under capitalism the owners of the means of production are completely differentiated from the workers, who become doubly

---

[21] Pearse (1930: 11) writes about the Japanese mill workers, in contrast to Indian operatives: 'National pride permeates all classes; it is almost a religion and has created a group instinct, all working like a trust.'

free—'free' in their social status from any bondage other than that of the wage–labour nexus, and 'free' in the sense of becoming totally separated from the means of production. The sale and purchase of commodities for the purpose of earning surplus value by using labour power as a commodity becomes the dominant motif binding and energizing the operation of different segments of a capitalist society.

Polanyi's formulation, however, abstracts from most of the elements of a capitalist society except the institution of the market, and the market itself is seen in rather abstracted terms. A capitalist society requires a particular set of political institutions, an ideological apparatus and an apparatus of coercion. In particular, once the worker has sold his labour power, he is, for the duration of the contract of employment, subject to the political power of the capitalist: he and the capitalist are willy-nilly involved in a relation of hierarchical subjection. The whole weight of the ideological and political institutions is directed towards the maintenance and legitimization of that hierarchy. Of course, this relationship of inequality is hidden in most advanced capitalist societies by a formal equality in the eye of the law. But it is often forgotten that democracy in the sense of government on the basis of universal adult suffrage was a rarity among the capitalist societies in their youth. Universal adult suffrage as the basis of government in most advanced capitalist countries was attained only after the Second World War. In earlier periods, unequal disposition of property rights often created a political inequality and inequality in civil status, and the working of the market was modified accordingly.

Under capitalism, the market structure itself varies from country to country and over time. This is not only because there are variations in the nature and degree of competition between firms in different countries and epochs, but also because the employer–worker relationship itself is conditioned by different degrees of coercion and different durations of contact and contract. The Polanyi-like conceptualization would have to reduce all such variations as departures from an ideal market economy. Marxian conceptualizations can take account of such variations. But much work still needs to be done on the nature of the variations and the influences acting on them. For example, under the stimulus of demonstrated Japanese competitive power, which is supposed to be strengthened by intimate worker–management relations, new work has been done on how the presence or absence of long-term 'implicit contracts' between management and workers assuring the latter of job security and a share in profits has shaped the labour processes in the US and Britain (cf. Lazonick 1987).

Both the Marxist and the post-Marxist formulations of the nature of a capitalist society are idealizations.[22] The civil society never achieved complete autonomy in relation to the state even in the first full-blown capitalist country that we know about, viz. Britain. The monarchy and the established church have continued to provide legitimacy to this first 'nation of shopkeepers'. When, in the nineteenth century, agnosticism and atheism seemed to threaten the ideological basis of the hierarchical society that England was, German idealism and *fin-de-siècle* aestheticism were brought in to lend a new respectability to the ideas of order and progress. More generally, positivism, idealism and a kind of apotheosis of science served as the ideology of the ruling class, as politics became secularized in Europe (Hobsbawm 1975; Bagchi 1997).

A purely mercantilist notion of capitalism *à la* Polanyi and Wallerstein is inadequate not only at the level of the integration of the state and society. At the core of the Marxist conception of the capitalist mode of production lies the labour process, which allows the capitalist to transform labour power into exchange value and earn surplus value therefrom. Within the firm, however, the market ceases to operate. The 'employment relationship' is one of the major relationships in a capitalist economy and, as we have argued earlier, it is not a short-run, arm's length relationship (Williamson 1975: Chapter 4). From that point of view, the jointly coercive, the familially coercive, the feudally coercive, or the racially coercive labour processes are not necessarily outside the broad class of capitalist labour processes. However, their operation affects social interactions outside the firm and extends beyond the binary relations of the worker and the employer.

---

[22] The legal requirements and social changes necessary for a full capitalist transformation had been formulated with stark clarity by the Scottish lawyers and reformers of the eighteenth century (Stein 1970; Hobsbawm 1980).

The employer–worker relation within the firm is inevitably a relationship of power and subordination. In colonial societies, whole groups of people are subjected to the same type of power–subordination nexus independent of whether the subordinated are formally incorporated in an employment relation or not. Under the social structures preserved, augmented or spawned by colonial systems, numbers of actual or potential employees are subordinated to their masters not just within their working hours, not just as individual workers, but as families, members of a class, caste or community. Of course, workers and peasants still retain their autonomous spheres of action and thought in spite of the subordination, and such autonomy is re-asserted in moments of conflict with the superior strata; moreover, moneylenders, village headmen, labour contractors, *mistris*, act as the intermediary conduits of exercise of power by the superior strata, and some of them may turn against their superiors in periods of conflict. But colonialism as a superordinate force continues to fix the outer limits of operation of such autonomy or such ambiguity in 'normal' times.

The development of 'capitalist' enterprises under colonialism involved numerous facets, many regional variations and many temporal changes. In the usual historical narratives, these multi-dimensional spaces of variation are often syncopated so that it becomes difficult to identify the processes leading to particular outcomes. On the other side, many structuralist accounts ride roughshod over certain basic temporal changes which altered the structures in significant ways. Moreover, the structuralist accounts slur over variables which the analysts find difficult to accommodate within their framework.

Conflicts occur not only between models using idealistic structures (such as the followers of Louis Dumont, 1970, or the followers of Americanized Weberianism) and those using some variant of materialist analysis, but also between analysts who agree on the fundamental relations to be incorporated in the analysis. For example, what importance is to be attached to the legal innovations by the British in India in different phases? How much of the stultification of capitalist development desired by many British administrators and politicians is to be attributed to the conflict between public and private law adduced, for instance, by Washbrook (1981)?

What role did ideology play in strengthening or undermining existing power relations and relations of production in general in the countryside in different regions of India?

Did the institutional innovations effected during the British period help or hinder the capitalist transformation of Indian society? For example, it has long been held by many economists and historians that the managing agency system was a means of mobilizing capital in a backward society, utilizing scarce managerial skills over a larger field of operation, and infusing the technology needed for exploiting the available resources of the country (Lokanathan 1935; Basu 1940; Kling 1966). Of course, there were severe critics of the system, ranging from the Bombay Shareholders' Association (ITB 1934) to Hazari (1966), but these tended to show up the limitations of the system in particular contexts rather than question its place in the development of the capitalist system in Indian industry. Recently, Rungta (1987) has assailed it as primarily a system of control with little demonstrable effect in quickening the flow of capital or technology or in upgrading the quality of management.

If it was a system of control, and it was perfected by the British managing agents though adroitly adapted also by their Indian imitators, the particular system of inequality created by colonial rule had probably an effect in keeping it alive and succouring it. Again, both conceptual clarification and extensive fact-gathering will be needed to proceed further along this line of enquiry. As in the case of technology in a narrow sense, in the area of management methods also, the relative regression of the metropolitan country may have induced a regression in the colonized country as well. It has been claimed (Littler 1982; Urry 1986) that in the adoption of 'scientific management' systems (such as Taylorism or the Bedaux system) Britain had fallen behind not only the US but also other advanced capitalist economies such as France, Germany and Japan. It is very unlikely that Anglo-Indian firms should have adopted any 'scientific management' or methods of multi-divisional organization of firms much before the Second World War.

Firms under Indian control sometimes adopted methods of management (in particular family control) which directly owed little to British models. In fact, the retention of non-individualistic laws of rights to property and inheritance helped many Indian business groups in retaining some riches against the onslaught of competition from metropolitan capitalists. But the organization of modern factories probably remained tied to Anglo-Indian models and thus suffered from the inertia characterizing their British counterparts. Again, this is an area which requires further intensive research.

The ideological and institutional aspects of the working of colonialism in tandem with the residues, transforms, or surrogates of the pre-colonial heritage in all relevant areas of human existence have to be studied together with the signal fact of colonialism in India, viz., that it was a system of exploitation of people of a geographically defined area with definite ethnic and cultural characteristics by an alien group that was ethnically and culturally distinct and which did not regard India as their home. That this rule was also exercised in a period in which large-scale manufacturing, transport and finance were conquering the whole world, added other characteristics to the colonial regime.

The thwarting of the growth of modern industry, the destruction of artisanal industry, the draining of the surplus for investment in other areas of the globe, were part and parcel of colonial exploitation as a process. The draining of an investible surplus and the continuous damping of the incentive to invest in turn hindered capitalist accumulation and rendered its transformatory potential at best sluggish and intermittent. The capitalist transformation of any one sector was in the long run slowed down by the failure of other sectors to be transformed. Only when one sector, for some reason, acquires an explosive motion of its own, can it drag other sectors along towards the same fate. This did not happen in any period over the whole subcontinent. While some regions from time to time grew fast and seemed to transform their social relations in the capitalist image, other forces (including their own past) dragged them back. This is one reason why I have regarded the search for capitalist relations in agriculture in isolation from the rest of the society and economy as foredoomed to failure (Bagchi 1975; see also, Bharadwaj 1985a, 1985b). Regional variations which ranged from developed capitalist pockets, such as the city of Ahmedabad, to the totally undeveloped heart of central India (which acted only as a reservoir of cheap labour) were also shaped by the overall constraints imposed by colonialism (Bagchi 1976).

Washbrook (1981) has made much of the conflict between the public laws relating to land revenue extraction introduced by the British and the private laws that militated against the implementation of purely individualistic, shall we say, bourgeois property relations. He has also claimed that the mercantilist role of the state ceased after 1857 and private (European) enterprise was established as the dominant form of British exploitation. In actual fact, however, the state remained the major receiver and remitter of the tribute of India through the fiscal apparatus, and continued as the patron of European private enterprise in such areas as plantations, railways and army supplies. The fiscal extraction of the state assumed enormous proportions in the late nineteenth and early twentieth centuries; this had a very definite role in retarding the development of the productive forces, the size of the domestic market and the base of accumulation.

The way in which even a limited domestic investment of the surplus could help change production relations when combined with appropriate institutional provisions, is exemplified very well by the case of Punjab (Bhattacharya 1983, 1985; Fox 1984). In colonial India, Punjab forged ahead of most other provinces in respect of agricultural growth (Blyn 1966). Most of this growth was in turn made possible because of investment in irrigation facilities linked to the Indus and its tributaries (Bagchi 1972: Chapter 4; Bagchi 1976). However, there were large regional variations within Punjab. Roughly speaking, the pre-Partition Punjab could be divided into three regions: south-eastern Punjab, which included Hissar, Rohtak, Karnal, Gurgaon; central Punjab, which included Gurdaspur, Hoshiarpur, Jullunder, Ludhiana, Ferozepur, Lahore and Amritsar; and the western region, which included Shahpur, Montgomery, Lyallpur, Multan, etc. (Fox 1984). The central region was the source of migration, whereas the western region was the major absorber of flows of migrants. The south-eastern region was the most stagnant in terms of both labour migration and productivity growth. This stagnation in turn was linked to the small value of investment in irrigation in this region before 1947.

In south-western and north-western Punjab, a planned development of canal colonies and the leasing out of land in parcels of 100 to 500 acres to large farmers or 'traditional gentry' led to a rapid growth of tenancy, especially in the form of sharecropping. The lessors were typically the large owners and the lessees were smaller men—often so-called low-caste people from central Punjab. Behind the government's decision to parcel out the land in large blocks, two conflicting ideologies were working. On the one hand, there were those who believed (plenty of evidence to the contrary), that control of land by moneyed men would lead to increased productivity and growth of capitalist farming in agriculture. On the other hand, there were others who wanted to strengthen those strata which were regarded as being naturally friendly to British rule. Since Punjab was a major area of army recruitment, loyalty of the Indian soldier and loyalty of the Indian nobility tended to coalesce into the image of the respectable and sturdy yeoman stock in the official mind. In practice, of course, the soldiers often came from poor families, and the canal colonies of Punjab became the breeding-ground of a new landlordism which has proved to be a major bulwark of army rule in Pakistani Punjab and an obstacle against rapid agricultural growth in western Punjab in the post-Independence period (Hamid 1980: Chapters 12–14).

In central Punjab also, tenancy tended to grow apace. Bhattacharya (1983) has shown that this often took the form of large farmers leasing in land from the small peasants, whereas typical sharecropping arrangements whereby substantial owners of land leased out land to small holders grew in the dry south-eastern region. In the canal colonies, the demand for labour raised wages and fed the growth of both wage-labour and sharecropping. The developments in Punjab have been viewed in apparently contrasting ways by Mishra (1982) on the one hand, and Hamid (1982) and Fox (1984) on the other. Hamid and Fox have tended to stress the increased differentiation among the peasantry and the renewed growth of debt bondage and the personal dependence of the small on the large peasants in the Punjab countryside. Mishra has stressed the virtual absence of a moneylending trading class holding the peasantry in thraldom, as in most other parts of India. (Mishra has explicitly brought out the contrast with the Maharashtra region.)

Bhattacharya (1983, 1985) has added three new dimensions to the picture: the regional variations, the link of caste with class, and the influence of ideology in maintaining the dominance of self-cultivating peasants in many parts of Punjab. Roughly speaking, the canal colonies came to be dominated by landlords. But in the other two areas, in spite of the growth of sharecropping over time, the ideology of *khudkasht* with its emphasis on the virtues of work in the field (except among the Rajputs) prevailed. Bhattacharya has shown that there was a close association between membership of one of the depressed castes (Chamar, or Chuhra) and of the class of landless workers. On the other hand, he has also shown that the process of differentiation among the peasantry under colonial rule and its accompanying institutional changes (including commercialization of many customary relations or their destruction) was creating *new* groups of landless labourers out of the 'respectable' castes.

Finally, while the ideology of *khudkasht* prevented the growth of absentee landlordism and infused an enterprising spirit among the substantial holders of land, it could not prevent the growth of a class of farmers who were also traders and moneylenders and whose income was derived from usury and trade as well as from exploitation of wage-labour or labourers subjected to debt bondage. Nor did it prevent the growth of rampant landlordism in western Punjab.

Punjab had a smaller proportion of landless agricultural labourers than most other parts of India. But this condition was sustained as much through the opening up of new areas for cultivation with the aid of investment in canal irrigation, as through the continuance of a pre-existing situation of relative labour shortage.

In Punjab, in common with many other parts of colonial India, labour in agriculture was subjected to a process of 'formal subsumption' while the existing labour processes remained virtually intact (for the distinction between 'formal' and 'real' subsumption of labour, see Marx 1976, Appendix: 1020–25). When irrigation and the growth of rural industry provided the base for higher productivity, labour was also subjected to real subsumption: it is interesting to note that the growth of formal contracts studied by Bhalla (1976) in Haryana (formerly a group of south-eastern districts of Punjab) can be traced back to the early twentieth century in Punjab, especially in the case of annual farm servants (Bhattacharya 1985: 126).

The backwash effects of stunting of growth under

colonialism in other parts of India and the slow pace of industrialization ensured that the substitution of formal subsumption of labour by real subsumption would be neither universal nor would it be an uninterrupted process. Ideological and institutional elements would often strengthen or hinder the processes of capital accumulation, class formation and peasant differentiation. But these ideological and institutional elements would be derived from the arsenal of the alien rulers as well as from the dominant or subordinate strata among the Indians.

Transition, Unequal Development and Underdevelopment

Our discussion of the peculiar nature of development of capitalist enterprises in India finds a resonance in the classical debates on the nature and causes of transition from feudalism to capitalism in Europe and elsewhere, on the phenomenon of unequal development and its extent, and on problems of underdevelopment and possible class and political strategies to break out of retardation or underdevelopment.

Within India itself it is possible to detect the germs of not one but many transitions, and of different kinds of obstacles against an uninterrupted transition, obstacles that are vitally linked to pre-colonial social formations but also to the constraints imposed by capitalist colonialism and international capitalism.

The debate on the transition from feudalism to capitalism is by no means over (for a summary of the major issues, see Sen 1984). The debate centres on three groups of issues: (a) the nature of the pre-capitalist society and polity and its effects on the speed and nature of the transition; (b) the relative roles played by internal and external factors—in particular, by inherent contradictions of a feudal society and by external trade, respectively, in the break-up or strengthening of the pre-capitalist system; and (c) the relative roles played in the transition by class struggles, ideological and institutional factors, and by 'purely economic' factors.

In the debate between Maurice Dobb, Paul Sweezy and other participants in the early fifties (Dobb 1946; Sweezy, Dobb et al. 1957), issues grouped under (b) played a central role; in the debate sparked off by Brenner (1976), issues grouped under (c) and less directly those grouped under (a) came to play a prominent role.

Issues arising from the alleged phenomena of 'proto-industrialization' and rural industrialization (Tilly and Tilly 1971; Mendels 1972; Kriedte, Medick and Schlumbohm 1981) have also figured in the transition debate. All these controversies have had their reverberations in the writings of Indian economists and historians in recent years (see, for example, JPS 1985).

Most of the questions involved in the transition debate can be seen to raise their head in the context of the history of colonial India. Did the pre-colonial history of India presage the development of market forces? Which regions were most affected by such forces? Which were the sectors most affected? Did they lead to peasant differentiation of a kind that might have developed into a capitalist transformation of agriculture? Or did political factors preclude such transformation? For example, it has been claimed that in the Maratha kingdom, large landlords were already concentrating land in their hands and land was becoming an alienable asset (Perlin 1978). On the other hand, Mishra (1982) has contended that the transformation of Maharashtrian agriculture through the agency of a group of thrusting large farmers in the late nineteenth century and early twentieth century is not a fact. If so, what was the route from increased peasant differentiation in the early nineteenth century to the failure of capitalist transformation in the late nineteenth and early twentieth centuries?[23]

Such questions indicate that the colonial experience in Indian history cannot be treated simply as continuation of earlier history. Colonialism created an absence—the absence of thrustful industrial and agricultural investment in the domestic economy, which is a precondition for the growth of a self-confident capitalist class. But it was also a Procrustean bed—a bed on which social formations were stretched, cramped and deformed to fit the demands of a colonial rule which was intimately connected with the dominant

---

[23] An implicit thesis of a Malthusian disaster negating productivity growth on the erstwhile Peshwa's dominions, put forward by Guha (1985), cannot be sustained: the demographic evidence adduced by him is highly suspect in nature. Rates of population growth exceeding 1.5 per cent per annum for decades together, which he claims for the region studied by him between the 1820s and 1872, have never been recorded for any sizeable region in India before the 1930s and 1940s.

tendencies of international capitalism of the time.

The 'peripheralization' of the Indian economy under colonial rule has been put forward as a fact by several analysts belonging to the 'world system' school (Wallerstein 1986; Palat, Barr et al. 1987). Many of the arguments that have cropped up in discussing the question of dependent development or peripheralization of India are similar to the arguments that were used to analyse the so-called 'second serfdom' in eastern Europe (Braudel 1982: 265–72). Using the history of Poland as the basic matrix, Witold Kula put forward an 'economic theory of the feudal system' (Kula 1976). One fundamental problem with Kula's framework is exemplified by the title itself; there can be no *economic theory* of the feudal system. At best one can hope for a theory of the economic aspects of the feudal system. Patnaik (1982) has pointed out inconsistencies in the framework and, in particular, in the schemata of economic calculation put forward by Kula. In the specifically post-colonial Indian context, Pradhan Prasad has, in many of his writings, pointed to the political aspects of what is often regarded as a semi-feudal social formation (see, for example, Prasad 1973–74). Usury or debt bondage is sustained by non-market power as well as by the threat of starvation of a peasant or worker who is denied employment or loans. There can be thus no purely 'economic' theory of agricultural backwardness or the so-called 'interlinkage of markets' (which is another name for the multiplicity of bonds by which peasants are enserfed).

Some of the difficulties faced in using Kula's framework to analyse either the structure of Polish feudalism or its dynamics should be cautionary lessons for social scientists trying to understand the structure and dynamics of British Indian colonial society. In sixteenth-century Poland, landlords were involved in market relations but only partially; they depended on serf labour who would be employed at a lower cost than was incurred by those who employed free labour. The manor was often a multi-crop enterprise but dominated by a single crop, viz. grain (Kula 1976: 40), which was the major marketable and exportable commodity. The involvement of a manorial system in both market relations and non-market coercion gave rise to peculiar conflicts: there were conflicts of interest between those proprietors who were mainly dependent on the market and those for whom market involvement was peripheral; and of course, there were those peasants and serfs whose freedom could be attained only with the break-down of the feudal system.

The 'huckstering' of land by landlords, the Janus-faced character of mercantile capital under feudalism, or the class struggle waged by the peasantry against the feudal lords, would all have been familiar to Marx—either the young Marx or the mature Marx—though in different degrees (see, for example, the extracts provided in Marx and Engels 1979). But the actual development in a particular society, for example, in seventeenth-century Poland, would still require detailed historical investigation and careful specification of the analytical categories used (a summary of the Polish debate on the question is given in Petrusewics 1978). In the Polish case, we would have to explain why greater exposure to the international market should tighten rather than loosen the feudal bondage. Here, as Brenner pointed out, the inclusion of the political dimension, including class struggle, would be crucial for a convincing analysis (Brenner 1976, 1978 and 1982).

Coming back to the Indian situation, it is easy to perceive that for every epoch of colonial history, we need a much more careful specification of the impact of the market under colonialism than is often given in the historical literature. In colonial India, did land become a fully fungible commodity? Was the legislation really aimed at this objective, or was the objective simply the maximization of a stable surplus obtained by the state in the form of land revenue? How far would the laws be actually implemented? Did the formal abolition of pre-colonial slavery really lead to the end of agrestic slavery? Which classes had surplus for accumulation? In which channels could investment flow? What happened to displaced labour? If a process of de-industrialization was let loose in the nineteenth century in many countries of Europe as well as the non-white colonies, such as India and China (Sabel and Zeitlin 1985), what were the circumstances favouring the re-industrialization of Italy, Austria or Spain in contrast with India and China? Is it enough to point to the unilateral, sustained transfer of a large portion of the investible surplus as an explanation of the Indian retardation?

There are many other questions surrounding the so-called process of commercialization. Did the failure to industrialize also lead to the permanent stunting of growth of capitalist classes and shortening of their time horizons, or was it simply a matter of the occurrence of a favourable conjuncture when the latent strata would surge forward? What kind of productivity-raising impulses were operative in the phase of proto-industrialization, if India did witness such a phase? Bagchi (1975) and Bharadwaj (1985b), among others, have pointed to the role of industrialization in keeping alive a strong process of capitalist transformation of agriculture. Does a process of growth of urban industry play a similar role in the period before the advent of steam or water-power-driven machinery? Or does the industry have to be located in rural areas in order for it to affect the production relations in agriculture?

The debate about the relation between the extraction of a very large fraction of the land revenue under Mughal rule and the terms of exchange between town and country may be enriched by raising questions about the mutual interaction between changes in labour processes in artisanal industry and changes in the market situation. Similarly, many of the questions raised by Bharadwaj (1985a) and others, such as the differential involvement of different classes or fractions of classes in exchange relations, the different degrees of subordination to which these fractions may be subject through both market and non-market coercion, can be raised also about the situation prevailing in the Mughal and the immediate post-Mughal period. These may in turn throw light on the precise nature of the alterations effected by colonial rule.

We have earlier noted that it is difficult to maintain a strict separation between market and non-market relations, or between 'purely economic' and non-economic relations, especially when we are observing situations in which capitalist transformation has remained seriously incomplete. In recent years, considerable interest has been shown in the ideological aspects of social change in colonial India. However, investigation of consciousness or class struggle will be but incompletely effective if it does not include the question of the existence of workers and peasants as producers of use value and exchange value, or of material goods and services in a broad sense. The structure of control utilized the legal apparatus at many different levels. The complexities of the change in the legal system brought about by colonialism cannot be captured simply as a change from status to contract.

It is ironical that Henry Maine and other jurists should have formulated the nature of the difference between pre-British and British India in these terms: in England, freedom of contract had hardly won its decisive battle over custom or precedent, before it was circumscribed again in the collective interest of the capitalists (Atiyah 1979: Parts II and III). Perhaps here again the conceptualization of the Indian society was used as a mirror for the theoretical musings on the uniqueness of the British (or European) miracle. Recent celebrants of the latter may have more ironies in store for them.

The full uncovering of the ideological feints of the rulers and the reading of the consciousness of the peasants and workers will require both a fresh investigation of the British and 'oriental' parentage of the feints and an investigation of the pre-colonial origins of the community and class consciousness of the Indians. In advanced capitalist countries, as mentioned above, not only is the labour process continually redesigned in the tussle between capital and labour, the system of 'manufacture' of 'consent' through the labour process itself can be observed directly (Burawoy 1979). How did the pre-colonial ruling classes try to effect such consent or establish their ideological hegemony? How did the colonial power try to acquire hegemony among both the property-owning and propertyless classes under its rule? How was the class or status-preserving ideology sustained and propagated by the upper-class Indians under colonial rule? What strategies did the subordinate classes adopt to fight such inequalizing ideologies?

The precise nature of the break between colonialism and post-colonial society has also to be theorized afresh. What did the change in the nature of the ruling class at the top signify? How was the structure of control modified? What kind of viscousness in social relations was needed to sustain a democratic form along with an authoritarian social structure? How do we set about analysing the resulting contradictions?[24]

---

[24] Baker's attempt (1984) to analyse the changes in the post-colonial economy of Tamil Nadu without theorizing the nature of the break in politics and society at the time of India's Independence, demonstrates that the thesis of continuity can be extended forward as well as backward. His failure to explain the quickening of a capitalist growth process in

Attempting to answer all these questions will require the gathering of new data and possibly new analytical techniques for interpreting them. Just as there is little systematic work available on the signs that indicate the consciousness of illiterate workers and peasants, so also there is little analysis of labour processes used by *karkhanas,* artisans, cottages, sweatshops run by merchants, and machine-based manufacturing enterprises in India. For most of nineteenth-century India, we do not even have a systematic account of the grosser aspects of births and deaths, prices and production movements against which to situate the finer analytical schemata. The current essay may be looked upon as an agenda for research as well as a contribution to the debate about the nature of colonial society and its changes.

Non-incriminating thanks are due to Ashok Sen for comments on an earlier version of the paper. I also benefited from comments made by participants in a seminar at the ANS Institute of Social Studies, Patna, held in February 1988.

References

Akerlof, G., 1970, 'The market for "Lemons": Quality, Uncertainty and the Market Mechanism', *Quarterly Journal of Economics,* Vol. 84, August.

Amin, S., 1984, *Sugarcane and Sugar in Gorakhpur: An Inquiry into Peasant Production for Capitalist Enterprise in Eastern India,* Oxford University Press, New Delhi.

Atiyah, P.S., 1979, *The Rise and Fall of Freedom of Contract,* Clarendon Press, Oxford.

Bagchi, A.K., 1963, *Private Investment and Partial Planning in India,* Ph. D. thesis, University of Cambridge.

———, 1972, *Private Investment in India 1900–1939,* Cambridge University Press, Cambridge.

———, 1975, 'The Relation of Agriculture to Industry in Context of South Asia', *Frontier,* Calcutta, Autumn.

———, 1976, 'Reflection on Patterns of Regional Growth in India under British Rule', *Bengal Past and Present,* vol. 95, January–June.

———, 1982, *The Political Economy of Underdevelopment,* Cambridge University Press, Cambridge.

———, 1985a, 'Merchants and Colonialism', in D.N. Panigrahi (ed.), *Economy, Society and Politics in Modern India.* Vikas, Delhi. (Also included in this volume.)

Tamil Nadu since the 1950s also demonstrates that we need explicit theorizing about the break rather than a 'maintained hypothesis' of continuity in order to achieve better understanding.

———, 1985b, 'The Ambiguity of Progress: Indian Society in Transition', *Social Scientist*, March. (Also included in this volume.)

———, 1987, *The Evolution of the State Bank of India*, Vol. I, *The Roots 1806–1876*, Parts I and II, Oxford University Press, Bombay.

Bagchi P.J., 1986, *Gem-Like Flame: Walter Pater and the Nineteenth Century Paradigm*, Papyrus, Calcutta.

Baker, C.J., 1984, *An Indian Rural Economy, 1880–1955: The Tamilnad Countryside*, Clarendon Press, Oxford.

Banerjee, A.C., 1981, *The Agrarian System of Bengal*, Vol. 2, K.P. Bagchi and Co., Calcutta.

Baran, P.A., 1962, *The Political Economy of Growth*, People's Publishing House, New Delhi.

Baran, T.J., 1987, 'Science and the Nineteenth Century Ceylon Coffee Planters', *Journal of Imperial and Commonwealth History*, Vol. XVI, No. i, October.

Bayly, C.A., 1983, *Rulers, Townsmen and Bazaars*, Cambridge University Press, Cambridge.

Beames, J., 1961, *Memoirs of a Bengal Civilian*, Chatto and Windus, London.

Bergquist, C. (ed.), 1984, *Labour in the Capitalist World Economy*, Sage, New Delhi.

Bhalla, S., 1976, 'New Relations of Production in Haryana Agriculture', *Economic and Political Weekly*, 27 March.

Bharadwaj, K., 1985a, 'A View on Commercialization in Indian Agriculture and the Development of Capitalism', *Journal of Peasant Studies*, Vol. 12, No. 4, July.

———, 1985b, 'A Note on Commercialization in Agriculture', in K.N. Raj *et al.* (eds), *Essays on the Commercialization of Indian Agriculture*.

Bhattacharya, N., 1983, 'The Logic of Tenancy and Cultivation: Central and South-East Punjab, 1870–1935', *The Indian Economic and Social History Review*, Vol. 20, April–June.

———, 1985, 'Agriculture, Labour and Production: Central and South-East Punjab', in K.N. Raj *et al.* (eds), *Essays on the Commercialization of Indian Agriculture*.

Bhogendranth, N.C., 1957, *Development of the Textile Industry in Madras (upto 1950)*, University of Madras, Madras.

Blyn, G., 1966, *Agricultural Trends in India: 1891–1947*, University of Pennsylvania Press, Philadelphia.

Braudel, F., 1982, *Civilization and Capitalism: 15th–18th Century*, Vol. II, *The Wheels of Commerce*, Collins, London.

Brenner, R., 1976, 'Agrarian Class Structure and Economic Development in Pre-Industrial Europe', *Past and Present*, No. 70, February.

———, 1978, 'Dobb on the Transition from Feudalism to Capitalism', *Cambridge Journal of Economics*, Vol. 2, June.

———, 1982, 'Agrarian Class Structure and Economic Development in Pre-Industrial Europe: The Agrarian Roots of European Capitalism', *Past and Present*, No. 97, November.

Buchanan, D.H., 1934, *The Development of Capitalistic Enterprise India*, Macmillan, New York, reprinted in 1966, Frank Cass, London.

Buckland, C.E., 1901, *Bengal under the Lieutenant Governors*, Vols I and II,

Calcutta, reprinted in 1976, Deep Publications, New Delhi.
Burawoy, M., 1979, *Manufacturing Consent: Changes in the Labour Process under Monopoly Capitalism,* The University of Chicago Press, Chicago.
——, 1984, '"The Contours" of Production Politics, in *Bergquist.*
Calvert, H.C., 1936, *The Wealth and Welfare of the Punjab,* Second Edition, Civil and Military Gazette Press, Lahore.
Chandavarkar, R., 1985, 'Industrialization before 1947: Conventional Approaches and Alternative Perspectives', *Modern Asian Studies,* Vol. 19, No. 3, July.
Chakrabarty, D., 1983, 'On Defying and Deifying Authority: Managers and Workers in the Jute Mills of Bengal, *c.* 1890–1940', *Past and Present,* No. 100, August.
Chowdhury, B., 1964, *The Growth of Commercial Agriculture in Bengal: 1757–1900,* Vol. I, Indian Studies, Calcutta.
Cohn, B.S., 1987a, 'Political Systems in Eighteenth Century India: The Benaras Region', in Cohn, *An Anthropologist among the Historians and other Essays.*
——, 1987b, 'Structural Changes in Indian Rural Society 1596–1885', in Cohn, *An Anthropologist among the Historians and other Essays..*
——, 1987c, *An Anthropologist among the Historians and other Essays,* Oxford University Press, New Delhi.
Darling, M.L., 1947, *The Punjab Peasant in Prosperity and Debt,* 4th edn, Oxford University Press, London.
Desai, M., 1987, 'Vladimir Iiyich (Ulyanov) Lenin', in Eatwell *et al., The New Palgrave Dictionary of Economics,* Vol. III, Macmillan, London.
Dobb, M., 1946, *Studies in the Development of Capitalism,* Routledge and Kegan Paul, London.
Dumont, L., 1970, *Homo Hierarchicus: The Caste System and its Implications,* Weidenfeld and Nicolson, London.
Eatwell J., Milgate M., and Newman P. (eds), 1987, *The New Palgrave Dictionary of Economics,* Vols 1–4, Macmillan, London.
Fisher, C.H., 1978, 'Planters and Peasants: The Ecological Context of Agrarian Unrest on the Indigo Plantations of North Bihar, 1820–1920', in A.G. Hopkins and C. Dewey (eds), *The Imperial Impact: Studies in the Economic History of Africa and India,* Athlone Press, London.
Fox, R.G., 1984, 'British Colonialism and Punjabi Labour', Bergquist, *Labour in the Capitalist World Economy.*
Friedman, A., 1977, *Industry and Labour,* Macmillan, London.
Guha, A., 1970, 'The Comprador Role of Parsi Seths', *Economic and Political Weekly,* Review of Management, 28 November.
Guha, S., 1985, *The Agrarian Economy of the Bombay Deccan 1818–1941,* Oxford University Press, New Delhi.
Hamid, N., 1980, 'Process of Agricultural Development—A Case Study of the Punjab', Ph. D. Dissertation, Stanford University.
——, 1982, 'Dispossession and Differentiation of Peasantry in the Punjab during Colonial Rule', *Journal of Peasant Studies,* Vol. 10, No. 1, October.
Hazari, R.K., 1966, *The Structure of the Corporate Private Sector,* Asia Publishing House, Bombay.
Hirschman, A.O., 1981, *Exit, Voice and Loyalty: Responses to Declines in Firms,*

Organizations and States, Harvard University Press, Cambridge, Mass.
Hobsawm, E.J., 1975, *The Age of Capital, 1848–75,* Weidenfeld and Nicolson, London.
———, 1980, 'Scottish Reformers of the Eighteenth Century and Capitalist Agriculture', in E.J. Hobsbawm et al (eds), *Peasants in History,* Oxford University Press, Calcutta.
Hossain, H., 1979, 'The Alienation of the Weavers: Impact of the Conflict Between the Revenue and Commercial Interests of the East India Company, 1750–1800', *Indian Economic and Social History Review,* Vol. XVI, No. 3, July–September.
Hunter, W.W., 1877a, *A Statistical Account of Bengal,* Vol. XI, *Patna and Saran,* Trubner and Co., London.
———, 1877b, *A Statistical Account of Bengal,* Vol. XIII, *Tirhut and Champaran,* Trubner, London.
Indian Tariff Board, 1934, *Cotton Textile Industry,* Vol. II, *Views of the Local Governments,* etc., Government of India, Delhi.
Joshi, C., 1985, 'Bonds of Community, Ties of Religion: Kanpur Textile Workers in the Early Twentieth Century', *Indian Economic and Social History Review,* Vol. XXIII, No. 3, July–September.
Byres, T.J., and H. Mukhia (eds), 1985, 'Feudalism and Non-European Societies', in *Journal of Peasants Studies,* Special Issue, vol. 12, January–April.
Kay, G., 1975, *Development and Underdevelopment,* Macmillan, London.
Kiyokawa, Y., 1983, 'Technical Adaptations and Managerial Resources in India: A Study of the Experience of the Cotton Textile Industry from a Comparative Viewpoint', in *The Developing Economies,* Vol. XXI, No. 2, June.
Kling, B., 1966, 'The Origin of the Managing Agency System in India', *Journal of Asian Studies,* Vol. XXVI, No. I, November.
———, 1977, *The Blue Mutiny: Indigo Disturbances in Bengal, 1859–62,* Firma KLM, Calcutta.
Kriedte, P. Medick, H. and Schlumbohm, J., 1981, *Industrialization before Industrialization,* Cambridge University Press, Cambridge.
Kula, W., 1976, *An Economic Theory of the Feudal System: Towards a Model of the Polish Economy, 1500–1800,* New Left Books, London.
Lazonick, W., 1979, 'Industrial Relations and Technical Change: The Case of the Self Acting Mule', in *Cambridge Journal of Economics,* Vol. 3, No. 3, September.
1987, 'Labour Process', in Eatwell, Milgate and Newman, *The New Palgrave Dictionary of Economics,* Vol. 3.
Lipietz, A., 1986, 'New Tendencies in the International Division of Labour: Regimes of Accumulation and Modes of Regulation', in Scott and Storper, *Production, Work, Territory, The Geographical Anatomy of Industrial Capitalism.*
Littler, C., 1982, *The Development of the Labour Process in Capitalist Societies,* Heinemann, London.
Marx, K., 1976, *Capital: A Critique of Political Economy,* translated by B. Fowkes, Penguin, Harmondsworth.
Marx., K., and F. Engels, 1979, *Precapitalist Socio-Economic Formations,* Progress Publishers, Moscow.

Mendels, F., 1972, 'Proto-Industrialization: The First Phase of the Industrialization Process', *Journal of Economic History,* Vol. 32.
Mishra, G., 1978, *Agrarian Problems of Permanent Settlement,* People's Publishing House, New Delhi.
Mishra, S.C., 1982, 'Commercialization, Peasant Differentiation and Merchant Capital in Late Nineteenth Century Bombay and Punjab', *Journal of Peasant Studies,* Vol. 10, No. 1, October.
Misra, B., 1985, *The Growth of Industries in Eastern India: 1880–1910,* Unpublished Ph. D. dissertation, Calcutta University.
Mitra, M., 1985, *Agrarian Social Structure, Continuity and Change in Bihar: 1786–1820,* Manohar, Delhi.
Noble, D., 1977, *America by Design: Science, Technology and the Rise of Corporate Capitalism,* Alfred A. Knopf, New York.
O'Malley, L.S.S., 1912, *Bengal District Gazetteers: Jessore,* Bengal Secretariat Book Depot, Calcutta.
Palat, R., K. Barr et al., 1987, 'The Incorporation and Peripheralization of South Asia, 1600–1950', in *Review,* Vol. X, No. 1, Summer.
Palit, C., 1975, *Tensions in Bengal Rural Society: Landlords, Planters and Colonial Rule, 1830–60,* Progressive Publishers, Calcutta.
Pearse, A., 1930, *The Cotton Industry of India: The Report of the Journey to India,* Manchester.
Perlin, F., 1978, 'Of White Whale and Countrymen in the Eighteenth Century Maratha Deccan', *Journal of Peasant Studies,* Vol. V, No. 2, January.
Petrusewics, M., 1978, *Polish Historians Debate the Seventeenth Century Crisis,* (mimeo), translated from the Italian by Bernd Wilm, 1980.
Polanyi, K. 1957. *The Great Transformation: The Political and Economic Origins of Our Time.* New York, Holt, Rinehart.
Prasad, P.H., 1973, 'Production Relations: Achilles' Heel of Indian Planning', *Economic and Political Weekly,* May 12.
———, 1974, 'Limits to Investment Planning', in A. Mitra (ed.), *Economic Theory and Planning, Essays in Honour of A.K. Das Gupta,* Oxford University Press, Calcutta.
Raj, K.N., N. Bhattacharya, S. Guha, and S. Padhi (eds), 1985, *Essays on the Commercialization of Indian Agriculture,* Oxford University Press, New Delhi.
Report on the Administration of Bengal in 1896–97, 1898, Bengal Secretariat Book Depot, Calcutta.
Report of the Indigo Commission, 1861, UK Parliamentary Papers, vol. XLIV.
Report on the Rail-brone Traffic of Bengal, 1889–90, Government of Bengal, Calcutta.
Rungta, R.S., 1970, *Rise of Business Corporations in India, 1850–1900,* Cambridge University Press, Cambridge.
———, 1987, *Structural Change in Indian Business: The Rise, Evolution and the Abolition of the Managing Agency System,* (mimeo), unpublished.
Sabel, C. and J. Zeitlin, 1985, 'Historical Alternatives to Mass Production', *Past and Present,* No. 108, August.
Sandberg, L.G., 1969, 'American Rings and English Mules: The Role of Economic Rationality, *Quarterly Journal of Economics,* February.
Schatz, S.P., 1972, 'Development in an Adverse Environment', in Schatz (ed.),

South of the Sahara: Development in African Economies, Macmillan, London.

Scott, A.J. and M. Storper (eds), 1986, *Production, Work, Territory: The Geographical Anatomy of Industrial Capitalism,* Allen and Unwin.

Sen, A. 1984, 'Transition from Feudalism to Capitalism', *Economic and Political Weekly,* Review of Political Economy, July 8.

Stein, P., 1970, 'Law and Society in Eighteenth Century Scottish Thought', in N.T. Phillipson and R. Mitchison (eds), *Essays in Scottish History in the Eighteenth Century,* Edinburgh University Press, Edinburgh.

Sulivan, R.J.F., 1937, *One Hundred Years of Bombay: History of the Bombay Chamber of Commerce 1836–1936,* Times of India Press, Bombay.

Sweezy, P., M. Dobb *et al,* 1957, *The Transition from Feudalism to Capitalism,* Sanskriti Publications, Patna.

Thorburn, S.S., 1886, *Mussalmans and Moneylenders in the Punjab,* William Blackwood and Sons, London.

Tilly, C. and R. Tilly, 1971, 'Agenda for European Economic History in the 1970s', *Journal of Economic History,* Vol. 31.

Todd, J.A., 1924, *The World's Cotton Crops,* Black, London.

Urry, J., 1986, 'Capitalist Production, Scientific Management and the Service Class', in Scott and Storper, *Production, Work, Territory: The Geographical Anatomy of Industrial Capitalism.*

Wallerstein, I., 1986, 'The Incorporation of the Indian Sub-continent into the Capitalist World Economy', *Economic and Political Weekly,* Review of Political Economy, January.

Warren, B., 1980, *Imperialism, Pioneer of Capitalism,* New Left Books, London.

Washbrook, D., 1981, 'Law, State and Agrarian Society in Colonial India', in *Modern Asian Studies,* Vol. XV, No. 3, July.

Watt, G., 1893, *A Dictionary of the Economic Products of India,* Vol. I–VI, reprinted in 1972, Cosmo Publications, Delhi.

Whitcombe, E., 1972, *Agrarian Conditions in Northern India,* Vol. I, *The United Provinces under British Rule 1860–1900,* University of California Press, Berkeley.

Labour in the Toils of Colonial and Global Capital

The Ambiguity of Progress
Indian Society in Transition

Most Indians have practised settled agriculture for several millennia, and been engaged for centuries in the making of tools and objects of everyday use. There have been towns in India for at least four thousand years and a written language for probably a longer period. Over a major part of the subcontinent, developed state systems have been in existence for more than two thousand years. With all these signs of what is called civilization as their heritage, the majority of Indians still drag on an existence which can only be called 'nasty, brutish and short'.

Thousands of writers (and, doubtless, even more numerous non-writers) have sought to provide an explanation for this paradox. For imperial law-givers and administrators, the paradox itself provided a justification for the alien rule and implementing measures to consolidate and strengthen that rule. For other observers from the west, in the eighteenth and nineteenth centuries the paradox was an object of curiosity, if also sometimes of disgust. The intellectual construct (or rather non-construct, since it was really a sign of refusal to engage in serious thinking) called the 'Changeless East' was the product of such an attitude.

We are not going to confront this attitude in this essay because it will divert us from our main theme, namely, the difficulty of reading the signs of progress in a society like ours. Let me only point out here that unfortunately for everybody, Indians still remain the kin of the majority of mankind in their misery. The poverty and

This essay is based on the Ranajay Karlekar Lecture for 1985, delivered on 9 February 1985.

the daily insult to human dignity suffered by us are shared by the majority of the people in Latin America, Africa and even the oil-rich Arab countries. That fact should at least warn us against accepting any explanation of our condition in terms of something quite unique in the Indian psyche, the Indian social system, or the Indian natural tradition. Both in our dignity and in our degradation, we share too much with most of mankind.

The mocking intellectuals and the rationalizers of the current social order find it easy to construct histories without any change. But even those people who want a decisive social revolution to occur in India but get tired of lamenting and tracing the stories of man's inhumanity to man (or woman) are tempted to see Indian society as essentially changeless. If there is no social change to explain, there is no real conflict between synchrony and diachrony—that favourite bugbear of philosophers of history and historians with a philosophical bent. All that then remains is to construct and reconstruct different versions of the same story. For all stories are then cyclical, and the same actors simply appear, disappear and reappear in the same tattered garments in an endless, boring sequence. The quest for a cause or a confluence of causes is then foredoomed *ab initio*. It all depends on which particular stretch of the sequence is observed and on the angle of observation of the bored spectator. The study of history does then become an incompetent variant of the writing of fiction. A purely formalist stance follows as a natural sequel: the attraction of the particular history lies entirely in the style, in the narrative structure, in the use of language for achieving particular effects. The content of history becomes analogous to the attempt to establish the relative truthfulness of the different chronologies of Suryavamsa and Chandravamsa, which are obligatory opening sequences in our epics and *puranas*.

What happens if we admit that in some significant sense Indian society has changed at least between the eighteenth century and today? Then we have to grasp the crux of the problem of conceptualization of Indian society, and its change. Many historians, sociologists and political activists, following in the footsteps of James Tod (1829) and using European analogies, have viewed the India that the British conquered as a feudal society. According to this view, there was the same kind of personal link based on loyalty and

The Ambiguity of Progress

the reciprocal grant of fiefs or rights to the use of land between the king, his vassals and a dependent or servile peasantry; the same predominance of direct methods of surplus extraction without a necessary intermediation of the market; the same rigidly hierarchical ordering of society with little mobility between the different classes or estates. This view has been challenged by many historians of modern India (see Thorner 1956), but the opinion that many of the methods of exploitation can be fruitfully compared with those which were characteristic of European feudalism in its most developed form survives among many economists and historians.

For another group of social scientists, any European analogy for Indian social development is anathema. According to them, Indian society is something *sui generis*. It is a hierarchical but, at the same time, segmented society. The logic of hierarchy and of segmentation is provided by one and the same ideology and a deeply ingrained institutional structure supporting that ideology, namely, the caste system. In fact, according to the formulation of the most famous theorist of the caste system in modern times, caste is '*a state of mind,* a state of mind which is expressed by the emergence, in various situations, of groups of various orders, generally called "castes"' (Dumont 1967: 34). It is symptomatic of this type of formulation that here society is supposed to have a view of itself collectively. The theory of the caste system, in this view, is not dominant ideology of the exploiting classes, nor even an ideology which retains its hegemony despite constant challenges, but somehow a construct that pervades the consciousness of everybody governed by the caste system. In the name of discovering the *differentia specifica* of the Indian society, this idealistic view abolishes the individual ideological conflicts and, above all, conflicts between classes.[1] It is typical of the disregard of real historical change displayed by the adherents of this school that they not only ignore the innumerable challenges to

---

[1] It was an Indian admirer of Louis Dumont, T.N. Madan, who edited a volume in his honour on his seventieth birthday and whose institute presumably bore the cost of publication of the volume. See Madan (1982). It is perhaps not accidental that there is no reference to the work of D.D. Kosambi in any of the articles collected in the volume, including that authored by the editor, who called, for the umpteenth time, 'for a sociology of India'.

the caste system in India as so many irrelevant bubbles on the stream of time. Even more comically, they are not even aware that just when they were gleefully celebrating the discovery of *homo hierarchicus* in India as against *homo equalis* in Europe and America, theorists of administrative and organizational behaviour were finding it necessary to conceptualize the nature of hierarchy in modern capitalist firms (Simon 1959; Williamson 1975).

It is important to emphasize that to challenge the validity of the caste system conceived as simply a state of mind somehow collectively, harmoniously embedded in so-called 'traditional societies', is not to deny the empirical importance of segmentation and incomplete ordering of Indian society in caste groups. The caste system has long invaded autochthonous peoples of the hills and forests and, according to many historians, has provided a method of incorporation of these peoples into the larger network of rule and exploitation spreading across the Indian plains. Even people owing allegiance to non-Hindu religions, such as the Buddhists, Christians and Muslims, have been affected by the system: they have internalized some of the characteristics of the system and even when they have not done that, they have had to come to terms with it since it prevailed among the majority religious group.

It is possible to admit all this and yet argue that a single homogeneous ideology, namely, that of the *varnasrama dharma*, is not sufficient to explain the processes of social change in pre-British and colonial India. For, we know that, to start with, the vast majority of the people were illiterate and did not have easy access otherwise to the texts expounding the ideology. While the ideology could be propagated successfully among illiterate people, it, in fact, was *interpreted* anew by a new sect: what came to be known in modern times as Hinduism was the conglomerate of all these accretions through the various *bhasyas* of the old texts and new texts propagated by new sets of religious leaders. There were also recurrent movements of protest against not only the dominance of particular castes but against the system itself (many of the protesting groups, of course, were incorporated as new sects). Furthermore, mobility of castes has been characteristic of most of the history we know. People also chose to change their religion rather than obey the *dharmasastra* edicts (so that these dissenting groups could not be incorporated into the system). Since the adherents of this remystifying ideology of the caste system are so fond of emphasizing the comparative method, it should be pointed out that the *homo equalis* of their domain of fantasy, the capitalist countries of the North Atlantic seaboard, is all the time disappearing into the maws of ever-renewed hierarchical structures of authority and control (I wonder whether they have heard of transnational corporations and their methods of organization and control).[2]

A third type of conceptualization of Indian society may be put forward which does not regard feudalism or the *varnasrama dharma* as holding the key to an understanding of Indian history since the eighteenth century. It accepts that India, in the early eighteenth century, had a state apparatus which extracted a large part of the surplus of the peasantry by using feudal methods and methods characteristic of absolute monarchies of western Europe. That grossly unequal society was maintained by using ties of loyalty and patronage, a military bureaucracy using mercenary armies or ties of supposedly extended kinship groups, and the working of a caste system which was rigid in the short run but fluid over longer stretches of time (fluidity generated through conquest, going up or down in the world or geographical mobility). Other important characteristics of eighteenth-century Indian society that must be made an integral part of the conceptualization are: important urban centres of crafts and commerce, and large numbers of merchants and bankers thriving on local and long-distance trade. Peasants were growing not only food crops for their own use but also special crops such as tobacco, cotton and sugarcane, which were treated by themselves and by the rulers as cash crops and favoured accordingly. True, wage-labour had not yet become the dominant form of work in the fields or perhaps even in towns, nor had land become a fully fungible asset. But, side by side with agrestic slavery and self-employment, wage-labour was prevalent in many parts of the country.

In this society, the *jajmani* system or, in a slightly less

[2] The objection may be raised that the hierarchy of modern corporations is not a social hierarchy but an organizational ranking only. But as the studies of urban society of the US and Japan have shown, the organizational hierarchy, in fact, dominates the social hierarchy, especially of small towns or towns centred on activities of big corporations.

rigorous form, the system of concurrently prevailing *haqs* or rights to specified shares of the crop or specified rewards, bound people pursuing particular craft or service occupations in the village economy to the people who were supposed to possess superior, though generally non-transferable, rights in the land. However, already in the eighteenth century, and perhaps even earlier, not only the rights to the fruits of the land or the rights to the revenue realizable from the land, but also whole bundles of rights connected with land had become transferable between persons for money. The right to transfer land through sale was often, however, restricted to certain superior right-holders such as *patidars* or *narwadars* in western India, and it was not alienable for all kinds of obligations (for example, not in settlement of a debt contracted with a village *sahukar*).

British rule introduced enormous changes in this society. Even this fact has been denied. I will not take up here that denial for specific rebuttal, for the voice of the 'no-changers' in this particular context is not as strident now as it seemed to be some years back. However, one reason for the semblance of validity acquired by the school claiming that colonialism did not effect any major social upheaval, was the difficulty of making out the direction of change. I will take up some issues in the sphere of economics and property relations because I have some familiarity with that domain, but similar points could be made with regard to changes in the educational system or changes in popular culture. It has been made out by many liberals and Marxists that the British introduced private property in land. As already mentioned, transferability of land had become common in many parts of India in the eighteenth century. Moreover, the British made payment of land revenue a prior condition for the retention of land by a private proprietor. Land as an asset could be alienated for the non-payment of land revenue alone. Furthermore, when it seemed that land would be sold by traditional landlords to moneylenders and other groups with no deep roots in the village society, the British intervened with Courts of Wards and laws restraining the sale of land for debt.[3] Only in plantation terri-

---

[3] For further discussion on some of the issues relating to property rights in land and their implications for conceptualization of Indian society, see Bagchi (1981).

tories, where European planters wanted a free hand, did the British confer absolute right on the buyer of the land on payment of a fee.

There are other areas of intended and unintended consequences of British policy and the general system of colonialism where we are uncertain both about the causes of certain phenomena and their implications. Contracting debts in money form and rules about servicing those debts have been subjects of law and discourse in India from the pre-Christian era. Losing personal liberty for failure to meet all kinds of obligations has been a matter of both history and fable. Customary practice often prescribed certain upper limits on the rate of interest that could be charged. Even in Britain, an upper limit on the nominal rate of interest prescribed by the medieval laws against usury was retained until the middle of the nineteenth century. After the abolition of usury in Britain, the British government in India abolished most of the customary restrictions on the rate of interest chargeable and on other conditions of servicing of debt. It is well known that in many parts of India, land passed out of the hands of landlords and peasants into those of moneylenders at a rapid rate, and these were among the potent causes of peasant revolts. However, the slowness of economic change, custom, old laws of inheritance, newly introduced legislation to curb land transfers and the inability of moneylenders to take possession rendered the process of alienation of land from the peasantry less precipitous than many observers supposed. Under the *Mitakshara* system of inheritance, creditors found it difficult to foreclose on the property of the debtors who had numerous coparceners in the property. But it is probable that illiterate and poor peasants could not take advantage of these laws and in many areas they became virtual serfs of their creditors.

Was debt bondage then a result of the commercialization process that was unleashed in British India? Where inhabitants of the forests, hills and more remote river valleys met carpetbaggers or *dikus* from the plains, it would seem that debt bondage was a direct result of this process. But then one has to admit the limited effectiveness of the legal abolition of slavery by the British in their dominions and a hiatus between the nominal index of progress and actual fact is revealed. On the other side, we know that hereditary bondage pre-dated the commercialization process in British India and debt was often a newly applied stigma to sanction such bondage.

Thus we do not really know how much of the debt bondage was a new development and how much of it was the continuation of an old servile status in a new form. All that we know is that under the dispensation of colonialism, the particular kind of bondage that was associated with debt obtained a new kind of sanction and spread into areas which had been unfamiliar with it earlier. Colonialism and colonial extraction of a surplus in the form of money was the overarching structure holding up the nexus between the moneylender, the landlord and the peasant. Although tributes had been extracted earlier, they had not always been extracted in the form of money, nor in particular units or media of exchange. Now tributes were defined and extracted in cash, often exactly at a time when the marketability of the main product in which the tribute was paid was sharply diminished, as direct or indirect result of colonial rule itself. This happened, for example, with the tribute in elephants paid by petty chieftains in eastern Bengal and Assam.[4]

This raising of 'transaction costs' of tribute through the working of the colonial state and commercial apparatus seeped into many different sectors and permeated even the exchanges effected by the tribal or semi-tribal peoples who hardly participated in regular market exchange. The extraction of all tribute in silver rather than *cowries* or gold imposed fresh transaction costs. Or the mutation of an own rate of interest in grains into money rates of interest gave the *sahukar* fresh opportunities to extract a *batta* every time the grain was converted into money or money into grain, and fattened him further because of the wide difference between the post-harvest and the scarcity-season prices of grain.[5]

---

[4] Some of these issues are discussed in more detail in Bagchi (1981a).

[5] There was a considerable discussion of the sources of the increased power of the moneylender in the colonial ethnographic literature. One of the most interesting of such analyses occurs in Russell and Hira Lal (1916: 131–34). Two passages are worth quoting from this source:

'The progress of administration, bringing with it easy and safe transit all over the country; the institution of a complete system of civil justice and the stringent enforcement of contracts through the courts; the introduction of cash coinage as the basis of all transactions; and the grant of proprietory and transferable rights in land, appear to have at the same time enhanced the *bania*'s prosperity and increased the harshness and rapacity of his dealings. When the moneylender lived in the village he had an interest in the solvency of the tenants who constituted his

The Ambiguity of Progress

Let us take another aspect of the subjection of workers or small peasants to landlords and moneylenders. Many of them started with a relation of formal or legal bondage. However, what has been called 'casual bondage' was not necessarily an inherited condition (Bremen 1974). Under 'casual bondage', workers become 'attached' to particular landlord households for specified, or undefined periods of time. Not only the workers but their families also are then regarded as virtually servile dependents of the landlord households. Colonialism and the international market adversely affected the conditions of living of millions of artisans. Agricultural growth in most areas remained too feeble to make an impact on the emerging reserve army of labour in the countryside. Faced with a condition of endemic unemployment and the threat of starvation almost every day, many working-class or small-peasant families were compelled to seek the patronage of landlords. Where the peasants had some land of their own, or 'sharecropped' some land of the employer or moneylender, sales of his labour power, of the produce of his land, and the terms and conditions of servicing of the loan he was forced to seek, became interlocked with one another. The observation of this interlocking

---

clientele and was also amenable to public opinion, though not of his own caste.... But with the rise of the large banking-houses when dealings are conducted though agents over considerable tracts of country, public opinion can no longer act. The agent looks mainly to his principal, and the latter has no interest, or a regard for the cultivators of distant villages.' (p. 131)

'Interest on money was probably little in vogue among pastoral peoples, and was looked upon with disfavour, being prohibited by both the Mosaic and Muhammadan Codes.... With the introduction of agriculture a system of loans on interest became a necessary and useful part of the public economy, as a cultivator could borrow grain to sow land and support himself and his family until the crop ripened, out of which the loan, principal and interest could be repaid. If, as seems likely, this was the first occasion for the introduction of the system of loan-giving on a large scale, it would follow that the rate of interest would be based largely on the return yielded by the earth to the seed. Support is afforded to this conjecture by the fact that in the case of grain loans in the Central Provinces the interest on loans of grain of the crops which yield a comparatively small return such as wheat, is twenty-five to fifty per cent, while in the case of those which yield a large return, such as *juari* and *kodon*, it is one hundred per cent. These high rates of return were not of much importance so long as the transaction was in grain. The grain was much less valuable at harvest than at seed time, and in addition the lender had

of markets has given rise to a large literature.[6] In much of this literature, what is studied is the landlord's trade-off between gains in different markets. But is it always possible to treat the interlocking of markets as the resultant of interlocking of market power? Is it also not affected by the pervasiveness of non-market power? Did not the same set of *lathials* or *paiks* enforce the performance of *begar,* supervise the garnering of the crop on the landlord's *khalian* and, when necessary, the forcible seizure of grain kept in the peasant's cottage?

Here there is ambiguity in both the genesis of casual and not-so-casual bondage, and the persistence of subjugation of the peasant in his roles as labourer, petty commodity producer and borrower of loans. The origin of bondage may have been in a voluntary surrender of freedom in the face of an intolerable uncertainty about survival. But probably for many families the bondage appeared to be hereditary, going back to the days when markets did not enter all the major aspects of their material existence. And where the power of the landlords, the *maliks,* is enforced by *pattas, kabuliyats,* mortgage bonds, as well as *chowkidars* or *paiks,* it is difficult to distinguish too clearly between market or contractual relations (the two are not synonymous) and non-market or openly coercive relations.

---

the expense of storing and protecting his stock of grain through the year. It is probable that a rate of twenty-five per cent on grain loans does not yield more than a reasonable profit to the lender. But when in recent times cash came to be substituted for grain it would appear that there was no proportionate reduction in the interest. The borrower would lose by having to sell his grain for the payment of his debt at the most unfavourable rate after harvest, and since the transaction was by regular deed the lender no longer took any share of the risk of bad harvest, as it is probable that he was formerly accustomed to do.' (pp. 132–33)

[6] Two of the major works on production relations in Indian agriculture in recent years are Krishna Bharadwaj, *Production Conditions in Indian Agriculture* (1974), and Amit Bhaduri, *The Economic Structure of Backward Agriculture* (1983). One major problem studied by Bhaduri is that of finding out when it suits the moneylender to make the borrower default. This question also has its historical dimension. For it is only when land becomes an easily saleable asset and when moneylenders can enter the circle of landlords without facing great difficulties that defaulting borrowers become attractive customers for them. The situation may be reversed again when peasants can put up an effective resistance against moneylenders and powerful landlords from grabbing their lands.

The Ambiguity of Progress

Yet another example of the difficulty of reading the sign of historical change occurs in the case of 'mixed occupations' in British India. Many peasants were observed to be following some specialized crafts as well. Did this indicate that these mixed occupations resulted from the process of de-industrialization which occurred in India after 1813 or so, when unemployed artisans were forced to take up agricultural occupations for survival? Or were mixed occupations the result of peasants taking up specialized crafts when they found it profitable to do so, as occurs during a process of commercialization, or what has been dubbed 'proto-industrialization'? The reading of Indian economic and social history since the eighteenth century would depend importantly on whether the first or the second proposition or a mixture of the two proves to be right.[7]

Much of our discussion so far has been carried on as if the oppressed classes passively adapted themselves to changes imposed from above or outside. That is partly a reflection of the fact that over the long period, the landlords, moneylenders and traders seem to have been able to maintain their stranglehold over the peasantry and the workers, so that the resistance put up by the latter does not leave any durable impact on the relationships, at least until the 1940s and 1950s. Partly it is the result of the fact that the documentation we have is generally far more eloquent (by conscious design and otherwise) on the control mechanisms of the exploiters than on the responses of the exploited. But it is also partly a defect of the linear style of discourse where the struggles waged by the exploited classes cannot be given their adequate weight in the unfolding story.

The instruments wielded by the exploited groups were of a myriad variety. There was the reluctance of the labourer to labour hard for somebody else's benefit—a reluctance that is portrayed in almost all written records as doltishness of the peasant. There are struggles for getting better deals within the existing structure of relationships. Much more infrequently and, of course, much more explosively, there are struggles to get the relationships themselves changed.

The ultimate goals of such movements were often not clear, and setbacks suffered in the struggle often rendered them much more

---

[7] The issue has been raised by Perlin (1983).

hazy except in the minds of a few. The instruments of these struggles were drawn not only from any embryonic consciousness of the exploited as a separate class of workers or poor peasants, but from their awareness also as human beings belonging to a larger society. The ties that bound them to the larger society were often those of caste, community, ethnic groups and habitation in particular regions. 'Pure' class relations as between individuals are only an abstract construct in most societies. But conversely, a community consciousness or caste consciousness transcending class relations in particular social structures is also an analyst's construct. To the extent that such consciousness can be posited at all, it often has a Janus-face. With one face it looks inward into the particular caste or community or ethnic group, and the other face is directed outward to the structure of society in which that group is located.

I have argued elsewhere that many of the conservative writers of Bengal in the nineteenth century were voicing the aspirations of a subjugated people (Bagchi 1984). Since their gaze was generally turned towards a vanished past they could not really point the direction towards progressive social change,[8] although this did not prevent them from portraying accurately the process of disintegration of the old social fabric. But the so-called 'modernizers' often expressed, objectively speaking, the aspirations and interests of a group whose fortunes were bound up with those of their colonial masters seeking to change India in tune with their imperial needs. Only an appropriation of the vision of a fractured society for effecting social change under the control of the workers and peasants could remove this type of contradiction between the conservatives and modernizers.

[8] It has been argued by some scholars that somehow a proletarian revolution could use a consciousness dating from pre-capitalist days to jump directly into socialism (Wertheim 1974). But, as Mao Zedong repeatedly warned, and as the Chinese experience has demonstrated, even when a revolution is effected under the leadership of a communist party, the consciousness of the people may retain many elements of the feudal past. The continuance of feudal infanticide in some regions of China despite decades of effort of the Communist Party of China and the government to stamp it out, is a tragic example of such survival. See Mao Zedong (1967). On the survival of pre-socialist relations of production and for a theory of 'stages of socialism' in China, see Xue Muqiao (1981).

The old society does impart a sense of community to the oppressed people because they need such a consciousness for survival. However, this collective consciousness could as well serve as an instrument in the hands of the rulers for forging new chains of control, as provide a vital weapon for cohesion and assault to the participants in a struggle against the old order, or particular elements in the old order (Bagchi 1984a).

In some recent conceptual attempts to break out of the rigid dichotomy between structure and superstructure and to put the role of structure in its proper place, the pendulum has sometimes swung too far. A kind of pure consciousness of the people detached from their material moorings is put forward as the protagonist of historical change.[9] If people's struggles are limited and shaped by their consciousness, the conditions of material existence of the people are part of the consciousness which is posited as an active element in these studies. A concrete example will perhaps help clarify my point. It has been pointed out that jute mill workers of Calcutta took a large time to form a 'pure' class consciousness, that is, consciousness as a group of people united simply because they are workers in jute mills and capable of joint action as workers against employers or the ruling classes in general when the need arose. In fact, there is some doubt as to whether they attained such a consciousness before Independence at all. These doubts spring from the fact that workers got involved in communal riots, and sometimes in riots between different linguistic groups, and in some cases in riots between groups distinguished by religion and language.[10]

It is important to analyse the consciousness of, or rather its expression by, the workers. But are most of these findings very surprising? Look at the way the workers were recruited, the way they lived in the jute mill localities, the way their life-cycles were shaped. They were recruited generally from villages several hundred miles away from Calcutta on the basis of ties with earlier recruits in the jute mills. They lived in abject poverty, mostly without their families

---

[9] For a discussion of the issues involved, see Guha (1983), S. Singh et al. (1984).

[10] Two important contributors to the recent discussion on the consciousness of the jute mill workers are Ranjit Dasgupta (1979) and Dipesh Chakrabarty (1981; 1983; 1984).

who stayed back in the villages. Most of them were illiterate and had little access to sources of information outside their own linguistic groups. There was no security of jobs for them, nor could they look forward to a future where they would settle down nearabout Calcutta and bring up their children as workers in mills or some other urban occupation. They could not even rise within the mills to the dignity of foremen or other supervisory staff, for all these positions were reserved for Europeans. The same kind of absolute barrier was faced even by the clerks or *babus*, though as white collar workers they had better pay than the people who operated the machines or worked in the preparatory or finishing departments of the mills. Their survival itself depended on keeping up their ties with the villages and with their extended kin groups defined in terms of community and language. Moreover, any sign of struggle on their part was met with massive repression and with threats of dismissal, since there was no dearth of workers to recruit from the vast and ever-expanding reserve army of labour.

Caught in a vicious demographic–political bind, workers in jute mills generally had a tough time voicing their minimum demands for survival. Unity on the basis of supra-regional and supra-religious class loyalties proved transient. Not only the mill authorities, but the police, the local owners of *bustee* hutments, and leaders of most of the traditional power-vendors often worked against them. The people who were giving vent to their grievances and trying to provide an organizational framework in the form of trade union activities were themselves part of the social hierarchy. Some of the *babus* might consciously try to de-class themselves, but most of them generally assumed a posture of authority over the workers they were trying to defend. Only sustained political education and work extending over generations could possibly eliminate some of these inconsistencies.

Such inconsistencies are characteristics of a situation in which not only capitalist style but also pre-capitalist style, and in fact colonially imposed rank orders, bound most of the struggling people. One could put it as the consequence of articulation of different modes of production, but such a language would not be very illuminating unless we could analytically characterize the different modes, and situate the transition process at each band of the feudal-

The Ambiguity of Progress

tribal–capitalist mode of production spectrum. I find it far more useful to regard it as a situation in which the exploiting classes use instruments of exploitation taken from arsenals of different social formations, and in which the oppressed themselves tragically and unwittingly allow their older loyalties to be used against them.

Any transitional society will be difficult to analyse, and any language used by participants in that society or observers of that society will have to be deciphered with caution. Such difficulties will be experienced both at the level of the structure and the superstructure, and at the crucial points of singularity where structural and superstructural elements blend and explode and create a new amalgam of structures and superstructures. But in a society which has been as heavily colonized as India, after experiencing several millennia of relatively autonomous but complicated evolution, the difficulty of reading the signs without leaving any ambiguous residue is really very great. Here a colonial state apparatus was sometimes preserving and sometimes destroying pre-capitalist structures to suit their own needs. Some of the members of the traditional upper classes were trying to become modern, but full modernity in the sense of a capitalist rationality that dissolves all ties between individuals except that of self-interest was forever denied to them. For, not only was capitalist development inhibited in the colonial environment, but world capitalism itself entered a defensive, though by no means moribund phase, where it tried to forge social and political structures which denied individuality to individuals but strenuously concealed that denial. The traditionalists could not recreate a past that had gone forever: they were often left in the position of decorators who provided the props of a court forever poised between tradition and modernity.

One could go on weaving these patterns of concealment and ambiguity in abstract. But it would be far more useful to concretely uncover these layers in the structures, superstructures and that dangerous zone, their areas of interaction, rather than resort to a mechanical determinism, or an idealist structuralism. Lurking behind much of the latter style of discourse there is ideology, an ideology that condemns all societies to search for an individualist haven—even though some of the self-appointed guides know that the peace of the haven is the calm of death for all mankind. There are others, however, who know that such a haven is forever unattainable and that the sailors would do much better to struggle for their common right to survival as human beings, however imperfect and rent by bickering such struggles may appear to a viewer watching them on the TV screen. *Cogito ergo sum,* yes, but we know that we live when we fight for our right to exist and to think, as human beings in the society of other human beings.

The author is indebted to several friends, including Javeed Alam, Himani Bandyopadhyay, Mihir and Malini Bhattacharya and Saugata Mukherjee, for probing questions and comments.

References

Bagchi, A.K., 1981, 'Daniel Thorner's India', *Economic and Political Weekly,* 28th March.

—— 1981a, 'Transition from Indian to British-Indian Systems of Money and Banking', *Modern Asian Studies,* April.

—— 1984, 'Ritwik Ghatak', *Frontier,* 7th July.

—— 1984a, 'The Terror and Squalor of East Asian Capitalism', in *Economic and Political Weekly,* January.

Bhaduri, A., 1983, *The Economic Structure of Backward Agriculture,* Delhi.

Bharadwaj, K., 1974, *Production Conditions in Indian Agriculture,* Cambridge.

Bremen, J., 1974, *Patronage and Exploitation: Changing Agrarian Conditions in South Gujarat: India,* Berkeley, California.

Chakrabarty, D., 1981, 'Communal Riots and Labour: Bengal's Jute Mill hands in the 1890s', in *Past and Present,* No. 91, May.

—— 1983, 'On Deifying and Defying Authority: Managers and Workers in Jute Mills of Bengal, *c.* 1890–1940', in *Past and Present,* no. 100, August.

—— 1984, 'Trade Unions in a Hierarchical Culture: The Jute Workers of Calcutta, 1920–50', in R. Guha (ed.), *Subaltern Studies III,* Delhi.

Dasgupta, R., 1979, *Material Conditions and Behavioural Aspects of Calcutta Working Class: 1875–99,* Occasional Paper No. 22, Centre for Studies in Social Sciences, Calcutta.

Dumont, L., 1967, *Homo Hierarchicus,* London.

Guha, R., 1983, 'The Prose of Counter-insurgency', in R. Guha edited *Subaltern Studies II,* Delhi.

Madan, T.N. (ed.), 1982, *Way of Life: King, Householder, Renouncer: Essays in Honour of Louis Dumont,* Delhi.

Muqiao, Xue, 1981, *China's Socialist Economy,* Beijing.

Perlin, F., 1983, 'Proto-industrialization and Pre-colonial South Asia', in *Past and Present,* No. 98, February.

Russell, R.V. and Hira Lal, 1916, *Tribes and Castes of Central Provinces of India,* Vol. II, reprinted in 1975, Delhi.

Simon, H., 1959, 'Theories of decision-making in economics and behavioural sciences', *American Economic Review,* June.

The Ambiguity of Progress

Singh, S. et al., 1984, 'Subaltern Studies II', in *Social Scientist,* vol. XII, no. 10, October.
Thorner, D., 1956, 'Feudalism in India', in R. Coulborn (ed.), *Feudalism in History,* Princeton, New Jersey.
Tod, J., 1829, *Annals and Antiquities of Rajasthan,* London.
Wertheim, W.F., 1974, *Evolution and Revolution,* Harmondsworth, Middlesex.
Williamson, O., 1975, *Markets and Hierarchies,* New York.
Zedong, Mao, 1967, 'The Chinese Revolution and the Chinese Communist Party' and 'On New Democracy', in *Selected Works of Mao Zedong,* Vol. II, Peking.

Wealth and Work in Calcutta
1860–1921

Calcutta, the Capital City

Calcutta was the seat of the government of British India until 1911, and the commercial capital of the British Indian empire down to the First World War. Except for two decades—the 1850s and 1860s—when Bombay overtook it, Calcutta was throughout the nineteenth century the point of largest outflow of exports from India as well as imports into the country. Until the development of the railway network in Punjab and Sind, and the rise of the port of Karachi, it was through Calcutta that the agricultural exports of the whole Gangetic basin, part of the Indus basin and central India found their way to East Asia, Europe and the USA. From the 1870s and 1880s, exports from Punjab, Sind and Rajasthan, as well as parts of central India and Uttar Pradesh, increasingly found their way abroad through Karachi and Bombay. But Calcutta added new exports to the list: tea, raw jute and, increasingly, jute manufactures. Calcutta was the *entrepôt* for imports of cotton piece-goods and other manufactures into its hinterland, consisting of Assam, Bengal, Bihar and Orissa, most of today's Uttar Pradesh, large parts of central India and, in the beginning, British Burma and parts of Madras Presidency as well.

Most of these exports and imports were controlled by British firms from the point of their entry into Calcutta and, in the case of such commodities as jute, tea, opium, mica and manganese, from the point of production or extraction as well. Many of those firms were domiciled in Calcutta, but not all. For a long time, tea companies registered in the UK controlled more acreage than those registered in India. These 'sterling' companies, as they were called, had their own marketing networks; their finances were handled mostly through banks registered in Britain. Moreover, the profits made in the Anglo-Indian rupee and sterling companies were regularly transmitted abroad, and contributed only a trickle to the accumulation of capital assets in India or to the disposable incomes of Indians. Hence the impact of the operations of the British (Anglo-Indian or sterling) firms was much smaller than might be guessed from the figures of the foreign, coastal or inland trade of Calcutta.

In order to understand the changing structure of the commercial and financial world of Calcutta, it is necessary to have some idea of the distribution of wealth and incomes in the city, for the character of local commerce was greatly influenced by that of local purchasing power and local custom.

The memory of Calcutta as the seat of empire inspires visions of grandeur and riches. Grandeur there was, and riches too. But, as H.E.A. Cotton put it at the time when its colonial glory was coming to a close, Calcutta was a 'queen of two faces: a city of startling contrasts, of palaces and hovels, of progress and reaction, of royal grandeur and of squalor that beggar[ed] description'. For eight months in the year, the seat of government was Simla and not Calcutta: an annual transplantation begun in the days of Sir John Lawrence and lasting right through the period we are covering.

The rich Europeans lived in the central part of the city. As the bureaucracy expanded and the wealth of the Europeans grew, the squalor in their part of Calcutta was removed and the face of the city changed noticeably. But, concomitantly, the poor were moved out to the periphery of the city—not only to the suburbs which were later incorporated within municipal limits but also to more outlying areas. Public amenities in Calcutta were very unequally distributed between the 'native' or 'Black' Town (chiefly the north of Calcutta and the more southerly portions of the southern part) and the parts where Europeans lived; also, within the Black Town, between those parts which harboured the mansions of the rich and those which housed only the poor.

Changes in Population and Occupational Structure

Originally, the 'town' of Calcutta, for which the various municipal acts were designed, consisted of twenty *mauzas* or nineteen wards. From 1888 onwards the Calcutta municipal area came to incorporate parts of Chitpur, Ultadanga, Maniktala, Beliaghata, Entally, Kashipur, all of Beniapukur, Ballyganj, Watganj and Ekbalpur, and parts of Garden Reach and Tollyganj. The population of Calcutta as enumerated by official censuses between 1872 and 1921 is given in Table 1.

TABLE 1 *The Population of Calcutta 1872–1921*

	(a) Old Town			(b) Calcutta Municipal Area		
	Males	Females	Total	Males	Females	Total
1872	299,857	147,644	447,601			
1876	282,506	147,029	429,535			
1881	288,817	144,402	433,219			
1891	318,739	149,813	468,552	446,746	234,814	681,560
1901				562,596	285,200	847,796
1911				607,674	288,393	896,067
1921				617,590	290,261	907,851

Notes: (a) Including the population of the Fort and the port area.
(b) Including the population of the Fort, the port area and the canals. The Census of 1872 was considered to be unreliable; hence a special, more carefully conceived census was carried out in 1876. Again, the Census of 1891 has been adjudged to be defective as compared with that of 1901; hence the growth of population between the two dates may have been overestimated by the census figures. However, the figures will serve for our present purposes.

Source: H.F.J.T. Maguire, *Report on the Census of Calcutta, 1891*, pp. 16–18; *Census of India, 1911,* Vol. VI, City of Calcutta, Part II, *Tables* by L.S.S. O'Malley; *Census of India, 1921,* Vol. V, Bengal, Part II, *Tables* by W.H. Thomson.

By the Municipal Consolidation Act of 1888, the area under municipal jurisdiction was increased from 11,954 acres to 20,547 acres, that is, by nearly 72 per cent; but the population added thereby was only 45 per cent. By and large, the density of population decreased from the centre of Calcutta to the more outlying wards. But the population density within the central area also varied greatly. It was far higher in wards inhabited mainly by Indians, such as Kalutola, Barabazar and Jorabagan, than in wards where the Europeans lived, such as Park Street, Waterloo Street and Victoria Terrace (formerly Bamun Bustee). Moreover, in the successive slum-clearance drives, the 'European' wards generally gained most in terms of space per resident, at the cost, of course, of *bustee*-dwellers who were expelled from the area.

While some of the northern wards were inhabited by families which had come there in the eighteenth or early nineteenth centuries, in most wards the immigrant element was very visible. The immigrants included Europeans, but also traders from Rajputana and other north Indian states, and general labourers and artisans from Bihar, the United Provinces (earlier called the North Western Provinces), Orissa, the Central Provinces and Madras. The immigrants were mostly male adult workers: taking immigrants and residents together, there were two males to every female, and there were far fewer children than in a population of normal, balanced age-structure. As a result, Calcutta's population failed to replenish itself through growth within the city: it was only the stream of immigrants that kept the population growing.

The high mortality rate also contributed to the situation; and here too, different Calcuttans faced different degrees of risk. Cholera took a toll every year, as did various unspecified 'fevers' including 'Burdwan fever', that is malaria. The northern or 'native' part of the town had far more than its fair share of these visitations. For example, out of 697 deaths from cholera during the fourth quarter of 1882, 'no less than 540 occurred in the north of the town, . . . against 157 in the nine wards of the south of the town. Only two deaths occurred in the Park Street ward and only four in the Waterloo ward' (*The Statesman,* 5 February 1883). When sanitation work was taken up in earnest and water supply improved, the European quarters and, to a lesser extent, the central district, benefited more than the outlying wards. More glaringly than ever, spatial patterns reproduced the inequality of the human condition.

Most Calcuttans made a living from work in trade, industry, transport and other services. Some made a living openly as rent-receivers; some others must have been 'agriculturists' (according to census returns) only in the sense of owning enough land or *zamindari* rights to preclude their having to work for a living. Successive censuses indicate the changes in the occupational structure of the city. But the concepts and schemes of classification differed from census to census. In Table 2, we have attempted a summary of the changes between 1891 and 1921 in the number of persons engaged or dependent upon two major occupations: trade or commerce (including banking, moneylending, etc.), and secondary industry, that is, the production of material substances other than agricultural products from the soil. The censuses of 1911 and 1921 conveniently separated the pure traders from manufacturers or manufacturers-cum-sellers. In 1891 and 1901 such separation had not been made consistently. Hence I have regrouped the data, adding the pure sellers of material substances to the category of general merchants, grocers, etc., and, conformably, grouping together all persons engaged in secondary industry as defined above.

The occupational structure of Calcutta changed under pressures of different kinds. First, Calcutta had a surprisingly large industrial population for an imperial capital, where we might have expected the apparatus of government and the residential demands of the bureaucrats to push most industries to outlying areas. Some industries catered to local demand, especially from the rich: carriage-makers, saddlers, jewellers, dress shops, ice factories, and shops turning out innumerable items of food and house furnishings. Building firms catered to the growth and improvement of the city. But there were also industries connected with exports, such as jute presses. The near-total lack of town planning regulations allowed any enterprise to be located anywhere: there was no separation of residential and industrial zones. As late as 13 September 1890, a correspondent to *The Statesman* complained about a chimney belonging to Mackintosh Burn and Co. belching out black smoke in the Bentinck Street area.

When the European wards of the town were improved, the more noisome industries moved to other parts of the city. In his 1914 plan for the improvement of the city, E.P. Richards, Chief Engineer of the Calcutta Improvement Trust, described the industrial belt of Calcutta as follows:

> The larger [manufacturing area] is formed along and between the railways and canals of north-east Calcutta. It extends north in a broad band ... from south of Sealdah station, right up to the northern limits of Calcutta. Still unbroken, it then turns west and continues south some distance down the Hooghly bank. It is

Wealth and Work in Calcutta

TABLE 2 Industry and Trade in the Occupational Structure of the City of Calcutta, 1891–1921

	Actual workers			Total no. of workers and dependants
	Males	Females	Total	
1891				
(1) Engaged in trade	54,135	3,480	57,615	116,263
(2) Engaged in industry	67,562	2,172	69,734	120,496
(3) All occupations	329,203	68,882	398,085	681,560
(4) Percentage of (1) to (3)			14.5	17.1
(5) Percentage of (2) to (3)			17.5	17.7
1901				
(1) Engaged in trade	86,890	5,970	92,860	179,062
(2) Engaged in industry	90,135	6,944	97,079	169,521
(3) All occupations	441,969	66,236	508,205	847,796
(4) Percentage of (1) to (3)			18.3	21.2
(5) Percentage of (2) to (3)			19.3	20.0
1911				
(1) Engaged in trade	88,102	6,530	94,632	169,286
(2) Engaged in industry	97,156	5,925	103,521	172,929
(3) All occupations	482,277	61,177	543,454	896,067
(4) Percentage of (1) to (3)			17.4	19.0
(6) Percentage of (2) to (3)			19.0	19.3
1921				
(1) Engaged in trade	91,893	6,335	98,228	184,537
(2) Engaged in industry	75,073	4,561	79,634	132,179
(3) All occupations	476,006	52,660	528,766	907,746
(4) Percentage of (1) to (3)			18.5	20.3
(5) Percentage of (2) to (3)			15.1	14.0

Note: The occupations had to be regrouped for 1891 and 1901, so as to separate, as far as possible, the pure sellers from makers and sellers, or makers of material substances.

Sources: Computed on the basis of Census Reports and accompanying Table volumes, cited under Table 1.

of horseshoe shape with the arms of unequal length, having the end of the long arm on Sealdah, the curve on Cossipore Bridge and the short arm finishing on the river bank near Aheeritollah Ghat. From the east, the Cornwallis Street residential area is now being seriously eaten into by this growing manufacturing district, which deals mostly with jute, cotton, ropes and flour manufacture.

This probably demarcates the greatest extent of manufacturing industries in the city proper. Apart from some new war-related engineering and other units, industry was henceforth slowly displaced from the heart of Calcutta by the demands of trade and the professions. However, the displacement was a long-drawn process and has not yet been completed. Manufacturing brought riches to a few and subsistence-level wages to others; but the crudeness of the manufacturing processes and the near-total absence of regulations on permitted processes posed serious health problems to the residents of the city.

The second factor that influenced the occupational structure of Calcutta was the character of the immigrant population. This in turn was doubtless influenced by pressures in their place of origin as well as the varying nature of demand for their services in the city. The Census Report of 1911 undertook a special return for 289,566 immigrants belonging to twenty-six large and representative castes. Here are some of their findings:

> There are only 2 females to every 5 male immigrants; over two-thirds of the latter are actual workers, but only one-fourth of the females are engaged in any occupation. Prostitutes alone account for one-fourth of the female workers, and their number is equal to one-seventh of the women of adult age. Altogether 15 per cent of both sexes are under 15 years of age. Half the women and two-thirds of the men are adults, i.e. aged 15 to 40; at this age period there are three males to every female. Trade engaged the energies of 19 per cent of the male workers. While 14 per cent are employed in domestic service, 13 per cent are day labourers and 7 per cent are clerks. Domestic service accounts for the largest population of female workers, viz., 42 per cent, and then come prostitutes with 25 per cent.

In fact, this census of immigrants in 1911 foreshadowed the direction of changes in the occupational structure of the city's population as a whole between 1911 and 1921. For example, the proportion of traders among the immigrant workers was six times that of workers in mills and factories. At a more disaggregated level, we find in 1911 the domestic servants among immigrant workers outnumbering the prostitutes virtually in a proportion of 2:1.

The census authorities were almost obsessed with caste at this time, creating new mischievous rigidities of segregation, and even generating new traditions and status symbols on an immense scale. Yet census after census found a number of castes to be engaged in every occupation: 'superior' castes such as Brahmins or Kayasthas were carrying out all kinds of menial or lowly tasks such as domestic service, daily-wage labour, begging and so on. Mills and factories provided employment for immigrants belonging to all the listed castes except the 'trading' castes of Agarwala, Gandhabanik, Maheshwari and Subarnabanik, and the Baidyas, the Shunris and the Dhobis. Prostitutes seemed to have come mainly from West Bengal districts, from typical peasant as well as upper-caste backgrounds.

Calcutta obviously acted as a melting-pot for all castes and communities, mixing and merging them in respect of occupations or avocations. Trading, for example, could be undertaken by almost any caste: in 1911 the Brahmins and the Kayasthas formed a third of the traders and outnumbered 'the members of all the mercantile castes, viz., Agarwalas, Gandhabaniks, Maheshwaris, Subarnabaniks and Telis taken together'.

However, 'traders' could designate both the haughty merchant princes or magnates of British business houses and banks, and the lowly pedlar hawking a basketload of wares on his head. In between came a whole range of shopkeepers, moneylenders and bankers, spread all over Calcutta but concentrated in the central districts. Increasingly, the wealthiest element among them was constituted by the Jains and the Hindu traders from Rajasthan. Between 1901 and 1911 the largest supply of immigrants, after the Bengal districts, Bihar, Orissa and the United Provinces, was provided by Rajputana, chiefly from Jaipur (8,000) and Bikaner (7,000). According to the 1911 Census Report, emigration to Calcutta from this area was growing in popularity: the number rose from 15,000 to 21,000 in the preceding ten years.

Calcutta's popularity with the Marwaris and north Indian traders continued to grow in the decade 1911–21. In the latter year, as many as twenty-three out of every thousand Calcuttans were found to have been born in Rajputana. According to the Census Report of 1921, they absorbed much of the piece-goods trade and were brokers in many other commodities. Their clerks and servants also generally came from Rajputana: 'They are almost the only Indian race which really favours the town life', said the report, 'and those who have settled in Calcutta are well off and have usually brought their families with them.' But their habit of saving space and preserving communal confidentiality by crowding into the areas where their clansmen had already settled doubtless increased the congestion of the central business district and adjoining areas.

Briefly, it can be said that the city passed the peak of its manufacturing and administrative functions by 1921, thereafter becoming more a city of traders, moneylenders, professionals and, of course, labourers. As the population became more settled and the sex ratio less unfavourable, the demand for prostitutes declined and that for domestic service increased. The departure of many Europeans after the transfer of the capital to New Delhi doubtless brought down the demand for many types of luxury goods, as for European prostitutes.

Living Space

How was the growing population of Calcutta accommodated? In terms of both space and civic amenities, the population fared poorly in most wards. The urban rich, who generally provide funds for the improvement of most cities, did not want to part with money at the best of times. According to the statistics cited by A.K. Ray in *A Short History of Calcutta* (1902), the revenues of the town administration (including ground rent) grew from Rs 2,84,000 only in 1821 to Rs 4,19,167 in 1850, in spite of the increasing need of funds for sanitation and public utilities of various kinds. Between 1875 and 1901, the municipal revenues (including ground rent) increased from Rs 21,79,589 to Rs 57,86,580. (Ground rent formed an increasingly unimportant part of the total, being Rs 18,000 in 1821 and Rs 19,113 in 1901.)

The increase in total revenue looks impressive until we remember that the backlog of public utility works in the pestilential city had accumulated at least since the late eighteenth century, and that both the overcrowding and the wealth of the central districts were increasing much faster than the population. To take just one instance of the increase of wealth, it has been estimated that the real value of jute manufactures from Bengal, which contributed so mightily to the wealth of the Anglo-Indian firms, was virtually doubling every ten years between 1880 and 1910. A similar story could be told about Anglo-Indian firms in the tea, coal and jute trading sectors: the bigger firms, of course, dealt in practically all those commodities. But the Europeans were birds of passage though their firms were not. They often left their families at home, visited them on furlough, and returned to them when they retired or took over as London (or Edinburgh or Manchester or Glasgow) partners of the firm. In any case, the British businessmen and bureaucrats, civil or military, had their children educated at 'Home'. Calcutta was not home for them, and they were not going to spend more money on it than they could help.

The European businessmen, of course, wanted better infrastructure for carrying on their trade. In particular, they wanted better port facilities. When, at one stage, there were proposals for combining the municipal and port facilities, the businessmen and their representatives protested through the newspapers controlled by them, as also through the Bengal Chamber of Commerce, and made their voices heard in the consultative councils of the Governor General and the Lieutenant Governor of Bengal.

A separate Port Trust with its own finances was created in 1870. It improved the docking, berthing, loading, unloading and warehousing facilities of Calcutta as a port, but left the civic facilities strictly alone. In the 1880s, there was a proposal to build a warehouse at the port exclusively for tea. The municipal commissioners and the British Indian Association protested, presumably on civic and environmental grounds, although the tea industry was almost wholly under British control. The warehouse was erected nonetheless.

The constitution of the Calcutta municipal administration was almost entirely bureaucratic, with the government nominating the commissioners and civil servants serving as chairmen. From the 1870s, the elective principle came to be more pronounced. As Indians acquired a stronger voice in the municipal administration, the implicit conflict of interest grew more and more apparent between the predominantly Indian owners of houses (including slum-dwellings rented out at exorbitant rates but with no civic amenities) and the European businessmen and bureaucrats. The Europeans wanted more spacious houses, wider streets and more sanitary conditions—for themselves—but were not prepared to pay for them in proportion to their wealth, income or exalted requirements. The Indians could not see much point in beautifying the European part of the city at a direct cost to their pockets: they would have to fork out higher rates, while losing out as slum landlords if the *bustees* were demolished. The slum-dwellers would lose out either way. If they remained where they were, they lived miserably and died like flies from cholera, smallpox, malaria and other fevers, and plague (though the last was a minor curse compared to its incidence in Bombay or Kanpur). When they were pushed out, they moved to equally noxious slums, and had to travel farther and spend more to go to work.

The natural solution for a city such as Calcutta was for the supreme government to spend generously for civic improvement. As Richards pointed out in his report of 1914, Calcutta did not have the financial resources 'to carry out, unaided, the reformation of fifty years of neglect'. Calcutta was neglected even when it was a capital city, and the neglect has continued ever since.

The Europeans now exerted *force majeure* to get what they wanted—mostly at the cost of the Indians. From the 1890s, the elected element in the municipal administration was virtually eliminated, and the Europeans (including representatives of their major commercial associations, the Bengal Chamber of Commerce and the Calcutta Trades Association) came to be the controlling element. The densely populated Bamun Bustee, for example, was removed to make way for Victoria Terrace; roads were widened in the mainly European wards (which included, in 1921, Ballyganj-Tollyganj, as well as Park Street, Waterloo Street and Victoria Terrace), and the benefits of sewerage and municipal water supply were more heavily

TABLE 3 *Density of Population per Acre in the Different Wards of Calcutta 1872–1921*

Ward	1872	1881	1891	1901	1911	1921
1. Shyampukur	71	70	90	115	130	139
2. Kumartuli	157	118	123	139	152	157
3. Bartala	74	72	90	125	136	152
4. Sukia Street	78	76	109	131	150	173
5. Jorabagan	161	149	161	202	214	216
6. Jorasanko	138	125	159	202	227	219
7. Barabazar	108	96	95	146	141	152
8. Kalutola	227	211	227	282	255	172
9. Muchipara	95	95	108	139	138	151
10. Bowbazar	160	147	154	184	170	184
11. Padmapukur	123	124	125	169	181	197
12. Waterloo Street	27	27	28	30	30	34
13. Fenwick Bazar	140	135	148	163	148	136
14. Taltala	137	132	148	163	162	160
15. Kalinga	71	66	74	94	64	66
16. Park Street	30	32	30	40	35	25
17. Victoria Terrace	51	48	36	43	24	25
18. Hastings	48	47	45	55	51	40
19. Entally	25	24	31	35	41	43
20. Beniapukur	24	23	28	34	46	43
21. Ballyganj–Tollyganj	11	10	11	13	19	25
22. Bhabanipur	45	47	52	61	67	70
23. Alipur	16	11	12	14	16	18
24. Ekbalpur	20	17	17	23	24	34
25. Watganj	32	38	37	52	60	47
Calcutta Municipal Area Average	51	48	54	68	72	74

Source: *Census of India, 1921,* Vol. VI, City of Calcutta, Part I, *Report,* p. 16.

concentrated in those wards. The unequal endowment of space per inhabitant in Calcutta can be gauged from the density per acre in the different wards between 1881 and 1921 (Table 3).

From Table 3 it can be seen that whatever increase in population took place in the half-century from 1872 to 1921 was mostly accommodated in those northern and central wards that were regarded as Indian quarters, or in the low-density peripheral wards. The

European-dominated wards hardly gained any population, and in some cases actually lost it. The only Indian-dominated wards to lose population significantly towards the end of one period were Kalutola and Watganj—the former because of the driving of Central Avenue through the area, and the latter because of a temporary depression of trade (owing to Non-Cooperation?) at the time of the 1921 Census.

Calcutta was a colonial city dominated by an alien minority, and with a highly heterogeneous Indian population constituting the other strata of society. At the top of the European society, as the fount of honour and patronage for the Europeans and even more for the Indians, were the Viceroy and his Council. The Viceroy's salary was Rs 10,000 a month, and that of the members of his Council appropriately graduated. The real incomes of the senior bureaucrats

TABLE 4 *Slum Life in Old Calcutta: Some Statistics*

Year	Number of kutcha houses		
1706	8,000		
1726	13,300		
1742	14,747		
1756	14,450		
1794	13,657		
	Tiled huts	Thatched huts	Total
1821	15,792	37,497	53,289
1831	19,419	35,354	54,773
1837	20,304	30,567	50,871
1850	48,314	—	48,314
1866	43,575	—	43,575
1872	18,421	—	18,421
1876	22,860	—	22,860
1881	20,667	—	20,667
1891	24,191	—	24,191
1901	49,007	—	49,007

Notes: (a) Thatched huts were prohibited by law in 1837.
(b) The sharp decline in the number of huts after 1872 seems likely to be caused by differences in the basis of enumeration more than by actual civic uplift.

Source: A.K. Ray, *A Short History of Calcutta,* 1902.

Wealth and Work in Calcutta

and judges were generally far higher than their official salaries (which ranged above Rs 2,500), as they were usually provided free or subsidized housing and an elaborate retinue of servants at public expense.

The European merchant princes, of course, earned considerably more than most of the civil servants. But their status was measured by the kind of honour that they received from the government houses at Esplanade or Belvedere. The expenditures made by the European merchant princes and civil servants helped to maintain their retainers and, as we have already indicated, numerous small-scale luxury industries. *The Friend of India* remarked that Calcutta was regarded as the 'Paradise of Swells'. But a major part (perhaps half) of the incomes of these grandees regularly leaked out to Blighty, to pay for the upkeep of their wives and children and for the accumulation of a fortune.

Even after such remittances to Britain, the Europeans managed to control larger and larger values of manufacturing, mining, planting and banking capital in eastern India, Calcutta in particular. Table 5 gives some idea of the distribution of control over enterprises above a certain size in Calcutta in 1911 and 1921. It must be remembered that most of the bigger enterprises were controlled by registered companies, the majority of which had Europeans as directors, and these companies employed a much larger number of persons on an average than an ordinary establishment. In 1911, for example, out of the 105 registered companies, 94 had Europeans (with a few Eurasians) as directors; four had a combination of European, Eurasian and Indian directors, and only seven had exclusively Indian directors. In 1921, the number of registered companies was 190; of these 119 had directors who were Europeans or Eurasians, forty had only Indians as directors and thirty-one had a mixed board of Indians, Europeans and Eurasians.

In some establishments, mainly the larger ones demanding newer types of technology, the managers were European or Eurasian even where the ownership was Indian. Among the Indians, Bengalis—especially Hindus—were more in evidence than most other groups. Between 1911 and 1921, the number of enterprises owned or managed by Marwaris or other north Indian trading groups grew; but even at the later date, the presence of these groups in industry of any kind was rather feeble. Table 6 throws some light on the changing

TABLE 5 *Ownership Pattern of Establishments in Calcutta and Suburbs Employing Twenty or More Persons in 1911 and 1921*

	Total number of establishments	Those directed by government or local bodies	Those directed by registered companies	Those owned by private persons		
				Europeans or Anglo-Indians	Indians	Others
1911	572	24	105	85	351	7
1921	643	20	180*	55	361	7

Note: *So printed here, although 190 in other Tables.
Source: *Census of India, 1921*, Vol. XI, City of Calcutta, Part I, *Report*, Chapter IX, Subsidiary Table VI.

TABLE 6 *Management Pattern of Establishments in Calcutta and Suburbs, 1911–21*

	Managed by						
	Europeans and Anglo-Indians	Hindu bhadralok groups (a)	Bengali trading groups and other Hindus (b)	Marwaris or north Indian trading groups (c)	Muslims (d)	Others (e)	Total
1911	202	160	134	8	22	47	573
1921	218	202	440	29	95	23	1007

Notes: (a) This is the classification used in 1921 but not in 1911; we have grouped the Baidyas, the Brahmins and the Kayasthas in 1911 as the *bhadralok*, for this is how the census authorities seemed to have grouped the castes. This may overstate the importance of this group since some 'Kayasths' may have been of non-Bengali origin.
(b) The 1921 Census gives 'Bengali trading classes' and 'other Hindus' separately; we have clubbed them and taken this category to be comparable to that of the total of 'Banias, Kalus, Kansaris, Chasi Kaibarttas, Sadgops, Subarnabaniks, Tantis, Telis and Tilis', whose numbers among managers are shown separately in the 1911 Census.
(c) For 1911, the only group shown was 'Marwaris'; we have taken this figure to be comparable to that of 'upcountry trading classes' in the 1921 Census.
(d) For 1911, the category given was of 'Sheikhs'; we have taken this to be synonymous with Muslims.
(e) 'Others' included Chinese and Parsis.
Sources: *Census of India, 1911*, Vol. VI, City of Calcutta, Part II, *Tables*, p. 114 (Table XV-E); and *Census of India, 1921*, Vol. VI, City of Calcutta, Part II, *Tables*, Table XXII, Part III.

management pattern of industrial enterprises between 1911 and 1921.

In interpreting the data in Table 6, it has to be borne in mind that only 623 out of the 1,007 enterprises in 1921 were at all comparable to the 573 enterprises of 1911; the rest were much smaller in size, and it is mostly these latter that were owned or managed by Indians. Considering their later record, the Bengali *bhadralok* and Bengali Hindu traders owned and managed a surprisingly large number of industrial enterprises. From more detailed data gathered in the censuses of 1911 and 1921, we know that Bengali Hindus were to be found in large numbers as managers and owners of printing presses, oil mills, bakeries, flour mills and rice mills; also, more surprisingly, iron foundries, iron and steel works, and a few tanneries or leather works. The Kalus were the only Bengali caste which seems to have adhered to their ascribed calling: all the seventeen owners or managers among Kalus in 1911 ran oil mills.

So the enthusiasm for *swadeshi*, fed both by the official propaganda of men like George Birdwood, E.B. Havell and Trailokyanath Mukherji (1847–1919), and the nationalist efforts of Jogendrachandra Ghosh, Manindrachandra Nandi (1860–1930), Satyasundar Deb (1880?–1971) and nationalist ex-officials such as Pramathanath Basu (1855–1935), had a wide social base. But this base was about to crumble in at least two of its bastions. The Bengal Tenancy Act of 1885 and the successive survey and settlement operations which limited the arbitrary rent-enhancing powers of the landlord, hit the old *zamindars* or lesser land-holding gentry very hard. So did the agricultural depression of the 1920s and 1930s. From the other side, the Marwaris and other north Indian traders gradually came to capture the inland trade of Calcutta's hinterland, including that in jute—the source of greatest lucre for the traders and of the greatest misery for the Bengal peasantry in bad years.

Willingness to take risks and acquire appropriate technical education were not equipment enough for lasting business success in a colonial economy where the government for a long time refused to patronize large-scale industry under Indian control. Only prowess in finance and marketing could have allowed any businessman to ride out trade cycles in such an economy. The weakness of the Bengalis in business had already been evident to discerning onlookers in the 1870s, when the 'young hopefuls' were advised by the editor of *The Statesman* to buy land and combine land-holding with the calling of a *bania*.

The 1890s and early 1900s seem to have still provided the Bengali upper classes with opportunities for small-scale industrial investment in the interstices of an agrarian economy. But when the Marwaris captured 'the commanding heights' of trade from the Europeans, the more enlightened form of capital of the educated Bengalis was overwhelmed by the less progressive form, which could better integrate itself with the changing demands of a late-colonial economy. A finer analysis of the data would reveal the symptoms of change already between 1911 and 1921.

The Muslims, whether Bengalis or from outside Bengal, fared badly as industrialists or traders. They constituted a much smaller proportion of factory-owners than of the population. There were some rich Nakhuda merchants who traded mainly with West Asia, but most others operated on a small scale. There were practically no bankers of importance among them. This was a major source of their weakness vis-à-vis the Marwaris, who combined both trade and banking. The latter financed the operations of the Nakhudas, to whom (as to Bengali traders) they offered worse terms than to the members of their own community. Of course there were rich Muslims, such as the descendants of Tipu Sultan or the Nawabs of Lucknow, the Nawab of Murshidabad, or the members of the Nawab family of Dhaka, who all maintained establishments in Calcutta. But few of these wealthy men engaged openly in trade, industry or banking, although the chief shareholders of the Dacca Bank (later absorbed by the Bank of Bengal) had belonged to the Dhaka Nawab's family. In the jute trade, Adamji Haji Dawood, a Muslim merchant from western India, became one of the biggest traders after the first World War, and his firm went on to found the Adamji Jute Mills. But one Dawood could not alter the relative positions of Hindus and Muslims among Indian businessmen.

The Condition of Wage-Earners

Our attention has so far been confined to the owners of land and capital. How did they fare who owned mostly nothing but their bodies (and sometimes not even that), and constituted the vast majority of Calcutta's population? A connected history of the labouring poor of Calcutta is still to be written, and we will not try to encompass the task here. Let us first try to figure out how much they earned and how their earnings varied over time. An idea of the monthly earnings and the cost of living can be obtained from Table 7.

TABLE 7 *The Monthly Wages of Syces, Common Masons, Carpenters and Blacksmiths in Calcutta, 1871–99*

	Average monthly wages (in Rs) of		Average price of common rice in terms of seers to a rupee
	Syces or grooms	Common masons, carpenters and blacksmiths	
1871	—	—	20.00
1873	6.5	7.5 to 10.0	—
1876	6	15.55	12.28
1881	7	12	16.80
1886	7	15	14.24
1891	6	15	13.38
1896	8	15 to 16	10.95
1899	8	18 to 20	11.85

Source: *Prices and Wages in India,* Seventeenth Issue, compiled under the supervision of the Director-General of Statistics, Office of the Superintendent of Government Printing, Calcutta, 1900, Tables 1 and 52.

In Table 7, syces or grooms are taken to represent unskilled workers, and common masons, etc., are taken to represent skilled workers. We take the price of common rice as a major component of the cost of living of ordinary workers, who spent most of their meagre earnings on food. On this basis, the cost of living almost doubled between the 1870s and the end of the century, whereas the earnings of unskilled workers increased in a much smaller proportion. Thus, the real income of such people, already low in the 1870s, fell further by the end of the century.

In the case of skilled workers, the trend was apparently different, since their money earnings, according to Table 7, rose in greater proportion than the cost of living. However, the figures are a little suspect. The publication from which the figures are taken also gives the figure for skilled and unskilled workers in a paper mill (probably the Bally Paper Mills). The wages of 'coolies' in that mill are almost identical with those of syces in Table 7. But the wages of mill carpenters and blacksmiths, while higher than those of skilled workers in Table 7 at the beginning of the 1870s, show virtually no trend thereafter, and are lower than those of skilled workers as given in Table 7 in 1899. Weighing the evidence, it is reasonable to conclude that skilled artisans may have just about maintained their real earnings but were very unlikely to have improved their condition in Calcutta of the 1890s. This inference is consistent with the stagnation of wages of jute-mill workers in Bengal after 1900.

How did the wages of unskilled workers in Calcutta relate to the cost of items other than food? I shall only cite the cost of internal transport. Horse-drawn tramcars appeared in Calcutta in the 1880s. In 1881, the fare from Kalighat to Tank Square (today's B.B.D. Bag) was 2 annas; but the fare from any intermediate point, such as Dharmatala, to Tank Square was also 2 annas. As the daily wage of an unskilled labourer then was about 4 annas, one ride would cost him half a day's wage, and a journey out and back, his earnings for the day. The fare was reduced in late 1881, but it still cost a minimum of 1 anna.

The reduction in fare was preceded by a drastic cut in conductors' and drivers' salaries: for conductors it went down from Rs 20–25 to Rs 14 per month. For both conductors and drivers, the company resorted to payment by trips: in order to earn Rs 20 per month under the new system, a conductor would have to work from 6 am to 10 pm, that is, sixteen hours at a stretch. Such actions of the Tramway Company provoked repeated strikes by the staff.

Workers in factories, steam-powered mills and other establishments resorted to strikes in protest against alterations in working conditions and wages, even though there were as yet few organized trade unions. For example, workers of Dykes and Co., a coach-building firm, went on strike in March 1881 because they were forbidden to go out to smoke a *hookah*. Several strikes by municipal sweepers and by the workers of Union Jute Mills (near Sealdah Station) and other establishments were reported in the newspapers of 1880.

Most Calcuttans—which obviously means most common workers—still lived in *kutcha* houses in 1891. Through their wretched living conditions and endemic poverty, apart from conditions in their places of work, the labouring men and women felt the brunt of the colonial, authoritarian rule even more keenly than did others. European foremen could kick them to death; policemen could beat them black and blue or warn them off public paths and gardens, under threat of an arrest or a beating. Slum-dwellers could be evicted by landlords, beaten up by their musclemen, and thrown out by the municipal administration bent on improving the city.

Not all workers actually had work. Technical and organizational changes were continually threatening the livelihood of workers, who had little job security. The advent of motor cars threw carriage-making firms out of business and, along with them, the thousands of workers engaged in the trade. Improvements in the port took away the jobs of thousands of porters, whose place was taken by hydraulic cranes and their few operators. Porters had been engaged earlier on to carry dignitaries from their boats to dry land, since there were virtually no jetties at many places. The advent of Portland cement took away the business of *surki* (brick-dust) works. The growth of Calcutta's population and the construction of palatial buildings partly compensated for these dislocations; but immigrants were steadily adding to the supply of workers, while the demand grew sluggishly, or in fits and starts. Workless people satisfied the desire for vicarious acquisition of virtue (*punya*) of rich Jains, who hired them to feed bedbugs on their own blood at the rate of 2 annas for two hours. Work in the factories was also affected by trade cycles; workers thrown out by trade depressions might go back to the villages or hang around in a half-starved condition in the hope of getting a job in some other establishment.

Calcutta's history is as much a story of the plight and struggle of such people, and of their enjoyment of life snatched from the jaws of misery, as of the doings of the great sahibs, maharajas and nawabs. But that story is yet to be told.

Working-Class Consciousness

I

Dipesh Chakrabarty has written an important and challenging book.* It is important because it incorporates aspects of the history of the working class which tend to be left out in more orthodox accounts. It is challenging because it raises new questions, and because it is theoretically ambitious. In particular, Chakrabarty challenges what he considers to be the methods of Marxian political economy, and seeks to demonstrate that 'the logic of a particular culture (or consciousness) cannot be explained by the methods of political economy which often fail to make a distinction between "function" and "reason"' (Preface, p. xii).

Let me first make it clear that I have serious disagreements with Chakrabarty about method. I share with him the perception that the methods of Marxian political economy as applied to many problems of Indian history (and of contemporary reality) are seriously incomplete. I do not, however, believe that the methods are themselves inappropriate. I would, in fact, suggest that the attempt to 'isolate questions of culture and consciousness' (Preface, p. vi) from the general existential problem of the working class as a method of enquiry, rather than as a provisional closure to a research programme, is a reductionist venture. This reductionism is responsible for some of the deficiencies of Chakrabarty's narrative that I will point to.

---

* Dipesh Chakrabarty, *Rethinking Working Class History: Bengal, 1890–1940*, Princeton University Press, Princeton, New Jersey, 1989.

Chakrabarty's ambition to view the problem of the working-class Indian man (or woman) in colonial India as a parable of the problem of the emergence of the Indian 'citizen' leads him to conceptual errors. Throughout most of the book, Chakrabarty's quarry is the nature of the 'state' and the demands of 'capital' or the relation of 'capital to labour'. Now, the 'nature of the state' is one of the grand questions of political philosophy, and the relation of 'capital to labour' is one of the central issues of classical political economy. Unless more historic specificities are imposed on the area to be investigated, the analyst is quite likely to be lost in the vast sea of enquiry. Casual asides cannot form the substance of such an enquiry. Much of that investigation in a colonial context must itself be a novel enterprise.

Chakrabarty fares best when he is being mainly 'a historian', or 'merely a historian', putting together a credible narrative. The reader understands at those points that Chakrabarty is dealing with not just any state but with a colonial state, not just with any capital but with colonial capital. But when he is wielding theory consciously his narrative lapses again and again into a historical amorphousness, or is betrayed into a rather one-sided view of how the experience of living by actual human beings is to be conceptualized.

Chakrabarty's ambition and his theoretical confusion are revealed in the 'Preface' itself. He cites Jean Jacques Rousseau on the origins of inequality. But Rousseau is a difficult witness for anybody theorizing about the nature of the state, or searching for the citizen. For, Rousseau regarded the civil society itself as the source of inequality. Whether we look at Rousseau's typology of man (for Rousseau it was always 'man' rather than 'woman' who was the subject) and his social and political environment as a series of stages through which he has passed (Hawthorn 1987: 21–24), or as a series of constructs on which he hangs his moral quest (Shklar 1969: Chapter 1), his thought can hardly be invoked to pinpoint the difference between the nature of inequality in a capitalist society and a pre-capitalist society. Chakrabarty cites Foucault to make the point that the 'individual' is itself a social construct—a construct which perhaps reaches its apogee in a pure capitalist society, and that the goal should be to transcend the individual. In fact, the same conclusion was reached by Rousseau, as indeed by Karl Marx. Rousseau's view of 'man in nature' was that of a patriarchal man, where woman existed only to sustain the quest of man to fulfil his nature. In the same year in which Tom Paine's *Rights of Man* was published, Mary Wollstonecroft (1791) published a trenchant critique of the patriarchal basis of much of the enlightenment philosophy of freedom. Chakrabarty might argue that he is only focusing on those aspects of inequality that are bred by the capital–labour relationship, or by the existence of a state. But does such a very general conception really help to illuminate the condition of jute-mill workers in Bengal so as to bring out their status as 'subjects', distinct from any other subjects in any modern society (since all modern societies are characterized by the possession of a state apparatus, and most are also characterized by a capital–labour relation)? Without further honing of such a theoretical tool, Rousseau's name becomes only an invocation in Chakrabarty's text.

It is difficult to know how Chakrabarty means to interpret the signs of the various saints he invokes. He knows that a capitalist individual is hardly the egalitarian individual he is looking for. Yet, he sets up the practice of that individual as a standard for comparison with the many pre-capitalist relations that he is castigating. Apart from the problem of how to read his hypothetical comparisons, there is a serious problem with his conceptualization of the colonial state and colonial capital. The relations observed by him are not just pre-capitalist relations: they are pre-capitalist and capitalist relations under the domination of a colonial state. Almost by definition, a 'citizen' in Rousseau's (or Bentham's or, for that matter, James Harrington's) sense cannot exist among the mere 'subjects' (*prajas*, not citizens) in a dependent colony of His (or Her) Majesty's Government. It is not enough to reply that only *prajas* and not 'citizens' are found among pre-capitalist social formations: for what is being observed is not the behaviour of people under pre-capitalist social formations *per se*. The data comes from, as I insisted earlier, a society composed of a state which is not answerable to any of the subjects it reigns over.

In an article (Chakrabarty 1988) which was published just before his book, Chakrabarty accused Marxist historians of Indian labour of harbouring 'the whole of English history' as 'a mythical model in explaining "problems" relating to workers' consciousness in India' (ibid.: 24). However, Chakrabarty himself seems to have a mythical view of what freedom and equality have meant in the theorizing of bourgeois philosophers, and how it has been actually realized in practice in the heartlands of modern capitalism. From Hobbes through Locke to Bentham, freedom or liberty was always the property of the propertied class (Macpherson 1962; Long 1979). In the text of his book Chakrabarty uses an untheorized, undefined 'bourgeois notion of equality' as the standard against which he judges his notion of the consciousness of the jute-mill workers (see, for example, p. 3). In actual fact, equality of any kind was not a voluntary gift of the bourgeoisie to the people, but was realized through long years of struggle. Some of the most aggressive capitalist societies (for example, Wilhelmine Germany or Meiji Japan) were built up on an explicit denial of the notion of equality of all citizens before law. The freedom of contract that was supposed to characterize all capitalist societies was qualified severely almost as soon as it began to operate in the first industrial nation (Atiyah 1979).

Chakrabarty stresses that real English history did not follow any set, oversimplified model of the working class gaining consciousness through the formation of centralized factories. Yet, when he comes to discuss Indian conditions, he conjures away many of the basic features of the construction of state, capital, working class, community, and so on. Take, for example, the notion of the state. Was it or was it not quixotic to search for a 'citizen' among a group of persons whose laws could be totally annulled, if it suited them to do so, by a group of legislators sitting 5,000 miles away? If a citizen must be a person who takes part in political decisions governing his own future, in concert with other citizens similarly placed under a set of constitutional provisions defining the rules of procedure and conduct, there was not a single citizen among the British Indian subjects of the Crown before 1947. The British Indian subjects of the Crown were doubly distanced from the citizens of the governing land: the former were a conquered people and, as blacks, the British regarded them as racially inferior. This was expressed not only in the conventions about what was due to a *sahib* as against a native (Bagchi 1970, 1972; Ballhatchet 1980), but also proclaimed in no uncertain terms whenever the British government tried to partially unify the apparatuses of legal practice applying to the 'natives' and to the Europeans. For example, at the time of the non-exemption debate of the 1850s, Theodore Dickens, a leading English lawyer of Calcutta, addressed the Indian claimants for equality under the law in the following words:

> You are one of the conquered race, who have therefore no original and strictly political right to be well-governed; you are at the mercy of the conquerors. But I am one of a nation who have their rights guaranteed by such things as Magna Carta, the Bill of Rights, the Act of Settlement and a few other conditions, upon whose due and faithful observance by the Crown, my allegiance to it depends. I cannot, therefore, admit that you are politically my equal. (Dickens 1857)

From his basically ahistorical notions of bourgeois freedom, equality, citizenship, etc., and his severely attenuated formulation of the characteristics of colonialism (which enters his discourse centrally only in Chapter 5), follows Chakrabarty's strategy of dumping all the features that seemed to have fractured a worker's capacity to act as a worker struggling against capital into the catch-all category of 'pre-capitalist' features. Take, for example, his notion of the '*babu–coolie*' relationship. Chakrabarty writes:

> This general aspect of the pre-capitalist relationship between the rich and the poor would thus appear to have constituted an important strand in the tradition that moulded the culture of trade unionism in colonial Calcutta. In the absence of a better name, let us call this the '*babu–coolie*' relationship in so far as it could be seen to exist in the practice of trade unionism. (p. 143)

Nowhere does Chakrabarty specify the generative processes of such 'pre-capitalist' relationships. If, by calling the so-called '*babu–coolie*' relationship a pre-capitalist relation, he implies that it was generated by the pre-colonial society and was a survival from those days, he is obviously wrong. Both the '*babu*' and the '*coolie*' were pre-eminently colonial terms and colonial creatures, and their coming into such close contact with each other that Chakrabarty can talk about a *babu–coolie relationship* was also a happening of the colonial experience. *Hobson-Jobson* (1903: 44) defines 'Baboo' as follows:

Properly a term of respect attached to a name, like Master or Mr, and formerly, in some parts of Hindustan, applied to certain persons of distinction. Its application as a term of respect is now almost or altogether confined to Lower Bengal (though C.P. Brown states that it is also used in south India for 'Sir', 'My Lord', 'Your Honour'). In Bengal and elsewhere, among Anglo-Indians, it is often used with a slight savour of disparagement, as characterizing a superficially cultivated, but too often effeminate, Bengali. And from the extensive employment of the class, to which the term was applied as a title, in the capacity of clerks in English offices, the word has come often to signify a native clerk who writes English.

A number of years before *Hobson-Jobson*, Bankimchandra Chattopadhyay, that unusual Bengali *babu* (he would always be Babu Bankim Chandra Chatterjee to his British contemporaries, though R.C. Dutt, ICS, would attain the dignity of Romesh Chunder Dutt, Esq.), had given more or less an exhaustive characterization of the *babu* in all his *avatars* (Chattopadhyay 1366 BS). The westernized *sahib*-imitating *babu*, callous to the misery of his fellow 'natives', became a figure of fun in a century-old tradition of writing in Bengal (see, for example, Amritalal Basu's farce, *Babu*). Chakrabarty sees the *babu* as the rich man as against the poor worker, or as the master as against his servant. Bankimchandra, however, also saw the *babu* as the mere clerk of the British employer, or his *bazar sarkar*, that is, the servant who was responsible for the marketing for the household. He also saw him as the enemy of various groups of victims, including the *daftary*, who was subordinate to the clerk. Unlike his great predecessor, Chakrabarty fails to see the *babu* as a creature *par excellence* of colonialism.

When we come to the '*coolie*', his colonial origins are also patent. A human being has to be completely dehumanized in order to be seen as a *coolie* (cf. Breman 1989). Let us look at *Hobson-Jobson* again, to find out how he is constituted by the *sahibs* (*Hobson-Jobson* 1903: 249):

> Cooly ... A hired labourer or burden-carrier, and, in modern days especially, a labourer induced to emigrate from India, or

from China, to labour in the plantations of Mauritius, Rangoon, or the West Indies, sometimes under circumstances, especially in French colonies, which have brought the *cooly*'s condition very near to slavery. In Upper India the term has frequently a specific application to the lower class of labourer who carries earth, bricks, etc., as distinguished from the skilled workman, and even from the digger.

The original of the word appears to have been a *nomen gentile,* the name *(Koli)* of a race or caste in eastern India, who have long performed such offices as have been mentioned, and whose savagery, filth and general degradation attracted much attention in former times. . . . The application of the word would thus be analogous to that which has rendered the name of the *Slav,* captured and made a bondservant, the word for such a bondservant in many European tongues.

The definition goes on to try to locate the exact habitat of the Kolis and the possible connection with the Kols of south-western Bihar. Notice, in this definition, the combination of a sophistication that recognizes the making of a stereotype, and the unabashed approval of the use of that stereotype. Notice, also, the attempt to deflect the opprobrium of inhuman usage on to another colonizing power, despite the existence of abundant evidence of similar behaviour on the part of the British (cf. Tinker 1974).

But note how the '*coolie*' was constituted. Even if he had existed in the colonizers' consciousness in an embryonic form earlier, he acquired prominence in their usage as a 'savage' or a 'beast' to be tamed only with his emigration, pre-eminently under colonial auspices, to distant lands (cf. Breman 1989). The *coolie* was already marked by the colonial branding-iron when he emigrated to Calcutta. When he, as a migrant labourer, was put in proximity with the colonial *babu,* it was not some pre-capitalist upheaval that caused this to happen; it was the needs of colonial capital and the colonial *raj* in the vast countryside of Bihar and Uttar Pradesh, and the colonial capital in the emerging jute mills, coal mines and tea plantations of Calcutta and western India that brought about that dehumanizing conjunction.

Chakrabarty is nowhere more eloquent in his outrage and

in his romanticized notions of bourgeois legality, culture, etc., as when he takes the fledgling trade union movement among the jute-mill workers to task (pp. 132–54). In his view (and he quotes Gramsci in his support), a real trade union must be a 'bourgeois-democratic organization'. By using this definition, of course, he would at once dismiss all workers' movements operating in authoritarian regimes as being other than trade union movements. In colonial India, before the Trade Union Act of 1926, trade unions were not legally recognized; soon after the passing of the Act, the major organizers of trade unions were tried in the Meerut Conspiracy Case, which went on until 1933. So, for most of the period studied by Chakrabarty, trade unions could but have only a semi-legal existence. Did Chakrabarty seriously expect to find 'bourgeois-democratic' trade unions in colonial India, especially in colonial Bengal, where the government had almost invariably adopted the viewpoint of the employers on every issue that involved the workers' welfare?

One possible objection to this type of critique of Chakrabarty's position could be that bourgeois culture, bourgeois legality, or bourgeois-democratic organizations are not made in a day; they have to be forged in popular struggles, elite re-adjustments and slow social processes. Surely, then, it is necessary to study these processes themselves rather than take a snapshot of an artificially immobilized formation and judge it against some kind of goal or entity that is fully formed. But such a processual study is conspicuous by its absence in Chakrabarty's book. Did the left organizers of the trade unions have any notion of eventual achievement of equality before law by workers as well as *babus*? (They might have flinched at the use of the word 'bourgeois legality'.) What conception of legality, if any, did the workers not embracing any kind of radical philosophy have? We do not get the answers from Chakrabarty's narrative, because he does not ask the questions.

The outrage Chakrabarty feels at the continuance of a hierarchical relationship between many (or even most) *bhadralok* or *babu* trade unionists and the workers constituted as *coolies*, betrays him into serious misuse of language. For example, he writes about Sibnath Banerjee, an important trade union organizer in the 1930s and 1940s:

> So it is not surprising that in spite of his ideology and sacrifices—in fact precisely because of his sacrifices—Shibnath Banerjee's union assumed no 'organizational form' for years and remained an 'out and out one-man-show', his *zamindari*. Even a 'real' representative turned out to be a master. (p. 153)

Now this is really confusing categories with a vengeance. Was Sibnath Banerjee a 'master' in the same sense as a manager or the managing agency of a jute mill? Did he have the power to hire and fire workers? Under another dispensation he might have been a master in this sense, but that is not the dispensation we are talking about.

When Chakrabarty pours scorn on the workers for representing themselves to a barrister as 'poor people' needing his help, or sneers at *babus* claiming the allegiance of workers because they had made sacrifices, he unfortunately sounds very much like a non-participant *babu* lecturing the participant *babu* on how to purify his practice. If this was only a matter of style, it would not matter. But perhaps because Chakrabarty is so aware of the need to sharpen his discourse to back up his critique of trade union practice, it also affects the quality of his analysis. His eloquence derives not only from the mis-specification of relationships, but also from the closing of several areas of discourse by simply remaining silent about them.

II

We have so far posed the problems that are created by the reified level at which Chakrabarty pitches his theoretical perspective. In doing so, we have seen how his unwillingness to take colonialism seriously enough has led him to mis-specify the genesis and the nature of relationships between *babus* as trade union organizers and the workers. The opacity of his lenses with regard to colonialism also affects some other parts of his narrative. One of the best chapters in the book—a chapter from which I have profited greatly—is on the evolution of the jute industry in Bengal. Chakrabarty has brought out better than anybody else before him how Dundee men had contributed to the growth of the industry on the banks of the Hooghly. He has also underlined 'the quick money mentality' of many of the early investors in jute mills, and the mismanagement of the mills by the likes of Richard Macallister. He brings out the fact that the establishment of Indian jute manufactures in foreign markets was a major act of entrepreneurship.

But Chakrabarty faces a conundrum when he tries to analyse why the Bengal jute mills failed to meet the challenge posited by substitutes or to effect any technical improvement in its manufacturing process. As a solution of this conundrum he evokes 'the mercantilist spirit' (p. 43) of the people running the industry, or, more elaborately, 'a deeply entrenched economic outlook that counterposed the cheapness of products and price-manipulation practices (like short-time working arrangements) to scientific and technological progress' (p. 40). However, Chakrabarty fails to answer the further query as to the rationale of the genesis and the persistence of such attitudes. We have to remember that the rate of growth of the jute industry was remarkably fast up to the First World War, the number of persons employed in the industry doubling every ten years or so (Bagchi 1989: 24). This bespeaks a high degree of confidence on the part of the British investors in the business environment they operated in.

The assurance of a cheap supply of labour was part of that environment. That was not taken to be just a passive function of the labour market. Several pieces of legislation had been passed in the nineteenth century permitting the indenturing of labour in the Assam tea plantations. The managing agency houses of Calcutta were allowed to recruit labour through *sardars* and other intermediaries over most parts of eastern and central India. The government instituted specific enquiries about labour supply whenever managing agencies complained of labour shortage. And, of course, the broader arrangements of a colonial state systematically pursuing a policy of 'one-way free trade' and maintaining a highly exploitative agrarian system, more or less guaranteed the cheapness of displaced labour (Bagchi 1972: Chapters 5 and 8; Bagchi 1976; Bagchi 1982: Chapter 4). And when the labourers came to work in the jute mills, the whole weight of the state apparatus curbed their attempts to raise wages, as Chakrabarty's own evidence (Chapter 5) and the evidence garnered by Parimal Ghosh (1984) have amply demonstrated. In and around the jute mills, the colonial state did not always resort to explicit coercion: that would have been too expensive. The imposition of an ideology of white superiority on the workers, the use of local taxes to effectively subsidize the housing of mill workers, wretched as it was, in the areas controlled by the mill municipalities, and the use, when it was necessary and feasible, of communal politics to deflect workers' struggles (cf. pp. 199–201)—all served their purpose.

The other parts of the business environment concerned the cheapness of raw material, and the maintenance of a quasi-monopolistic structure regulating the prices and quantities of jute manufactures. I have discussed elsewhere in some detail how the latter was kept in place (Bagchi 1972: Chapters 6 and 8). The control over purchase of jute and its sale in foreign markets by a few large European companies also ensured that the price of jute remained low; and when an attempt was made to provide some holding power to the peasants through government loans, the government of Bengal effectively quashed the movement, at the behest of the Bengal Chamber of Commerce (Bagchi 1972: 269n).

So long as the controllers of the jute mills had confidence in the stability of the business environment as outlined above, extensive growth could take place at a rapid pace. With cheap labour, cheap raw materials, unchanging technical equipment, and with relatively cheap supervisory personnel (for, however lordly the white supervisors in jute mills might have been, these semi-skilled or unskilled recruits from the north of Scotland must have been cheap in comparison with, for example, a trained British engineer), the rates of profit in the jute industry could be maintained at a high level; and as one senior partner of the managing agency house after another returned to Britain, they could take a tidy fortune with them.

The requirements of intensive growth, with rapidly changing technologies and investment for effecting technical change from within, were quite different from those of extensive growth with unchanging, rather labour-intensive techniques. Intensive growth of this kind would have meant employment of really skilled personnel, longer time horizons for investment (that is, longer pay-off periods) and explicit investment in R and D. The latter would have required not only that the oligopolistic managing agency houses assume greater risks, but also that their controlling partners be prepared to commit their capital for more or less permanent lodgement on the Indian soil. Even if some of them had been prepared to do that before 1914, none but the foolhardy would have been so inclined after 1919. This does not mean that there could have been no technical progress in any industry controlled by European capital before 1914. Technical progress was achieved where it was the result of learning by doing, and where no major capital cost was incurred in bringing it about. This condition was fulfilled in the plantation industries, where productivity grew through precisely such processes (see, for example, Misra 1985: Chapter 2).

I have analysed this issue at some length to show that even where Chakrabarty is breaking new ground, he could have brought his analysis into sharper focus if he had taken the specificities of colonial capital more seriously, and had not lapsed again and again into talking about 'capital' as an abstract category.

III

I now turn to an issue posed in Chakrabarty's book, which is one of its most distinctive and most contentious features. This is his treatment of 'Class and Community', the subject of Chapter 6. He contests the claim made in some of the communist or, more broadly, Marxist, literature, that there was an evolution in the consciousness of the jute-mill workers such that their identification with a class transcended their identification as Hindus or Muslims.

Chakrabarty's central argument is best given by a quotation from the book:

> ... all collective public actions of the workers were marked by an inherent duality. An act of revolt against the authorities, such as a strike, always had the potential of turning into its opposite, a fight among the workers themselves, a religious riot; a religious or racial riot, on the other hand, contained a necessary element of rebellion against authority, an extreme manifestation of which were the strikes based on 'religious' or 'racial' demands.
>
> This duality, characteristic of the collective and public acts of the working class, prompts explanations that are either political or political–economic in orientation. None of these explanations ... gives us any clue to the nature of the consciousness that was expressed through the 'duality' in question. (p. 198)

Then Chakrabarty quotes from an article (Bagchi 1985) which had been critical of some of his earlier formulations. I had written, among other things: 'The old society does impart a sense of community to the oppressed people because they need such a consciousness for survival' (ibid.: 10). Chakrabarty is censorious about such statements:

> 'Needs', that is, 'utility', the celebrants of political economy will tell us, is the key to the secrets of consciousness. Yet it empties 'culture' of all specific content. Serving the 'needs of survival' is a function universal to all cultures in all historical settings. This functionalist understanding can never be guide to the internal logic of a culture, the way it constructs and uses its 'reason'. (p. 211)

I shall defer for the moment an analysis of whether invoking 'needs' is equivalent to using the notion of 'utility'. I had expected at this moment that Chakrabarty would tell us how the consciousness of the worker was constructed. Instead he offers his residual category, 'pre-capitalist' or 'pre-bourgeois', as a sufficient characterization: 'The jute workers ... acted out of an understanding that was pre-bourgeois in its elements' (p. 212). He then proceeds to give examples of such a 'pre-bourgeois' culture: a Brahmin who spends more than an average person in order to preserve the honour of his caste, a Bengali worker who would not allow his wife to work in a mill. He also cites the statement of a woman from Chapra who would 'bring her daughter to work when she [was] sufficiently old' (p. 213; the quotation is from evidence tendered before the Indian Factory Labour Commission of 1890). Did this woman, incidentally, become 'bourgeois' by making such a statement?

Chakrabarty then goes on to cite instances of protest by the workers of a particular community because its honour was violated by various acts of individuals of another community: a Hindu throws coloured water on a Muslim during the *holi* festival, or the honour of a woman of one community is violated by a man of another community. In this 'communal sense of honour' Chakrabarty finds evidence of the 'non-individualistic, pre-bourgeois nature of the identity' (p. 215) of the jute-mill worker.

Let us grant that all this kind of behaviour is 'pre-bourgeois'.

But how does such an adjectival exercise bring out the 'reason' of such a consciousness? The inadequacy of Chakrabarty's explanation becomes obvious as soon as we ask two questions. Are all characteristics of consciousness which are implicated in religion and a sense of solidarity bred out of that consciousness necessarily pre-bourgeois? In that case almost everything that was written during the Puritan Revolution in England down to the days of Edmund Burke have to be considered 'pre-bourgeois' in origin. Barring Thomas Hobbes, the arguments of virtually every political philosopher in Britain before David Hume and Adam Smith were couched in a religious idiom (see, for some of the latest debates in this area, Pocock 1985; Tully 1988). Similarly, the consciousness of the emerging working class of England was manifested in religious idioms, as E.P. Thompson has so eloquently brought out. If the use of a religious idiom should be considered a bar to the formation of a bourgeois society, then Calvin's Geneva would never qualify as even a proto-bourgeois city.

The second question, which is connected with the first but is even more relevant for Chakrabarty's enquiry is, why should workers' movements have so often assumed a 'communal' form rather than an ethno-linguistic form cutting across religious boundaries? In a study of the Yorubas of Nigeria, David Laitin found that although the former were divided between Christians and Muslims, when it came to political loyalties, it was their (real or mythic) city of origin rather than religion that became a decisive factor (Laitin 1985). Why did the jute-mill worker not behave in the same way as the Yorubas? Moreover, being religious is not synonymous with being communal. If, in moments of stress, the religious consciousness broke out occasionally in communal violence, that *was* connected with the 'political' and 'political–economic' factors on which Chakrabarty pours so much scorn. However, these political and political–economic factors were themselves intimately linked to religious movements, to effects of colonial rule and to movements against that rule. For all his concern with 'the reason' of the workers' consciousness, Chakrabarty totally omits any mention of these, except in some casual asides.

If we look at the consciousness of the Muslim workers in the late nineteenth century, we see that it was being stirred through a series of reform movements starting generally from Delhi and Uttar Pradesh, but gradually spreading throughout northern and eastern India. These were the *tariqah* movement, the *taiyuni* movement, the *faraizi* movement (which probably had its greatest impact in Bengal) and the movement of religious instruction diffused from the Dar-ul-Ulum of Deoband (Robinson 1975; Ahmed 1981; Metcalf 1982). Some of them were primarily anti-British in origin. Some also took on a communal tinge when the major oppressors of the Muslim peasantry were found to be Hindu landlords and moneylenders (cf. Pandey 1981). Fundamentalist Islam held that it was religion that formed the basis of a political community. Accordingly, the British doubly violated Islam by being foreign aggressors and by flouting the principles of Islamic theocracy. This lent a special edge to the anti-British and, where they identified the Hindus as siding with or benefiting from British rule, the anti-Hindu stance of many of the reformist Muslims. Similarly, the portrayal of the Muslim as a foreign intruder and as a destroyer or polluter of the *sanatan dharma* also inflamed many Hindus with anti-Muslim sentiments (McLane 1977; Yang 1989). These currents had been at work in many parts of northern India long before the Muslim League or the Hindu Mahasabha came into existence.

Colonialism made an impact on the living conditions of the groups from among whom migrant workers were recruited, and left many of them extremely insecure in their rural bases. In Bihar and eastern Uttar Pradesh were to be found some of the most oppressive *zamindaris* in alliance with European planters (see, for a recent study, Yang 1989). While their oppression bore down hard on groups who were still outside the pale of the major religions, they could also create divisions among the oppressed through differential treatment in terms of caste and community. Moreover, there were other ways in which colonialism threatened different groups differently. While the colonial land revenue system led to a rapid depletion of pastures and other common lands (Bagchi 1976), it was the *goalas* who would be most threatened by this process, and semi-nomadic *goalas* and settled cultivators would often come into conflict. When the latter happened to be Muslims, the conflict would assume a communal aspect, as most of the *goalas* were Hindus. The cow then became a symbol to be fought over, since it was a source of livelihood to the one and the pre-eminent sacrificial animal to the other (the pre-eminence arising from the need of a Muslim to distinguish himself decisively from the other). In the same way, the *jolaha* or Muslim weaver, who in pre-colonial days was close to the sources of court patronage, would perhaps be most affected by the disastrous decline of handloom weaving in the nineteenth century. On the other side, his major source of credit or major channel of marketing would be the Hindu merchant, whose power waxed as the condition of the *jolaha* worsened over time. Here, again, any communal conflict would gain an added degree of fierceness from the perception of conflicting economic interests; in some cases, conflicts over economic interests would turn into communal conflicts.

Chakrabarty, in his utter disdain of 'political' or 'political–economic' analysis, does not even bother to enquire into the specificities of the belief systems or social organizations of the migrant workers that made them enter into communal conflicts from time to time. His discourse is squarely in the line of official discourse, as exemplified in the *Report of the Royal Commission on Labour in India* (1931), which saw the Indian mill worker as the Indian peasant uprooted. He basically treats the uprooted peasants as an undifferentiated mass liable to be governed by 'primordial' loyalties, and break out into primeval violence from time to time.

I now have to condemn myself for using the phrase 'primordial loyalty' in my brief critique of Chakrabarty's earlier work (Bagchi 1985). I find that Chakrabarty also uses the same or very similar phrases in his book. There are two problems in using such phrases to describe the jute-mill worker's (or any other human being's) consciousness. One is that 'primordial loyalties' are themselves liable to change through new cultural and, *pace* Chakrabarty, political–economic experience. The second is that it is not enough to characterize some attitudes or loyalties as 'primordial'. It is necessary to enquire as to how and why such 'primordial loyalties' are likely to be brought into play in a new setting.

Chakrabarty dismisses as mere 'economism' or 'political economy' any discussion of the living conditions of the workers as irrelevant to the constitution or reproduction of their consciousness. I would still maintain that in order to retain any consciousness at all, the workers need to live. There is abundant evidence that the

Bengal jute-mill worker's chances of survival were even slimmer than those of the ordinary villagers of Bengal. The mortality rates (per 1,000) in the urban areas of Howrah and Hooghly districts, for example, in 1894–95 and 1895–96, were as follows:

	1894–95	1895–96
Hooghly	47.8	41.3
Howrah	25.0	41.3

Source: *Annual General Administration Report,* Burdwan Division, 1895–96, paras 30, 31, 37; as quoted by Ghosh 1984.

These were by no means abnormal years. The census reports on Calcutta—taking into account the abnormal male–female ratios, and the toll taken by cholera, malaria and other endemic diseases on the urban population—show that without a net influx of immigrants every year, Calcutta and its mill-suburbs could not have reproduced their population (for documentation, see Ghosh 1984: Chapter 3).

The mill workers were men living mostly without their families in the mill-suburbs in unhygenic conditions without minimum sanitation facilities. There was little medical attention available in case of disease. They were liable to be kicked out any time by the *sardars* or *sahib* bosses. Under these circumstances, the mosques or the temples would provide several points of contact and solidarity to the workers. In the mosques they would meet people of their own locality and religion, talk about their need for mutual help, pray and try to find solace in religion when worldly goods were so patently short: the mosques would also often have attached to them *mullahs* who would practise the *tibbia* system of medicine (cf. Metcalf 1982: 103–04). These were also places where financial help would be given out to the needy. Some mosques also provided temporary living quarters.

Chakrabarty too readily dismisses the materiality of religious practices as he also somehow thinks that the only consciousness that matters is the one that is expressed in riots and strikes. Radical social scientists have long ceased to accept that workers are always manipulable according to the needs of capital. They have also ceased to accept that the capitalist is an undisputed despot even within the factory gates, as Marx (1867: Chapters 13–15) had claimed, and have extended their view of the area of struggle to the whole of society, including the factory and the farm. There is an abundance of literature now on the politics of the workplace (for example, Burawoy 1984; Friedman 1977; Lazonick 1979). Because Chakrabarty depends so much on official sources which also reflect a preoccupation with law and order, the areas of silence in the official accounts also become the areas of silence (and blindness) for Chakrabarty.

We go back to the question of Chakrabarty's understanding of the vocabulary of political economy. He writes: '"Needs", that is, "utility", the celebrants of political economy will tell us, is the key to the secrets of consciousness' (p. 211). It is a sign of his lack of familiarity with the relevant literature that he confuses 'needs' with 'utility'. The literature on utilitarianism is strewn with mangled corpses of 'utility', 'needs', 'well-being', 'functioning', etc., which started out as the major protagonists around which the discipline of economics was to be built. But, at the same time, they are revived from time to time to act as foot-soldiers in some major theoretical debate, or to form the phalanx in support of some major welfare programme. 'Freedom' and 'capabilities' are domains that are favoured by an influential group as the foundation concepts of welfare economics. (For a sampling of the controversies, see, Sen and Williams 1982; and Sen 1985 and 1987.)

Few economists would maintain that 'needs' are 'the key' to the secrets of consciousness. But most students of society, whether trained in political economy or not, would find it surprising to be told that the experience of living perilously near the margin of subsistence, of being exposed to the threats of disease and death, or living away from their nearest family members year in and year out, should somehow not enter into the consciousness of these people. Chakrabarty has a mishmash of philosophical-sounding phrases to invoke in support of his stance, but no logically defensible argument that I can lay my hands on.

IV

I come now to the methods of investigation employed by Chakrabarty. This book is supposed to be about working-class consciousness. Yet virtually all the evidence comes from official reports about the working class. There are other kinds of accounts which Chakrabarty has ignored (see, for example, Ahmad 1974; Pachhal 1987; the latter may have been published after the manuscript of Chakrabarty's book was ready, but the former was available to him). Perhaps there is no way but to depend on the official record most of the time. But then he should have been careful in interpreting the record. Take, for example, his treatment of the 'traditional *ma–baap* relationship' that was supposed to exist between managers and workers in jute mills (p. 163).

From Chakrabarty's account it appears that the workers must have believed in such a relationship. Yet, all the evidence comes from the accounts given by mill managers or persons taking their testimony as unvarnished truth. In the first place, workers must have expressed their thoughts in Hindi, Bengali, Oriya, Telugu or any other Indian language, rather than in English. Even if the officials knew any of the vernaculars, it was generally a pidgin version in which they would communicate with the workers. So when we get official versions of workers' thoughts, we should expect them to reach us through layers of transcription, translation and distortion at several stages. Does a researcher really hope to get at the 'workers' consciousness' by using such methods, even when augmented by the strategy of inversion?

Moreover, we would expect a considerable amount of dissimulation in the workers' publicly-expressed attitudes. It does not seem to have occurred to Chakrabarty that the workers' supposed invocation of a *ma–baap* relationship might well have been a strategic choice: to appear defenceless in the face of terroristic authority, to introduce conflicts between managers and *sardars* and try to find chinks in the monolithic structure of authority. A *ma–baap* relationship was a construct that many workers might have wanted the managers to believe in, without they themselves giving much credence to it. There would also be differences between different workers in the degree to which they would have internalized such a strategic construct as part of their verbally-expressed belief system. If

Chakrabarty does believe in the complexity of working-class culture, he should not rush to take literally the English translation of statements made by workers in a different language and idiom in front of official bodies, which would themselves have been antagonistic entities to them most of the time.

Similar exception can be taken to his treatment of the workers' supposed attitude to persons like A.C. Banerjee, K.C. Roy Chowdhury, or Prabhabati Dasgupta. The workers sought their help because they were supposed to be rich or powerful, and willing to fight on behalf of the workers. Chakrabarty comments on their attitude in the following fashion: 'The poor man making a spectacle of his sufferings, and thus obtaining the compassion of the rich, was, and still is, a familiar sight in societies marked by pre-capitalist cultures' (p. 143). If that is so, Britain has been a hotbed of pre-capitalist culture for as long as we can remember. Has Chakrabarty never come across the appeals of numerous distressed gentlefolks' associations? Has he not even heard of women with children at their breasts begging in the streets and underground stations of London and Paris today?

Apart from the peculiar locution Chakrabarty resorts to, this kind of treatment again betrays his failure to fully grasp the authoritarian order that the British maintained in India. Inside the gates of the factory or the workers' *bustees,* the authority of the *durwan* or the *sardar* was the one the worker was governed by, as Chakrabarty has so well brought out. Only rarely would this authority need to be backed up by the *sahib*. If the *sahib* or the *durwan* did something that went beyond the usual bounds of terror under which the workers laboured, there was virtually no appeal against him. The police constable would normally simply obey the orders of a *sahib*, and would reinforce his authority with virtually unlimited physical violence (for a graphic account of the violence perpetrated by the police nearabout the time of the Talla riots, see, Atarthi 1351 BS: 14–18). The 'law' part of the 'law and order' enforced by the British was virtually inaccessible to a mill worker living on the margin of subsistence. The British had succeeded in making 'law' so expensive and so distant that workers needed special help in order to secure whatever relief it could give them. Chakrabarty would have spent his time better if, instead of venting his contemptuous anger against the workers who were so damned by 'pre-capitalist culture', he had tried to unravel the toils of oppression which bound the workers in an authoritarian state.

It may be claimed that the author's enquiry was into the 'moment' of consciousness of the workers; and that it was not incumbent on him to ask questions about the aetiology of consciousness, or to give an account of the temporal antecedents of that consciousness. The structuralist or post-structuralist nuances of the author's discourse might incline a reader to use this excuse. The trouble with this way out of Chakrabarty's difficulties is that he uses a chronological characterization of consciousness all the time. His 'pre-capitalist culture' cannot be transformed into 'non-capitalist' or 'post-capitalist' entities through any known logical transformation. Moreover, he explicitly dates the origin of particular manifestations of culture authority, power relations, etc. For example, he writes:

> There is no denying that the authority of the mill manager was bolstered by his position as a member of the ruling race. But, in some respects, one also cannot help noticing the 'Indian' elements of this authority. Hence the close resemblance—often commented upon in the nationalist press—of the jute-mill manager's authority to that of the nineteenth-century indigo planter in Bengal, who in turn modelled himself on the Bengali (or North Indian) landlord. (p. 166)

So, in Chakrabarty's discourse, the jute-mill manager harked back to his predecessor—the indigo planter in Bengal. In fact, indigo planters in Bihar and jute-mill managers were contemporaries over a long period; and both groups lorded it over workers and peasants from very similar backgrounds. The indigo planter, poor creature that he was, had to model himself on the Bengali landlord!

Thus for Chakrabarty chronology *is* important. But he practises a double sleight-of-hand even as he uses the chronology. The Bengali landlord on whom the indigo planter modelled himself was, in fact, a creature of British dominion. And did the cousins and business associates of planters from the slave-using West Indies really need the Bengali landlord for a lesson in brutality? Did the indigo planter know that he was modelling himself on the Bengali or north Indian landlord? On the contrary, the indigo planter or any other true-born European, regarded the prospect of 'going native' as 'one of the worst states to fall into' (see Yang 1989: Chapter 1, for references to middle and late nineteenth-century accounts of the typical Europeans' attitude to Indian customs). Chakrabarty stresses conscious intention at various points of his discourse. But when it suits him, he often lapses into portraying the colonial rulers as creatures of the society they have fallen into.

Through such sleights-of-hand Chakrabarty simultaneously recognizes and negates the importance of the colonial character of the state apparatus. Chakrabarty's reductionist methodology does not allow him to analyse the transformations brought about by social and economic processes, or lay bare the structures that enable certain processes to be reproduced. Many economists and historians have in the past tried to analyse how the apparatus of British rule and the spread of international capitalism at the same time transformed and preserved many elements of the pre-capitalist social structure, modes of exploitation and ideology (see, for example, Bagchi 1982: Chapters 2 and 6; Bagchi 1988). Historians of northern India have underscored the modes of control instituted by the major landlords under the aegis of the British *raj* (Ghosh 1984: Chapter 1; Mitra 1985; Yang 1989). The racialist ideology of the British ruling class in India has also received attention from radical observers and social scientists (House 1949; Bagchi 1970; Bagchi 1972: Chapter 6; Ballhatchet 1980; Chattopadhyay 1990). I had hoped that a historian with Chakrabarty's sophistication would add a new dimension by illuminating the area of workers' consciousness for us. But by failing to search out the workers' real voice, as opposed to the voice recorded in the official discourse, by using the workers more as exemplars of Chakrabarty's method and as mute witnesses to his *angst* about the state of the world, and by refusing to situate the human condition of the workers in their changing historical context, Chakrabarty has disappointed the great hopes he had aroused.

However, the arousing of hopes and bringing to the surface new questions are in themselves a considerable contribution. Despite my reservations I found his discourse never dull—a compliment that cannot be paid to the work of many a worthy social scientist. I also think that the legacy of colonialism is still a potent force in Indian society. Just as the British could not entirely negate India's pre-colonial past in spite of many efforts to the contrary, in post-Independence India we have inherited the problems of barriers created by class, by ethnic and linguistic differences, by differences in patterns of living of different communities and by numerous untheorized prejudices and superstitions. The task of building in the ideology of *Homo equalis* as the foundation of a democratic society remains largely unfinished. But I would maintain that it serves no purpose, either for scholarship or for effectiveness of contemporary ideological intervention, to treat our ancestors as edifices for projection of our anxieties. They also need to be treated as human beings of flesh and blood, and endowed with minds constantly grappling with their own destinies. If workers turned communal and were unable to defend their interest as workers, or as people striving for freedom, they were victims of a vicious system. As Judith Shklar (1984: 18) has pointed out: 'To blame the victims for their own suffering is simply an easy way to distance oneself from them. Blaming the victims is just like idealizing them.' The difficulties faced by those among them who strived for a better future for the workers need also to be analysed objectively. There is a tendency to condemn them in blanket terms just because they belonged to the same class or status group to which the more radical social scientists studying their efforts belong. I do not see any serious objective served by that kind of attitude either.

References

Ahmad, Muzaffar, 1974, *Amar Jeeban O Bharater Communist Party* (in Bengali), Vol. 2 (incomplete), National Book Agency, Calcutta.

Ahmed, R., 1981, *The Bengal Muslims 1971-1906: A Quest for Identity*, Oxford University Press, Delhi.

Atarthi, Premankur, 1351 BS, *Mahasthabir Jatak* (in Bengali), *Pratham Khanda* (Vol. 1), reprinted, 1393 BS (1986), De's Publishing House, Calcutta.

Bagchi, A.K., 1970, 'European and Indian Entrepreneurship in India: 1900-1930', in E. Leach and S. N. Mukherjee (eds), *Elites in South Asia*, Cambridge University Press, Cambridge.

—— 1972, *Private Investment in India: 1900-1939*, Cambridge University Press, Cambridge.

—— 1976, 'Reflections on Patterns of Regional Growth in India under British Rule', *Bengal Past and Present*, January-June.

—— 1982, *The Political Economy of Underdevelopment*, Cambridge University Press, Cambridge.

—— 1985, 'The Ambiguity of Progress: Indian Society in Transition', *Social Scientist*, No. 141, February.

―――― 1988, 'Colonialism and the Nature of "Capitalist" Enterprise in India', *Economic and Political Weekly*, Review of Political Economy, 30 July.
―――― 1989, *The Presidency Banks and the Indian Economy, 1876–1914*, Oxford University Press, Calcutta.
Ballhatchet, K., 1980, *Race, Sex and Class under the Raj*, Weidenfeld and Nicolson, London.
Basu, Amritlal, n.d., 'Babu' (a Bengali play), in *Amrita Granthabali, Tritiya Khanda* (Vol. 3), Basumati Sahitya Mandir, Calcutta.
Breman, J., 1989, *Taming the Coolie Beast: Plantation Society and the Colonial Order in South-East Asia*, Oxford University Press, Delhi.
Brewer, A., 1980, *Marxist Theories of Imperialism*, Routledge and Kegan Paul, London.
Burawoy, M., 1984, 'The Contours of Production Politics', in C Bergquist (ed.), *Labour in the Capitalist World Economy*, Sage, Beverly Hills.
Chakrabarty, D., 1988, 'Class Consciousness and the Indian Working Class: Dilemmas of Marxist Historiography', *Journal of Asian and African Studies*, Vol. XXIII, No. 1–2.
―――― 1989, *Rethinking Working-Class History: Bengal 1890–1940*, Princeton University Press, Princeton, New Jersey.
Chattopadyay, Bankimchandra, 1366 BS, 'Babu' (in Bengali), *Lokrahasya*, in *Bankim Rachanabali*, Sahitya Sansad, Calcutta.
Chattopadhyay, Basudeb, 1990, *Changing Inter-Racial Relationship in Nineteenth-Century Calcutta*, unpublished paper, presented at the seminar on Calcutta's history, held at the Department of History, University of Calcutta, Calcutta, March.
Dickens, T., 1857, 'A Letter to the Rt. Hon. Vernon Smith M. P. Upon the Professed Judicial Reform in India, 1857', IOL Tract, quoted in N.S. Bose, 1981, *Racism, Equality and Indian Nationalism*, Calcutta, p. 101, and further cited in Chattopadhyay, 1990.
Dunn, J., 1969, *The Political Thought of John Locke: A Historical Account of the Argument of the 'Two Treatises of Government'*, Cambridge University Press, Cambridge.
Friedman, A., 1977, *Industry and Labour*, Macmillan, London.
Ghosh, Parimal, 1984, *Emergence of an Industrial Labour Force in Bengal: A Study of the Conflicts of Jute-Mill Workers with the State, 1880–1930*, Ph.D. dissertation, Jadavpur University, Calcutta.
Hawthorn, G., 1987, *Enlightenment and Despair: A History of Social Theory*, second edn, Cambridge University Press, Cambridge.
Hobson-Jobson (1903), *Hobson-Jobson: A Glossary of Colloquial Anglo-Indian Words and Phrases, and of Kindred Terms, Etymological, Historical, Geographical and Discursive*, by H. Yule and A.C. Burnell (1886); new edn, edited by W Crooke; reprinted, 1968, Delhi, Munshiram Manoharlal.
House, Humphry, 1949, 'Bengal Lights', in *Listener*, March 10; reprinted in House, 1955, *All in Due Time*, Hart-Davis, London.
Laitin, David, D., 1985, 'Hegemony and Religious Conflict: British Imperial Control and Political Cleavages in Yorubaland', in P.B. Evans, D. Rueschemeyer and T. Skocpol (eds), *Bringing the State Bank In*, Cambridge University Press, Cambridge.

Lazonick, W., 1979, 'Industrial Relations and Technical Change: The Case of the Self-Acting Mule', *Cambridge Journal of Economics*, Vol. 3, September.
Long, D., 1979, 'Bentham on Property', in A. Parel and T. Flanagan (eds), *Theories of Property: Aristotle to the Present*, Wilfrid Laurier University Press, Waterloo, Canada.
McLane, J.R., 1977, *Indian Nationalism and the Early Congress*, Princeton University Press, Princeton, New Jersey.
Macpherson, C.B., 1962, *The Political Theory of Possessive Individualism*, Clarendon Press, Oxford.
Marx, K., 1867, *Capital: A Critique of Political Economy*, Vol. 1, translated from the German by B. Fowkers and introduced by E. Mandel, 1976, Penguin, Harmondsworth.
Metcalf, Barbara D., 1982, *Islamic Revival in British India: Deoband, 1860–1900*, Princeton University Press, Princeton, New Jersey.
Misra, B., 1985, *The Growth of Industries in Eastern India: 1880–1910*, Ph.D. dissertation, Calcutta University, Calcutta.
Mitra, M., 1985, *Agrarian Social Structure: Continuity and Change in Bihar, 1786–1820*, Manohar, Delhi.
Olson, M., 1971, *The Logic of Collective Action*, Harvard University Press, Cambridge, Mass.
Pachhal, 1987, 'Surath Pachhaler Smriticharan' (in Bengali), compiled by Amitabha Chandra, *Baromas*, Nabam Barsha, Pratham Sankhya, pp. 41–69, Calcutta.
Pandey, G., 1981, *Rallying Round the Cow: Sectarian Strife in the Bhojpur Region, c. 1888–1917*, Occasional Paper no. 39, Centre for Studies in Social Sciences, Calcutta.
Pocock, J.G.A., 1985, *Virtue, Commerce and History: Essays on Political Thought and History Chiefly in the Eighteenth Century*, Cambridge University Press, Cambridge.
Robinson, F., 1975, *Separatism among Indian Muslims: The Politics of the United Provinces' Muslims, 1860–1923*, Vikas, Delhi.
Sen, A., 1985, *Commodities and Capabilities*, Elsevier Science Publishers, reprinted, 1987, Oxford University Press, Delhi.
—— 1987, *On Ethics and Economics*, Blackwell, Oxford.
Sen, A. and B. Williams (eds), 1982, *Utilitarianism and Beyond*, Cambridge University Press, Cambridge.
Shklar, Judith N., 1969, *Men and Citizens: A Study of Rousseau's Social Theory*, Cambridge University Press, Cambridge.
—— 1984, *Ordinary Vices*, The Belknap Press, Cambridge Mass.
Tinker, H., 1974, *A New System of Slavery: The Export of Indian Labour Overseas 1870–1920*, Oxford University Press, Oxford.
Tully, J., (ed.), 1988, *Meaning and Context: Quentin Skinner and His Critics*, Polity Press and Blackwell, Oxford.
Wollstonecroft, Mary, 1791, *A Vindication of the Rights of Women*, reprinted, 1974, Garland Publishing Co., New York.
Yang, Anand A., 1989, *The Limited Raj: Agrarian Relations in Colonial India, Saran District, 1793–1920*, Oxford University Press, Delhi.

Dualism and Dialectics in the Historiography of Labour

Dualism Rampant

Aristotle, one of the two founding fathers of western European philosophy, in his *Politics,* classified human beings into natural lords and natural slaves: 'that which can foresee by exercise of mind is by nature lord and master, and that which can with its body give effect to such foresight is a subject and by nature a slave; hence master and slave have the same interest' (Aristotle 1988: 2). Thus, in one sentence, he gave an ideological justification for a society based on slavery and for ruling out master–slave conflicts. Even in his time there was a contrary view, and Aristotle was aware of it. So he wrote, a few paragraphs later: 'Others affirm that the rule of a master over slaves is contrary to nature and that the distinction between slave and freeman exists by convention only, and not by nature; and being an interference with nature is therefore unjust' (ibid.: 5).

The Aristotelian distinction between natural masters and natural slaves, and the more general Greek distinction between barbarians who could not speak the logos and Greeks who could, percolated into Christian (especially Thomist) theology and provided the basis for sixteenth-century Spanish debates about the right of American Indians to be treated as free human beings rather than as creatures fit for enslavement (Pagden 1986).

The Aristotelian (and Thomist) dualism was reinforced in the seventeenth century by Rene Descartes, whom Bertrand Russell regarded as the founder of modern (presumably, western) philosophy. Descartes posited a rigid dualism between mind and body, and regarded the mind essentially as a ghost in the machine. Hence there was no human reason why the body of one man could not be directed by the superior ghost living in the body of another man.

The Aristotelian, Thomist and Cartesian distinctions were handy for marauding European explorers, soldiers and sailors in the centuries since Henry the Navigator of Portugal first went looking for gold and slaves down the coast of Africa. Even without any explicit formulation of the labour theory of value, they knew that wealth could be produced only by labour, that those who could effectively mobilize and put to use the largest numbers of workers would in the long run come out victorious. One of the simplest ways of converting thinking and feeling human beings into labour was to ethnicize and dehumanize whole peoples—all non-Christian Africans, for example, and in most cases, Christian Africans as well—into 'barbarians' or 'natural slaves'.

The historiography of labour has not been able to escape the influence of this dualism which lies at the ideological and structural foundation of modern capitalism. Some historians (and economists) have regarded workers as just bodies who respond to changes in wages and behave like inanimate machines once they enter the workplace. Other social scientists regarded them as not fully deserving the name of 'workers' because they failed to respond only as 'economic' men/women to economic stimuli and seemed to have other preoccupations as well. A sub-group among this last class have treated workers as fancy-free beings whose behaviour can be explained entirely by invoking their presumed states of mind, without reference to the way they live, work, socialize or die.

The historiography and the economics of labour are dotted with conceptual frameworks that posit any (or several) of the following kinds of dualism:

(a) Dualism of body and mind.
(b) Dualism of unfreedom and freedom under fully-developed capitalism.
(c) Dualism of unfree (pre-capitalist, pre-colonial) and free (capitalist, colonial) markets.
(d) Dualism of industry and agriculture (as in Lewis-type models of dualistic growth and development).
(e) Dualism of formal and informal markets of labour.

(f) Dualism of primary and secondary markets in models of segmented labour markets and segmented space.

The mind–body duality in the absolute sense will not stand up to serious philosophical or scientific scrutiny. But there is a core of truth in the dualism posited in the different—and sometimes overlapping—frameworks. The spread of capitalist colonialism across the world with its repeated drive to subordinate whole groups of people to the dictates of capital, and the creation and re-creation of new reserve armies of labour within a capitalist society, lie at the heart of dualistic, or more generally, segmented structures. No dualism is entirely static, however, nor is it the case (as is often assumed in Lewis-type models of dualistic growth) that dualism suddenly ceases some day because of the operation of the market, the graduation of a peripheral country to a semi-peripheral status, or because of the exhaustion of the secondary market for labour. Moreover, dualistic phenomena in labour markets are often subordinate to overarching structures of other kinds—such as imperialism, or the operation of a racially-governed system. Completely 'denatured' capital and labour are rarely found, and the operation of the capital–labour relationship is imbricated with discrimination or exclusion based on race, linguistic or regional affiliation and, last but not the least, gender. The results of such discriminatory or exclusionary practices show up also as dualistic or, on closer examination, multiple segmented structures. Uneven processes of growth under capitalism inevitably reproduce and create patterns of dualism. But every kind of dualism produces its own contradictions and, in some cases, the sustaining structures break down or are transformed through the working of a dialectical process. The propositions advanced above will be illustrated with examples from the historiography of Indian labour and also that of the historiography of labour in Africa and Latin America.

Dualism of Mind and Body and Slave Workers

The postulated dualism between mind and body in the field of labour studies is connected with intimations of breaks between European Enlightenment and non-European—Oriental, or barbaric, in an inclusive sense—superstition, between freedom and unfreedom, between supine acceptance by workers of hegemonic constructions and their resistance. As we have seen, the mind–body dualism for slaves was advanced by Aristotle in the first book of his *Politics*, and the Aristotelian tradition was followed in Europe for more than two millennia after its formulation. Slaves were a form of property. Even if slaves were 'property with a soul', that soul was only to be at the service of the master whose living tool the slave was (Finley 1980: Chapter 13; Sabine and Thorson 1973: Chapters 6, 9). Moreover, the people who were peculiarly suitable for being natural slaves were 'barbarians'. By definition, the latter did not speak the Greek language. Since Greek was the sole instrument and medium of communication of reason, therefore, the barbarians were without reason, and fit for enslavement (Pagden 1986: Chapters 2, 3). However, there were barbarians who might still not be suitable for enslavement. In the case of the American Indians after the Spanish conquest of America, it was argued by leading clerics and theologians such as Francisco de Vitoria and Bartolome de Las Casas, that the Spaniards had no right to enslave them. But they could be treated as 'nature's children' and subjected to the discipline of an authoritarian parent (Pagden 1986: Chapter 4).[1]

The doctrine of natural slavery was used to justify the fresh enslavement of millions of people conquered by the Europeans and the Atlantic slave trade in which around 12 million Africans may have been transported to the Americas. In the Arab world and in Asia and Africa, slavery generally took a different form from the chattel slavery of the American plantations (Smith 1954). Moreover, until the rise of plantations in Africa under the stimulus of expanding commerce, slaves in that continent were used for domestic service

---

[1] Stoics and most sects of Christians advanced many arguments for treating all men as equals. However, it is not always clear whether women were subsumed under the general category of 'man'. It is characteristic that in the widely-used textbook on political theory by Sabine and Thorson (1973), there is no entry for 'woman' in the index, nor is there any discussion on the position of women in society and politics. Despite the Stoic–Christian ideals of equality among men, enslavement of Europeans survived in many European countries down to the Renaissance times. Serfdom in eastern and south-eastern Europe was abolished only in the second half of the nineteenth century, and women did not attain political equality with men until the twentieth century.

and for military and administrative purposes, rather than for producing surplus value.

The Africans transported across the Atlantic and employed in the plantations and mines of the Caribbean, North America, Brazil and Peru were probably the largest mass of black workers employed in capitalist enterprises before the rise of capitalist-style plantations, mines and factories in Asia and Latin America from the nineteenth century. Most planters tried to practise the theory of natural slavery or natural childhood on the lives of the slaves employed by them (Craton 1978; Dunn 1987). However, the slaves resisted, most often in the mode of daily and silent protest, by 'idling', shirking the more arduous kinds of labour, running away, refusing to produce children, and dying untimely, thus damaging the valuable property of the slave-owners (of course, slave prices would adjust to reflect this unruly behaviour of the living tools). But slaves also revolted. The first act of abolition of large-scale, western-style plantation slavery was carried out not through white, anti-slavery propaganda or legislation, but through a revolt organized by the slaves themselves. In 1791, the slaves of the French colony of St Domingue (today's Haiti) rose in revolt; by 1803, they had established the first black republic in the western hemisphere, three years before the British abolished trade in slaves in their dominions (James 1989).

The revolution led by Toussaint L'Ouverture was the most famous of the slave revolts. But there were many others, big and small (Genovese 1979; Craton 1982 and 1987). In most of these revolts, one of the rights the slaves demanded was the right to strike: they obviously saw themselves first and foremost as workers, exactly as in fact their owners did. Thus, in British Guyana, on 16 August 1823, slaves of 60 estates, 30,000 in number, rose in revolt, and when the British Governor of the colony met them, the rebels told him: 'God has made them of the same flesh and blood as the whites, that they were tired of being slaves to them, that their good King had sent orders that they should be free and they would not work no more' (Craton 1982: 283).

Again, in Jamaica, around Christmas 1831, about 60,000 slaves from 200 estates rose up in what was essentially a strike action, and bound 'themselves by oath not to work after Christmas as slaves, but to assert their claim to freedom, and to be faithful to each other' (Craton 1982: 291–321; Craton 1987: 273).

In all the three major slave revolts in the British Caribbean—Barbados in 1816, Guyana in 1823, Jamaica in 1831—the black workers on the plantations took care not to damage property or the plantations, and only used the threat of force as a backing for strike action and for their bid for freedom (Craton 1982 and 1987). But all three were suppressed by the planters and the British colonial authorities with exemplary ferocity; in each case, they shot down and executed several hundred revolting slaves, and sent countless others to jail. The ferocity was provoked by the challenge to white racism, the threat to their profits and, above all, the perceived danger to an order based on naked coercion rather than consent. However, the revolt of 1834 sealed the fate of slavery in the British Caribbean. It was seen that neither Christianizing the slaves nor ameliorating their condition would save the existing order, and that the greed of the plantocracy might endanger British imperium in the region—the fate of the erstwhile French St Domingue was fresh in everybody's memory. Thus, the mind–body dualism, in the case of the slaves in the British Caribbean, ended in the termination of slavery and the gaining of legal freedom by the plantation workers.

The Dualism of Freedom and Unfreedom under Capitalism

In Marx's definition, capitalism in a pure form is a system under which the whole society is polarized into two classes, namely, a class of capitalists who own and control the means of production, and a class of workers who are free in a civil sense—in daily life they are not subject to the arbitrary power of any individuals or private organizations—but who are dispossessed of all means of production and can survive only by selling their labour power. These workers are thus doubly free, in the sense that the only authority that can regulate their daily life is the state—within a framework laid down by law—but they are also freed of all their means of production, and hence survival, other than their labour power.

What seems to have escaped the notice of many observers is that workers are also doubly unfree under the capitalist system. First, when the workers sell their labour power and enter into an employment relationship with a capitalist, the latter can exercise an arbitrary authority (within widely defined legal limits) over the workers (Marx 1887/1960: Chapters 13–15; Coase 1937; Simon 1982; Bagchi 1997). Essentially, the worker is subjected to the political authority of the capitalist for the duration of the relationship. This authority can extend outside the workplace, as in many company towns, or as in the relation prevailing between managers of large Japanese firms and their workers. But even without such an extension of the political relationship outside the labour process, the political nature of the worker's surrender of his freedom to the employer remains an irreducible core of the employment relation.

Second, workers are forced to sell their labour power in order to survive, and have very little control over the way they want to live. As Marx (1857–58/1973: 488) put it in the *Grundrisse*, the worker is denied the possibility of realizing his full potential, viz., 'the full development of human mastery over the forces of nature as well as of humanity's own nature and the absolute working out of his creative potentialities'.[2]

As in the case of other dualisms, the contradiction between capitalist unfreedom and nominal freedom in the marketplace, unfreedom within the labour process and apparent liberty within the broader society, lead to tensions and struggles. The history of the workers' struggle for more control over their lives in the workplace has been the subject of extensive research by Braverman (1974), Friedmann (1977), Burawoy (1983), Elbaum, Lazonick, Wilkinson and Zeitlin (1979), Elbaum and Wilkinson (1979), David Noble (1979) and others, and we will not try to summarize that literature here. Similarly, the struggles for trade union rights, social democracy and socialism in western European countries and other advanced capitalist countries can be regarded as struggles for workers to attain greater control over their lives outside the workplace (and inside as

---

[2] Interestingly enough, Sen's idea of freedom is much closer to Marx's idea of emancipation or end of alienation for class-bound human beings, than to the bourgeois–liberal idea of freedom as a mere absence of arbitrary interference with people's lives (Sen 1987, 1993). A person's agency and her well-being are both involved in the concept of freedom. The denial of well-being can restrict freedom just as the denial of agency fractures it. For a slightly different view of capitalist unfreedom, see Cohen (1983).

well) and to acquire a greater share of labour power. Since my focus is on third world countries, I will leave aside these very big areas of debate with the comment that when all the so-called pre-capitalist forms of unfreedom are ended, problems of capitalist unfreedom within the workplace, in the broader society and within the family still remain and appear in their stark form.

Unfreedom within the family should be included as the inevitable accompaniment of capitalism as we have known it. Although Marx and Engels predicted in the *Communist Manifesto* the disappearance of the family itself before the onslaught of capitalism, patriarchy has in fact served as a powerful lever of labour control and a device for subsidizing the social reproduction of labour, and hence capital itself, in all capitalist countries. Engels (1884/1970) laid the basis of the Marxist theory of the family as a system of control and reproduction in class societies, but it has been only in the last thirty years or thereabouts that radical social scientists and feminists have laid bare the tentacles of patriarchy and their transformations in advanced capitalist societies. In all colonial and ex-colonial countries, the alien rulers and indigenous ruling strata have collaborated in the reproduction of patriarchy, even as they have striven to individuate labour power including that provided by women; we will illustrate this later with the help of Sen (1996).

Marxist Historiography and Mind–Body Dialectics

Frederick Engels wrote the first systematic biography of the workers as a class (1845/1962). Marx and Engels devoted their lives to the study of workers in their subjugation to the capitalist mode of production, and their potential as the creators of a new mode of production and a new society where the subjection of the workers to the capitalists and to the imperatives of a profit-driven market would be ended. In Marx's single-minded concentration on illumining the nature of the working of the capitalist mode, he did not pay much attention to the workers' agency, even when they are subject to the dictates of capital. His attention was centred on the social and political devices by which capital seeks to bind them down. But Marx and Engels certainly did not believe in mind–body dualism, or in the thesis that workers, as soon as they become sellers of labour power, miraculously shed all their other identities except in relation to their fellow-workers, and the capitalist control they have to confront daily. In his astonishingly precocious book on the working class, Engels fully recognized the cultural identity of particular groups of workers—the Irish as against the English, for example—and similar references recur in their works and correspondence in later years also.[3]

In his path-breaking work, Engels commented extensively on the degraded living conditions of Irish workers in England (Engels 1845/1962: 124–27). But unlike cultural determinists, he did not attribute the degradation of the Irish to culture but traced it to the degraded conditions under which they lived in Ireland. He went further and drew the connection between absentee landlordism and British colonialism in Ireland and the desperate poverty of the Irish. Engels, and later Marx, traced the huge waves of immigration from Ireland to the Irish famine, caused by the failure of the potato crop, against the backdrop of the abject poverty of the ordinary Irish (Marx 1853; Marx 1857: Chapter 25).

Thus, Marx and Engels were fully aware of the actual working person's cultural conditions and his/her further degradation caused by enforced competition with one another. It is surprising, therefore, that Marxists should be accused of being, in a sense, corporeal determinists. That is to say, the opponents of Marxism as a framework of conceptualization (and, hopefully, organized action) have often accused Marxist scholars and activists of neglecting the thought processes of workers except in so far as they should be (without finding out whether they actually are) directed towards the overthrow of the capitalist order. Certainly, the activists among the Marxists consciously or unconsciously attributed to the workers a degree of class consciousness they might not possess, and prolepsis was a method of exhortation for them. Marxist or radical scholars also often tended to focus more on the emergence of the 'new man', unfettered by the trammels of the old society, than on the actual

---

[3] Engels may have been influenced in some of his views on Ireland by the authors he consulted and used, such as James Kay Shuttleworth (1832) and Thomas Carlyle (1840). But, of course, he drove his analysis down to the social and economic roots of the problems of the workers (including Irish workers), and would not rest content with moralizing on the evils of modernity, or with meliorist prescriptions.

nature of consciousness of the workers (Gorky's *Mother* is a celebration of the 'new woman' as well).

Such accusations, however, cannot be made about the three most prominent Marxist historians of labour, society and consciousness in the first industrializing society in our times. Christopher Hill's primary focus, throughout a long and active career, was on the state of consciousness of the revolutionaries and their opponents, the artisans and the magistrates, the country and the court in Britain between the 1640s and the 1760s (Hill 1940, 1974, 1975). Eric Hobsbawm has written as much about the consciousness of the labouring poor as about their material conditions of living (see, for example, Hobsbawm 1962: Chapters 11–13). E.P. Thompson made his mark as a major historian of post-war Britain with his magisterial *The Making of the English Working Class* (1963). The investigation of the consciousness of the British workers and the poor in general has since then become a major preoccupation among non-Marxists as well as Marxists.

Mind–Body Dualism in the Indian Historiography of Labour

What can we say about the mind–body dualism in the Indian historiography of labour? In this field, as in most other fields of academic studies, Marxists were (and probably still are) in a grievous minority. But almost from the beginning of serious academic discussion of Indian labour history—starting with Rajani Kanta Das (1923)—studies covered wages and working hours, the work environment, and the constraints workers were subjected to or the protection they were given by legal measures adopted by the colonial state. Those studies, however, tended to be bounded by data thrown up by official inquiries into the conditions of labour instituted by a number of Factory or Plantation Labour Commissions, or by officials looking into complaints of shortage of labour, or finally, by the Royal Commission on Labour.

The legislative protection given to labour, say, in the form of limits on the hours of work, or safety provisions, was limited to those factories which were subject to the jurisdiction of official inspectors of factories. Data on wages and employment were also collected on the basis of the same jurisdiction but were periodically supplemented by information collected during the censuses or occasional inquiries into conditions of labour. Moreover, the attention of the major trade union movements and organizations was primarily focused on getting workers in organized factories into their fold. These limitations of the inquiries and trade union activities tend to be reflected also in works on labour history. One part of the history would cover wages and other conditions of work in factories, and another part would deal with the trade union movement (cf. Singh 1965).

However, the more perceptive historians of workers' conditions, while in the main sticking to this kind of bifurcated description and analysis, also inquired into the ways in which the so-called organized and unorganized sectors interacted. For example, Buchanan (1934) devoted four chapters in his book to 'Labour: Sources and Conditions', 'Wages and Subtractions: Debt', 'The Worker's Standard of Living', and 'The Labour Movement'. In these chapters he inevitably had to glance over the factory walls towards the larger world the workers came from, the selection process in which the jobber played a prominent part, and the occasional strikes in which the workers' local environment and loose associations played a role. Out of eighteen chapters in Mukerjee (1945/1951), three were devoted to 'agricultural background' and to the methods of recruitment in plantations and mines, one to female and child labour, one to the standard of living of the workers (in addition to several chapters on the wages of labour), and one to trade unionism. The world outside the factory gates made its appearance in virtually all these chapters, and the interaction between the organized and the unorganized sectors made its presence felt in a separate chapter devoted to contract labour.

Other examples of this genre include the chapters on 'Trade Union Movement' by V.B. Singh, 'Condition of Workers: 1880–1950' by Jurgen Kuczynski, and on 'Levels of Living of Industrial Workers' by K. Mukerji, in Singh (1965). While none of these books devoted separate chapters to the workers' consciousness, none of them treated the workers as simply animate machines either. And none of them can be accused of treating an organized trade union movement as the only evidence of workers as thinking beings. Virtually all of them pointed out that workers resisted through unorganized, or rather non-visibly organized, strikes or work stoppages and other kinds of protest. They also pointed out the difficulty of workers organizing themselves when they had to work up to fifteen hours a day under inhuman conditions, on a pay which did not allow them to live for long.[4]

In later years, a number of sociologists carried out 'social–anthropological' studies of Indian labour. Lambert (1963), Seth (1968), Holmstrom (1976, 1985) and Ramaswamy (1977) are some of the leading examples of such studies. They looked at the workers' immediate work environment, the workers' response to that environment, and their consciousness in general. Not all of them, however, tried to relate the workers' consciousness to the larger socio-economic environment or to their historical origins.

The question of the proletarian consciousness of plantation, mining and jute-mill workers has come up in the books and articles of Amalendu Guha (1977) and Ranjit Das Gupta (1984, 1985, 1994). The issue of worker consciousness became the fulcrum of Chakrabarty's study of jute-mill workers (Chakrabarty, 1989). More recently, Chandavarkar has published his study of the work environment, the habitat and consciousness of the cotton-mill workers of Bombay, and assessed the influence of E.P. Thompson on Indian history in general and historians of Indian labour in particular (Chandavarkar 1994, 1998).

Hopefully, the age of mind–body dualism in Indian historiography of labour is over. The task in the future will be to relate the worker's consciousness to her environment in the workplace, her home and familial environment, her existential links, and to see all of them in relation to the continuities and changes in the politics and economics of the region and the country as a whole.

Debates continue, however, about the nature of worker consciousness, and the means employed to read that. In spite of the

---

[4] These examples again demonstrate the hollowness of the claims of the more strident proponents of the Subaltern School of historiography that it was only the advent of that school that restored the notion of agency to peasants and workers. Of course, these proponents do not hide their intention of trashing Marxist and radical historiography (see, for example, Prakash 1994; Chakrabarty 1998). But one could wish that they were less cavalier in their treatment of historical evidence.

work of social anthropologists and the increasing use of the resources of private papers and oral history, the chief sources of historians' evidence are official documents of the British period. These documents reflect the pre-occupations of the officials and the (mostly European) employers and managers, rather than those of the workers. The reports purport to reproduce workers' statements; but we must remember that those statements were made in the presence of people whom the workers saw as their bosses or rulers, rather than as interlocutors before whom they could express themselves freely. Moreover, the statements would have been made overwhelmingly in the vernaculars and the process of translation into English itself would produce meanings that the workers may not have had in their minds. For example, when the workers made statements to the effect that they regarded their European managers as their *'ma-baap'* (that is, their parents), were they expressing what they truly believed or were they saying what they thought the *'sahibs'* expected to hear, knowing they would be annoyed if the workers did not profess such sentiments (Bagchi 1990)? Moreover, attributing a univocal meaning to workers' statements in such contexts is to miss the dialectical tensions that mark the relations between workers and managers, the propertyless and the propertied, the ruled and the rulers. As Thompson (1991: 66) noted, in eighteenth-century England, 'The same man who touches his forelock to the squire by day—and who goes down to history as an example of deference—may kill his sheep, snare his pheasants or poison his dogs at night' (see also Sarkar 1997: 58–59).

Apart from how we read the officially recorded evidence, there is also the question of how the workers express their will as free agents. There are at least two different issues involved here. The first is the role of so-called 'outsiders'. The second is the way the workers vent their protest when they find their lot unacceptable.

On the question of the role of 'outsiders', some of the best evidence and arguments were recorded by the witnesses before the Indian Factory Labour Commission of 1908 and the Minute of Dissent to the *Report* written by T.M. Nair, M.D. (Nair 1908/1990; see also Bhattacharya 1985; Upadhyay 1990). Nair summarizes the evidence regarding the excessively long hours (going up to thirteen to fifteen hours in the case of cotton mills, and even up to twenty hours in the case of some other factories); the helplessness of the illiterate, ill-nourished and overworked operatives; and the callousness of the general run of managers and mill-owners regarding the housing conditions and health of their operatives (including children not yet in their teens). At the same time, there were mill-owners, such as the Tata group, who themselves wanted legislative restriction of hours of work. They realized the efficiency of shorter hours in the long run, but they knew that if hours were not regulated for all factories, the Tatas by themselves could not go very far in restricting hours of work in their own factories. Legal restriction of working hours of adults was also after all 'outside' interference, instigated not by the organized movement of workers but by the lobbying of Lancashire interests, and desire for amelioration of workers' conditions by the government and a few far-sighted Indian capitalists. Moreover, if any workers were found capable of reasoning on the basis of legal enactments and other supposed measures of protection for workers, they would have been thrown out by the management and probably have faced imprisonment by the state as well. Thus, if any such persons had somehow found employment in the mills, they would no doubt become 'outsiders' soon. Mukerjee (1945/1951: 364–66) expressed alarm at the fact that 'men [had] entered into the field of trade unionism in India who [were] indoctrinating the workers with ideas and beliefs that [ran] counter to such fundamental institutions as property and the state'. However, he commented cannily:

> The employer's objection to 'outsiders' is largely based on his expectation and experience that the executive formed from among the rank and file of the workers will be docile and accommodating. This, if true, would nullify the aims of the trade union which has to conduct negotiations with the employers with courage and determination, not only in times of peace but even during strikes and lock-outs. (ibid.: 364–65)

Thus, historians of labour who bristle at the evidence of social inequality between workers and their spokesmen, ignore the more basic inequality between employers who were supported by a highly coercive state apparatus, and workers with few resources at their command.[5]

There is plenty of evidence of workers' agency, with or without the help of 'outsiders', in the history of labour in colonial India (Punekar and Varickayil 1990: 303–41). And it is not only in the major textile centres of Bombay and Calcutta that we find numerous examples of strikes and other protest action by the workers (Chakrabarty 1989; Bagchi 1990a; Das Gupta 1994). All over India, even with exiguous records, we find evidence of workers in plantations, mines, quarries, and small and large factories, resorting to peaceful protests, and sometimes riots, in redressing their grievances.

In 1904, for example, a seven-month-long strike at the Government Press, Madras, was entirely conducted by the worker leaders. In 1913, the workers of the Perambur workshop of Madras and Southern Mahratta Railways struck work for more than six months, under a leadership from among their ranks (Veeraraghavan and Thankappan 1990). In 1930, the workers of the Kolar Gold Fields (KGF) stopped work in protest against a new registration system introduced by the mine managers. Under this system, all miners would be regarded as criminals unless proved otherwise (Nair 1990). The solidarity between the permanent workers of KGF and the contract labourers proved strong, and the workers were able to continue the strike despite the adoption of highly repressive measures by the mine authorities. The Mysore government became alarmed, however, by the disruptive effect of the strike and deputed an official, M.A. Sreenivasan, to investigate the living conditions of the workers (Sreenivasan 1980). The authorities were perturbed by the invisibility of

[5] In colonial countries, where state coercion of workers in the interest of capitalists was a common practice, capitalists and their agents refused to tolerate a situation in which workers might have something to say about the management of an enterprise. Thus, in the Indian cotton textile industry, when in course of the great Bombay mill strikes of 1928–29, leaders of militant workers acquired better knowledge of managerial practices, the mill-owners took the first opportunity to dismiss them and convert them into 'outsiders'. Schemes of rationalization very often fell through because of the unwillingness of the mill-owners and their managers to negotiate with leaders or engage in collective bargaining on any matters involving internal management procedures (Chandavarkar 1994: Chapter 8).

the workers' leaders (Nair 1990: 79). In this case, it was the authorities rather than the workers who conjured up 'outsiders' as representatives of the workers, for easing their negotiating strategy. In the Meerut Conspiracy Case, by contrast, the authorities damned the 'outsider' leaders of the workers as conspirators against the state —in order to demonize them and curb the militancy of the workers.

Outsiders, of course, could not just impose themselves on the workers; they had to prove their worth in the course of workers' struggle. We cite here just one example of a workers' movement which has been carefully analysed by two scholars, Vinay Bahl (1995) and Dileep Simeon (1995). The Jamshedpur Labour Association (JLA) was set up in 1920 to organize the workers of the Tata Iron and Steel Company (TISCO), with the help of the Indian National Congress. The JLA then led the 1920–21 strike of the TISCO workers (Bahl 1995: Chapter 4). During the course of another major strike, which took place in 1928, however, the workers repeatedly rejected the JLA leadership. They followed leaders either from among themselves, or the leadership of 'communist outsiders', or of Maneck Homi, a local advocate (Bahl 1995: Chapter 6; Simeon 1995: Chapter 2). In many recent accounts of workers' consciousness (for example, Chakrabarty 1989), community affiliation has been generally seen as a barrier to workers' solidarity and as an enemy of the consciousness of workers as a class. However, during the 1928 strike of the TISCO workers, places of worship, such as the Golkhali Jhopra mosque, and ethnic networks, such as those of the Punjabis and Pathans, were utilized to support the striking workers (Simeon 1995: 52–53). This is not to deny that in other contexts, community affiliation could turn into communalism. It is in the nature of the difficult terrain that workers in India and other third world countries inhabit that workers' solidarity can turn into fissiparousness. But the opposite also happens in the crucible of struggle. The political and economic context has to be analysed in every case.

Dualism and Dialectics of Freedom and Bondage

In the historiography of colonial workers, another frequently posited duality is that between free labour under capitalist colonialism and bonded labour in pre-capitalist, pre-colonial times. This dualism is linked up in the conceptual apparatus of the analysts with pre-capitalist values of pre-colonial labour and society. These values are regarded as leftover baggage impeding the thinking and actions of the workers, and the generation of values imparted by pristine capitalism. These values are also regarded as a major obstacle to the attainment of civil freedom that capitalist colonialism seeks to foster (cf. Chakrabarty 1989). The origins of ideas of civil freedom can be traced to the thinkers of the Scottish and the French Enlightenment, and more proximately to European liberalism of the nineteenth century, and finally to Marx and Marxism. Hence, the indignant analysts hold the workers guilty of violating the ideal of attainment of civil rights that they should have guarded as the inheritors of this hallowed heritage.

An initial stumbling block in disentangling the various strands out of which this brand of dualism has been composed, is the unquestioning acceptance by this group of analysts of two related propositions: (a) European (and white North American) workers enjoyed civil freedom in a real sense at the time the major parts of the third world were colonized; (b) there was a ruling-class discourse of freedom which included both property owners and the propertyless in its fold.

Both of these propositions have to be substantially qualified, however, before we reach the second half of the nineteenth century. Irish Catholics were repeatedly subjected to the loss of their civil freedom between the reconquest of Ireland by Oliver Cromwell's army in the 1650s and the passing of the Catholic Emancipation Act in 1829 by the British parliament. This Act was not simply an expression of the enlightenment associated with liberalism. This was produced by the threat of an Irish insurrection. The Duke of Wellington, then Tory Prime Minister of Britain, in introducing the bill for Catholic Emancipation in the House of Lords, noted that civil war was the only alternative to emancipation, 'This is the measure [namely, civil war] to which we must have looked, these are the means which we must have applied . . . if we had not embraced the option of bringing forward this measure' (cited in Beckett 1981: 303).

British colonialism in Ireland, starting from the Norman invasion of that country in the twelfth century, is almost a case study of colonial unreason, denial of civil freedom to the conquered people, and ideological and legal buttressing of that denial through the device of racism. For example, there is clear evidence that from the middle of the thirteenth century, an Englishman could claim 'that he [was] not held' to answer a case on the ground that the plaintiff was Irish 'and not of free blood' (cited by Bartlett 1994: 215). An exactly similar argument would be used in 1851 by Theodore Dickens, an English lawyer practising in Calcutta, when he argued that the Indian subjects of the British Crown could not claim the same benefits of the law and the law courts, as could true-born citizens of Britain (Bose 1981; Bagchi 1998).

In the sixteenth century, when Europeans, led by the Portuguese and the Spaniards, began conquering lands outside Europe, virtually all of Europe, except England and the Netherlands, were governed mainly by feudal institutions. In Spain and Portugal, feudal obligations restricted the civil freedom of a major fraction of the population. Civil freedom was enjoyed by ordinary people in the Netherlands, and to a lesser extent in Britain, at the time they acquired their major colonies in Indonesia, India, Africa, and the Caribbean and its littoral. However, in both countries, the rule of the propertied very greatly restricted the reality of civil freedom for the property-less workers (Boxer 1973; Parry 1973; Schama 1987: Chapters 1–2; Thompson 1991; Corrigan and Sayer 1985: Chapter 5).

If we confine ourselves to Britain, we find that while the remnants of feudalism were terminated by the short-lived Commonwealth and the Restoration monarchy instituted in 1660, an Act of Settlement and Removal was passed in 1662, with the main object of exercising surveillance over the poor (Porter 1990: 127–28). Every native of England was deemed to possess a 'settlement' in one parish, and in one parish only. Tax rates for succouring the poor were levied on property owners since 1597. They were fixed by overseers working under the supervision of magistrates. 'In law a person needed a certificate before leaving his parish of settlement to seek work.... Officers had the power to drive back to their native parish vagabonds and all those without a settlement, liable to become a burden on the rates' (Porter 1990: 128). These powers of the magistrates and the overseers could lead to enormous cruelties, including the death of unmarried pregnant women whose children the parishes did not want to be burdened with. In England, the eighteenth century witnessed criminalization of a whole range of offences against property —and many of them invited the death penalty. Most of the laws, excluding those whose infringement led to capital punishment or long jail sentences, were administered by magistrates who were chosen from among the propertied men of the locality. During his travels in England and Ireland in the 1830s, Tocqueville remarked that 'The whole of English society [was] based on privileges of money' (Tocqueville, note dated 11 May 1835, 1958: 90–91). He then proceeded to provide a catalogue:

> A man must be rich to be a Minister since the style of living expected from him runs him into expenses much greater than what he receives from the State . . .
> A man must be rich to get into the House of Commons because election expenses are immense.
> A man must be rich to be a Justice of the Peace, Lord Lieutenant, High Sheriff, Mayor, or Overseer of the Poor as these duties are unpaid.
> A man must be rich to be a barrister or a judge because the education necessary to enter these professions costs a lot.
> A man must be rich to be a clergyman again because the necessary education is expensive.
> A man must be rich to be a litigant since one who cannot give bail must go to prison. There is not a country in the world where justice . . . is more the privilege of the rich. Apart from the Justices of the Peace, there is no tribunal for the poor man.

The extreme inequality between the propertied and the property-less not only deprived the latter of any political power (since they were all excluded from the franchise till perhaps the Act of 1867), but also seriously restricted their civil freedom. Through all the centuries when capitalism was emerging as the dominant mode of production, women enjoyed few freedoms. They could not assume any powers of the ruling class even if they had property (the monarch in England was an exception). In England, marriage meant a civil death for woman, since a married woman could hardly enter into any legally valid contract without her husband's explicit consent. If freedom meant command over an adequate range of 'functionings'

(Sen 1987, 1993), then, of course, before the advances in sanitation and medicine and the spread of education to all ranks, that is, before the last quarter of the nineteenth century, very few people even in England enjoyed adequate freedom.

When we turn to the discourse of freedom in Europe, we find the real-life difference between the propertied and the property-less being mirrored in that discourse, especially from the time capitalism became triumphant. The political theory in England from the time of Hobbes down to Mill's *Representative Government* was concerned as much with the nature and necessity of political authority, as with the rights of persons subject to that authority. Political theorists are still debating the exact manner in which Hobbes' or Locke's theory of political obligation is to be interpreted. But it is rarely denied that most theorists of democracy or republicanism set out to defend the right to property against arbitrary authority; and many theorists, including the seventeenth-century proponents of republicanism during the English Civil War, equated property and 'propriety' (Macpherson 1962; Dunn 1969, 1984; Pocock 1985). Of course most of the theorists, including Locke, would confine the right to rule to men of property, but would not deny civil liberty to the property-less. But they had a horror of a situation in which the latter could have a part in decision-making regarding the affairs of the realm. For radical republicanism—extending to advocacy of universal male suffrage—we have to wait for Rousseau in the eighteenth century and James Mill in the nineteenth. Locke explicitly denied 'that a man who has been deprived of the means of production [given by God to all men] can be forced into subjection through control over these means' (Dunn 1984: 43). However, few of the theorists who influenced public policy paid much attention to the liability of freedom to be abridged by extreme inequality of economic conditions. Only in the nineteenth century would the horrors of child labour and the killing factory towns of industrial England throw such concerns into relief, and lead to measures to curb the freedom of contract in the interest of the right to life and the minimum requirements for the toiling poor to enjoy civil liberty (Atiyah 1979).

Thus, the ruling classes of the colonizing European powers harboured at best a paternalistic, and at worst a disdainful attitude towards the poor or the lower orders of society. Hence it would be strange if their officials in the dependencies were not imbued with very similar ideas regarding the lower classes under their tutelage (cf. Cain and Hopkins 1993). Although the imperatives of sustaining colonial rule modified some of these attitudes, they coloured the colonizers' treatment of labour and property in the dependent territories.

If the civil and political liberty of workers was systematically breached in nineteenth-century Europe, the workers did not fare much better in the USA, as the long struggle of US workers to gain recognition for trade unions and collective bargaining demonstrates. The USA did not have formal colonies until the acquisition of Cuba and the Philippines in the closing years of the nineteenth century. But US workers could not escape the consequences of racism which had laid the foundation of the prosperity of slave-run plantations, or of colonialism. The Irish immigrants, fleeing from poverty, English landlordism and famine to the land of promise, soon tried to prove that they were 'white' by distancing themselves from anti-slavery campaigns in the USA, and they very often drove the blacks out of their craft occupations. Capitalists were happy to use those among them who were willing to be so used, to displace black workers and resort to wage-cutting. Racism long remained a problem fouling white workers' struggle to gain civil freedom, effective political rights and a decent standard of living (Roediger 1991; Ignatiev 1995). Thus, colonialism and racism had a major impact on capital–labour relations in the most advanced capitalist country without any trammels of formal feudalism. Capitalism created new structures of unfreedom in that land even as it promised unlimited freedom for capital to expand.

In the formal colonies of the imperial countries, of course, 'freedom' for the native was often regarded as a prize to be handed out by the rulers for good behaviour, or withdrawn as a measure of punishment. Moreover, there were at least three different ways in which the imperatives of colonial rule induced the imperial proconsuls to take a nuanced view of how much freedom could be given to workers in the colonies. The first was the imperative of public works. In all colonial territories, in the beginning, the new conquerors wanted to impress workers forcibly for building roads, carrying loads, acting as carters and often as foot-soldiers. They also often commandeered carts, draught animals, boats and fodder from the hapless subjects. In some cases, this was justified as a continuation of the practice of the indigenous rulers whom the colonial power had displaced. But, in many cases, the practice was renewed and expanded under colonial rule. The *mita* exacted from the Amerindians for work in the mines and building roads in Spanish America is a prime example of such extensions (Bagchi 1982: Chapter 3). This cannot be regarded as an exception to be found only in the colonies of backward Spain and Portugal. In 1806, Bengal Regulation XI laid down that it was the duty of the 'native' officers 'to provide troops with whatever bearers, coolies, boatmen, carts and bullocks which may be desirable for the troops to prosecute their route' (Das 1941: 154). Bengal Regulation III of 1820 rescinded some of the provisions but retained others, and 'the impressment of bearers, coolies, and boatmen found sanction alongside the appropriation of carts and bullocks' (Anderson 1993: 98). Similar legislative measures were passed in Bombay and Madras.

Secondly, explicit legal provisions and practices in the colonies restricting the freedom of the workers were introduced and sustained in the interest of white employers—mainly owners of plantations, forests and mines, but in some cases, also of factories. While a strong anti-slavery agitation was building up in England, equally strong opposition was offered by the planter interests of the Caribbean. Even if, ultimately, slave trade was banned in British territories in 1807, actual slavery even in the Crown colonies was not abolished until 1833. As we have seen, this legislation was the direct outcome of the perceived threat to empire portended by the Jamaican slave revolt of 1831.

The abolition of slavery in the Caribbean was followed by the introduction of indentured labour mainly from British India into European-owned plantations and mines in the West Indian islands, Mauritius, Fiji, Ceylon and South Africa (Tinker 1974). Thus, slavery was followed not by a system run on the basis of free wage labour, but unfree migrant labour. A system of indentured labour was also introduced into the Assam plantations from the 1860s. In South Africa, southern Rhodesia and Kenya, government measures deliberately restricted the access of Africans to land. In South Africa and southern Rhodesia, of course, the system evolved into one of a strict separation between whites, blacks and the so-called 'coloured', on strict racial lines. South African apartheid did not have its origin solely in the racism of the Dutch settlers—the Boers. A series of measures taken by the British officials of the Cape Colony and British settlers also hastened the process. In 1820 the British government of the Cape Colony introduced new white settlers into the territory occupied by the African peoples such as the Ngunis, the Khois and the Sans. The settlers ruthlessly dispossessed these peoples through so-called frontier wars, and African land and herds were systematically taken over by settlers of both Dutch and British origin. The British authorities also introduced a Masters and Servants Act, and laws against vagrancy; it became illegal for proletarianized Africans to live in any place without a proof of employment by somebody.

Between 1845 and 1876, in Natal, another British colony, Theophilus Shepstone, a British administrator and the self-proclaimed Great White Chief of the Natal Zulus, provided a model of labour control along racial lines. He created 'reserves' for the black Africans, from where they could be drawn for servicing the white-controlled commercialized sector (Welsh 1971; Freund 1984: Chapter 4; Sparks 1990: 32, 66; Worden 1995). Following the same model, the administration of Cecil Rhodes' South Africa Company imposed a hut tax on the Africans, confined them to reservations, and introduced pass laws to control their movements (Ranger 1969; Chanaiwa 1985: 202–07). Thus the twentieth-century horrors of apartheid and racist rule in South Africa and Zimbabwe were built on the foundations of the British colonial regime of the nineteenth century. Proletarian workers were created by depriving Africans of their possessions, and they were subjected to extreme degrees of unfreedom almost at once. In the Belgain Congo, an extremely coercive state power put itself behind private enterprise bent on extracting as much profit as possible from exploitation of forest and mineral products. These 'new systems' of African slavery led to extreme cruelty and to genocide (Conrad 1899/1902; Stengers 1969; Coquery-Vidrovitch 1985). These restrictions on worker freedom were operating, be it noted, not in the benighted seventeenth or eighteenth centuries, but in the age of liberalism in Europe, and in South Africa, down to the 1980s (Sparks 1990).

Restrictions on the freedom of the Africans and their access to land in the white-settler economies of Africa were motivated in the first place by the need to make white plantations viable; without a forcibly proletarianized and low-wage labour force, those plantations would not have been feasible in the first place. The same observation may apply to gold mining in South Africa. However, in many of the settler economies, contradictions built up as conflicts of interest surfaced among the white capitalists, particularly when global crises and African resistance reduced the effectiveness of coercive measures over time (Mosley 1983: Chapters 2, 4). But while colonial or white-settler control lasted, coercive methods of labour and land control remained on the statute books, if not always on the ground.

Territorially, the most widespread factor motivating colonial rulers to restrict the civil liberties of the workers was the need of governance itself. The colonial rulers had to generate revenues for maintaining the apparatus of government and the flow of tribute to the metropolitan country. The imperatives of governance also required the local collaborators to be kept content with the colonial dispensation. In the nineteenth century, for example, Africans in territories occupied by Republican France were from the beginning defined as subjects rather than citizens because, it was argued, the latter were too primitive to be given political rights. In French West Africa, slavery was legally recognized down to 1905, when legislation was passed to make it no longer legally enforceable. However, the practice of using forced labour, or the so-called *prestations*, for public purposes was continued (Conklin 1998). In a decree passed in 1912, '*prestations* were defined as annual labour requisitions owed by each African over the age of fifteen to the administration, and were not to exceed a maximum of twelve days a year' (Conklin 1998: 439). The French colonial government at Dakar, by means of a new labour code, put *prestations* at the disposal of private enterprise (a practice that had grown through official connivance without explicit legal backing). Forced labour was receiving official sanction down to the 1930s—in the name of improving the condition of the conquered peoples (Conklin 1998: 440).

When the British launched their final drive for the conquest of Nigeria in the 1890s, the Sokoto Caliphate was the nominal sovereign of most of northern and central Nigeria and the neighbouring territories of Niger and Cameroon (which came to be occupied by the French and the Germans). These territories together had a huge slave population, estimates varying from 1 million to more than 2.5 million (Lovejoy and Hogendorn 1993: 1). From 1890, George Goldie, as the head of the Royal Niger Company, became the spearhead of British expansion in the emirates owing allegiance to the Sokoto Caliphate. Goldie's forays and annexations seemed to threaten the stability of the Sokoto Caliphate itself. Concerned at the prospect of French expansion at the cost of the Caliphate, the British government then authorized the raising of a West African Frontier Force, and appointed Frederick Lugard as its commander. Lugard completed the final overthrow of the Caliphate and installation of British rule by 1903 (Lovejoy and Hogendorn 1993: Chapter 1).

During these campaigns, Goldie and Lugard used anti-slavery rhetoric as one of the main justifications for their annexation policy, and in many cases sheltered and used fugitive slaves as soldiers and auxiliaries. In 1897, Goldie abolished 'the legal status of slavery in the conquered territories. Under this approach, slavery was no longer recognized as a legal institution in the courts, although slavery itself was not abolished and slaves were not emancipated' (Lovejoy and Hogendorn 1993: 6). This approach was first tried out in India, as we shall presently see.

The colonial government was concerned to contain the desertion of slaves because it adversely affected production in the conquered territories. Moreover, revolting or absconding slaves posed a threat to colonial rule. In 1905–06, at Satiru in northern Nigeria, revolt broke out against both the Caliphate, which had surrendered to the British, and the conquering British. This revolt was inspired by radical Muslim clerics, who freed the slaves, and the latter flocked to the banner. The revolt was put down by the British, and they remained wary of fugitive and potentially rebellious slaves.

The dilemma posed to the colonial authorities in managing the transition from production based on slavery to that based on nominally free workers has been well put by Lovejoy and Hogendorn (1993: 65–66):

> Once slave status was abolished, slaves wanted to desert their places of work, concubines began to move off for other men, the supply of food failed because land fell out of cultivation, the once-

powerful and proud became desperate, and ex-slaves began to take the law into their own hands. The proto-colonial state was put into serious jeopardy, since it lacked sufficient soldiers of its own to control the vast spaces, and it was unsure if it had local allies enough to sustain order, let alone trade, food, markets, and prosperity. In short, the old system—slavery by any other name—had to be maintained for the transition.

The British colonial authorities took only one step in the direction of ending slavery after the abolition of the legal status of slavery, and that was to prohibit the enslavement of children born after 1901. However, they sought to curb any tendency the slaves had to run away, by two major items of legislation. One was a vagrancy act, which empowered the government and the Islamic courts to arrest and return vagrants to their places of origin. The other move was effectively to make the state the owner of land, recognize the rights of the older, mainly slave-holding, aristocracy or free peasants to land only on payment of a tax (called 'rent', as in British India), and to deny runaway slaves or vagrants access to waste land. This system kept slavery in place. With further progress of commerce, and economic crises, slavery as an institution declined; but economic crises, insecurity on the side of the poor, and the scarcity of labour experienced by some land-owners tended to reproduce slavery in a 'voluntary' form, and gave rise to a clandestine slave trade. In an enquiry made by the League of Nations in 1936, Nigeria was reported to have about 120,000 slaves, but the real number would come to 400,000 or thereabouts (Lovejoy and Hogendorn 1993: 270–80). Only in that year did the government feel forced to bring in an ordinance freeing all slaves. But from the way in which the real numbers of slaves had been concealed from the official gaze, it would appear that unofficial slavery remained in place even after that date.

In northern India, except in Bihar, most slavery was of the domestic variety. But there was a large number of agrestic slaves in the south. The abolition of legal status slavery by the British government in 1843 had been preceded, as in the case of Nigeria later, by considerable debate in official circles. The majority of the Indian Law Commission submitting their report in 1841 recommended the legal abolition of slavery. But most officials were concerned to protect the integrity of the existing provisions of 'traditional' family laws of Hindus and Muslims (which provided for slaves as heritable property), and the property rights of the masters of slaves (Anderson 1993: 100–03).

In south India, unfree labour was known as *banniyals*, *parakudis* or *puliyas*, and in Bihar as *kamias* (T. Sarkar 1985; Prakash 1990). Their condition could not easily be slotted into the categories of Roman or British jurisprudence. The British produced approximations which did not fit the ground reality. Moreover, right after the termination of 'legal status' slavery, the British were almost immediately forced to interpret 'the freedom of contract' to mean the possibility of being forced into unfreedom by contract because of debts as per terms of contract, or if the persons concerned had incurred obligations they could not discharge (Prakash 1990). Although British Indian courts denounced the 'perpetuity' implied in the setting up of *waqfs* or other religious trusts (Kozlowski 1985), they often recognized hereditary or perpetual bondage contracted through debt (Bagchi 1992; Bhattacharya 1983, 1985; Fox 1984).

Ironically enough, although British India had no contract act before 1874, the unfreedom and criminalization of labour found to be guilty of breach of contract were legalized as early as 1819 by the Bengal Regulation VI of that year (Das 1941: 154–55). That regulation was abolished in 1862. But other items of legislation such as the Masters and Servants Act and legislation authorizing the recruitment and indenture of labour for the Assam plantations and for employment overseas, and criminalizing breach of contract had been already put in place (Tinker 1974; Guha 1977; T. Sarkar 1985; Anderson 1993; Das Gupta 1994).

Hence the history of labour in India can hardly be written in the idiom of civil rights bursting forth under colonial rule. The duality of freedom and unfreedom often got blurred in ideology, legislation and practice. The attainment of civil freedom by workers had often to await struggles by the workers themselves, the perceived threat to imperial rule posed by workers' protests and wider political movements aimed at redressing the workers' grievances, and contradictions within the policy framework of imperial rule.

One of the paradigmatic examples of such conflicts has been

provided by Samita Sen (1996). She has shown that there was a three-way conflict raging behind the framing and implementation of the Assam Labour and Emigration Act (Act VI of 1901). First, in order to redress the sex imbalance in the plantations in Assam and overseas colonies, the Assam planters and the suppliers of indentured labour wanted to recruit as many Indian women as possible. Secondly, however, the Indian patriarchal society was determined to assert the right of husbands and fathers to decide the fates of women of the household. And third, the British Indian government was committed to upholding the sanctity and integrity of the Indian family and also to protecting the freedom of choice of the intended recruit. The Act was an uneasy compromise between the three objectives and the three kinds of interests, with provisions for registration of the intending migrants and establishing the nature of their migration. In many cases, the interests of the recruiting agencies and the callousness or collusion of the district administration defeated the patriarchs, and allowed the recruiters' interests to triumph. Were these instances to be regarded as the victory of freedom (as a wage labourer) over bondage (in the household)? How free would the woman be to exercise her choice or how much 'freedom of well-being' (to use a phrase from Sen 1993) did she possess, once she got to the plantation in Assam, Natal or Mauritius? Once she was taken to the plantation, she would have no means at her disposal to seek other employment, or indeed to physically leave the plantation and go somewhere else. Suppose, on the other hand, patriarchy triumphed, how free, either in terms of well-being or exercise of choice, would the woman remain, if she was simply kept as an exploited drudge of the household? The posing of the duality of freedom and unfreedom by linking it to the other duality of the enlightenment of European rule and the benighted nature of pre-colonial rule misses out these dimensions of the meaning of freedom altogether.

The persistence of personal and familial bondage into a period when private property became the dominant mode of control of assets and unfree persons were regarded as the private property of their masters meant that, even when such bondage was abolished by legislation, the legally free ex-bondsmen (and ex-bonds women) did not really come into the possession of their full civil rights, let alone human freedom in the fullest (Marxist or Amartya Sen's) sense.

In the USA, slavery was abolished during the course of the American Civil War. But it was not until the passing of the Civil Rights Act (1964) exactly a century later, that African–Americans could enjoy their minimal rights as US citizens. Moreover, as an ethnic minority at the bottom of the social ladder the African–Americans had lost, by the 1980s, many of the gains they had made up to the 1970s (Carnoy 1994; Darity and Mason 1998).

In colonial and pre-colonial India, while not all untouchables were bondsmen, virtually all bondsmen belonged to the so-called untouchable castes. Of course, 'untouchability' itself was a severe infringement of civil freedom. The practice of untouchability was made into a legally cognizable offence only after India's Independence. But the so-called untouchable or scheduled castes (so-called because their caste names were entered in a separate schedule of the Indian Constitution, as deserving of special consideration in the way of affirmative action), who are now designated as Dalits (the oppressed), were overwhelmingly property-less and illiterate. There have been no land reforms benefiting the poor or landless peasants, including the Dalits, except in the states of Jammu and Kashmir, Kerala, West Bengal, Tripura and, to some extent, Karnataka. As a result, the Dalits are regularly denied their civil and political rights. In such states as Bihar, Andhra Pradesh, Madhya Pradesh, Uttar Pradesh, Orissa and Rajasthan, they have also been targets of violence by landlords. This violence has also been one of the major reasons for the ability of Naxalite groups in Bihar and Andhra Pradesh to rally peasants in acts of counter-violence against the landlords. Dualism has generated its own particular variant of dialectics in the Indian countryside.[6]

The Dualism of the Formal and the Informal, or the Primary and Peripheral Sectors

Economists, historians and social theorists have postulated another class of dualisms pervading the structure, behaviour and condition of the working class. These have been characterized

---

[6] I have not cited any specific references here, for *The Economic and Political Weekly* regularly contains numerous articles bearing on this theme.

variously as workers belonging to the (a) traditional versus modern sectors, (b) agriculture versus industry, (c) unorganized versus organized (and, equivalently, formal versus informal) sectors, (d) workers with political connections and workers without such connections, and (e) casual versus permanent workers. These postulated dichotomies bear a close family resemblance to the family of models of segmented labour markets, segregated places of residence of workers, and primary versus peripheral or secondary sectors of industry or services in advanced capitalist countries.

In the historiography of Indian labour (and money markets) the distinction between organized and unorganized labour (and money) markets precedes the coining of the distinction between the formal and informal sectors by Keith Hart and its popularization by the International Labour Office, followed by the World Bank (Hart 1973; ILO 1972). However, early historians of Indian labour were aware of the close interconnection between the unorganized and organized sectors, and between conditions in rural and urban areas (Das 1923; Buchanan 1934: Chapters 14–15; Mukerjee 1945/1951: Chapters 1–2 and 14–15). It is now fairly widely recognized that the conditions and standards of living of the workers in formal and informal, or the organized and the unorganized sectors are closely linked. Any differential between the conditions and standards of living of workers in the two sectors in the colonial dependencies or in the developing countries today has more to do with the compulsions of capitalist growth and the nature of the society the workers belonged to, than with 'illegitimate' protection given by the government or won by the trade unions (see, for an excellent discussion of these issues, Portes and Schauffler 1993; Chandavarkar 1994: Chapter 3). However, with decreasing rates of growth of employment in most developing countries, the World Bank, governments and policy advisers of those countries continue to regard the 'informal sector' and dismantling of the few measures of legal protection accorded to a small group of workers in the so-called formal sector as the panacea for employment growth (for an extreme, but by no means atypical statement of this position, see De Soto 1989).

Along with differences in wages, general working conditions, location and general standards of living, the difference between the formal and informal sectors has also been linked to supposed differences in culture, for example, attitude to work, propensity to form trade unions, tendency towards and against riotousness, acceptance or rejection of urbanity, and so on. As serious students of Indian labour history have pointed out, however, such a picture misses out the numerous ways in which the workers in the two sectors interact socially, politically and culturally, and share the vicissitudes of living in an urban environment (Holmstrom 1985: Chapter 6; Chandavarkar 1994: Chapters 3, 5).

The postulation of a difference between the formal and informal sectors builds (although not always consciously) on a generalization about the history of industrialization in western Europe. The creation of a stable and increasingly immobile labour force in factory towns and villages required their deliberate disciplining to the hours of the clock rather than roughly measured movements of the sun across the sky, and assurance of more stable employment at a higher wage than the perceived opportunity cost of labour (Thompson 1967; Hicks 1977). Since skill formation within the new industries was very often an idiosyncratic affair, with considerable dependence on in-house learning by doing, upgrading of the skills of labour went hand-in-hand with the formation of an increasingly disciplined, 'committed' labour force, leading eventually to what have been dubbed as internal labour markets.

However reasonable this may seem, even this bit of the folklore of history cannot be applied to the history of the Indian, or more generally, colonial work forces. First of all, in many cases workers were forcibly pushed into wage employment in factories and mines by various fiscal devices, and through public regulation authorizing coercion (Arrighi 1970, 1973; Bagchi 1982: Chapter 6; Freund 1988: Chapters 3–4). The denial of access to land and forests to a large section of the colonial peoples on the grounds of lack of title, conformity to customary usage, or even conservation of resources (some of these grounds have been referred to earlier) served the same purpose of impressment of the colonial peoples into barracks, '*coolie*' lines, mining settlements, or other slums.

Secondly, in most colonial countries with settled agriculture and large artisanal populations, workers, many of them skilled in craft-work, were rendered destitute through processes of deindustrialization (Bagchi 1976). I have argued earlier that de-industrialization in the regions and phases in which it occurred was basically caused by an absolute fall in demand for artisanal products due to a contraction in domestic demand. The latter was in turn caused by an absolute fall in the incomes of consumers and penetration of the domestic market by factory produce from abroad. There was an associated fall in exports caused by competition from foreign factory goods. This kind of displacement of workers cannot be looked upon as an inevitable preparation for the rise of factory industry, or as a process of substitution of more profitable agricultural exportables for the less profitable artisanal products (Bagchi 1976).

Thirdly, in many colonial countries, including India, before the trade unions made their presence felt, employers were rarely prepared to pay an increasing or even a steady premium for skilled as against unskilled labour. In fact, it has been contended that in the initial years factory industry tended to pay 'too high a wage' in order to attract labour, and the margin between factory and nonfactory wage was eroded over the years (Buchanan 1934: Chapter 14). The quality and availability of data on wages in colonial India or other colonial countries remain problematic (for a useful discussion of the nature of the relevant data in India, see Mukerji 1965). But careful scrutiny of these data has failed to reveal any large or persistent difference between the earnings of labour classed as 'general labour' or '*coolies*' in the factories, and the wages of unskilled labour in the surrounding area (Mukerji 1965; Bagchi 1990a).

In colonial countries, the duality of wages and living conditions of urban versus rural labour, 'advanced and traditional' sector workers, or even skilled versus unskilled labour, was conditioned and even reversed by various constraints of unfreedom and stigmata of discrimination under which workers lived. European planters in Assam or Ceylon planters imported labour from, say, central or southern India, under conditions of indenture, rather than employ local labour, because agricultural wages in surrounding areas were higher than in the plantations. It was the same kind of reverse differential between industrial and agricultural wages that led to the increasing substitution of non-Bengali for Bengali labour in the Bengal jute mills (Bagchi 1972: Chapters 4, 5). The use of trained engineers and technicians in jute mills or other British-owned factories in eastern India was minimal because the racist governance structure of those factories would not allow the employment of such personnel in the mills if they happened to be black or 'native' (Bagchi 1972: Chapter 5; Bagchi 1976a; Chakrabarty 1989). As Mukerjee (1945/1951) remarked, the highest position to which Indians could aspire in most European-controlled factories was that of the *sardar*, who acted as the intermediary between the European supervisory staff and the general run of Indian manual workers. In South Africa the racist regime sustained itself by systematically bribing the white workers with higher wages and better opportunities of moving to supervisory positions, and denying the latter to the blacks, however skilled they might be. Systematic discrimination in wages and employment on the basis of gender was, of course, a universal phenomenon. But appeal to the special nature of being 'white' would have been elicited when the employers faced special challenges from women workers (see, for example, Hyslop 1995).

Finally, capitalism all the time tends to reproduce duality between advancing and declining sectors, and privileged and underprivileged workers, by continually and unpredictably changing the structure of production, and making the workers with no other assets than labour power compete among themselves for jobs and better deals (Shulman 1984; Botwinick 1993; Mason 1995). This is where Marx's macro-economic theory of the capitalist reproduction of the reserve army of labour combines with his theory of capitalist competition to provide us with an analytical framework for discussing segmentation and dualism at many levels—in terms of sectors, race, caste, gender and locality (on the last aspect, see, for example, Tabb and Sawers 1984).

Conclusion

We have been concerned, in the present essay, primarily with the historiography of labour. But our analysis has implications for current dilemmas before labour movements everywhere. Through improvements in medical technology, advances in education and improvement in nutritional standards—however unevenly distributed that improvement is—advanced capitalism has overcome the problem of reproduction of labour. It now seeks to reduce labour power everywhere to a commodity sold in auction markets without any legal or trade union protection. On the other side, by making capital fully mobile while imposing ever-increasing restrictions on immigration of workers from poorer countries, they have now inflicted a double disability on workers in those countries. The workers can neither depend on protection from a disarmed nation-state which is supposed to govern them, nor can they look forward to a better standard of living by moving to countries with higher wages, as European workers did between the 1850s and the 1920s (Hatton and Williamson 1994). Moreover, by seeking to incorporate so-called labour standards in the regime regulating international trade, the G–7 countries are trying to further curtail the markets of less developed countries which are in the throes of a massive recession. Unfortunately, some trade union leaders of the advanced capitalist countries are collaborating in these policy initiatives that would effectively deprive all workers of their well-being, freedom and agency, without realizing that they are helping to further enfeeble the power of resistance of workers in the advanced capitalist countries. It is hoped that recalling the historiography of elite-imposed dualism on workers' lives and consciousness and the resistance provoked by them will help to render more transparent the terms of the current policy debates facing trade unionists and supporters of an egalitarian and free society everywhere.

Non-incriminating thanks are due to Raj Chandavarkar for his comments on an earlier version of this essay.

References

Anderson, M.R., 1993, 'Work Construed: Ideological Origins of Labour Law in British India to 1918', in P. Robb (ed.), *Dalit Movements and the Meanings of Labour in India,* Oxford University Press, New Delhi.
Aristotle, 1988, *The Politics,* S. Everson (ed.), Cambridge University Press, Cambridge.
Arrighi, G., 1970, 'International Corporations, Labour Aristocracies and Economic Development in Tropical Africa', in R.I. Rhodes (ed.), *Imperialism and Underdevelopment,* Monthly Review Press, New York.
——— 1973, 'Labour Supplies in Historical Perspective: A Study of the Proletarianization of the African Peasantry', in G. Arrighi and J. Saul (eds), *Essays on the Political Economy of Africa,* Monthly Review Press, New York.
Atiyah, P.S., 1979, *The Rise and Fall of the Freedom of Contract,* Clarendon Press, Oxford.

Bagchi, A.K., 1972, *Private Investment in India: 1900–1939*, Cambridge University Press, Cambridge.

——— 1976, 'De-industrialization in India in the Nineteenth Century: Some Theoretical Implications', in *Journal of Development Studies*, Vol. 12, No. 2, pp. 135–164.

——— 1976a, 'Reflections on Patterns of Regional Growth in India During the Period of British Rule', *Bengal Past and Present*, Vol. 95, No. 1, pp. 247–89.

——— 1982, *The Political Economy of Underdevelopment*, Cambridge University Press, Cambridge.

——— 1990, 'Working Class Consciousness', in *Economic and Political Weekly*, Vol. 25, No. 30, PE 54–PE 60.

——— 1990a, 'Wealth and Work in Calcutta: 1860–1921', in S. Chaudhuri (ed.), *Calcutta: The Living City*, Vol. I, *The Past*, Oxford University Press, Calcutta, pp. 212–23.

——— 1992, 'Land Tax, Property Rights and Peasant Insecurity in Colonial India', *Journal of Peasant Studies*, Vol. 20, No. 1, pp. 1–40.

——— 1997, *Economic Theory and Economic Organization, I: A Critique of the Anglo–American Theory of Firm Structure*, Occasional Paper No. 165, Centre for Studies in Social Sciences, Calcutta.

——— 1998, 'Workers and the Historians' Burden', in *Bengal Past and Present*, Vol. 117, No. 9, pp. 9–56.

Bahl, V., 1995, *The Making of the Indian Working Class: The Case of the Tata Iron and Steel Company*, Sage, New Delhi.

Bartlett, R., 1994, *The Making of Europe: Conquest, Colonization and Cultural Change: 950–1350*, Penguin, Harmondsworth.

Beckett, J.C., 1981, *The Making of Modern Ireland: 1603–1923*, Faber and Faber, London.

Bhattacharya, N., 1983, 'The Logic of Tenancy Cultivation: Central and South-east Punjab', *Indian Economic and Social History Review*, Vol. 20, No. 2.

——— 1985, 'Agricultural Labour and Production: Central and South-east Punjab 1870–1940', in K.N. Raj et al. (eds), *Essays in the Commercialization of Indian Agriculture*, Oxford University Press, Delhi, pp. 105–162.

Bhattacharya, S., 1985, 'The Outsiders: A Historical Note', in A. Mitra (ed.), *The Truth Unites: Essays in Tribute to Samar Sen*, Subarnarekha, Calcutta, pp. 90–100.

Boahen, A.A. (ed.), 1985, *Africa under Colonial Domination 1880–1935*, Vol. VI of *UNESCO General History of Africa*, Heinemann, Paris and London.

Botwinick, H., 1993, *Persistent Inequalities: Wages Disparity under Capitalist Competition*, Princeton University Press, Princeton.

Bose, N.S., 1981, *Racism, Struggle for Equality and Indian Nationalism*, Firma KLM, Calcutta.

Boxer, C.R., 1973, *The Portuguese Seaborne Empire*, Penguin, Harmondsworth.

Braverman, H., 1974, *Labour and Monopoly Capital*, Monthly Review Press, New York.

Buchanan, D.H., 1934, *The Development of Capitalistic Enterprise in India*, Macmillan, London.

Burawoy, M., 1983, 'Between the Labour Process and the State: The Changing

Face of Factory Regimes under Advanced Capitalism', *American Sociological Review*, Vol. 48, pp. 587–605.
Cain, P.J. and A.G. Hopkins, 1993, *British Imperialism: Innovation and Expansion 1688–1914*, Longman, London.
Carlyle, Thomas, 1840, *Chartism*, London.
Carnoy, M., 1994, *Faded Dreams: The Politics and Economics of Race in America*, Cambridge University Press, Cambridge.
Chakrabarty, D., 1989, *Rethinking Working Class History*, Princeton University Press, Princeton.
——— 1998, 'Postcoloniality and the Artifice of History: Who Speaks for Indian Pasts?', in R. Guha (ed.), *A Subaltern Studies Reader: 1986–95*, Oxford University Press, Delhi, pp. 263–293.
Chanaiwa, D., 1985, 'African Initiatives and Resistance in Southern Africa', in Boahen (ed.), *Africa under Colonial Domination*, pp. 194–220.
Chandavarkar, R., 1994, *The Origins of Industrial Capitalism in India: Business Strategies and the Working Classes in Bombay: 1900–40*, Cambridge University Press, Cambridge.
——— 1998, *Imperial Power and Popular Politics: Class, Resistance and the State in India, c. 1850–1950*, Cambridge University Press, Cambridge.
Coase, R.H., 1937, 'The Nature of the Firm', in *Economica*, Vol. 4.
Cohen, G.A., 1983, 'The Structure of Proletarian Unfreedom', in *Philosophy of Public Affairs*, Vol. 12, No. 1, pp. 3–34.
Conklin, Alice, L., 1998, 'Colonialism and Human Rights, a Contradiction in Terms? The Case of France and West Africa, 1895–1914', *American Historical Review*, Vol. 103, No. 2.
Commander, S., 1983, 'The *Jajmani* System in North India: An Examination of its Status and its Logic Across Two Centuries', *Modern Asian Studies*, Vol. 17, No. 2.
Conrad, Joseph, 1899, *The Heart of Darkness*, serialized in *Blackwood's Magazine*, published and reprinted as a book in 1902, , London.
Conquery-Vidrovitch, C., 1985, 'The Colonial Economy of the Former French, Belgian and Portuguese Zones: 1914–35', in Boahen (ed.), *Africa under Colonial Domination*.
Corrigan, P. and D. Sayer, 1985, *The Great Arch: English State Formation as Cultural Revolution*, Blackwell, Oxford.
Craton, M., 1978, *Searching for the Invisible Man: Slaves and Plantation Life in Jamaica*, Harvard University Press, Cambridge, Mass.
——— 1982, *Testing the Chains: Resistance to Slavery in the British West Indies*, Cornell University Press, Ithaca, New York.
——— 1987, 'What and Who to Whom and What: The Significance of Slave Resistance', in Solow and Engerman (eds), *British Capitalism and Carribbean Slavery*.
Darity, W.A. Jr and P.L. Mason, 1998, 'Evidence on Discrimination in Employment: Codes of Colour, Codes of Gender', *Journal of Economic Perspectives*, Vol. 12, No. 2, pp. 63–90.
Das, A.N., V. Nilakant and P.S. Dubey (eds), 1984, *The Worker and the Working Class: A Labour Studies Anthology*, Public Enterprises Centre for Continuing Education, New Delhi.
Das, R.K., 1923, *Factory Labour in India*, Walter de Gruyter, Berlin and Leiden.

―――― 1941, *History of Indian Labour Legislation*, University of Calcutta Press, Calcutta.
Das Gupta, R., 1984, 'Poverty and Protest: Calcutta Working Class and the Labouring Poor', in Das, Nilakant and Dubey (eds), *The Worker and the Working Class*, reprinted in Das Gupta 1994, pp. 315–405.
―――― 1985, 'Migrants in Coal Mines: 1850s–1947: Peasants or Proletarians?', *Social Scientist*, December, reprinted in Das Gupta 1994, pp. 175–208.
―――― 1986, 'Factory Labour in Eastern India: Sources of Supply', *Indian Economic and Social History Review*, July–September, reprinted in Das Gupta, 1994, pp. 1–55.
―――― 1994, *Labour and Working Class in Eastern India: Studies in Colonial History*, K.P. Bagchi &Co., Calcutta.
De Soto, H., 1989, *The Other Path: The Informal Revolution*, Harper and Row, New York.
Dunn, J., 1969, *The Political Thought of John Locke: An Historical Account of the 'Two Treatises on Government'*, Cambridge University Press, Cambridge.
―――― 1984, *Locke*, Modern Masters Series, Oxford University Press, Oxford.
Dunn, R.S., 1987, '"Dreadful Idlers" in the Cane Fields: The Slave Labour Pattern on a Jamaican Sugar Estate, 1762–1831', in Solow and Engerman (eds), *British Capitalism and Carribbean Slavery*, pp. 163–190.
Elbaum, B., W. Lazonick, F. Wilkinson and J. Zeitlin, 1979, 'The Labour Process, Market Structure, and Marxist Theory', in *Cambridge Journal of Economics*, Vol. 3, No. 3, pp. 227–30.
Elbaum, B. and F. Wilkinson, 1979, 'Industrial Relations and Uneven Development: A Comparative Study of the American and British Steel Industries', *Cambridge Journal of Economics*, Vol. 3, No. 3.
Engels, F., 1845, *The Condition of the Working Class in England*, translated from the German edn of 1891 and reprinted in Marx and Engles, 1962, pp. 3–338.
―――― 1884, *The Origin of the Family, Private Property and the State*, translated from the fourth German edn of 1891, reprinted in Marx and Engels, 1990, pp. 191–334.
Finley, M.I., 1980, *Ancient Slavery and Modern Ideology*, Chatto and Windus, London.
Fox, R.G., 1984, 'British Colonialism and Punjabi Labour', in C. Bergquist (ed.), *Labour in the Capitalist World-Economy*, Sage, Beverly Hills, CA.
Freund, B., 1984, *The Making of Contemporary Africa*, Indiana University Press, Bloomington.
―――― 1988, *The African Worker*, Cambridge University Press, Cambridge.
Friedmann, A., 1977, *Industry and Labour*, Macmillan, London.
Gann, L.H. and P. Duignan (eds.), 1969, *Colonialism in Africa*, Vol. I, *The History and Politics of Colonialism 1870–1914*, Cambridge University Press, Cambridge.
Genovese, E.D., 1979, *From Rebellion to Revolution: Afro–American Slave Revolts in the Modern World*, Louisana University Press, Baton Rouge.
Guha, A., 1977, *Planter Raj to Swaraj*, People's Publishing House, New Delhi.
Hart, K., 1973, 'Informal Income Opportunities and Urban Employment in Ghana', *Journal of Modern African Studies*, Vol. II.

Hatton, T.J. and J.G. Williamson (eds), 1994, *Migration and the International Labour Market, 1850–1939,* Routledge, London.

Hicks, J., 1974, 'Industrialism', *International Affairs,* April, reprinted in J. Hieks, 1977, pp. 20–24.

——— 1977, *Economic Perspectives: Further Essays on Money and Growth,* Clarendon Press, Oxford.

Hill, C., 1940, *The English Revolution of 1640,* Lawrence and Wishart, London.

——— 1974, *The Century of Revolution 1603–1714,* Sphere Books, London.

——— 1975, *The World Turned Upside Down: Radical Ideas During the English Revolution,* Penguin, Harmondsworth.

Hobsbawm, E., 1962, *The Age of Revolution,* Weidenfeld and Nicolson, London.

Holmstrom, M., 1976, *South Indian Factory Workers: Their Life and Their World,* Cambridge University Press, Cambridge.

——— 1985, *Industry and Inequality: The Social Anthropology of Indian Labour,* Cambridge University Press, Cambridge.

Hyslop, J., 1995, 'White Working-Class Women and the Invention of Apartheid: "Purified" Afrikaner Nationalist Agitation for Legislation against "Mixed" Marriages, 1934–39', in *Journal of African History,* Vol. 36, No. 1, pp. 57–81.

Ignatiev, N., 1995, *How the Irish Became White,* Routledge, London.

ILO, 1972, *Employment, Incomes and Inequality: A Strategy for Increasing Productive Employment in Kenya,* International Labour Office, Geneva.

James, C.L.R., 1989, *The Black Jacobins: Toussaint L'Ouverture and the San Domingo Revolution,* W.H. Allen & Co., London.

Kay, J, 1832, *The Moral and Physical Condition of the Working Classes Employed in the Cotton Manufacture in Manchester,* London.

Kozlowski, G.C., 1985, *Muslim Endowments and Society in British India,* Cambridge University Press, Cambridge.

Lambert, R.D., 1963, *Workers, Factories, and Social Change in India,* Asia Publishing House, Bombay.

Lovejoy, P.E. and J.S. Hogendorn, 1993, *Slow Death for Slavery: the Course of Abolition in Northern Nigeria: 1897–1936,* Cambridge University Press, Cambridge.

Macpherson, C.B., 1962, *The Political Theory of Possessive Individualism: Hobbes to Locke,* Clarendon Press, Oxford.

Marx, K., 1853, 'Forced Emigration: Kossuth and Mazzini: The Refugee Question: Election Bribery in England: Mr. Cobden', in *The New York Daily Tribune,* 22 March; reprinted in Marx and Engels, 1971.

——— 1857–58, rpt. 1973. *Grundrisse,* translated with a foreword by M. Nicolaus, Penguin, Harmondsworth.

——— 1887, rpt. 1960. *Capital,* Vol. I, translated from the third German edition by S. Moore and Fl Aveling; reprinted, by Foreign Language Publishing House, Moscow.

Marx, K. and F. Engels. 1962. *Marx and Engels on Britain,* Moscow: Progress Publishers.

——— 1970. *Selected works of Marx and Engels,* Vol. 3, Progress Publishers, Moscow.

—Rpt., 1971. *Marx and Engels on Ireland and the Irish Question,* Progress Publishers, Moscow.

Mason, P.L. 1995, 'Race, Competition and Differential Wages', *Cambridge Journal of Economics*, Vol. 19, No. 4, pp. 545–67.
Mosley, P. 1983. *The Settler Economics: Studies in the Economic History of Kenya and Southern Rhodesia 1900–63*, Cambridge: Cambridge University Press.
Mukerjee, R.K. 1945, 3rd edn. 1951. *The Indian Working Class*, Bombay: Hind Kitabs.
Mukerji, K. 1965. "Levels of Living of Industrial Workers," in Singh (ed.), 1965, pp. 638–60.
Nair, T. M. 1908, rpt. 1990. *Minute of Dissent to the Report of the Indian Factory Labour Commission (1908):* reprinted in Punekar and Varickayil (eds), 1990, pp. 41–62.
Nair, J. 1990. "Representing Labour in Old Mysore: Kolar Gold Fields Strike of 1930," *Economic and Political Weekly*, 25,30: PE 73 PE 86.
Noble, D. 1979. *America by Design: Science, Technology, and the Rise of Corporate Capitalism*, New York: A.A. Knopf.
Oliver, R. and A. Atmore, 1981. *Africa Since 1800*, Cambridge University Press, Cambridge.
Pagden, A., 1986, *The Fall of Natural Man: The American Indian and the Origins of Comparative Ethnology*, Cambridge University Press, Cambridge.
Parry, J. H. 1973. *The Spanish Seaborne Empire*, Harmondsworth, Penguin.
Pocock, J.G.A. 1985. *Virtue, Commerce and History*, Cambridge University Press, Cambridge.
Porter, R. 1990. *English Society in the Eighteenth Century*, rev. edn, Penguin, Harmondsworth.
Portes, A. and R. Schauffler, 1993, 'Competing Perspectives on the Latin American Informal Sector,' *Population and Development Review*, Vol. 19, No. 1, pp. 33–60.
Prakash, G. 1990. *Bonded Histories: Genealogies of Labour Servitude in Colonial India*, Cambridge University Press, Cambridge.
———— 1994. 'Subaltern Studies as Postcolonial Criticism,' *American Historical Review*, Vol. 99, No. 5, pp. 1475–90.
Punekar, S. D. and R. Varickayil, (eds), 1990, *Labour Movement in India: Documents, 1891–1917*, Vol. II, *Factories*, Popular Prakashan for the ICHR, Bombay.
Ramaswamy, E. A. 1977. *The Worker and His Union: A Study in South India*, Allied Publishing House, New Delhi.
Ranger, T. O. 1969. 'African Reactions to the Imposition of Colonial Rule in East and Central Africa,' in Gann and Duignan (eds), 1969, pp. 293–324.
Roediger, D. R. 1991. *The Wages of Whiteness: Race and the Making of the American Working Class*, Verso, London.
Sabine, G.H. and T.L. Thorson. 1973. *A History of Political Theory*, Oxford & IBH Publishing Co., New Delhi.
Sarkar, T. 1985. "Bondage in the Colonial Text," in M. Dingwaney and U. Patnaik (eds), *Chains of Servitude: Bondage and Slavery in India*, Sangam Books, Madras, pp. 97–126.
Sarkar, S. 1997. "The Relevance of E. P. Thompson," in S. Sarkar, *Writing Social History*, Oxford University Press, Delhi.
Schama, S. 1987. *The Embarrassment of Riches*, Collins, London.

Sen, A. K. 1987. *On Ethics and Economics,* Blackwell, Oxford.
—— 1993. 'Capability and Well-Being,' in Martha C. Nussbaum and A. Sen (eds), *The Quality of Life,* Clarendon Press, pp. 30–53, Oxford.
Sen, S. 1996. 'Unsettling the Household: Act VI (of 1901) and the Regulation of Women Migrants in Colonial Bengal,' *International Review of Social History,* Vol. 41, pp. 135–56.
Seth, N. R., 1968, *The Social Framework of an Indian Factory,* Manchester University Press, Manchester.
Shulman, S., 1984, 'Competition and Racial Discrimination, The Employment Effects of Regan's Labour Market Policies,' *Review of Radical Political Economics,* Vol. 16, No. 4, pp. 111–28.
Simeon, D., 1995, *The Politics of Labour under Late Colonialism: Workers, Unions and the State in Chhota Nagpur,* Manohar, Delhi.
Simon, H. A., 1951, rpt. 1982. 'A Formal Theory of the Employment Relationship,' *Econometrica,* Vol. 19, reprinted in H.A. Simon: *Models of Bounded Rationality,* Vol. 2, MIT Press, Cambridge, MA, pp. 11–23.
Singh, V. B. (ed.), 1965. *Economic History of India (1857–1956),* Allied Publishers, New Delhi.
Smith, M.G., 1954, 'Slavery and Emancipation in Two Societies,' *Social and Economic Studies,* Vol. 3, No. 3–4, pp. 239–90.
Solow, Barbara L. and S. L. Engerman (eds), 1987, *British Capitalism and Caribbean Slavery: The Legacy of Eric Williams,* Cambridge University Press, Cambridge.
Sparks, A, 1990, *The Mind of South Africa: The Story of the Rise and Fall of Apartheid,* Heinemann, London.
Sreenivasan, M.A., 1980, *Labour in India: Socio-Economic Conditions of Workers in the Kolar Gold Mines,* Vikas, New Delhi.
Stengers, J., 1969, 'The Congo Free State and the Belgain Congo before 1914,' in Gann and Duignan (eds), 1969, pp. 268–92.
Tabb, W. K. and L. Sawers (eds), 1984, *Marxism and the Metropolis: New Perspectives in Urban Political Economy,* 2nd edn., Oxford University Press, New York.
Thompson, E. P., 1967, 'Time, Work-Discipline, and Industrial Capitalism', *Past and Present,* Vol. 38, pp. 56–96.
——, 1991. *Customs in Common,* Merlin Press, London.
Tinker, H. 1974. *A New System of Slavery,* Oxford University Press, Oxford.
Tocqueville, A. de., 1958, *Journeys to England ad Ireland,* translated from the French by G. Lawrence and K. P. Mayer, ed. by J.P. Mayer, Yale University Press, New Haven.
Upadhyay, S. B., 1990, 'Cotton Mill Workers in Bombay, 1875 to 1918: Condition of Work and Life,' *Economic and Political Weekly,* Vol. 25, No. 30, PE 87-PE 999.
Veeraraghavan, D. and T. Thankappan, 1990. 'Class Conflict and the Colonial State in Madras up to 1918,' *South Asia Bulletin,* Vol. 10, No. 1: pp. 1-11.
Welsh, D., 1971, *The Roots of Segregation: Native Policy in Colonial Natal, 1845–1910,* Oxford University Press.
Worden, N., 1995, *The Making of Modern South Africa,* 2nd edn, Blackwell, Oxford.

Neo-liberal Economic Reforms and Workers of the Third World
At the End of the Second Millennium of the Christian Era

Goals, Arguments, and Issues: Contradictions in the Process of Social Reproduction of Labour under Capitalism

In this essay, we briefly sketch the history and recent experience of the social reproduction of labour under capitalism. On the basis of the experience of labour in Africa, Asia and Latin America, we argue that until the twentieth century, capital faced severe problems in creating and mobilizing a free labour force. Hence, in order to secure its own ends, capital owners imposed various kinds of bondage, stretching from slavery to the denial of basic civil and political rights to ordinary people. The subjection of women to men became almost universal under the dispensation of capital. Race, ethnicity and other differentiating characteristics of workers also came in handy under this programme. Uneven development under capitalism continually reproduced and transformed the nature of segmentation of the working class. However, in some advanced capitalist economies, workers won better living conditions through their own struggles and as part of the agenda of nation-building. In the last two decades, under the programme of free capital and internationally immobile labour, however, workers' living standards have come under attack, and the future of wages and working conditions of labour, especially third-world labour, appears to be bleak unless this trend of international policy-making can be reversed in the interest of the prosperity of ordinary people everywhere.

At the end of the second millennium of the Christian era, according to its eminent official biographers (Karl Marx, Frederick Engels, Maurice Dobb, Fernand Braudel, Immanuel Wallerstein et al.), capitalism is only 500 years old. Most archaeologists and historians of human evolution have dated the origin of human beings as between 5 and 9 million years, when they became differentiated from the great apes, and most of the authorities agree that the first great-grandmother of *Homo sapiens* grew up in Africa (Diamond 1998). Village life and rudimentary agriculture are supposed to have originated in several areas of the world, more or less at the end of the last Ice Age, around 11000 BC. Compared with these dates, capitalism is a very young entity. Judging by capitalist political domination over the most populated parts of the world, namely, the continent of Asia, capitalism is just about 250–300 years old.

Within this period, the production, communication and social systems of the world have been revolutionized. Marx and Engels (1848) memorably described the nature and impact of that revolution 150 years back. The laws of population growth, the quality of life of the more fortunate sections of human beings, and the technologies and organization for mass destruction of human beings and the environment they live in, have also been thoroughly altered by capitalism.

The contrast between the rich and the poor, the fortunate and the unfortunate, the owners and controllers of the means of production and the masses who labour for them, has probably never been more stark and more geographically pervasive than at the end of the second millennium. The claim can be credibly advanced that the worst sufferers of the contradictions of capitalism have been the poor and the working classes of the third world (about three-fourths or more of the global population).

While capitalism penetrated all the cells of daily life in the countries that came under its sway, the vast majority of the people in the dependent colonies experienced it primarily as deprivation: deprivation of land, of occupations, of social status, of dignity as human beings, and of life itself. There were increases in productivity and in some amenities of daily existence, but the latter were reserved for the colonial rulers and the collaborating elite of the respective countries.

The upturn in the rates of population growth in Africa and Asia is a twentieth-century—and in many countries, a post-Second World War—phenomenon. The paradox of capitalism is that at one time capitalists scoured and pillaged whole continents, such as Africa and many parts of Asia, in search of labour. Now the same system increasingly treats labour as an eminently disposable agent and a nuisance, especially if workers demand their rights and dignity as human beings. Just as the law of expanded reproduction of non-human capital under capitalism works only by producing periodic crises, the law of social reproduction of labour and labour power has also been working itself out by creating contradictions in families, workplaces, neighbourhoods, countries and international relations.

The so-called Golden Age of Capitalism (Marglin and Schor 1990) lasted roughly from 1946 to 1973, just a little more—and in some countries a little less—than a quarter century. Labour in the advanced capitalist nations of the North Atlantic seaboard made substantial gains in real earnings, with shorter working hours and better social security, through state policies and their own struggles. During the same period, labour in some developing countries, such as Argentina, Mexico, Chile and Brazil in Latin America, acquired some political influence, and in the phases of 'go' in the stop–go cycles of those economies, obtained higher real wages and some rudimentary social insurance. In most other developing countries (for example, India and Turkey), only labour in the bigger, often state-owned, enterprises secured substantial wage increases and some health and social insurance. In the so-called Four Tigers of East Asia, namely, South Korea, Hong Kong, Taiwan and Singapore, real wages of labour went up very substantially, but labour was put under strong repression by the state and state-related apparatuses (including the legally-recognized trade unions). In Thailand and Malaysia, major sections of labour made substantial gains, again with the state often acting as patron and controller of trade unions. With the onset of the so-called Asian economic crisis from the latter half of 1997, however, labour in even these East and Southeast Asian countries has lost out substantially, in terms of employment and real earnings (Lee 1998: 35–53).

The capitalist system, dominating the developing as well as the developed economies, is driven by ceaseless competition, and continually produces and reproduces structures of uneven development—structures that get transformed to produce other patterns of uneven development. Even as capitalism frees labour in some directions, it enslaves them in other ways and, in doing so, it often mimes and takes over structures of oppression preceding the onset of capitalist-style competition and regulation. For example, most less developed countries suffer from endemic underemployment and seasonal unemployment. In such situations, labour often enters into relations of bondage or attachment with landlords (Bagchi 1973). Such relations are, of course, embedded in pre-existing systems of inequality—caste oppression, hereditary debt, servitude, or peonage (Breman 1974). Workers often have no real access to legal mechanisms of redress or alternative avenues of employment (Brass 1990: 36–37). Thus racism, ethnic exclusion, patriarchy, peonage and patron–client relations, all become part of the processes associated with the evolution of capitalism.

Crises of Accumulation, Corporatism, Authoritarianism and the Fortunes of Labour in the Third World

The 1930s produced widespread crises of accumulation in Latin American countries and a very large number witnessed changes of regime, often from military–authoritarian to civilian–authoritarian rule, or from democratic to authoritarian rule (Hobsbawm 1994; Skidmore and Smith 1989). The attitude of most of these regimes to labour was generally repressive. But in Mexico, the presidency of Lazaro Cardenas witnessed a systematic attempt to incorporate labour in the task of nation-building. Corporatism became far more widespread after the Second World War, for example, in Peronist Argentina, and the developmentalist state of Brazil, up to the military take-over in the 1960s. For a patronage system yielding better wages and working conditions, labour accepted the guidance of the state (Roxborough 1994).

However, corporatism did not make the state or labour immune to crises of accumulation. These crises led the patron state very often to resort to wage repression (as in Argentina in the 1950s), or to severe curtailment of civil and political rights of all the people (as under the military regimes in Argentina and Chile).

The 1980s witnessed widespread recession, amounting in many cases to the virtual decimation of major parts of economies in the third world (Dornbusch 1993; Camargo, Jatoba and Mezzera 1995). Many countries in Africa and Latin America went through a decade-long decline in per capita incomes and even aggregate national incomes. But a group of countries and city-states in East and Southeast Asia, such as China, Taiwan, South Korea and Singapore, seemed to buck this trend, and proved to be the major dynamic force in the global economy. As we have pointed out already, workers' freedom was severely restricted in most of these countries or city-states.

When the debt crises broke out in 1982 and entrapped the whole of Latin America and Sub-Saharan Africa in its toils, the working class, of course, were the worst sufferers. In Chile, for example, GDP contracted by 23.6 per cent in 1982 and 1983, unemployment reached a level of 31.3 per cent of the labour force in 1983 and, for four years, ran at more than 24 per cent of the work force. Real wages of those who were lucky enough to have jobs declined by almost 20 per cent, and health, education and housing budgets were cut by 20 per cent (Meller 1992). In Brazil, real wages declined by 18 per cent over 1979–83, and after some recovery over 1983–87 (when real wages rose by 37 per cent), they fell again by 11 per cent over 1986–89. In Argentina, real wages fell almost continuously from 1980 to 1991, except for the years 1983 to 1986, but, at the same time, urban unemployment levels rose to 81 per cent over the period 1980–83, 19 per cent over 1983–86, 36 per cent over 1986–89, and declined by only 13 per cent over 1990–91 (Altimir 1994: 41–52). The Mexican story is a compound of the experiences of Chile, Argentina and Brazil.

In the neo-liberal theology of adjustment in developing countries, the informal sector has been assigned a special place at the altar. It is supposed to correct the rigidities in the labour market introduced by government regulations, and act as a shock absorber when the economy is rocked by the need to correct serious imbalances. Some protagonists, such as Hernan De Soto (1989), the World Bank and others, have even regarded the informal sector as a major dynamic force in developing economies. It is characteristic of the disingenuousness of the neo-liberal theology that the view of the informal sector as the positive force in developing economies and the formal sector as the negative element holding back their growth acquired salience, even as another group of economists were busy elaborating the theory of efficiency wages (Leibenstein 1957; Prasad 1970; Akerlof and Yellen 1986; Bowles and Boyer 1990:

187–217). A major base of that theory is a long-term relationship between the employer and the employee—a relationship that is protected by the 'formal sector' in an industrialized or industrializing economy.

The 'informal sector', as it has been defined in much of the mainstream literature, is a sector that is left strictly alone by the state, with no regulation of the terms of employment, wages, safety conditions, retrenchment and maternity or retirement benefits for the workers. It is supposed that without state regulation, workers and their employers will work out the best bargains for themselves, and everybody will gain in the process.

This line of reasoning ignores the long-range, often path-dependent nature of development of productivity and skills, and fails to recognize the peculiar nature of labour power as a commodity. Productivity grows in modern industrial ventures through investment in fixed capital, through investment in the skills of production and management inside or outside firms, and through idiosyncratic, path-dependent learning in particular firms and factories. All of these require long-range decisions by the controllers of firms and long-term relationships between at least a core group of workers (including supervisors and managers) and the owners. Moreover, uninterrupted working of plants and/or continuous attention to design and fabrication of products are essential for many process industries and for bulk delivery or customized manufacture or provision of technically complicated products and services. Thus, bargaining in an auction market with the work force on a daily basis is not the mode of working of capitalist firms employing wage-labour. Capitalists, in their own interest, had generally assured more or less permanent tenure to their skilled workers, and many of them had provided housing, medical facilities and other benefits to their workers long before the state undertook the regulation of conditions of work (Hicks 1974: 20–44; Lee 1970: 442–91). The labour welfare practices of Robert Owen and his followers in England, or the early industrialists in Germany such as the Krupps or the Fabers, and the so-called 'life-time employment' system for skilled male workers in Japan, all pre-dated or grew outside the system of government regulation of industrial relations.

Secondly, most of the regulations governing wages, working

conditions, tenure, or minimum provision of welfare services, such as maternity benefits, were introduced in the interests of capital, although the workers also benefited in the process. If workers gained skills while working in a particular enterprise, and have an incentive to walk away and work elsewhere, the original employer in whose workplace the skills were acquired would have less incentive to invest in such skills. If workers worked twelve or fifteen hours a day, as they did in many of the early capitalist enterprises, and lived in insanitary neighbourhoods, their health and productivity would suffer, and the property owners might have to fork out more money in the long run for recruiting labour and for reclaiming degraded slums and squatments. If product quality was lowered as a cost-cutting device, then not only would consumers suffer but the reputation of the whole neighbourhood or industrial sector in which some firms resorted to such quality erosion would also go down. Thus, an umpire would be needed to set the rules and limits of inter-capitalist competition, which also induced competition among workers at their mercy. The history of labour-market regulation is thoroughly misrepresented implicitly or explicitly by many of the proponents of total deregulation in the interest of removing so-called 'distortions' in the labour market.

This does not mean that there are no regulations that redound to the benefit of a small privileged minority and create unnecessary obstacles against the entry of dynamic entrepreneurs. But when they are closely examined, they will be found to have been created in the interests of capital. If they were retained when they ceased to promote the growth of capital (and even more, of the employment or earnings of labour), it was in the interest of particular sections of capital or the ruling apparatus (Hirschman 1968: 531–62). If public enterprises are built up and used to subsidize private enterprise by supplying cheap power or raw materials to it, or channel illicit gains to corrupt politicians and bureaucrats, the workers in such enterprises only get the scrapings of the pork barrel. Under corporatist management of industrial relations, trade union bosses may get a share of the spoils. But as the case of the CTM in Mexico clearly showed, in the event of an economic crisis or a conflict with the top managers of the political apparatus (the PRI and the President in Mexico, for example; see Patroni 1988), bosses can be changed and the earnings of workers can be drastically reduced. Such situations, of course, can also incite fresh struggles of the workers seeking to establish trade unions that are independent of the establishment unions and their federating bodies, as happened in Mexico and South Korea from the 1980s (Roxborough 1994; Park 1997).

We can obtain a true perspective on the roles of the so-called formal and informal sectors if we keep the above considerations in mind and if, additionally, we grasp the continual ebb and flow from the formal to the informal sectors and vice versa produced by the forces of capitalist competition and competition among workers induced by the capitalist rules of the game. When industrial and economic growth is strong enough, a larger fraction of the work force will be sucked into the formal sector, and capitalists will have to offer higher wages to attract new workers and retain those already employed, especially if they happen to be endowed with scarce skills. When, however, the growth of the labour force far outpaces the expansion of employment, even in phases of high growth, the real wages or working conditions may stay stagnant even when the earnings of skilled labour move upward. In the case of a serious recession and contraction of the economy, as happened in so many parts of Latin America and Africa in the 1980s, and in East and Southeast Asia from the middle of 1997, the formal sector spews workers into the informal sector, and the latter swell the ranks of the self-employed or workers in micro-enterprises (those employing, say, ten persons or less). As a result, the earnings of the self-employed in those sectors which require little start-up capital go down, and so do the wages of employees in micro-enterprises (Portes and Schauffler 1993: 33–60).

Many third-world governments have instituted legal minimum wages as a way of protecting workers in the informal sector. But apart from the fact that in a typical third-world country, neither the government nor trade unions nor peasant organizations have enough monitoring capacity even when they have the incentive to try and observe these minima, the minimum wages effectively serve as ceilings rather than floors of the wage levels as they did, for example, in Brazil and Indonesia (Portes 1989; ILO 1996a).

Workers Caught in the Web of Mobile Capital and (Im)mobile Labour

In addition to national conditions and policies, major international constraints inevitably impinge on the conditions of workers in the third world. The most obvious ones have been already referred to: if a country gets caught in the build-up of unsustainable debt levels and has thereafter to enforce structural adjustment policies as conceived by the Washington twins (viz., the IMF and the World Bank), the real wages of workers suffer, trade union organizations come under attack, unemployment increases and the prospects of future growth become dimmer than before.

The Atlantic slave trade, ending only in the nineteenth century, depopulated Africa and left African societies carrying burdens of polygyny, agrestic and domestic slavery, and disrupted ecology. Not all migrations were, however, inimical to labour or to the home countries of the migrants. The biggest migration of peoples in recent times took place from Europe to North and South America, Canada, Australia and other colonies of white settlement. Between the late nineteenth century and the middle of the 1920s, about 40 million Europeans migrated overseas (Woodruff 1966).

The impact of this massive flow of migrants from Europe on the home countries was profound. By increasing the demand for labour in relation to supply on a sustained basis, it helped raise real wages—through market processes and workers' struggles. It influenced government policies which had to be directed, as in Sweden, to special care of older people, as their children left to seek their fortunes overseas (Massey 1988; Hatton and Williamson 1994). The migration lessened the pressures on urban facilities in the home countries, even as both local and national governments woke up to the consequences of unplanned urbanization associated with industrial development under capitalist auspices (Szreter 1996).

By contrast, the borders of all countries at the end of the twentieth century were closed to immigrants from abroad, and especially to the poor of the third world. Over the last two decades, this exclusion has grown stronger in intensity even as capital has increasingly freed itself from the usual regulations, national and international. The enforced licentiousness of capital and the rigorous immobilization of ordinary workers across national boundaries are encoded in national laws, regional agreements such as the North American Free Trade Agreement (NAFTA), and in the clauses of the infant World Trade Organization (WTO). The United States militia and police have with impunity killed Mexicans trying to illegally cross the border to the north. NAFTA, by completely freeing trade and finance while keeping the immigrant-exclusion laws and practices in place, has further emphasized the asymmetry of legal treatment of capital and labour. The WTO, with its so-called trade-related investment measures (TRIMs), has taken away the power of governments to introduce any special regulations on the movement and behaviour of foreign capital. The attempt is now being made to introduce multilateral investment guarantee agreement (MIGA) clauses that would put virtually all capital beyond the regulatory reach of governments.

If capital becomes more mobile across a national border, and there is a sizeable reserve army of labour on one side of it, it could be predicted that the wages of labour on both sides would tend to slide down (except for the resistance put up by organized labour), and the wages of unskilled workers or workers with skills specialized for declining industries would especially suffer. This is exactly what has tended to happen in the case of wages of unskilled or low-skilled workers in Mexico and the United States (Lustig 1992; Pastor Jr 1994), and the NAFTA and the Mexican crisis of 1994–95 have aggravated these tendencies.

Large flows of migrants also enter developing countries, especially West Asia and some countries of East and Southeast Asia. According to an estimate published by the secretariat of the International Confederation of Free Trade Unions (ICFTU) in 1998, there were about 30 million 'illegal' immigrants all over the world. These 'illegal' workers are generally much more at a disadvantage compared with domestic workers and the much less numerous 'legal' immigrants, since they are at the mercy of their recruiters and their masters, and face the threat of expulsion if they dare to protest against the often inhuman working conditions (Park 1997; Jomo and Kanapathy 1996). With the onset of the Asian economic crisis, and with low rates of growth in the rest of the world, the plight of the immigrant workers has become even more tragic than before.

Social Reproduction of Stigmata of Working-Class Differentiation: Gender, Ethnicity and Class under Capitalism

Many scholars believed that capitalism would eradicate all distinctions between people, except those of class. However, gender discrimination and differences of treatment based on ascribed racial, religious and ethnic distinctions continue to thrive in most contemporary societies. One reason for this is that capitalists and their managers have found these ascribed differentials useful for dividing the workers, curbing their resistance and controlling them (for examples from Britain, see Elbaum, Lazonick, Wilkinson and Zeitlin 1979; for colonial India, see Bagchi 1972: Chapter 5; Chakrabarty 1989; Bagchi 1998a).

Secondly, capitalism by its nature produces and reproduces uneven development (for recent expositions of this line of reasoning, which goes back to Lenin and Rosa Luxemburg, see Shulman 1984). In many countries of Latin America, people of Amerindian origin had lost entitlements to their land and resources during Spanish colonialism and under the rule of various successor regimes run by the Creole ruling classes in the nineteenth and twentieth centuries. In most countries, they also had lower degrees of access to education, credit, market and infrastructural facilities. As a result, they are highly over-represented among the lower-paid workers. Similarly, in most parts of India the people of the so-called scheduled castes and scheduled tribes (targets of affirmative action under the Indian Constitution) are over-represented among the poor, ill-educated, low-paid and insecure workers on casual employment in the informal or formal sectors (Psacharapoulos and Patrinos 1994; ILO 1996; and Bagchi 1999).

Uneven development can also occur across sectors, regions and nations. As particular industries decline, workers formerly employed by them face unemployment, those who are still lucky enough to find jobs suffer wage-cuts and deteriorating terms of employment. Particular groups of workers suffer unemployment more intensely. Women employees all over the world are generally retrenched before their male colleagues. Afro–Americans in the United States similarly face greater bouts of unemployment and are usually among the first to be laid-off when a recession hits a particular sector or region. Uneven development across regions produces waste lands, especially in cities or neighbourhoods which suffer disproportionately from bad and deteriorating housing and public infrastructure.

As we pointed out earlier, in advanced capitalist countries uncontrolled urbanization produced a host of ill-effects (Bairoch 1988; Massey 1988; Szreter 1996). Typically, third-world countries (barring such exceptions as Singapore or Hong Kong) often lack the resources for dealing with an increasingly overcrowded and degraded urban environment. Under the theology of profit-seeking as the *summum bonum* of successful governance, the ruling classes have been extremely unwilling to tax themselves and find the resources needed to overcome the urban crisis. The international watchdogs of capitalism have regularly preached to them the virtues of environmental protection. But they have effectively negated any such protection by forcing or inducing these countries to sell their timber, minerals and farm produce at ruinously low prices, thus taking away the resources needed for environmental sustenance and forcing further millions of landless people into overcrowded cities.

These processes have produced widespread social disarray in third-world countries, and criminalized whole neighbourhoods (UNRISD 1995). Moreover, such social dislocation has been a fertile breeding-ground for the culture and politics of exclusionary identity formation, as in the case of Nazi Germany or the Taliban regime in Afghanistan.

Women in the Maelstrom of Competition

Internationally, capitalism evolved as a system of competitive conquest of markets, and sources of labour and raw materials and arms often decided the conquest. Britain, the first nation to industrialize its economy fully (in the sense that industry provided the major fraction of national income and employment), also became the biggest formal empire the world has ever seen. In the twentieth century, as the United States became the top capitalist nation, it also became militarily the most powerful nation on earth. For instance, the military expenditure of the United States as a proportion of global defence spending increased from 30.4 per cent in 1985 to 33.3 per cent in 1996. Furthermore, the combined defence spending of the United States and other members of NATO, as a proportion of total global spending, increased from 50.8 per cent in 1985 to 62.8 per cent in 1996 (Achcar 1998).

This continued armed competition under the capitalist system has provided a major, generally unstated reason for subjection of women to men. Women have to guard the home-front while men go out as conquering or defending heroes to the battlefields and theatres of war. Even in the countries of the North Atlantic seaboard, women's shares of earned income or positions of power, such as managerial posts and seats in parliament, remain much smaller than those of men (see *HDR 1998*). In Japan, after waging several large-scale wars between the nineteenth and twentieth centuries, the position of women still remains extremely inferior compared to men: women had only 7.7 per cent of the parliamentary seats, and 8.9 per cent of administrative and managerial posts. But, because of the high levels of women's education and their paid employment, women's share in earned income was 34 per cent, as against the corresponding average of 35 per cent for countries with high human development indices (*HDR 1998*).

In the other countries of East and Southeast Asia, which managed to grow fast during the last twenty years or so (Amsden 1989; Bagchi 1987), women's position measured by most indices remains inferior compared to their levels of development. The UNDP *Human Development Report* includes a gender development index (GDI) and a human development index (HDI). If we subtract GDI from HDI, a negative figure means that, relatively speaking, compared with its level of human development, the country treats its women worse than average. The gaps between HDI and GDI for Japan, Hong Kong (China), Singapore and the Republic of Korea were −5, −8, +1 and −8 respectively. The figure for Singapore is misleading, because when it comes to a measure of gender empowerment, Singapore ranks 42nd, whereas its HDI and GDI ranks are 28 and 29 respectively (*HDR 1998*). These countries have proved to be highly aggressive penetrators of foreign markets, by using the values of male dominance as battering rams.

If we take South Korea as a typical developmental state, we see that its economic success has been contingent upon its ability to pursue the goal of economic development in a coherent manner, and use state power to regulate, promote or supersede the market—depending on the requirements of development. However, geopolitical security considerations of the United States and its allies, especially Japan (and of an embattled South Korean military regime confronting the hostility and threat of a communist North Korea) had a considerable role in the construction and sustenance of a developmental state in South Korea (and Taiwan as well) (Cumings 1984; Woo-Cumings 1999).

Another, often overlooked, bastion of the South Korean (and East Asian) politico–economic structure has been the patriarchal family, with women subordinated to men in most areas of life. While the participation rate of South Korean women in paid employment was quite low by the standards of advanced market economies to start with, it progressively rose over the years from around 36.5 per cent in 1965 to about 47.9 per cent by 1994 (Bagchi 1987; ILO 1995). Young women join paid employment in factories and offices, but a large proportion leave when they marry in order to look after household chores and children. At every level of education, women receive only a half or a little more of the wages of their male counterparts. The levels of education of South Korean women have gone up along with those of men, but this has not altered the situation that women are virtually never to be found in any decision-making position in business firms, administration or, of course, the military establishment (Bagchi 1987; Lindauer et al. 1998). In every major economic crisis in South Korea, women have generally tended to be laid-off in greater numbers than men, and the crisis that erupted in November 1997 is no exception. According to a report in the *Asian Wall Street Journal*, 4 May 1999, an advocacy group, the Seoul Women's Trade Union, pointed out that women are the first to lose jobs as companies seek to cut costs. In October 1998, for example, nine commercial banks laid off 4,463 low-level employees, and 87 per cent of them were female, though only 29 per cent of the banks' low-level staff were female.

In South Korea, Taiwan, Hong Kong, and now in China, economic growth is pursued through competitiveness and minimum state expenditure for social insurance, with only male children being supposed to raise or keep up the family's position in society and support parents in their old age (Zeng Yi et al. 1993; Park and Cho

1995). Most of these changes have occurred during the last twenty years, when the competitiveness of East Asian countries allowed them to forge ahead and buck the trend of global recession.

In other third-world societies, women fare no better, and in most cases, fare even worse than South Korean women do. The so-called 'feminization' of the labour force generally means that more and more women lose access to land or other productive assets and crowd into low-paid casual jobs in order to maintain themselves and their family (for the Indian situation as an example, see Bagchi 1999). Female foeticide and even female infanticide are common practices in the poor, patriarchy-ridden societies of West Asia and North Africa.

Workers under the Heel of Capitalism Face the Third Millennium of the Christian era

Capitalism has, after a long time, succeeded in speeding up human development, increasing longevity and bringing down infant and adult mortality all across the world. But most countries of Sub-Saharan Africa and South Asia still have unacceptably high levels of infant and adult mortality. Precisely when labour has become more abundant than ever before, the capitalist system is unable to utilize this increase in labour power.

In western Europe, since the nineteenth century, state action has played a very important role in raising the standards of living and productivity of workers. Heavy migration to countries of white settlement aided this process. Labour in the third world now faces the prospect of withdrawal of state protection and severe restrictions on their movement to countries offering higher standards of living, even as all restrictions on the mobility of capital are removed and capital gains unfettered licence in its treatment of national governments and labour. With global recession and international competition reaching new heights of ferocity, women and ethnically disadvantaged minorities get the worst of the deal. Almost alone among the large countries of the third world, China has tried to regulate the mobility of capital, even though it has become a favoured destination of international capital. The high rate of growth of China's economy has led to growth of incomes and of employment, even in the recession of the 1990s. But this has also been accompanied by increasing casualization of labour and the loss of job security, especially in the case of joint ventures (Bagchi 1998b; Sargeson 1999).

The increased mobility of capital with immobile labour may provide some protection for people with skills (Wood 1994), but capitalist competition can lead also to the oversupply of skills and downgrading of previous skills. No country entering the arena of international competition for markets can escape these processes.

It is ironical that international bodies became vociferous about the necessity of protecting human rights in all countries and improving labour standards precisely in a period when many thirdworld countries have suffered so much from economic dislocation, rising criminality, ethnic fissiparousness and fundamentalism of one kind or another (UNRISD 1995). If child labour is to be abolished or labour standards to be raised, the societies and states must have enough resources and autonomy to do it in their own way. The debt crisis and continuing weakness of primary commodity markets have led to a massive haemorrhage of resources from the third world to the capitalists of the G-7 countries (and the rich of all other countries who stash their wealth in the safe havens of New York, London, Paris, Zurich or Frankfurt). Greater internationalization of capital in the form of the rise of transnational corporations and their increasing domination of the world economy have led to greater violations of human rights rather than less. Transnational corporations were happily doing business under the apartheid regime until economic problems and the rising tide of revolt of the people of South Africa made it unviable. It was Shell's violation of the rights of the Ogoni people in Nigeria that led to protests by the poet Farowiwa and his comrades, and to their execution by the military regime of Sani Abacha. The Enron Corporation's Dabhol power plant in Maharashtra, India, has been guilty of serious violations of human rights (Human Rights Watch 1999).

Given this background, the international surveillance of human and labour rights against the will of the people, including workers, of the third world is likely to be either ineffective or lead to distorted results. They can be used as protectionist devices as the United States has done under its 301 and Super 301 provisions; or more grotesquely still, for protecting the human rights of Albanians in Kosovo, the NATO has resorted to massive destruction and violation of human rights in Yugoslavia (and Kosovo as well).

Improvement of the condition of workers all over the world requires at a minimum the reining in of the licentiousness of capital, forcing capitalists in third-world countries to assume the responsibility of paying their taxes and obeying the laws of the land, strengthening the foundations of national states through social reforms carried out by the people themselves, and increasing the power of such a socially-reinforced state to adopt policies for upgradation of the skills, education and life chances of male and female workers. Removing many of the hindrances against labour mobility will also lead to lesser violations of human rights in the form of maltreatment of 'illegal' immigrants, and produce greater solidarity among workers of different ethnic groups and religious affiliations. At the close of the second millennium, the slogan 'Workers of the world, unite', has not lost its relevance, but has to be given a new content, keeping in mind both the new opportunities and the new dangers posed by development under capitalist auspices.

References

Achcar, G., 1998, 'The Strategic Triad: The United States, Russia and China', *New Left Review*, 118, March–April, pp. 91–126.

Akerlof, G.A. and J.L. Yellen (eds), 1986, *Efficiency Wage Models of the Labour Market*, Cambridge University Press, Cambridge.

Altimir, O., 1994, 'Income Distribution and Poverty through Crisis and Adjustment', *CEPAL Review*, 50, August.

Amsden, A.H., 1989, *Asia's Next Giant: South Korea and Late Industrialization*, Oxford University Press, New York.

Bagchi, A.K., 1972, *Private Investment in India 1990–39*, Cambridge University Press, Cambridge.

———, 1973, 'Some Implications of Unemployment in Rural Areas', *Economic and Political Weekly*, Vol. 8, Nos. 31–33, August, pp. 1500–10.

———, 1987, *Public Intervention and Industrial Restructuring in China, India and the Republic of Korea*, ILO–ARTEP, New Delhi.

———, 1998a, 'Workers and the Historians' Burden', *Bengal Past and Present* 117, pp. 9–56.

———, 1998b, *Globalization with Equity: Policies for Growth* (mimeo), ILO–SEAPAT, Manila.

———, 1999, 'Economic Reforms and Employment in India' in *South Asia under the Economic Reforms*, edited by Fumiko Oshikawa, The Japan Centre for Asian Studies, National Museum of Ethnology, Osaka, pp. 15–64.

Bairoch, P., 1988, *Cities and Economic Development: From the dawn of history to the present*, translated from the French by C. Braider, University of Chicago Press, Chicago.

Bowles, S. and R. Boyer, 1990, 'A Wage-led Employment Regime: Income Distribution, Labour Discipline, and Aggregate Demand in Welfare Capitalism', in S. Marglin and J. Schor (eds), *The Golden Age of Capitalism: Re-Interpreting the Postwar Experience*, Clarendon Press, Oxford, pp. 187–217.

Brass, T., 1990, 'Class Struggle and the De-proletarianization of Agricultural Labour in Haryana', *Journal of Peasant Studies*, 18 (1), October, pp. 36–37.

Breman, J., 1974, *Patronage and Exploitation: Changing Agrarian Relations in South Gujarat*, Manohar, Delhi.

Camargo, J.M., J. Jatoba and J. Mezzera, 1995, *Stability, Growth, Modernization and Pervasive Flexibility: Feasible Combination?*, International Labour Organization, Santiago, Chile.

Chakrabarty, D., 1989, *Rethinking Working Class History*, Princeton University Press, Princeton, N.J.

Cumings, B., 1984, 'The Origins and Development of the Northeast Asian Political Economy: Industrial Sector, Product Cycles and Political Consequences', *International Organization*, 3, pp. 1–40.

De Soto, H., 1989, *The Other Path: The Invisible Revolution in the Third World*, Harper and Row, New York.

Diamond, J., 1998, *Guns, Germs and Steel: A Short history of everybody during the last 13,000 years*, Vintage, York.

Dornbusch, R., 1993, *Stabilization, Debt and Reform: Policy Analysis for Developing Countries*, Harvester Wheatsheaf, London.

Elbaum, B.W., F. Lazonick , Wilkinson and J. Zeitlin, 1979, 'The Labour Process, the Market Structure, and Marxist Theory', *Cambridge Journal of Economics*, 3 (3), September, pp. 227–30.

Hatton, T.J. and J.G. Williamson, 1994, 'What Drove the Mass Immigration of the Nineteenth Century?', *Population and Development Review*, 20 (3), September, pp. 533–59.

Human Development Report, 1998, Oxford University Press for UNDP, Oxford.

Hicks, J., 1974, 'Industrialism', in J. Hicks (ed.), *Economic Perspectives*, Clarendon Press, Oxford, pp. 20–44.

Hirschman, O., 1968, 'The Political Economy of Import Substituting: Industrialization in Latin America', *Quarterly Journal of Economics*, reprinted in S. Haggard–Aldershot (ed.), *The International Political Economy and the Developing Countries*, Edward Elgar, UK, pp. 531–62.

Hobsbawm, E.J., 1994, *The Age of Extremes: A History of the World 1914–91*, Pantheon Books, New York.

Human Rights Watch, 1999, *The Enron Corporation: Corporate Complicity in Human Rights Violations*, Human Rights Watch, New York.

ILO, 1996, *Yearbook of Labour Statistics: 1995*, Vol. I, International Labour Office, Geneva.

——, 1996a, *The Impact of Globalization on the World of Work*, ILO Regional Office for Asia and the Pacific, Bangkok.

——, 1997, *World Employment Report 1996–97*, International Labour Office, Geneva.

Jomo, K.S. and V. Kanapathy, 1996, *Economic Liberalization and Labour in Malaysia: Efficiency and Equity Considerations in Public Policy Reform*

(mimeo), Institute of Strategic and International Studies, Kualalumpur, Malaysia.
Lee, E., 1998, *The Asian Financial Crisis: The Challenge for Social Policy*, International Labour Office, Geneva.
Lee, J.J. 1970, 'Labour in German Industrialization', in P. Mathias and M. Postan (eds), *The Cambridge Economic History of Europe*, Vol. VII, Part I, Cambridge University Press, Cambridge, pp. 442–91.
Leibenstein, H., 1957, *Economic Backwardness and Economic Growth*, John Wiley, New York.
Lindauer, D.L., J.G. Kim, J.W. Lee, H.S. Lim, J.Y. Son and E.F. Vogel, 1998, 'Labour Market Outcomes: An Overview', in D.L. Lindauer, Song-Gie Lim, Song-Woo Lee, Hy-Sip Lim, Jac-Yong Son and E.F. Vogel (eds), *The Strains of Economic Growth: Labour Unrest and Social Dissatisfaction in Korea*, Harvard Institute for International Development, Cambridge, Mass, pp. 35–53.
Lustig, N., 1992, *Mexico: The Remaking of an Economy*, Brookings Institution, Washington D.C.
Marglin, S. and J. Schor (eds), 1990, *The Golden Age of Capitalism: Re-Interpreting the Postwar Experience*, Clarendon Press, Oxford.
Marx, K. and F. Engels, 1969, *Manifesto of the Communist Party*, reprint, Progress Publishers, Moscow.
Massey, D.S., 1988, 'Economic Development and International Migration in Comparative Perspective', *Population and Development Review*, 14 (3), September, pp. 383–413.
Park, Y., 1997, 'Globalization with Equity: The Korean Case', paper prepared for JIL/ILO National Institute for Labour Studies in Asia and the Pacific, Korea Development Institute, Seoul.
Park, C.B. and N.H. Cho, 1995, 'Consequences of Son Preference in a Low-Fertility Society: Imbalance of Sex at Birth in Korea', *Population and Development Review*, 21 (1), March, pp. 59–84.
Pastor, Jr., M., 1994, 'Mexican Trade Liberalization and NAFTA', *Latin American Research Review*, pp. 153–73.
Patroni, V., 1998, 'The Politics of Labour Legislation Reform in Mexico', *Capital and Class*, 65, pp. 107–32.
Portes, A., 1989, 'Latin American Urbanization During the Years of the Crisis', *Latin American Research Review*, 23 (3), pp. 7–44.
Portes, A. and R. Schauffler, 1993, 'Competing Perspectives on the Latin American Informal Sector', *Population and Development Review*, 19 (1), March, pp. 33–60.
Prasad, P.H., 1970, *Growth with Full Employment*, Allied Publishers, Bombay.
Psacharapoulos, G. and H.A. Patrinos (eds), 1994, *Indigenous People and Poverty in Latin America*, World Bank, Washington D.C.
Roxborough, I., 1994, 'The Urban Working Class and Labour Movement in Latin America since 1930', in L. Bethell (ed.), *The Cambridge History of Latin America*, Vol. VI, *Latin America*, Part II, Cambridge University Press, Cambridge.
Sargeson, S., 1999, *Rethinking China's Proletariat*, Macmillan, London.
Shulman, S., 1984, 'Competition and Racial Discrimination: The Employment

Effects of Reagan's Market Policies', *Review of Radical Political Economics,* 16 (4), Winter, pp. 111–28.

Skidmore, T.E. and P.H. Smith, 1989, *Modern Latin America,* Oxford University Press, New York.

Szreter, S., 1996, *Fertility, Class and Gender in Britain 1860–1940,* Cambridge University Press, Cambridge.

UNRISD, 1995, *States of Disarray: The Social Effects of Globalization,* United Nations Institute for Social Development, Geneva.

Woo-Cumings, M.J., 1999, 'National Security and the Rise of the Developmental State in South Korea', in H.S. Rowen (ed.), *Behind East Asian Growth: the political and social prosperity,* Routledge, London, pp. 319–37.

Wood, A., 1994, *North–South Trade, Employment and Inequality: Changing Fortunes in a Skill-driven World,* Clarendon, Oxford.

Woodruff, W., 1966, *The Impact of Western Man,* Macmillan, London.

Zeng Yi, Tu Ping, Gu Baochang, Xu Yi, Li Bohua and Li Yong Ping, 1993, 'Causes and Implications of the Recent Increase in the Reported Sex Ratio at Birth in China', *Population and Development Review,* 19 (2), June, pp. 283–302.

Multiculturalism, Communalism and the Bourgeoisie

Predatory Commercialization and Communalism in India

I

The word 'communalism' can be interpreted in numerous ways. In one sense it can mean any feeling of animosity that the members of any community (a *bhaichara biradari*, a linguistic group living side by side with other linguistic groups, a group claiming to belong to a particular 'race' as against other people belonging to other 'races', and so on) entertains against members of any other community defined by criteria that establish the distinctiveness of the latter. But in the Indian context, it has come specifically to mean the feelings of animosity between people who profess different religions. In particular, in post-Independence India, it has come to mean feelings of animosity between Hindus and Muslims, and in the 1980s between Sikhs and Hindus in particular pockets of the country. This does not mean that either the Hindus, or the Muslims, or the Sikhs, present a monolithic front to the rest of the world. Apart from the fact that there are many people nominally belonging to each of these communities who do not define their own identities in terms of the religion they actually or nominally profess, there are also divisions within each of these communities. The most pervasive division is between the upper-caste Hindus and the Harijans or Dalits—people who are legally defined as the scheduled castes. The division between the Sunnis, who form a majority of the Muslims in India, and the Shias, has sometimes expressed itself in acts of violence; so has the division between the orthodox Sikhs and the Nirankaris. The divisions between the upper-caste Hindus and the Dalits in many parts of the country has led to a conversion of the latter to Buddhism or Islam, and the older conflicts have then manifested themselves as communal conflicts defined in nominally religious terms.

We have already referred to acts of violence resulting from communalism. How do we, in fact, detect the expression of communalism? I may feel contemptuous or envious of a neighbour who flaunts his wealth or his social standing too blatantly for my taste, but unless he or I have a violent disposition, such a feeling may never come out overtly in public action or behaviour. So it is necessary to gather evidence of public acts or symptoms of feelings of animosity designated as 'communalism'. It might be thought that if we find a group of Hindus indulging in violence against a group of Muslims, it is the clear sign of a communal clash. But this is also not certain: the conflict may arise purely out of a private quarrel, and the Hindus might simply be associates of the Hindu protagonist, and the Muslims those of the Muslim protagonist. It is when these immediate associates are joined by other people with the same religious affiliation, and attack people belonging to another religious community, whether they are associates of the antagonists or not, that the private quarrel turns into a communal conflict.[1] There could also be situations in which members of a particular community would be protesting against the action of a particular individual or a group; when the antagonist has a different religious affiliation, the conflict might appear to be a communal one. This is apparently what happened in the so-called Talla riots of 1897 in Calcutta (Dasgupta 1984). That was, properly speaking, a riot of a group of Muslims against the police who had demolished a mosque on disputed ground. In these cases, the specification and the explanation of the so-called communal incident or communal riot are inextricably linked; for, a wrong specification would at once litter the investigator's path with red herrings and the answers would also be misleading.[2]

---

[1] This is apparently how the communal conflict originated in the walled city of Delhi in 1974 (Krishna 1985).

[2] According to the official data, during the ten years from 1954 to 1963, an average of 62 riots took place annually and the number of those killed in these riots was forty on an average. From 1964 to 1970 the number of communal riots rose to an annual average of 425 and the number killed increased even faster, to a figure of 467 persons killed annually. With some improvements from 1971 to 1978, the situation again deteriorated drastically from 1979. If we take the killing of Sikhs in the wake of the assassination of Indira Gandhi into account, the figure

Two communities may live side by side with feelings of their own identity, and some disdain or contempt for members of other communities, without there being any communal incident or a communal riot. Such, after all, has been the situation of most Hindus, Muslims and Sikhs for most of the period they have lived in the same locality. There may also be communal 'incidents' without there being communal riots. Very often those who fish in troubled waters try to provoke communal incidents, hoping that there would be a communal riot, or the assertion of the might of one community in relation to the other. What we are concerned to explore here are the conditions that permit mischief-making or politicking by provoking communal incidents. In this exploration we shall confine ourselves mainly to incidents of communalism involving Hindus and Muslims.

Very broadly, the following alternative sets of conditions seem to be necessary for communalist elements to be able to provoke communal incidents and riots. First, the leaders of the community (political or spiritual) perceive themselves and people belonging to their community as losing out in relation to the people of another contiguous community. Second, the ordinary people of one community suffer a major erosion of their standard of living and identify some or all of the members of the other community (through guilt by association or through personification of a whole community) as being the cause of that erosion. Third, traders or merchants belonging to the two separate but contiguous communities engage in competition and suffer losses through competitive pressures or through the working of exogenous forces, see themselves as competing for the same economic and physical space, and try to use communal solidarity and political instruments to serve their own ends. Finally, there is the ubiquitous fact of politics—whether in a democratic set-up or under a military regime as in Pakistan under Zia-ul-Haq—

---

in the 1980s must have averaged more than 600 a year.

With increasing politicization of communal issues, the figures of communal incidents and deaths from communal riots have become far more unreliable in recent years. But our discussion in the text suggests that earlier also, a purely personal, sectional or economic conflict was often presented as a communal incident. Such mistaken identification can be the source of further communal conflicts. See also, Brass 1990: Table 6.3; and Saksena 1990.

where some political leaders act as the champions of one community, some others act as the protectors of a threatened community, and still others pose as the champions of communal unity, all the while making sure that the cauldron of communalism continues to simmer.

II

I take a quick look in this section at some of the ways in which communal conflict erupted under British colonialism. Under British-style capitalist colonialism, predatory commercialization was let loose in an almost unhindered fashion in most regions of India, and it affected most areas of life. The continued operation of a process of commercialization under which the losers are simply proletarianized, or worse, pauperized, is one of the basic continuities between pre-Independence and post-Independence India. Pauperization is a process under which the property-less losers do not even have access to employment; this can happen both when the losers are willing to behave as 'free' labourers and when they cling to an ascribed status in society and refuse to accept the employment open to them. Ashrafs and Brahmins have often starved rather than accept jobs as unskilled labourers; of course, social mores have also prevented their employment in such capacities, at least within the immediate neighbourhood.

Capitalist colonialism and its inevitable partner, predatory commercialization, did not start out to destroy all communities; they attacked those communal or status attributes that stood in the way of tribute extraction or private profit-making. But they affected different communities differently, depending on where they happened to be. Take the case of the weavers, for example. Both the Hindu and the Muslim weaver communities were affected by the decline of hand-spinning and hand-weaving after the Indian market was flooded by machine-made yarn and cloth from Britain. However, in eastern Bengal there was a sizeable amount of forest and swamp land which could be opened up for cultivation. Many peasants moved to clear this land. Some displaced weavers also became cultivators—more often as agricultural labourers than as land-owning peasants. Even when the peasants or weavers held land, it was on insecure tenure. This also created problems which took a communal turn when the landlords happened to be predominantly Hindus, and the peasants Muslims. However, the impact of loss of craft occupations was partially absorbed by this kind of population movement. In areas where such prospects of occupational changes were bleak, or where the weavers were highly skilled—urban artisans used to a very different life-style from that of the cultivators—they continued to practise a diminishingly remunerative profession. Under Indian conditions, this would mean that they would become even more dependent than before on traders and moneylenders for advances and loans, generally at usurious rates of interest. If, again, many of the weavers were Muslims and the traders and moneylenders were Hindus, tensions between the weavers and moneylenders in the area of commerce and finance would take on a communal turn, especially if the only supervisory authority with which the weavers were in touch happened to be religious leaders. Such conflicts which had a dual edge—an economic and a religious one—have been recorded and analysed by many historians (Hardy 1972; McLane 1977; Pandey 1982, 1983; Chatterjee 1984; Ghosh 1984; Sarkar 1987; Das 1990).

But British colonialism damaged the fortunes of many others besides the weavers. The system of revenue extraction and the processes of commercialization instituted under colonialism affected all Indians. But the effects were felt differentially by different groups. Under the Mughals, revenue was collected only from the land that was cultivated. The effect was that with a relatively sparse population, cattle, sheep and goats had abundant pastures to feed on; peasants owning livestock and shepherds, especially in northern and north-western India, did well out of this differential treatment, and India perhaps had one of the highest ratios of livestock to people in the world. Under the British, every piece of land was supposed to be owned by a private person or the state. If any piece of land was claimed by a private person, he had to pay rent on it, whether he cultivated it or not. If the land was government-owned, the peasants or shepherds had to pay for the use of any of its produce—be it timber or fodder. The relatively favourable treatment of pastures for revenue purposes virtually ceased under this dispensation.

This meant that, over time, it became more and more difficult to keep livestock. As a result, the ratio of livestock to people and of livestock per acre of cultivated land came down (Bagchi 1976). This was because there was pressure to cultivate every piece of land that could yield anything above the cost of cultivation. Earlier on, in many areas, peasants on *khudkasht* (land to which a person has a hereditary right and which he is supposed to cultivate himself; or may designate land tenure incorporating such a right) tenure, *patidars* (persons claiming to belong to the group which has hereditary right to the ownership of the land in a particular area; a term used in Gujarat), or otherwise privileged peasants, could often claim the right to cultivate a piece of land, even if they had not cultivated it for a long time or had not paid taxes on it, provided they could establish an ancestral claim to that piece of land. Under the British, land-ownership became conditional on prompt payment of the land revenue not just every year, but every *kist* (instalment of payment of land revenue in British India). Thus, even if a particular piece of land gave no certain promise of yielding a surplus above the cost of cultivation, the peasant dare not let it lie fallow. For, he hoped that it would yield some surplus at some future date, and if he failed to meet his revenue demand for a single year he would lose that land forever, and with that his chance of survival would also decline by a significant margin. The peasants' proverbial attachment to land was reinforced by the insecurity created by the revenue system.

More livestock for most Indians meant more milk and more butter or *ghee*, and these were major sources of protein and fat. More livestock also meant more manure for the peasants' fields in areas where tillage and pasture were combined. But for shepherd communities—*goalas, yadavs,* etc.—livestock was also the source of livelihood. When the government took over common pastures as its own property, or when pastures or forest lands were parcelled out as private domain, the graziers found it increasingly difficult to feed their livestock without encroaching on land claimed by others. Traditional usage, such as keeping the stubble on the fields and keeping the fields open after harvest, provided some relief, but it was not enough. With the low level of monetization in the village economy, the graziers often could not grow fodder crops and make a living after paying for the cost of cultivation and for the state's revenue demand on the land put to fodder. The herdsmen moved from one area to another in search of empty fields on which they could feed their herds. Often there were no social conventions or regular policing to keep them from letting loose their herds in fields under crop. This led to clashes between peasants and graziers. When the peasants happened to be Muslims and the graziers Hindus, the clashes took on a communal complexion.

However, the 'cow protection movement'[3] in the late nineteenth century, which gave rise to a number of communal incidents and helped spread communalism in many parts of northern and eastern India, should not be seen simply as a reflection of the sectional conflict between semi-nomadic graziers and sedentary peasants. The cow, of course, was for ages a symbol of prosperity in Hindu India—both as the source of milk (hence as surrogate mother), and as the mother of oxen, the chief source of power for cultivation. (It is interesting to speculate as to why the buffalo never occupied that space. Was it because Aryan colonizers had already domesticated kine, whereas they had met the buffalo first in their wild state and because the domesticated buffalo was the chief wealth of people who were for long beyond the pale of brahminical dominance?) Hence when the peasants and pastoralists saw one of the main sources of their wealth threatened by alien rule, in a tragic mode of transference of anger to a visible imagined enemy from an invisible system, they took the cow-eaters as their target of attack. Of course, the white rulers also ate cows, but the whites were few and scattered and, in any case, were mostly beyond the threat of violence by the means at the peasant's command. So the Muslim neighbour became the chief target of attack as the cow protection movement lost its focus.

Neither the anti-Muslim attacks of the cow-protectors nor the anti-Hindu *jehad* (holy war waged in the defence of Islam) of the *julahas* and other poor Muslims, were 'spontaneous'. For anger to express itself in communal violence, some organization and planning are almost always necessary. The brahminical hierarchy of the Hindus, strongly supported by the upper-caste landlords (the Maharaja of Darbhanga and his kin were Brahmins and, along with

---

[3] This apparently originated as a movement among the Kuka Sikhs of Punjab in 1870 or so. But it was taken up as a slogan by Dayanand Saraswati and his followers. It then assumed the character of a movement in virtually all parts of north India in the 1880s and 1890s. It thrived often on the patronage of the Hindu *zamindars* and *rajas*. A major part of the early Congress leadership was imbued with an ideology of Hindu revivalism of which cow protection was a part. See, in this connection, Hasan 1979.

the Rajputs and the Bhumihars, constituted the dominant landlord element in Bihar and eastern Uttar Pradesh—the chief trouble spot of the anti-cow slaughter riots), provided the ideological underpinnings and the muscle-power of the communal riots triggered by the derailed cow protection movement. Similarly, the *ulamas* (plural of *alim*: person learned in Muslim scriptures and other traditional Islamic studies) took up the *jehad*—initially against the British who, in their eyes, had converted India from a land favourable to Islam to a country favouring the infidels. But they found it easier to imbue the faithful with a hatred of the infidel next door rather than with a determination to fight the infidel occupying (symbolically speaking first, and literally, from 1911) the *masnad* of Delhi. Moreover, the *ulamas'* movement was soon supplemented by the Anglo–Orientalist movement of Sir Syed Ahmad. The Anglo–Orientalist movement, and the rise of an Anglicized but separatist politics among the upper-class Muslims of Uttar Pradesh, illustrate the point that communalism may arise not from processes of absolute deprivation but from perceptions of relative deprivation. According to Paul Brass, the Muslim gentry and the landlords of Uttar Pradesh in the latter half of the nineteenth century were not doing badly at all as compared to their Hindu counterparts.[4] But they felt degraded by British rule since at one time a Nawab had ruled in Lucknow or a Mughal emperor had ruled from Delhi, and this was the major cause of their anti-Hindu sentiments. Of course, not all Muslim gentry or landlords behaved in the same way: there were many who joined the nationalist struggle, just as on the other side many Hindu landlords and professionals remained loyal to the British government till the very end. Moreover, much of the majority 'nationalism' remained implicated in religious symbolism, vocabulary and sentiment. But among the Muslim masses in most parts of India, it was the communalist ideology of the *ulama* or the Anglo–Orientalist perception of the upper-class Muslims of Uttar Pradesh that came to prevail.

[4] According to Brass (1975: Chapter 3), Muslims in the United Provinces before 1900 held more than a disproportionate share of the government jobs open to the Indians, and they were also better educated in terms of western learning than the Hindus. According to Robinson (1975), they also formed a disproportionate share of the land-holding aristocracy of the province, especially in its western part.

After Independence, there was a large-scale migration of the professionals among the Muslims to Pakistan. Along with that, *zamindari* rights and the rule of Indian chiefs over their territories ended in the Republic of India. These particular changes hit hard some sections of the Muslims in Uttar Pradesh, the province in which the Muslim landed aristocracy and the professionals had first spearheaded the demand for separate privileges for Muslims and then for Pakistan (Brass 1975: Chapters 3 and 4). Those institutions which had depended on the patronage of the Muslim landlords were impoverished by the changes. Similar changes occurred, though to a lesser extent, in other parts of India also. This meant that, even if there were no concealed processes of discrimination against Muslims working under the surface, with the normal rules of competition in an increasingly commercialized society, the percentage of Muslims making it to the professional classes would decline. Combined with such processes of social discrimination as were operating in predominantly Hindu-administered institutions, the proportion of Muslims in the professional classes could also be expected to be lower than their proportion in the general population. This meant that the average Muslim perceived his advancement being barred in this society, which professed to be secular, but which practised systemic, if not systematic, discrimination against an underprivileged minority.

III

In this section we turn to an examination of some aspects of the economic and demographic setting in post-Independence India, which would help us depict the operation of predatory commercialization in its true magnitude. If we look at the distribution of the Muslims and Hindus in India as between rural and urban areas (Table 1), it becomes obvious that Muslims are a far more urbanized community than the Hindus. In some states (such as Maharashtra), there are more Muslims living in urban areas than in villages (Table 1). It is not accidental that most of the communal riots in India have been urban. However, the Bhagalpur riots[5] demonstrate that we should not harbour the illusion that if we understand the pre-

---

[5] For a graphic description and analysis of the Bhagalpur riots, see People's Union for Democratic Rights, *Bhagalpur Riots*, 1990.

disposing conditions of urban riots, we will understand the pathology of communal riots in general. Where so many people are dispossessed or threatened with dispossession by processes of predatory commercialization, and where society and the state take little note of the need to succour the victims of such commercialization, the material conditions facilitating communal riots are present all the time.

As we have pointed out earlier, capitalist colonialism under the British already affected the people's livelihood in numerous ways. It led to the erosion of the protection given to members of many communities in pre-colonial days—however inadequate and unequally distributed such protection might have been in practice—without putting any new protective structures in place. New patronage linkages grew around the *zamindari* structures and the structures revolving around the more important native princes. But in most cases, the *zamindars'* economic position deteriorated over time. Moreover, threatened with relative impoverishment, the *zamindars* increased their demands ferociously—until they were stalled by the resistance of the suffering peasants.

British rule produced landlord domination. This domination was not, however, automatic, and contradictory pulls acted on it: when the *zamindars* were threatened too extensively with bankruptcy because of their extravagance and because of the newly-instituted right of the moneylender to take over mortgaged properties, the British rulers rushed with Courts of Wards and with special legislation to try and save them as a class. In Punjab the British brought in special measures to protect land from being taken over by non-agriculturists. The imperatives of imperial rule led to authority structures and measures that mainly subserved the colonial regime but could, on occasion, be used to defend some particular rights of members of the patronage network latticing those structures. However, predatory commercialization acted as a corrosive acid on most existing structures, throwing handicraft workers out of work, dispossessing peasants, ruining petty landlords, enriching traders and moneylenders, and leading to new alignments of power under the overarching framework of colonial rule and landlord domination.

After Independence, predatory commercialization continued to work through the new structures of a post-colonial mimetic state apparatus, thrusting forward nodes of industrialization, a countryside dominated by landlords and rich peasants, and urban centres with numerous, jostling, petty merchants and monopoly capitalists. It is a characteristic of predatory commercialization that, acting by itself, it tends to convert people into paupers rather than proletarians. As we have noted already, pauperization is a process under which owners of means of production—whether artisans, peasants or petty landlords—are dispossessed but are not absorbed in alternative gainful occupations even in the long run. This can happen because the potential employment in alternative occupations does not grow at a sufficiently high rate. This can also happen because the losers refuse to accept the employment open to them, because it does not satisfy the requirements of their ascribed status in the old society. Ashrafs and upper-caste Hindus have often starved (literally to death, in times of famines in colonial India) rather than accept jobs as unskilled labourers, or in menial occupations—at least in the same neighbourhood. One of the motives of migration of such threatened groups has been to achieve a relative freedom from ascriptive status away from prying eyes.

We must not, of course, exaggerate the importance of such cultural barriers. If the searches for jobs have failed, in most cases it is because there are not enough new jobs when old ones are destroyed by shifts in market conditions. Capitalist colonialism and predatory commercialization adversely affected the fortunes of millions of Hindus, Muslims, Sikhs, Christians, Buddhists and people outside the reach of the major religions.

Let us try to see whether we can say something more about the predisposing conditions for communal riots by using the data on the urban–rural distribution of populations by community ascription. If we look carefully at Tables 1 and 2 we will see that, with the sole exceptions of Assam and West Bengal, among the more populous states of India Muslims are a more urbanized community, in the sense that their proportion in urban population is higher than their proportion in total population. In the more urbanized states, such as Gujarat and Maharashtra, the urban Muslims constitute the majority of the Muslim population. The degree of urbanization of Indians is increasing over time, but in some states the degree of urbanization of Muslims is increasing at a faster rate.

In the jargon of economists, both push and pull factors are

TABLE 1 Total population of Hindus and Muslims in different states and their urban areas 1961-81 (in '000)

	Total population						Urban population					
	1961		1971		1981		1961		1971		1981	
	Hindus	Muslims	Hindus	Muslims	Hindus	Muslims	Hindus	Muslims	Hindus	Muslims	Hindus	Muslims
India [a]	366,527	46,941	453,437	61,418	541,779	75,512	60,336	12,698	83,195	17,685	120,653	25,678
Andhra Pradesh	31,814	2,715	38,791	3,520	47,526	4,534	4,759	1,219	6,328	1,667	9,623	2,393
Assam [b]	7,885	2,766	9,490	3,592	—	—	719	114	1,115	145	—	—
Bihar	39,346	5,786	42,589	7,594	58,011	9,875	3,095	691	4,442	986	6,953	1,504
Gujarat	18,356	1,745	17,949	2,249	30,519	2,908	4,108	905	5,887	1,218	8,512	1,647
Haryana [c]	—	—	7,341	405	11,548	524	—	—	1,615	16	2,586	40
Himachal Pradesh	—	—	3,113	50	4,100	70	—	—	211	6	290	9
Jammu & Kashmir	1,013	2,432	1,404	3,040	1,930	3,843	197	370	298	519	420	784
Kerala	10,283	3,028	12,683	4,163	14,801	5,410	1,521	527	2,018	765	2,779	1,048
Karnataka [d]	20,583	2,328	25,332	3,113	31,907	4,105	3,952	1,014	5,227	1,496	7,936	2,198
Madhya Pradesh	30,426	1,318	39,024	1,816	48,505	2,502	3,649	708	5,372	1,009	8,520	1,496
Maharashtra	32,531	3,034	41,307	4,233	51,109	5,806	8,064	1,671	11,195	2,497	15,675	3,552
Manipur	—	—	633	71	853	99	—	—	120	2	296	23
Meghalaya	—	—	187	26	241	41	—	—	71	4	99	7
Nagaland	—	—	59	3	111	12	—	—	28	2	44	5
Orissa	17,123	215	21,121	327	25,162	422	994	81	1,678	100	2,849	159
Punjab	12,930	393	5,087	114	6,200	168	3,117	45	2,135	42	2,982	60
Rajasthan	18,133	1,315	23,094	1,778	30,604	2,492	2,543	518	3,489	757	5,639	1,169

Sikkim	—	—	145	*	213	3	—	—	13	*	33	2
Tamil Nadu (e)	30,297	1,559	36,674	2,104	43,017	2,520	7,485	900	10,323	1,256	13,246	1,579
Tripura	—	—	1,394	104	1,834	139	—	—	157	5	218	6
Uttar Pradesh	62,437	10,788	73,998	13,677	92,366	17,658	6,451	2,765	8,408	3,657	13,856	5,667
West Bengal	27,523	6,985	31,612	9,064	42,007	11,743	7,388	986	9,564	1,243	12,458	1,768

* Less than a thousand

Notes: (a) The population of India includes that of all the component states and union territories, except in 1981, when no census operation could be conducted in Assam.
(b) No census operation could be conducted in Assam in 1981.
(c) Haryana was included in Punjab in 1961.
(d) Karnataka was named 'Mysore' in the census of 1961.
(e) Tamil Nadu was named 'Madras' in the census of 1961.

Sources: Census of India 1961, Vol. 1, Part II, C (i); *Social and Cultural Tables*, Manager of Publications, Delhi, 1963, Table CII, Religion, pp. 488–90; *Census of India 1971*, Series 1, Part II, C (i); *Social and Cultural Tables*, Manager of Publications, Delhi, 1974, Union Table CVII, Religion, pp. 92–95; *Census of India 1981*, Series I, India, Paper 3 of 1984, Household Publication by Religion by Household, Manager of Publications, Delhi, 1984, Table H H, 15, pp. 6–9.

acting to affect the process of urbanization. In many states, the proportion of landless labour to the total rural working force has increased. There is also evidence that in Haryana, Punjab and western Uttar Pradesh, the employment of labour per hectare has tended to fall over time. The rate of growth of employment in agriculture has tended to decline drastically in recent years. Along with these developments, unemployment has tended to increase in both urban and rural areas.[6]

On the basis of the data gathered by the 43rd Round of the National Sample Survey (NSS), it is found that in 1987–88, the total unemployment was 12.43 million person-years, according to the Usual Principal Status (UPS) criterion, 15.3 million according to the Weekly Status (WS), and 18.95 million according to the Daily Status (DS).[7] The proportion of the labour force unemployed was higher in urban than in rural areas and, interestingly enough, higher among females than among males, both in rural and urban areas. A more alarming fact is that the numbers of unemployed, especially by the UPS criterion, have been rising all through the 1970s and 1980s, as Table 3 demonstrates. The only break in the series is for unemployed females between 1977–78 and 1983, but it is not clear as to how much this decline in their numbers is a statistical artefact and how much it reflects a real improvement. The rates of unemployment as a proportion of the work force have risen between 1983 and 1987–88, except for unemployment by the DS criterion. This seems to indicate a greater degree of casualization of the work force. (We have other evidence of such casualization, such as the growth in the numbers of registered and unregistered non-factory enterprises

---

[6] Usual Principal Status: a person is considered unemployed according to this concept if he/she is available for but is without work for a major part of the year. Weekly Status: a person is considered unemployed according to this concept if he/she, though being available for work, does not have paid work for even one hour during the reference week. Daily Status: it is a measure of unemployment in terms of person-days of unemployment of all persons in the labour force during the reference week. See Planning Commission (1990: 14).

[7] These findings are based on the 32nd, 38th and 43rd Rounds of the National Sample Survey and have been summarized in ibid. The only exception to the increasing trend is the measure of unemployment by Daily Status.

TABLE 2: *Percentage of Hindus and Muslims in total population and urban population of India 1961-81*

	Percentage of total population						Percentage of urban population					
	1961		1971		1981		1961		1971		1981	
	Hindus	Muslims	Hindus	Muslims	Hindus	Muslims	Hindus	Muslims	Hindus	Muslims	Hindus	Muslims
India [a]	83.4	10.7	82.7	11.2	82.6	11.3	76.4	16.1	72.2	16.2	76.5	16.3
Andhra Pradesh	88.4	7.5	87.6	8.1	88.7	8.5	75.8	19.4	75.3	19.8	2.2	19.1
Assam [b]	66.4	23.3	72.5	24.6	—	—	78.7	12.5	86.5	11.2	—	—
Bihar	84.7	12.5	83.4	13.5	83.0	14.1	79.1	17.6	78.8	17.5	79.7	17.2
Gujarat	89.0	8.4	89.3	8.4	89.5	8.5	77.3	17.0	78.5	16.2	80.3	15.5
Haryana [c]	—	—	89.2	4.0	89.3	4.0	—	—	91.1	0.8	91.4	1.4
Himachal Pradesh	—	—	96.1	1.4	95.7	1.6	—	—	87.2	2.1	88.9	2.8
Jammu & Kashmir	28.4	68.3	30.4	65.8	32.2	64.2	33.2	62.4	34.7	30.5	33.2	62.2
Karnataka [d]	87.3	9.9	86.5	10.6	85.9	11.0	75.0	19.2	73.4	21.0	73.9	20.5
Kerala	60.8	17.9	59.4	19.5	58.1	21.2	59.6	20.6	58.2	22.0	58.2	22.0
Madhya Pradesh	94.0	4.1	93.6	4.4	93.0	4.8	78.9	15.3	79.2	14.9	80.5	14.1
Maharashtra	82.2	7.7	81.9	8.4	81.4	9.2	72.2	15.0	71.2	15.9	71.2	16.1
Manipur	—	—	50.9	6.6	60.0	7.0	—	—	85.1	1.4	78.9	6.1
Meghalaya	—	—	18.5	2.6	18.0	3.1	—	—	48.3	2.7	41.1	2.9
Nagaland	—	—	11.4	0.6	14.3	1.5	—	—	54.9	3.9	36.7	3.3
Orissa	97.6	1.2	96.2	1.5	95.4	1.6	89.5	7.2	90.9	5.4	91.6	5.1
Punjab	63.7	1.9	37.5	0.8	36.9	1.0	76.2	1.1	66.4	1.3	64.1	1.3
Rajasthan	90.0	6.5	89.6	6.9	89.3	7.3	77.5	15.8	76.8	16.5	78.2	16.2
Sikkim	—	—	68.6	0.2	67.4	0.9	—	—	65.0	1.02	64.7	3.9
Tamil Nadu [e]	89.9	4.6	89.0	5.1	88.9	5.2	83.2	10.0	82.8	10.1	83.0	9.9
Tripura	—	—	89.6	6.7	89.3	6.7	—	—	96.3	3.1	96.5	2.6
Uttar Pradesh	84.7	14.6	83.8	15.5	83.3	15.9	68.0	29.2	67.9	29.5	69.6	28.5
West Bengal	78.8	20.0	71.3	20.4	77.0	21.5	86.5	11.5	87.2	11.3	86.2	12.2

Notes and Sources: As for Table 1

TABLE 3 *Number of unemployed by the usual status criterion (excluding subsidiary occupations) from 1972–73 to 1987–88 (in million)*

	Rural		Urban	
	Male	Female	Male	Female
1972–73 (27th Round of NSS)	1.5	0.3	1.6	0.5
1977–78 (32nd Round of NSS)	1.8	1.8	2.0	1.3
1983 (38th Round of NSS)	2.2	0.5	2.5	0.6
1987–88 (43rd Round of NSS)	3.0	2.3	3.0	1.0

Source: National Sample Survey Organization (NSSO), *Key Results of Employment and Unemployment Survey, All-India (Part-I)*, NSS 43rd Round, July 1987–June 1988, Department of Statistics, Ministry of Planning, Government of India, January 1990, Statement 39, p. 113.

and growth in employment in such enterprises even while employment growth in the private factory sector has become negative.[8])

Of course, unemployment in rural and urban areas is not spread evenly across the states. Nor does the rate of unemployment by itself indicate the degree of insecurity of the poor. It can be argued that in regions where the proportions of the poor are low, various informal social mechanisms, and the prospect of a relatively high-wage casual work may sustain the morale of the poor. But such a general statement cannot be fully trusted without further investigation. What I am doing here is to pull in certain kinds of data relating to the living conditions of the poor, to see whether the degree of insecurity as such provides an approximate index of the proneness of the region to communal violence.

In Table 4 we have reproduced the percentages of persons in the lowest three expenditure classes (in terms of per capita expenditure) in rural and urban areas in the major states of India during the 43rd Round of the NSS (1987–88). (The population is divided into twelve expenditure classes in both rural and urban areas; but since prices and money incomes tend to be higher in the urban areas, the lowest expenditure class and the highest one [open-ended], both have higher cut-off points for urban areas. For rural areas, the upper

---

[8] See Appendix Table 3.2, in Government of India (1990).

limit of the lowest three expenditure classes is Rs 95 per capita, and for urban areas it is Rs 135 per capita.)

One inference follows directly from Table 4. In both relatively urbanized and non-urbanized states, there is a large proportion of people who can be regarded as desperately poor by any standard. (Here, I am not entering into a technical discussion of the comparison of degrees of poverty in real terms as between different states: relative price structures, absolute price levels and differences in the consumption baskets of the poor, all enter into the picture.) The only major states in which the proportion of the very poor as defined above is less than 10 per cent of the rural population are Haryana, Himachal Pradesh, Jammu and Kashmir and Punjab in the north, and Kerala in the south. Some of the populous states, such as Bihar, Madhya Pradesh, Orissa and Uttar Pradesh in northern and central India, and Karnataka and Tamil Nadu in the south, have more than 25 per cent of the rural people in the three lowest expenditure classes. Maharashtra and Andhra Pradesh have their corresponding figures lying between 20 and 25 per cent. Low figures of population in the lowest expenditure classes of Assam are more in line with those of the north-eastern states than with those of the other eastern states. (This largely explains the attraction of immigrants to Assam from Bangladesh and from other neighbouring states within India.)

If we look at the figures of the population in the lowest expenditure classes in urban areas, we find that they vary largely, though not wholly, with the corresponding figures for the rural areas of the respective states. The figures for the proportion of the poor in the urban areas tend to be higher—in some cases, for example, Andhra Pradesh, Bihar and Uttar Pradesh, considerably higher—than for the corresponding figures of the rural areas. The exceptions are Himachal Pradesh, Karnataka, Madhya Pradesh, Maharashtra and Tamil Nadu. But since in the case of Madhya Pradesh, the proportion of the urban poor exceeds 25 per cent of the total urban population, this is little comfort. It does seem, however, that the above-average industrial growth of Karnataka, Gujarat and Maharashtra has helped keep the numbers of the urban poor lower than they would otherwise have been.

We will add another table of figures to illustrate the asymmetries of the grid against which the deadly politics of communalism

TABLE 4: *Percentage of population in the lowest three expenditure classes (in terms of monthly per capita expenditure) in rural and urban areas of major states of India in 1987–88*

States	Rural: monthly per capita expenditure less than Rs 95	Urban: monthly per capita expenditure less than Rs 135
Andhra Pradesh	23.4	31.7
Assam	12.2	16.4
Bihar	29.3	40.5
Gujarat	13.8	16.0
Haryana	7.8	15.0
Himachal Pradesh	5.4	5.4
Jammu & Kashmir	8.7	12.0
Karnataka	25.8	20.2
Kerala	9.8	14.0
Madhya Pradesh	32.9	28.0
Maharashtra	24.0	21.0
Orissa	25.4	27.4
Punjab	5.1	12.2
Rajasthan	19.1	22.5
Tamil Nadu	29.2	27.0
Uttar Pradesh	26.4	35.3
West Bengal	19.0	25.9

Source: National Sample Survey Organization (NSSO), *Key Results of Employment and Unemployment, All-India,* NSS 43rd Round, July 1987–June 1988, Statement 8.

and casteism is being played, and then begin to draw out some of the social, political and ideological implications. Table 5 reproduces the state-wise figures of the urban unemployment rate and the total numbers of unemployed in urban areas as estimated by the 43rd Round of the NSS (1987–88). For this purpose, we took the Usual (Principal) Status criterion of unemployment. One of the most striking features of the array of figures in Table 5 is that urban unemployment rates among males are the highest in the two states governed by the left parties, namely, Kerala and West Bengal. These two states also have the two largest masses of unemployed females in the country. The number of unemployed women is low in most of the north Indian states, not because women face alluring prospects of employment but because the female participation rate in the work force outside the household is low.

TABLE 5 *Usual Status unemployment rates (as percentages of the work force) and numbers of persons unemployed (in '000s) by sex in urban areas of major Indian states in 1987–88*

States	Unemployment Rates (%)		No. of Persons Unemployed	
	Males	Females	Males	Females
Andhra Pradesh	6.4	9.0	269	134
Assam	5.3	28.4	41	25
Bihar	6.4	3.3	190	11
Gujarat	4.7	2.2	169	12
Haryana	4.6	9.6	55	13
Himachal Pradesh	6.9	10.5	7	3
Jammu & Kashmir	4.7	15.5	22	10
Karnataka	5.6	4.1	209	47
Kerala	14.1	33.8	239	211
Madhya Pradesh	4.3	5.6	158	47
Maharashtra	6.5	5.0	496	88
Orissa	7.1	14.0	87	27
Punjab	4.8	14.7	84	28
Rajasthan	4.7	1.4	119	9
Tamil Nadu	7.3	9.1	413	175
Uttar Pradesh	3.4	2.9	250	25
West Bengal	9.0	21.4	492	188

Source: NSSO, *Key Results of Employment and Unemployment Survey, All-India (Part 1)*, NSS 43rd Round, July 1987–June 1988, Statement 40.

IV

Let us now look at the rough grid of communal and caste violence in recent years against the information about insecurity and poverty culled so far. Uttar Pradesh and Bihar would seem to fit a hypothesis that links the potential for communal violence to the incidence of poverty. Moreover, the massive numbers of unemployed men confined in overcrowded urban slums also provide frequent occasions for the flaring-up of tempers or for deliberate mobilization of ignitable materials required for such flare-ups. But Gujarat does not conform to this stereotype at all. The state has witnessed some of the worst communal riots in recent years (Engineer 1985a 1985b; Iyengar and Patel 1985). Yet, the incidence of poverty and the incidence of urban unemployment among males in Gujarat are below the average for the major Indian states (the all-India average computed by the NSSO and reproduced in Table 3 seems to be biased downward because of a large weight accorded to the north-eastern states—out of proportion to their population). One clue to all this is to be found in the general climate of opinion among the upper classes (and castes) of Gujarat, which have practised a policy of social Darwinism over a number of years (Breman 1990; Patel 1983; Kalathil 1990). 'If the existing local population cannot be exploited at low wages, and labour can be obtained from elsewhere at lower wages, the local exploitable population might as well die off.' This is the implicit ideology of the thrusting predatory commercialization process almost everywhere in India. But its ideology can be seen nakedly in operation in Gujarat, in the consistent and open violation of most of the minimum wage and social security regulations by local capitalists—with the deliberate connivance and collusion of the state apparatus.[9] This is also the state that witnessed one of the worst carnages instigated by members of the upper castes protesting against reservation of some jobs for the backward castes; this casteist hatred later turned into communal violence in which again the poor suffered most of the casualties and loss of belongings.

Is there any way of countering this ideology? Activists in Gujarat have tried public interest litigation. The government of Gujarat was the first state government (apart from Tamil Nadu) to try and reserve jobs for backward castes other than scheduled castes and tribes, and there has been a proliferation of non-governmental organizations taking up the cause of women, the poor and tribals. But most of these moves have again and again been swamped by casteist riots and communal riots engulfing the major cities and towns of Gujarat, which have even spread to the rural areas.

Let us look at neighbouring Maharashtra. There, in spite of a high rate of industrial growth and burgeoning of trade related to West Asia, massive urban unemployment continues to persist. Rural male unemployment rates in Maharashtra, however, are pretty low, according to the NSS 43rd Round, much lower, say, than in Kerala and West Bengal. In the wake of a major drought in Maharashtra, the government of Maharashtra launched the Employment

---

[9] For a discussion of the linkages between caste, class and dominance in Gujarat, see Desai 1984; Shah 1985; Baxi 1985.

Guarantee Scheme, which has been hailed as 'perhaps the first programme which guarantees the right to work as a basic right in a developing country' (Acharya 1990: Preface). Yet, rural wages in Maharashtra often remain far below the minimum legal level, workers wait vainly for the employment guaranteed to them, and the proportion of people in the lowest three expenditure brackets was 24 per cent (see Table 4)—much higher than in Kerala and West Bengal, both states that have done far worse in terms of industrial and commercial growth than Maharashtra. Maharashtra has been repeatedly embroiled in massive communal riots, mostly in and around Bombay, but these have also spread to other areas from time to time. Admittedly, the number of urban unemployed males (UUM) in Maharashtra is the largest among all the major states. But Maharashtra, with 496,000 UUM, is closely followed by West Bengal with 492,000 UUM, and we have to remember that the latter's population is considerably less than that of Maharashtra. The ideological and political aspects of communal violence acquire significance when we see that despite the poor record of urban unemployment, at least since the middle of the 1970s, West Bengal can claim the best record in terms of keeping communal peace.

Let me now put forward several propositions without claiming more than that the picture presented above provides only a suggestive support for them. The first proposition is that in most states of India the insecurity of the poor, as indicated by their meagre daily earnings when they are lucky enough to find a job, the threat of unemployment to which they are continually exposed because of predatory commercialization,[10] and the continual threat of disease and death under which they spend their daily lives, maintain a fertile ground for *agents provocateurs* to prod them into divisive conflicts of all kinds.

---

[10] Degrees of poverty and infant mortality rates both in urban and rural areas are closely related. See World Bank (1990: 30). When talking about unemployment, we have to remember that most of the poor face a positive threat of unemployment and starvation practically all the time. The threat may be caused by droughts, floods, disabling diseases, sudden loss of assets through seizure by moneylenders, and so on. Thus, while some people stay desperately poor all the time, there are others who may move out of poverty in one year to find themselves again pushed below

The second proposition is that the overcrowded conditions of most cities and the competition for valuable urban space which can be monopolized, speculated with, divided and redivided to profit the greedy, constitute powder-kegs for generating various petty conflicts. Adroitly exploited, such petty conflicts can be made to snowball into a major communal conflagration.

The third proposition is that any measures that improve the chances of upward social mobility for the poor and accord them increased bargaining power against the rest will help to make the environment less congenial to fomenting communal violence. These measures include pro-peasant land reforms that effectively eradicate landlordism, a continuous campaign for universalizing literacy, removing the special position of women as both the victims and hostages of communal violence and hostility and making them fully equal citizens with men, and providing everybody with a guarantee for the basic necessities of life. The first three sets of measures will themselves reduce poverty and insecurity of life by giving more land to the small peasants, who will cultivate it more intensively by raising productivity through the spread of literacy among workers and by releasing the productive energies of women, a large number of whom are immured within walls as the ultimate victims of exploitation, and the residuary legatees of the all-oppressive systems. A uniform civil law which abolishes the special pre-bourgeois privileges enjoyed by propertied Hindus (under the *Mitakshara* system) in most parts of India, and render their positions of vantage relatively immune to competition from other groups which are not similarly placed, will increase the chances of upward mobility of disadvantaged groups. A civil law that makes women equal sharers in property and the fruits of work with men will fully liberate the energies of half of the population. (India shares with West Asia the dubious distinction of having one of the worst records of treatment of women in terms of work, health services and literacy.)

---

subsistence levels of living the next year. For a study of this kind of instability around the poverty line, see ibid., p. 35, which summarizes the findings of a study of 211 agricultural households in drought-prone areas of central India between 1975 and 1983, carried out by the International Crops Research Institute for the Semi-Arid Tropics (ICRISAT) based in Hyderabad.

But this package of social and economic reforms must be accompanied by a basic but comprehensive social security system which will guarantee that nobody need starve to death or die of exposure to cold and heat, or from easily preventable diseases. This system will be necessary because unemployment will not go away soon, landlessness or property-lessness will continue to increase, and we cannot depend on market forces alone to raise wages to the minimum standards laid down, as we saw from the examples of Gujarat and Maharashtra.

The importance of a civil law that distances itself from arbitrary religious criteria needs to be emphasized again. The landlord lineages and trader lineages of northern and central India have effectively used non-market power and the power of restrictive organizations and practices to keep their vantage positions. Intermediary rights were abolished in many states. But landlordism survived wherever land-ceiling laws and tenancy legislation were weak or were badly implemented. But that landlordism now required the exercise of political power, including local administrative and police authority, and in turn shored up the political power of landlord lineages in a nominally democratic society. Muslim landlords in Uttar Pradesh and Madhya Pradesh lost their pre-eminent positions. Many migrated to Pakistan, and those who remained found it difficult to maintain their position through lineage ties or links to the local administration and the police. The migration of their co-religionists in erstwhile strategic positions in administration and their weakening ability to maintain patronage networks for their dependents sapped their muscle power and their shouting prowess, both of which counted in an imperfect democracy.

With the declining fortunes of Muslim landlords, the continued erosion of the livelihood of Muslim artisans and the diminished opportunities for public employment of a community which suffered renewed educational backwardness in states such as Hyderabad and Uttar Pradesh—areas where the Muslim elite had been earlier the dominant section—the major avenue of upward mobility for Muslims could have been trade. Here the dominant position maintained by particular groups of Hindu traders, with the help of their early start and the special advantages conferred on them by the *Mitakshara* law of property inheritance and partition, erected strong barriers against the entry of not only non-trading Muslim groups (that is, all except Bohras, Khojas and Memons), but also against Hindu castes or ethnic groups that had not acquired a major position of vantage. In states in which trade was not already monopolized by all-India lineages of Hindu traders, new trading (and industrial) groups came up by using the resources of local politics and various government subsidies and contracts. Tamil Nadu and Andhra Pradesh would provide many examples of such upward mobility. This avenue was not and is not generally open to Muslim groups, although some particular groups or individuals may be cited as exceptions. This means that without conscious public action to counter the trend, the vast majority of Muslims in urban areas can only hope to hold on to what they have, or worse, expect to come down in the world. This pauperized mass, along with their Hindu brethren in similar situations, then become available as the frontline operators in smuggling, drug-peddling, protection rackets, and other illegal or semi-legal activities that thrive in a regime of predatory commercialization. They also, of course, become available for manipulation by politicians who use communalism for their own ends.

Using impoverished Muslims and Hindus as the infantry of contraband trade is the most obvious aspect of predatory commercialization that I referred to earlier. The point about the process of commercialization that is occurring in India today is that there is no social institution or mechanism to ensure the minimal needs of the losers in the game. Although commercialization as a process is fairly blind, there are differences in institutional structures that different groups use in order to find footholds for advance on the slippery terrain. The use of intra-caste and intra-clan networks, the use of trade unionism with close-shop policies by employees in many public and private organizations, the wielding of political and muscle power by lineages of big landlords and rich peasants—all these permit particular sections of the community to keep their existing positions and allow other members to get into protected niches. In this situation of prevailing insecurity, especially for the poor of the minority communities, it is easy for communalist organizations and politicians to pose as champions of the minorities. They can launch schools, colleges, hospitals to cater especially to members of those communities. However marginal these gains may be, they still loom large in relation to the efforts of a government that does little to succour the poor. Many religious institutions also, besides seeking to provide a psychological solace, dole out alms and medicines and provide other real or illusory services, and thus strengthen their hold on the consciousness of the poor.

The greatest threat to communal peace in India today is the communalization of politics. The state of West Bengal in recent years provides one clear case where an ideological battle supported by the state administration has been able to stem the tide of communal violence. However, the ideological base of such struggles needs to be strengthened by a massive effort to secularize people's consciousness; and this ideological deepening needs to be sustained by changes in the legal apparatus, the social structure and the political arrangements, that will make the whole society attuned to the needs of the poor, and the requirements of sustained economic growth whose effects are diffused through all the layers of the social system. No state can be an island in an all-India context; nor can pure ideological work be sustained in the long run without changes in the material conditions of living.

V

I will end this essay by making concrete some of the implications of the propositions just put forward. The major ideological influence on the consciousness of the poor in our country still stems from religion. However, such ideological influences are not immutable. Hinduism has been at best a congeries of faiths and practices, with intermittent attempts to re-assert the authority of some ancient text, or to invent a new tradition in the name of either reform, devotion or orthodoxy, while popular practice has again and again strayed beyond all those carefully constructed boundaries. Brahminical Hinduism has also had one of the most inegalitarian ideologies and social hierarchies associated with it, namely, the caste system, including the practice of characterizing a vast number of people as untouchables (or even 'unseeables', as in the case of the Nayadis of south India). As a result, religions which preach equality before God, at least for men, has claimed adherents away from this amorphous mass of Hindus: this has certainly been one factor responsible for the steady increase in the number of Muslims in South Asia. For very similar reasons, vast numbers of Dalits converted to Buddhism in the 1950s.

The Arya Samaj, and modern political movements such as the Rashtriya Swayamsevak Sangh (RSS), the Vishwa Hindu Parishad (VHP) and the Bharatiya Janata Party (BJP), have tried to create a militant Hinduism in the mirror image of a militant Islam. Hinduism is not a religion with a single creed or with a single focus of authority. Not only are there multiple interpretations of sacred texts but new sacred texts have been created within the fold of the religion every few centuries. The disputes between Shaktas and Vaishnavas in Bengal, or between the Veera Shaivas and traditional Brahminical Hindus in the south, have been on occasion no less acrimonious than those between Muslims and Hindus. Moreover, a Hindu often harbours beliefs and traditions that are mutually contradictory with one another. The attempt to impose a single belief system or a single authority structure on the people belonging to such a religion (or rather such a congeries of religions), is likely only to produce a new sectarian division at a tremendous cost to the society and polity. The onslaught on the fabric of the Indian polity mounted by the RSS, the VHP and the BJP in their attempt to impose a single ideology on Hindus and, by extension, on the rest of the population, has been a prime cause behind the flaring-up of communal violence in recent years. Their ideological onslaught is bound to fail for at least two reasons. In spite of Swami Dayanand Saraswati's preaching against caste, the insignia of caste are treasured highly for both narrow materialistic reasons and for reasons of status by members of higher castes, as the recent anti-reservation movement has demonstrated with gruesome vividness. The second reason is that a majority of the Hindus would be unwilling and perhaps even unable to convert themselves into mono-credal people of the book with a single historical tradition, especially when most of that tradition is based on myth—some of it concocted before their very eyes.[11]

---

[11] I cannot here resist reproducing a story (in free translation) from Charuchandra Datta's *Purano Katha* (1343 BS or AD 1936, reprinted 1962, Visva Bharati, Calcutta, p. 24), which illustrates the contradictions and the amorphousness of popular Hinduism. On a rainy and stormy night a (Muslim) *fakir* took shelter in a dilapidated temple, which still housed a

It is necessary, ideologically, to confront the ventures of both militant Islam and militant Hindutva. That confrontation is not achieved by writing learned essays in English or even in the vernacular. Perhaps the liberal and radical propagandists of secularism can take a leaf out of the practices of the Faraizi and Taiyuni movements in Bengal in the nineteenth century. The preachers affiliated to these movements literally became 'fish in the water' (as Mao Tse-tung advised his followers to become, in a later and much bigger movement), lived at the level of the common people, and tried to spread Islam by using vast numbers of vernacular tracts (as well as ill-understood texts of the Koran in Arabic), and frequent formal and informal meetings (A.M. Ahmed 1970; R. Ahmed 1981).

Militant and reformist Islam preached equality before God, and gave the poor a collective identity as an *umma,* but, unfortunately, left the women in a permanently inferior position even in terms of religion and, of course, in terms of rights to property and income. In other respects, the practice of societies dominated by a theocratic Islamic ideology has remained as unequal and as undemocratic as ever. If militant Hindutva succeeds in its endeavour, it will produce at best the same results as reformist Islam attained, and at worst, will also perpetuate caste-based inequalities.

A militantly secular ideology has to be diffused into the people's consciousness, and the defaults of the religion-oriented ideologies which promise paradise to the poor after death but nothing at all on earth, have to be clearly pointed out. The political activities of most of the left-oriented parties have studiously avoided such substantive issues of ideology. The cadres have also tended most of the time to distance themselves, however marginally, from most of

---

Shiva-*linga*. The *fakir* did not know the *linga* from any ordinary stone. He sat down on it, and ate some *kebabs* that he was carrying. The rain and the storm continued to rage. A Hindu peasant also ran into the temple to get some relief from the inclement weather. He was flabbergasted by the sight of the *fakir* with his white beard, and became transfixed in the doorway from fright. The *fakir* did not open his mouth, but the god was less kind. In a dreadful accent the *linga* spoke thus, 'My dear *fakir*, move your feet a bit. Let me go and break the neck of the Hindu. How dare he, a low-born fellow, enter my temple with muddy feet and dirty clothes?'

the poor villagers and town-dwellers. Secularism has meant for most of them allowing all religious claimants to acquire more and more public space at the cost of other citizens. This sort of tolerance cannot be extended indefinitely without the claims over public spaces of different religions coming into conflict, as they have already done with tragic consequences. (Associated with many of the so-called religious activities are very narrow private interests, such as claims over prime land occupied by temples or mosques, or the right to raise protection money in the name of subscriptions—but I am leaving such issues aside.) Are these cadres ready to take up the cause of secularizing people's consciousness with the same zeal and commitment as the *sadhus* and the *fakirs* had in the past?

Finally, in all the states, including those such as Kerala and West Bengal which have had some success in resisting communalism, we need a strong positive growth of employment and of the incomes of poor people for secularism to gain any ground. Pro-peasant land reforms and universal literacy will go a long way towards creating the conditions for such growth. Such social changes will also directly hit at the conditions that allow communal violence to be provoked.

References

Ahmed, A.M., 1970, *Amar Dekha Rajnitir Panchash Bachhar* (Bengali), Nawroz Kitabistan, Dhaka.

Ahmed, R., 1981, *The Bengal Muslims 1871–1906: a quist for identity*, Oxford University Press, New Delhi.

Acharya, S., 1990, *The Maharashtra Employment Guarantee Scheme: A Study of Labour Market Intervention*, mimeo, ILO (ARTEP), New Delhi, May.

Bagchi, A.K., 1976, 'Reflections on Patterns of Regional Growth in India under British Rule', *Bengal Past and Present*, Vol. 95, Part 1, No. 180, January–June.

Baxi, U., 1985, 'Caste, Class and Reservations (In Memory of I.P. Desai)', *Economic and Political Weekly*, Vol. 20, No. 10, March.

Brass, P.R., 1975, *Language, Religion and Politics in North India*, Vikas, Delhi.

———, 1990, *The Politics of India since Independence: The New Cambridge History of India*, IV.1, Cambridge University Press, Cambridge.

Breman, J., 1990, *'Even Dogs are Better Off': The On-going Battle Between Capital and Labour in the Cane Fields of Gujarat*, mimeo, Indian Council of Social Sciences Research, New Delhi and Institute for Social Science Research in Developing Countries, The Hague, April.

Chatterjee, Partha, 1984, *Bengal 1920–1947*, Vol. I: *The Land Question*, Centre for Studies in Social Sciences and K.P. Bagchi, Calcutta.

Das, S., 1990, 'Communal Violence in Twentieth-Century Colonial Bengal: An Analytical Framework', *Social Scientist*, Vol. 18, Nos 6–7, June–July.

Dasgupta, R., 1984, 'Poverty and Protest: A Study of Calcutta's Working Class and Labouring Poor (1875–1900)', in A.N. Das, V. Nilakanth and P.S. Dubey (eds), *The Worker and the Working Class*, Public Enterprises Centre for Continuing Education, New Delhi.

Datta, Charuchandra, 1936, *Purano Katha*, reprinted in 1962 by Vishva-Bharati, Calcutta, p. 24.

Desai, I.P., 1984, 'Should "Caste" be the Basis for Recognising Backwardness', *Economic and Political Weekly*, Vol. 19, No. 28, July.

Engineer, A.A., 1985, 'Ahmedabad: From Caste to Communal Violence', *Economic and Political Weekly*, Vol. 20, No. 15, April.

——, 1985, 'Communal Fire Engulfs Ahmedabad Once Again', *Economic and Political Weekly*, Vol. 20, No. 27, July.

Ghosh, P., 1984, *Emergence of an Industrial Labour Force in Bengal: A Study of the Conflicts of the Jute-Mill Workers with the State, 1880–1930*, Ph.D dissertation, Jadavpur University, Calcutta.

Government of India, 1990, *Economic Survey 1989–90*, Ministry of Finance (Economic Division), New Delhi.

Hasan, M., 1979, *Nationalism and Communal Politics in India*, Manohar, New Delhi.

Hardy, P., 1972, *The Muslims of British India*, Cambridge University Press, Cambridge.

Iyengar, S. and S. Patel, 1985, 'Gujarat: Violence with a Difference', *Economic and Political Weekly*, Vol. 20, No. 28, July.

Kalathil, M., 1990, 'Gujarat: Everyday Discrimination Against Tribals', *Economic and Political Weekly*, Vol. 25, No. 47, November.

Krishna, Gopal, 1985, 'Communal Violence in India: A Study of Communal Disturbance', *Economic and Political Weekly*, Vol. 20, Nos 2 and 3, 12 and 19 January.

McLane, J.R., 1977, *Indian Nationalism and Early Congress*, Princeton University Press, Princeton, N.J.

Pandey, G., 1982, 'Rallying Round the Cow: Sectarian Strife in the Bhojpur Region, 1888–1917', in R. Guha (ed.), *Subaltern Studies II*, Oxford University Press, New Delhi.

——, 1983, 'The Bigoted Jolaha', *Economic and Political Weekly*, Vol. 20, No. 5, Review of Political Economy, 29 January.

Patel, S., 1983, 'Gujarat: Contract Labour and Public Interest Litigation', *Economic and Political Weekly*, Vol. 18, No. 51, December.

Planning Commission, 1990, 'Employment: Past Trends and Prospects for the 1990s', Working Paper, New Delhi, May.

Robinson, F.S., 1975, *Separatism among Indian Muslims: The Politics of the United Provinces' Muslims, 1860–1923*, Vikas, Delhi.

Saksena, N.S., 1990, 'Anatomy of Communal Riots', *Indian Express*, New Delhi, 31 March.

Sarkar, T., 1987, *Bengal 1928–1934: The Politics of Protest*, Oxford University Press, New Delhi.

Shah, G., 1985, 'Caste, Class and Reservation', *Economic and Political Weekly*, Vol. 20, No. 3, January.

World Bank, 19900, *World Development Report*, Oxford University Press.

Multiculturalism, Governance and the Indian Bourgeoisie

Dense, Regimented and Democratic Multiculturalism and Slippage into Intolerant Identity Politics

Human beings have been migrants for most of their history. They have struck roots, assumed new identities—constructed by themselves and constructed for them by others—and moved on and assumed yet other identities. In the process they have often invented origins, whole histories and believed them, until some upheaval has destroyed or radically altered all these carefully constructed myths, histories and identities. In many different geographical locations, groups with different identities have mingled, jostled with one another, engaged sometimes in armed conflicts, but have often worked out codes for co-existence, in tolerance, if not always in friendship.[1]

The Indian subcontinent has seen almost as much intermingling of different migrant streams and settled populations, with their assumed identities, life-styles and belief-systems, as the whole continent of Europe. This intermingling did not take place without a great deal of armed conflict, domination of one group over another, and the subjugation of whole groups for centuries under some code of hierarchical order (mostly the caste system but also distinctions between the Arya and Dasyu, *ashraf* and *ajlaf*, *bhadralok* and *chasa*, and so on). But for ages together, communities with different assumed identities and belief-systems have lived cheek-by-jowl with one

---

[1] For a fascinating sketch of the intermingling of the city-dweller and steppe pastoralist, of Greeks and Scythians, Khazars and Varangians, Muslims and Byzantine Christians, see Ascherson 1995.

another in what could be called a system of dense multiculturalism, where different communities exchanged rituals, put on some of the outer garments and took over parts of the belief-systems of other communities.

Indian business communities lived in this milieu for hundreds, if not thousands of years. Many members of the business community adopted Jainism or Buddhism when these belief-systems came up in protest against the *sanatana dharma* characterized by a Brahmin–Kshatriya-centred hierarchical order. Many of them remained faithful to Jainism even when a refurbished Brahminism triumphed over Buddhism and Jainism. When most of northern India and parts of southern India came to be ruled by Sultans or Padshahs who professed Islam, the major business communities remained Hindu or Jain in their religious beliefs. Despite the urgings and the ideological preaching of some Islamic clerics who wanted to convert all the subjects under a Muslim king to 'the true faith' and treat the infidels harshly, most rulers tolerated and some positively encouraged a diversity of beliefs among their subjects. (For a fascinating account of the contention of approaches to multiculturalism and governance in medieval India, see Alam 1996.)

The British practised a more schematized form of secularism, overtly putting the state above the contending faiths. However, in some ways, the very attempt to make a watertight distinction between affairs of the state and affairs of the society—and at the same time exercise absolute dominion over the subject peoples—led to the outbreak of conflicts which acquired a communal hue (Pandey 1990). The Indian business communities, partly under the compulsion of authoritarian foreign rule, partly under a traditional dissociation from the mechanics of the exercise of political power, and partly under the influence of such leaders as Mahatma Gandhi and Jawaharlal Nehru, practised an uninvolved multiculturalism, although a few among them became militantly Hindu or Muslim at critical political junctures.

The newly-independent Indian Republic enshrined a variant of secularism in the Constitution of the country. By and large, in overt conflicts over religion the state apparatus adopted a neutral stance, at least so long as Nehru was alive. The Indian business community acquiesced in this democratic multiculturalism even when privately they might have shared a different view of how the Indian state should behave.

In recent years, however, this pragmatist multiculturalism has often been replaced among a section of the business community by an overt espousal of identity politics and support for parties and organizations which would convert India into a polity of majoritarian despotism, a majority which claims to represent all Hindus. The present essay seeks to understand the many gradations of multiculturalism among the Indian business communities and the structural and ideological limits of that multiculturalism, and advance some hypotheses regarding the fracturing of pale multiculturalism by, say, the horrors of the Bombay riots of 1992–93.

The Indian Bourgeoisie in a Multicultural Setting

Most of the rulers in non-socialist states and most capitalist states have believed in some religion or other. But not all religions have had a single organization or a religious head acting as the supreme authority. Nor have all religions been guided by a single text or set of texts. In societies without a church or a book ruling a religious community, the relation between religious organizations and the state has been a rather loose one. Where the rulers have felt secure by virtue of their control of the army and the other visible paraphernalia of rule, the people of different religions have been allowed to practise their worship of God or gods any way they pleased. Where the rulers have felt an urge to convert their subjects to their mode of worship out of either a spiritual need or a conviction that subjects of a different religion pose a threat to their secular authority, the relations between rulers and subjects of a different faith have been fraught with contention in the religious arena. These complexities mean that, unlike in most European settings since the sixteenth century, the question of the place of religion in the beliefs and practices of subjects, citizens and rulers in South Asia cannot be posed simply as that of relations between church and state. Once we grasp that, we will also see that posing the problem of making room for multiculturalism in the subcontinent of India cannot be couched entirely in terms of the European debate. In India the problem was not that of a religiously-oriented ideological make-up breaking through to the simple duality of religion as the sphere of private faith and the state as the sphere of exercise of public virtue or civic consciousness. Here the problem often has been that the subject who was denied all political rights earlier has, as a citizen, wanted to engross both private and public space in the name of a religious faith.

To point out these differences is not to claim that the place of religion in the history of the Indian state and society during the last two centuries can be discussed without invoking some terms of the debate that has been carried on in Europe over the same, or a longer span of time. But we must watch out for any unjustified extrapolation of the European terms to the Indian scene and unfounded expectation of modes of resolution of the conflict between private faith and public virtue.

Before we proceed, we would like to introduce yet another set of distinctions into the usual debates on multiculturalism. These are the distinctions between multiculturalism as a belief-system, multiculturalism as private and social practice, and multiculturalism as public policy. Very often people who invoke a notion of Hinduism as multiculturalism embodied fail to see that this was often only a recognition of plurality in the realm of beliefs, with no recognition of deviant practices in rituals or quotidian social behaviour. In this essay I shall discuss the situation of business communities in India in a multicultural setting in pre-colonial, colonial and post-colonial epochs, and the way these business communities have negotiated the plurality of religious beliefs in different political settings.

India had recognizably distinct business communities long before the European merchants penetrated the Indian market or established their political hegemony in the country. There were Hindu *bania* communities all over India, but there were merchants, shipowners and bankers who professed Islam as their faith, and there were bankers and merchants among Hindus whose ascribed caste was not that of a *bania* or a Vaishya. Most of the merchants and bankers in the immediate pre-British period had a subordinate relation to the state apparatus. They would service the armies and the courts of the Mughals and their *subahdars* or *fauzdars*, or those of the successors to the Mughals, or those of the southern principalities under the sway of other rulers. Some even used their position as courtiers and generals to further their mercantile interests

(Subrahmanyam 1990). But there is no record of any group of merchants who wanted to control the state apparatus as merchants rather than as surrogate *rajas* or *nawabs*.

Under the Mughals, especially since the days of Akbar, the spheres of religion and politics were generally kept separate. Akbar, of course, had a remarkably ecumenical attitude towards all religions (see the citations of Akbar's reported sayings, in Moosvi1994: 126–29). Even after the re-imposition of the *jizyah* on Hindus under Aurangzeb, Islam did not become the state religion in the sense in which Anglicanism became the state religion of England under Elizabeth I. Along with other subjects of the Padshah in Delhi, Indian Hindu and Muslim merchants could expect even-handed treatment from the civil authorities. That treatment could be arbitrary on occasion, but the arbitrariness was not systematically related to the religious faith of the victim.

The merchants, by and large, especially the Hindus among them, eschewed the use of armed violence and resorted to threats of migration, *hartals, dharnas,* fasts and boycotts, as instruments of protest or pressure (Bagchi 1985). It is significant that the leading Muslim merchants of Surat who did resort to arms in the 1730s in order to enforce their claims were utterly routed and became completely marginalized when the British established their hegemony (Das Gupta 1970, 1979; Bagchi 1985). The British, of course, had even less tolerance for armed Indian merchants than their immediate predecessors. But even peace-loving merchants fared badly when they posed any threat to the European aggrandizement of trans-oceanic trade from the time Vasco Da Gama found the route to India round the Cape of Good Hope. For that reason Indian ship-owning merchants almost everywhere in India suffered severely after the establishment of British paramountcy, since the British exercised a virtual monopoly on most trans-oceanic routes between India and foreign countries.

In pre-British days, especially since the later stages of the Mughal empire, Indian bankers had a close relationship with the revenue-raising activities and the finances of Indian rulers. When the British overthrew those rulers, these financiers went into a rapid decline. This happened with the Maratha bankers of the Peshwa's court, as had happened with the family of Jagatseth Mahatabchand in Bengal (Jenkins 1827; Little 1967; Divekar 1982). However, many of the bankers continued to service the operations of the surviving and subordinate Indian princes and princelings, and found new avenues of profit as suppliers of credit to the landlords and owner-occupiers who had to pay land taxes to the British.

The British used Indian merchants and bankers as collaborators at a time when they were still to establish a political presence in the country. But once British rule was established, these collaborators were subordinated by them and converted into junior partners or eliminated them altogether when the Indians proved to be threatening competitors, or were rendered irrelevant because the new rulers controlled the major resources of the government, including the enormous land revenues of Bengal and of the rest of British India. However, even in British territories, bankers and moneylenders remained important for servicing the revenue-extracting mechanism. Not only the poor peasants but many of the substantial landlords (variously known as *zamindars, talukdars, mirasdars*) also were dependent on loans extended by the *sahukars* or *mahajans* for payment of the land taxes to the superior right-holders or the government.

It is necessary to recall these situational characteristics of the majority of Indian merchants and bankers during the colonial period in order to grasp that while religion and the state were kept separate under the colonial dispensation, the latter presided over a social and political order in which capitalist and pre-capitalist elements, tributary or pure rent-receiving and entrepreneurial ingredients, were intertwined at all levels of society and in all the mechanisms for the exercise of power. Unlike in Europe, the merchants were not struggling to break the links between religion and a state controlled by feudal lords aided by the bureaucracy of emerging absolutist states.

Gandhi and the *Bania* Practice of Multiculturalism

The analytical separation of the roles of individual or micro-level movements in society, and the macro-level movements which are generally more, or less, than the sums of the micro-level changes, is tricky, and it cannot be theorized as mere summations of the micro-level interactions. This issue crops up also in analysing the social and political changes which brought about the transformation of western European societies that allowed capitalists to become the most important controllers of power in those societies. We can then see that the Weber–Sombart–Tawney problematic of the role of the Protestant (or Jewish or Old Believer) ethic in capitalist transformation is not likely to throw up an easy answer, however massive the evidence accumulated is about the exact nature of that ethic, or the power and character of the capitalist class and changes in those characteristics over time.

In the Indian case, the role of the bourgeoisie in fostering or hindering a democratic, multicultural society has not even been posed, although the role of big and small Indian merchants in financing and sometimes directing the activities of communalist organizations seeking to establish the dominance of a particular brand of, say, Sikhism, or much more menacingly, Hinduism, has been observed by all serious students of Indian politics and sectarian violence.

It is necessary to recall the moral values of the Indian merchants and bankers who still constitute the predominant sector of the Indian bourgeoisie because they indicate how implicated they were with pre-capitalist and colonial state apparatuses and social formations. At the same time, of course, not only the functions but also the values and social practices of the mercantile communities were in many ways different from those of the traditional rulers and military functionaries, and in some ways closely approximated to many of the values designated as the 'protestant ethic' by Max Weber (1925).

A provisional beginning for such a discourse may be provided by examining some of the statements of Mahatma Gandhi regarding Hinduism and multiculturalism. Gandhi is important for several reasons. He was, of course, the most important leader of the struggle for Independence in India. He often used religious idioms for conveying his social and political messages, and these idioms made sense to most Indians for whom a language of modernity remained as foreign as the English tongue. (For a powerful portrayal of how the Gandhian message was conveyed to and interpreted by a community of Tatmas—a depressed community of north Bihar—see the novel *Dhorai Charit Manas*, in Bengali, by Satinath Bhaduri.) Finally, Gandhi was in communication with influential groups of Indian merchants and some of them avowed themselves to be followers of Gandhi. They included, among others, G.D. Birla and Jamunalal Bajaj, whose families are counted among the most important business groups of modern India. It is perhaps not an accident in this context that Gandhi was born into a Hindu *bania* family of Gujarat—which can claim to have been one of the major cradles of Indian capitalism—and went out to South Africa as a lawyer employed by another Gujarati *bania*, though the latter was a Muslim rather than a Hindu in his professed faith.

In Gandhi's writings we can find plenty of statements of the 'protestant ethic' which was claimed by Max Weber to have been one of the impulsive forces of western capitalism:

> Action is my domain, and what I understand, according to my lights, to be my duty, and what comes my way, I do. All my action is actuated by the spirit of service. Let anyone who can systematize ahimsa into a science do so, if indeed it lends itself to such treatment. . . .
>
> God alone is omniscient. Man in the flesh is essentially imperfect. He may be described as being made in the image of God, but he is far from being God. God is invisible, beyond the reach of the human eye. All that we can do, therefore, is to try to understand the words and actions of those whom we regard as men of God. Let them soak into our being and let us endeavour to translate them into action, but only so far as they appeal to the heart. (Gandhi 1946)

Again, in response to some questions put by Sarvepalli Radhakrishnan, Gandhi answered in 1935:

> My religion is Hinduism, which for me, is the religion of humanity and includes the best of all the religions known to me. . . .
>
> Denial of God we have known. Denial of Truth we have not known. The most ignorant among mankind have some Truth in them. We are all sparks of Truth. The sum total of these sparks is indescribable, as yet-unknown Truth, which is God . . .
>
> The bearing of this religion on social life is, or has to be, seen in one's daily contact. To be true to such religion one has to lose oneself in continuous and continuing service of all life. . .

Hence for me, there is no escape from social service. . . . (Iyer 1991: 158–59)

Similar statements about an inner vision of truth, the necessity of non-violence, or abstinence, especially *brahmacharya* (or abstinence from sexual intercourse), could be culled from innumerable passages in Gandhi's writings (Prabhu and Rao 1946; Iyer 1987, 1991). Gandhi's idioms were imbricated with Hindu traditions, especially the Vaishnavite tradition which he explicitly acknowledged (Gandhi 1920). A poem by Narasimha Mehta (1414–79), the Vaishnavite saint-poet of Gujarat, formed part of the daily prayers of Sabarmati Ashram (Iyer 1991). Most of the Hindu *banias* of Gujarat in the nineteenth century were followers of Vallabhacharya of the Vaishnava sect; the rest were Jains or Shravaks (*Gazetteer of the Bombay Presidency* 1901: 69). They all believed in *ahimsa*, and were vegetarians, and within their own communities or in dealings with other businessmen they mostly relied on trust and word of honour, often without any written documents. In addition, the thriftiness or miserliness of the merchant was part of the *bania* stereotype virtually all over India. Hence, practically all the virtues extolled by Gandhi (except perhaps social service) were part of the value-system of a well-brought-up Hindu *bania*.

Even in the middle of the nineteenth century, in many parts of India, following earlier traditions when land was either not transferable property or transferable under rather strict conditions, moneylenders and bankers kept aloof from direct land-ownership (Kolff 1980). However, with the British bringing in legislation which made rights to the produce of the land and the right to pay taxes on it transferable and heritable property, moneylenders and bankers also became land-owners.

Whether the bankers and merchants were or were not distanced from the ownership of land, they could not insulate themselves from the social practices of the landlords who were the dominant strata in most parts of colonial India. For example, the immigrant Marwari community in the Central Provinces (today's Madhya Pradesh), which dominated the trade and banking of that province, might be thrifty, but would go on a splurge when a marriage or some other social event was celebrated (Russell and Hiralal 1915;

see also (*Gazetteer of the Bombay Presidency* 1901: 90–93, for a description of the elaborate marriage ceremony of the Meshri or Vaishnava *banias*). The marriage of the thirteen-year-old Jamunalal Bajaj, a Marwari *bania* and the adopted grandson of Seth Bachhraj of Wardha, to Jankidevi, the daughter of Girdharilal Jajodia, another Marwari Vaishnava *bania* of Rajasthan, in 1902, was celebrated with 'great pomp'. 'The festivities continued for several days, with dinners, nautch performances (dance) and fireworks' (Nanda 1990: 9). In conformity with the status-ranking of the time, G.D. Birla, possibly the most powerful businessman of his age, and R.K. Dalmia were regularly described as *zamindars* and not just as businessmen and industrialists.

The self-definition of Indian businessmen as belonging to particular communities characterized by the same caste, originating in the same region and speaking the same language, was reinforced by British business practices in India. The Banks of Bengal, Bombay and Madras would often treat, especially in periods of crisis, whole communities, such as Chettiars, Marwaris or Multani *banias*, with the same degree of favour or disfavour, without scrutinizing their credentials as individuals or even as separate joint families. Interestingly enough, one aspect of Mahatma Gandhi's espousal of *varnashrama dharma* would be the retention of the separate identities of particular business communities. Thus, the pre-Independence plurality and co-existence of separate business communities can be seen both as a device for preserving internal cohesion and as a way of confronting a generally haughty, if not hostile, alien ruling class and dominant business community. The separate existence of business communities as identifiable groups was also facilitated by the presence of a powerful group of landlords and 'native princes' who generally regarded the profession of businessmen with condescension, if not disdain. A 'semi-feudal' and colonial structure of society facilitated the separation of the profit-earners as identifiable groups.

Gandhi and Tagore as Exponents of Hinduism as Multiculturalism, and the Ambivalence of the Hindu Merchant Community towards Secularism

Independence was followed by the abolition of legally recognized intermediaries between the government and the legal occupant or owner of the land. But it did not see, except, in a few states such as West Bengal, Kerala and Jammu and Kashmir, the abolition of landlord power in the countryside and its extension into most of the small towns and even state capitals of northern, and to a lesser extent, southern India. The abject poverty of the vast majority of small peasants, artisans, casual workers in the formal or informal sectors and agricultural labourers continued to provide the base for a social, economic and political nexus between the power of the landlord, the trader and the moneylender—sometimes augmented by the power of the bureaucrat or politician, and often embodied within the confines of the same family. The law relating to ownership and inheritance within the Hindu undivided family—a law which is applicable to practically all property-owning Hindus except Bengali Hindus—also allowed *bania* and landlord families to erect various kinds of barriers against challenges from outsiders, including the state, creditors in business relations and competitors in business. The post-colonial governments sought to promote business. But their initiatives augmented the non-competitive, non-entrepreneurial characteristics of the Indian business community, and allowed them to enjoy both profits and luxury. Especially since lavish subsidies were given for construction of hotels and most of the real incomes of businessmen went untaxed (through tax forgiveness, allowances for expenditure, exemption of trust properties, etc.), the life-styles of the erstwhile Maharajas have been emulated by the businessmen of India. Many of the trading communities in northern, eastern and western India claim a Rajput or Kshatriya descent and are not happy if they are described as Vaishyas.

The Indian Hindu bourgeoisie, with perhaps a few exceptions, has been intensely religious. This religiosity has been expressed in their strict obedience to the rituals of religion, but also in the endowments they have made to temples and in the foundation of new temples: the Birlas have dotted the landscape of big Indian cities with temples founded by them. These temples or their appurtenances have been means of earning incomes or avoiding taxes, and have often obtruded into public space. While G.D. Birla and Jamunalal Bajaj were followers of Gandhi, the simplicity of the latter's religious beliefs has obviously not satisfied them or their families.

In a period of spiritual crisis during the last days of his life, Bajaj found his 'guru' in Anandamayi Ma (she had also been the 'guru' of Kamala Nehru).

In many parts of Gujarat, the Meshri and Shravak *banias* enjoyed a higher social status than the Brahmins (*Gazetteer of the Bombay Presidency* 1901: Section III). Yet they were bound by the brahminical code for sustaining a patriarcal, hierarchical and ritualistic social order. In medieval and modern Rajasthan, the top crust of society is constituted by the Rajputs, the ruling group, the *banias*, their financiers and revenue farmers, and the Brahmins, who provided the rationale for the rank ordering of access to private and public goods on the part of the different castes and sub-castes. Rajputs may be displaced by *bania sarpanches* as the effective voice of secular authority. But the Brahmin provides the (often invented) justification for the burning of widows (such as the case of Om Kanwar in Jhardli village of the Shekhawati region in 1980, and of Roop Kanwar in Deorala village of the same region in 1987), and *banias* mime the traditions of Rajputs (Vaid and Sangari 1991).

We have already seen how the religiosity of the Indian *banias* could go along with occasional splurges in life-styles. This belies Mahatma Gandhi's stress on correct practice (embodied in the phrase 'experiments with truth') as the true expression of a belief-system. How did the apparent catholicity of Hinduism as a congeries of belief-systems, rather than as a set of rigid precepts guiding the thoughts and practices of believers, fare among the *banias* or among the upper-class and upper-caste Hindus in general?

The answer to this question is not easy. Attempts were made in colonial India to convert Hindus into a sect swearing by a set of agreed texts and following them in their daily lives. This can be seen in the emergence of the Arya Samaj movement initiated by Swami Dayanand Saraswati (for his career and beliefs, see Sharma 1972; Yadav 1978). Dayanand too was born in Gujarat but in a Brahmin family, and he attacked the Vallabhacharya sect, with a large following among Gujarati *banias*. It is also interesting that Gandhi should have specifically distanced himself from Arya Samaj and called himself a follower of *sanatana* (that is, traditional) *dharma,* even while applauding some of the work in the field of education done by the followers of Dayanand (Gandhi 1916: 333–38). One reason given by Gandhi for differing from Arya Samaj is worth quoting:

> For me Hinduism is all-sufficing. Every variety of belief finds protection under its ample fold. And though the Arya Samajists and the Sikhs and the Brahmo Samajists may choose to be classed differently from the Hindus, I have no doubt that at no distant future they will all be merged in Hinduism and find in it their fullness. Hinduism, like every other human institution, has its drawbacks and its defects. Here is ample scope for any worker to strive for reform but there is little room for secession. (ibid.: 333).

Rabindranath Tagore, another major influence on the ideology of nationalism in India, had in many ways a very different outlook on politics from Gandhi. Despite occasionally contradictory statements, Tagore was almost entirely free of religious sectarianism. But he expressed his beliefs in very similar terms to those of Gandhi on a number of occasions. In an essay which was originally published around April–May 1912 (Baishakh 1319 of the Bengali era), with the title 'Self-identification' ('Atmaparichay'; Tagore 1361 BS: 452–87) Tagore, who had been born into a Brahmo family, identified himself as a *Hindu Brahmo*.

Tagore was here consciously or unconsciously echoing his contemporary, Brahmabandhab Upadhyay, who edited the nationalist paper *Sandhya* during the Swadeshi movement in Bengal. Upadhyay had, a few years back, called himself a Hindu Catholic or Catholic Hindu, after his conversion to Roman Catholicism. (Upadhyay renounced Christianity later.)

In a controversy which arose because of critical comments on Tagore's essay by an orthodox Brahmo, Tagore further defended his position (Tagore 1361 BS: 580–88). Tagore's arguments are quite detailed and in parts subtle, involving criteria for identification in terms of the self and the other, the nature of religious belief, and the evolution of Hinduism as a complex of belief-systems. He claimed that it was possible to remain a Hindu even if somebody embraced Islam or Christianity (Tagore 1361 BS: 464). If somebody calls himself a Brahmo and not also a Hindu simply because he (she) has abjured superstition and adopted a code of conduct which is superior to that of the average practising Hindu, he (she) denies his (her) identification as a brother (sister) of those Hindus who were steeped in superstition and misery. Believers in monotheistic faiths such as Christianity, Islam or Sikhism might resent what appeared to be the imperialistic tendency of the syncretic religious belief-systems proclaimed by Gandhi and Tagore. But the religious reformers who wanted to convert Hinduism into a religion of a single creed and single set of practices would resent them even more. Tagore's novel *Gora* portrays the conflicting ways in which Brahmoism and orthodox Hinduism were expounded by the dogmatists and the liberal humanists in contrast for whom secularism and tolerance of other belief-systems became the only acceptable norm (see, in this connection, J. Bagchi 1996).

Gandhi's and Tagore's difference from militant brands of Hinduism also stemmed from their opposition to any use of force or state power for purposes of religious propaganda or the enshrining of religious orthodoxy. Neither of them could have any truck with the use of the state apparatus, or any force other than that of moral persuasion and inner conviction, for empowering one set of religious beliefs at the cost of the other. Hence the support of sectarian or, in the Indian parlance, communalist organizations such as the Rashtriya Swayamsevak Sangh, the Vishwa Hindu Parishad or Jamaat-e-Islami by anybody and, most of all, in Gandhi's case, by the capitalist 'trustees' of property on behalf of the labouring poor would have been anathema.

The discourse of Gandhi and Tagore on multiculturalism is important because their writings show the way in which deeply-held religious beliefs could be combined with genuine belief in multicultural democracy. The idiom of the Indian bourgeoisie has remained religious in its phraseology with but a few exceptions. But they have not shown themselves responsive to the kind of openness that permeates Gandhi's and Tagore's discourse.

Before we leave this section, it would be interesting to note that Gandhi's lukewarmness with regard to affirmative action in relation to the Dalits and the Muslims has been criticized by later analysts and younger contemporaries, such as B.R. Ambedkar (cf. Ambedkar 1932; Baxi 1995). His attitude sprang at least partly from his distrust of state action, especially under colonial auspices, for addressing social wrongs.[2] But it is probable that he had genuinely underestimated the influence of an initially extremely inequitable distribution of assets on the attainability of Swaraj (that is, the acquisition of the ability to control one's destiny). If Gandhi had not convinced the majority of the Indian bourgeoisie of the virtue of multiculturalism, still less could he convince them of the need for such affirmative action as might threaten their entrenched positions which they had tried to defend through two centuries of colonial rule.

Gandhi was regarded as a godhead by many Indians, including many Indian businessmen. This was quite consistent with the infringement of most of the canons of the Gandhian philosophy of praxis. The bestowal of many Hindu spiritual leaders (godmen or more rarely, goddess-women) with attributes of godhead has been quite usual among the Indian bourgeoisie. Of course, in some cases, the circles of godmen such as Dhirendra Brahmachari, who was at one time close to Indira Gandhi, or Chandraswamy, who is close to numerous politicians, from the ex-Prime Minister Narasimha Rao to Subramanian Swamy, also serve as networks of power: in India's political and business milieu they are probably more puissant than Rotary Clubs or Lions Clubs. G.D. Birla was unusual in ordering statues of Marx and Lenin as incarnations of Saraswati, the goddess of learning, to be erected at the university founded by him at Pilani (the village to which the Birlas trace their origin). One of his spiritual mentors, Swami Chinmayananda, who was invited to unveil G.D. Birla's statue in the garden of the Golders Green crematorium, later became a major figure in the Vishwa Hindu Parishad, an organization that gained special notoriety through its involvement in the illegal demolition of the Babri Masjid at Ayodhya in 1992 (T. Basu, P. Dutta, S. Sarkar, T. Sarkar and S. Sen 1993: 65).

If we except the community of Parsis, it was the temple-

---

[2] Of course those nationalists who were fervently Hindu—in an orthodox or militant sense—would have no truck with any affirmative action for the Muslims, which they generally branded as 'appeasement'. For example, Lala Lajpat Rai broke with C.R. Das in 1923 because the latter wanted to work out a Hindu–Muslim pact embodying some bold measures of affirmative action favouring the Muslims (Nayar1977: 123). On the other hand, unlike Gandhi and Tagore, and following the tenets of the militant Arya Samaj, he wanted Hinduism to be a proselytizing religion (ibid.: Chapter 10).

erecting and socially and politically conformist group of Hindu traders and bankers who were responsible for most of the modern industrial firms erected or acquired by Indians before Independence (Bagchi 1972: Chapter 6). After Independence too, in the private sector, it is the same group that has dominated Indian industry. If anything, their predominance and their publicly-displayed religiosity have increased. The laying down of foundation stones of factories or business premises by politicians and the performance of a religious ceremony on such occasions have become almost compulsory rituals (cf. the photograph of Arvind Mafatlal and his wife at the premises of the National Organic Chemical Industries Ltd., in Herdeck and Piramal 1986).

Before we turn to the final tier of my argument, it should be emphasized again that the Indian bourgeoisie as bourgeoisie had only a minor share in the running of the state apparatus before Independence. They did not have to agitate to separate the state from the church or, rather, the organizational apparatus of a religious denomination, because the British had already done so. The first real opportunity for exercising a determinate influence on state policies came with Independence. In the initial period, during the prime ministership of Jawaharlal Nehru, the Indian bourgeoisie went along with the largely secular policies followed by the government. However, fissures in the coalition of ruling classes led to a section of the coalition using religion as a political weapon, and a section of the big bourgeoisie—and a very large section of the smaller businessmen—financed and actively supported political parties that used religious idioms and religious slogans as means of consolidating electoral support and exercising undemocratic power over large sections of religious minorities.

The Cosmopolitanism of Bombay's Indian Capitalists and Its Fragility

The roots of the sectarian use of religion by the Indian bourgeoisie and by Hindu nationalists and loyalists alike for purposes of self-definition go back to the days before Independence. In this conflation of nationalism or national identity with a particular view of what true religion is, neither the Hindu bourgeoisie nor the other protagonists in the pre-Independence conflicts can claim any uniqueness. Martin Luther's campaign against the papal control over western Christianity was often conducted in the name of the freedom of the German nation (Tawney 1926–38; Sabine and Thorson 1973: 336–39). In the formulation of Sir Lewis Namier, as quoted by Christopher Hill, religion was 'a sixteenth-century word for nationalism'. In England, 'after or before 1640, any threat, real or imagined, to Protestantism at once rallied the majority, as Laud, Charles I and James II all found to their cost' (Hill 1986: 19–20). It took three centuries from the time of the first reformation of the English church under Henry VIII for full toleration of all sects of Christianity to be established in England, after all. Even in those enlightened lands of western Europe, the equality of access of all religious or ethnic groups to civil and political rights still remains a matter of periodic contention.

In colonial India, the state often went by expediency, here recognizing the special privileges claimed by a particular religious denomination, and there refusing to grant similar privileges in the name of equality before law or the preservation of civil peace ('law and order'). The allowance of cow slaughter was one of those contentious issues. On that issue, many towns and some villages of northern India found rich Hindu merchants and landlords ranged against Muslims—mostly poor artisans and peasants. If the exploited weaver tried to target the merchant and convert his struggle into a *jehad* against the infidel, the latter tried to have cow slaughter banned and use the ban as yet another weapon with which to beat down the rebellious artisan (Pandey 1990).

The Marwari *banias* constitute the most important business community of northern and eastern India. Among them, social reform or religious reform meant adjustment to changing economic conditions, especially in the big cities and towns, with minimum disturbance to their habitual ('traditional') mode of life. Modernity or western education was to be resisted rather than embraced (Timberg 1972). In the generation of G.D. Birla, R.K. Dalmia or Jamunalal Bajaj, a business career began at the age of ten or eleven, with little time for elaborate formal schooling. It is not surprising that such early apprenticeship, combined with the astonishing cohesiveness among the Marwari migrants, should have made them formidable traders and financiers. But it is remarkable that Bajaj or Birla should have also picked up a very broad education through their sheer drive and curiosity. However, such education did not urge them to break the barriers erected by the injunction of a male-dominated, socially conservative religious ethos (ibid.: 90–105 and Appendix B).

This conservativeness of the Hindu business community in most parts of India contrasts sharply with the social ferment that prevailed among the business communities in late nineteenth-century Bombay (Dobbin 1992: Chapters 3–4). That ferment may have been due to the fact that Bombay had several Indian business groups, professing different religions, contending in business and politics. But the fact that the British did not dominate the business life of Bombay to the same extent as they did in the other major port cities of Calcutta, Madras, Rangoon or Karachi, also contributed to the upsurge of social movements among Bombay's indigenous businessmen. Hence the Indian business groups in Bombay did not have to define their own identities in contradistinction to the 'modernity' flaunted by the British as yet another sign of their superiority as the ruling race. Among the Bombay business groups at that time were the Parsis, who through their earlier and closer contact with the British had adopted western-style education and so-called 'female emancipation' much more whole-heartedly than the others. Among the Bhatias or Kapol Banias, the major Hindu *shetias* of Bombay, the move towards social reform was much more tentative. Even more tentative was any attempt to reform the religious practices of Muslim business communities such as the Dawoodi Bohras or the Ismaili Khojas. There was also some inter-community tension between the different groups (ibid.: Chapter 4). However, all those communities had some role to play in Bombay's business world, and in municipal, and later on, national politics. All of them—and not just the intelligentsia, as in Calcutta—were touched by various social and religious reform movements.

The cosmopolitanism of the Bombay business community was displayed in the way the leading *shetias*—or rather, the men among them—constantly intermingled with one another socially as well as in business (ibid.: Chapters 1 and 4). It was also demonstrated in the way in which the three major Indian business communities—the Parsis, the Gujarati Hindus and the Gujarati Muslims—were represented in the direction of the Bank of Bombay (the leading domestic bank) from 1868 to 1920, that is, till the time it was merged with the Imperial Bank of India. Similarly, the Bombay Chamber of Commerce and the Bombay Millowners' Association were far more cosmopolitan bodies than their counterparts in Calcutta.

However, the cosmopolitanism of the Bombay elite, even in colonial times, had very strait limits: these are illustrated by the difficult relations that Mohammad Ali Jinnah had with his Parsi father-in-law and, later on, with a daughter who insisted on marrying a Parsi convert to Christianity against her father's wishes. Jinnah had owed his first step up in his career to the patronage of a Scotsman, Sir Frederick Leigh Croft, who recommended the young Mohammad Ali for employment in the London office of his firm, Douglas Graham and Co. There, Jinnah developed his liberal political views, qualified as a barrister, made friends with the wealthy and the powerful, who included Dinshaw Manockjee Petit, the second baronet and one of the top leaders of the Parsi community and cotton mill-owners in Bombay. In 1916, fresh from his triumph in forging the Lucknow Pact between the Congress and the Muslim League, Jinnah offered for the hand of Ruttie, the sixteen-year-old daughter of his friend, Sir Dinshaw, and was rudely rejected. After overcoming all the social and legal obstacles, Jinnah married Ruttie in 1918. But the marriage ended in divorce in a few years' time, and Sir Dinshaw never recognized his daughter after her marriage. When Dina, the daughter born of the marriage of Jinnah and Ruttie, married Neville Wadia, another Parsi mill-owner but a convert to Christianity, Jinnah in turn forswore his relationship with his daughter. Although father and daughter wrote to each other occasionally, Dina never set foot in Pakistan while Jinnah lived, and went there only to attend his funeral (Wolpert 1984: Chapters 2–4 and 23). The tragedy of the dis-harmony of the upper classes in the subcontinent and of its partition on the basis of ascribed religious community was reflected in the tragedy of the loneliness in the life of the man who carved Pakistan out of this multicultural subcontinent.

In Calcutta, there was little multicultural sociability among the Indian business communities to start with. The dominant business associations in the city were British, and the new associations set up by Indians either started as bodies dominated by one Indian business group belonging to one religious or linguistic group, or became such one-denomination or uni-ethnic bodies through splits or secession. The Bengal National Chamber of Commerce came to represent the Bengali-speaking, mostly Hindu, businessmen; the Oriental Chamber of Commerce, Muslim businessmen; and the Bharat Chamber of Commerce, the Marwari businessmen. Among the Marwaris themselves there were differences between the loyalists and the nationalists (Herdeck and Piramal 1986: 109), as indeed there were between the smaller and more nationalistically inclined merchants of Bombay and the big mill-owners organized in the Bombay Millowners' Association (Gordon 1978: Chapters 4–5). But these conflicts were over political tactics rather than about social reform or the opening up of the community to welcome outsiders as social equals.[3]

Indian business communities, however socially conservative, had learned how to negotiate with different political parties with different ideologies. This is typified by the statement attributed to Sardar Vallabhbhai Patel regarding the Walchand brothers, who were leading entrepreneurs in the fields of shipping, construction, sugar and automobiles: 'Gulabchand belongs to the Hindu Sabha, Lalchand belongs to the Congress, Ratanchand belongs to no party, and Walchand belongs to every party' (Herdeck and Piramal 1986: 404). True to this practical political philosophy, Indian businessmen by and large supported the Congress after Independence, and did well out of the policies pursued by it, even though individual businessmen might have railed against particular government restrictions. However, Nehru's apparent fraternization with the communists during the heyday of the non-aligned movement made some erstwhile followers of the Congress rebellious and look for allies among the non-communist opposition parties. Two of the parties in this group operating in western India were the Swatantra Party, which was self-consciously for free enterprise, and the Shiv Sena, which wanted Maharashtra to be ruled exclusively by Maharashtrians (by their

[3] One of the cartoons reproduced from the *Maheshwari Bandhu* in Timberg (1972: Appendix B), caricatures inter-dining with people from outside the caste of Maheshwarias, such as Muslims, Europeans and Parsis; and another caricatures a rabble-rousing social reformer speaking against the caste system.

construction only Hindus could be true Maharashtrians). Kamal Nayan Bajaj and Ramkrishna Bajaj, sons of Jamunalal, hobnobbed with these parties, and supported J.B. Kripalani against V.K. Krishna Menon, the official Congress nominee, as parliamentary candidate for the North Bombay constituency (Kamath 1988: 166–88). The Swatantra Party collapsed but the Shiv Sena has remained as a highly chauvinist and sectarian political party; it was one of the major forces behind the Bombay riots of December 1992 and January 1993.

Businessmen and politicians consciously used the Shiv Sena to try and break up communist-dominated trade unions. The Shiv Sena used a Maratha-supremacist ideology, and major Congress leaders such as Y.B. Chavan and his powerful successors such as Sharad Pawar used the same idioms of Maratha prowess and the need to recover lost glory. The Shiv Sena found its financial backers among capitalists and the middle classes in Bombay, and its constituency in an enlarged non-Brahmin, non-Dalit conglomerate of castes led by the Marathas and *kunbis*, and its storm-troopers among the disaffected, casually employed or unemployed and often criminalized slum-dwellers. The parallel economy of Bombay generated a parallel politics, which likewise thrived on blatant breaches of the law, generally with the connivance—as in the case of the Bombay riots of 1992–93—and active assistance of the custodians of the law. The scapegoats or the other of the Shiv Sena were not, of course, the moneyed real-estate speculators or smugglers or owners of declining textile mills wanting to build housing complexes on the grounds of the mills, but militant trade union leaders, Dalits and Muslims. The 'saffronization' of the Shiv Sena, and the fusion of its Maratha–*kunbi* chauvinism and communalism were natural outcomes. Of course, ironically enough, many Dalits also served as its storm-troopers in the Bombay riots, and upwardly-mobile Dalits seeking to turn themselves into respectable Hindus may have found a welcome embrace in the Shiv Sena or the BJP (Lele 1981, 1995; Gupta 1982; Hansen 1997: Chapters 8–10).

As the hegemony of the Congress Party over the apparatus of rule was seriously challenged and occasionally fractured, Congress politicians consciously used slogans appealing to different religious denominations: multiculturalism became an arena of manipulation as well as conflict (Lele 1995). The few businessmen who openly sided with the opposition often suffered discrimination at the hands of the Congress government.[4] Tensions in urban India mounted with the growth of unemployment, the massing of the lumpen-proletariat, and the scramble for ever-appreciating urban land, including slums that could be converted into office complexes or affluent residential localities. This provided an ideal milieu for politicians to foment communal trouble with a view to mobilizing a particular community as a captive electoral constituency and, as we have indicated earlier, many businessmen were only too willing to go along with this game (Bagchi 1991).

It came about in this way that not only Uttar Pradesh—which had witnessed a number of riots, some of them deliberately provoked by the provincial police—but also western India—the capital of Indian big bourgeoisie and the land of Mahatma Gandhi—became a scene of regular riots since the late 1970s. These anti-Muslim riots reached a peak in the city of Bombay in the wake of the demolition of the Babri Masjid. This riot had two phases. In the first phase, riots were relatively unorganized. In the second phase, the Shiv Sena, the BJP and the Bombay police played a major role in instigating violence, burning and damaging the slums and houses of Muslims and killing scores of them (IPHRC 1994: esp. 95–116). This could be seen as a replay of the riots that occurred in Bombay in August 1893 as a fall-out of the so-called cow protection movement, but on a much larger scale altogether.

We have referred earlier to the remarkable atmosphere of cooperation among the leading businessmen of Bombay in the late nineteenth century. The cooperation generally took the form of choice of representatives from separate business communities in elective bodies or business organizations. This propensity for cooperation (or collusion) at the top did not automatically translate into a similar attitude among the poorer people, a very large proportion of whom were immigrants. They were badly housed, had practically no public sanitary facilities, and no security of employment. Some of them were regularly organized into syndicates of musclemen willing to defend the *mohalla* or the community as the occasion arose

[4] See the story of the persecution of the Bajaj family by Indira Gandhi's government during the Emergency of 1975–77 (Kamath 1988: Chapter 8).

(Chandavarkar 1994: esp. Chapter 5). The official *Gazetteer of the Bombay City and Island,* while giving accounts of the various kinds of riots or civil disturbances in the city, repeatedly cited overcrowding and inhospitable living conditions as contributing factors (Edwardes 1909: 150–96). In 1851 and 1874 there were riots between Parsis and Muslims, provoked by indiscreet (indeed, in one case, according to Edwardes, 'scurrilous') remarks on Islam or Prophet Muhammad by a Parsi journalist or a Parsi publicist (ibid.: 156 and 179–80). There were also riots between rival factions of Khojas and between Shias and Sunnis (ibid.: 156, 179, 195). But these were rather minor affairs, in most cases resulting in injuries and damages to property (including temples and mosques) rather than to loss of life. But the riot of 1893 was far more serious, leading to an estimated 80 fatalities and enormous damage to property (ibid.: 193). This riot demonstrated not only that collaboration among big businessmen did not trickle all the way down, but that some businessmen were quite prepared to aid and abet the rioters. Some *shetias* (mostly belonging to Gujarat) funded the agitation of the cow protection society, which led to the riots of 1893, and later gave money to the rampaging masses (Upadhyay 1989; see also Masselos 1993, for another view of the riot).

The Structural Determinants of the Choice of a Stance on Multiculturalism by the Indian Bourgeoisie

It is probably not coincidental that the 1893 riot in Bombay occurred at a time when, because of the monetary and tariff policy followed by the government, the major industry of Bombay, the cotton mills, had entered into a period of crisis. The Bombay industry was plagued by slow growth and falling exports for a decade after that date. (Not only economic distress but plague played a role in all this, but the effects of plague were aggravated by the wretched living conditions of mill workers.) The 1992–93 riots came almost a decade after the collapse of the great Bombay textile strike of 1982–83 and the quickening of the pace of land speculation within the erstwhile mill areas. The Bombay riots of 1992–93 also damaged the growth of Indian exports.

The 1992–93 riots were, however, distinguished from their century-old counterpart in several major respects. First, they lasted longer and caused much more damage to life and property. Second, the forces of so-called law and order were, for a time at least, on the side of the rioters rather than on that of peace-loving citizens. Third, the Indian big bourgeoisie, led by their doyen, the octogenerian J.R.D. Tata, became almost helpless spectators, pleading vainly with the government to stop the riots (see also, in this connection, Sharma 1995: 268–86).

J.R.D. Tata's career in some ways illustrates the problems of operating as a secularly-minded industrialist in the Indian milieu (see Lala 1992, for Tata's career). Born in 1904 of a Parsi father and a French mother, who was received into the Zoroastrian faith after her marriage, Tata spent the first eleven years of his life in Paris, another four years (from about 1915 to 1919) in India. He was then enlisted into the French army when he was back in Europe and was preparing for admission into the University of Cambridge. But then he was called back home. He trained as a civilian pilot and came to control the first Indian-owned civilian airline. Apart from S.L. Kirloskar, J.R.D. Tata was the only big industrialist of his time who had a technical background. His group was the only one to have trained a cadre of professional managers within the conglomerate. He followed other Parsis, including the founders of the Tata group, in giving large sums for secular philanthropy, including the promotion of science and the arts.

However, the Indian law of Hindu undivided family, which also applies with some variations to Parsis, accords unusual privileges to ownership of property within the family. So while Tata could professionalize his top management and recruit people from all communities, the ultimate control of the group was left with a family member—a cousin (since Tata was childless). Moreover, the secularization of Tata's public works did little to change the sectarian orientation of other members of the Indian big bourgeoisie. (G.D. Birla's motto was to save, to invest in profit-making enterprises or to build temples—which could also, of course, yield profits.) A life of Brajmohan Birla (in Hindi) by D.B. Taknet gives pride of place to his association with glittering gods in temples and such conservative Hindu gurus as a Sankaracharya of one of the four major Saiva *maths*, and has little room for his wordly concerns.

J.R.D. Tata also tried to keep a distance from individual

politicians, though, of course, he had often to collaborate with the government and operate through it. In this too he differed from most other successful big businessmen. Finally, his attempt to create an internal labour market for managers in the group was not emulated by other Indian businessmen. Moreover, investment in the training of cadres of workers and managers with firm-specific or group-specific skills would not yield noticeable dividends if the general environment was suffused with a sea of undifferentiated unskilled labour or skilled labour, with unreliable certification.

The Bombay riots of 1992–93 are a vivid illustration of the contradictions of the social order that the Indian bourgeoisie did so much to create through active manipulation of the state apparatus and passive acquiescence in the consequences of the failure of the post-Independence ruling classes to provide security of life and existence to major sections of a fast-growing population. A combination of the decline of Bombay's major manufacturing industry, namely, the cotton textile industry, and unplanned growth of the city at the service of rich property developers rendered life highly insecure for most workers. Moreover, nominal prohibition, bootlegging and smuggling easily made Bombay the capital of economic crime in India (Banerjee-Guha 1995: 100–20). The ideological ground was prepared by the rise, first, of militant Hindutva as espoused by the Rashtriya Swayamsevak Sangh, the cult of Shivaji embraced by virtually all political parties except the communists, the anti-communism of all capitalists eager to ward off militant trade unionism, and finally, the growth of the militant chauvinism of the Shiv Sena. The latter thrived among the deprived who would wreak injustice on selected 'others' in quest of justice for themselves. (For succinct accounts of the economics, culture and politics of manipulation as revealed in the Bombay riots of 1992–93, see Banerjee-Guha 1995; Lele 1995; Heuze 1995; Sharma 1995.) The Bombay riots are both a metaphor and a concrete manifestation of the fracturing of multiculturalism among the Indian bourgeoisie and the masses they manipulate.

The unemployed and unemployable mass of unskilled labour in the slow-developing poor country that India is, would always attract speculators in land or politics and would endanger the secularist aspirations of individual businessmen. As it is, most of India's big bourgeoisie are far from embracing a doctrine of strict separation between the public sphere of politics and the private sphere of religion. Those businessmen who tried to operate as individualist professionals venturing into industry before Independence found that in a country in which trade rather than manufacturing skill, family or clan loyalty rather than professional excellence, conformity to obscurantist social norms rather than conspicuous display of enlightenment prevailed, they were likely to be soundly beaten by the traders and financiers: their enterprises were almost invariably taken over by the latter (Bagchi 1990: 212–23; Ray 1992: Introduction). As the prota-gonist in H.G. Wells' story found out, in the country of the blind the one-eyed man cannot be king.

There are enormous differences, however, in the attitudes of the big and small bourgeoisie to collaboration with foreigners, or the role of the state. Many members of the bourgeoisie are adopting liberal or 'modern' codes with respect to marriage or social behaviour. But the core of control in business matters or social power remains in the family. Adopting or inventing conservative codes for family behaviour in the face of challenge remains the strategy of defence and can become a weapon of aggression. Multiculturalism for the big or middle bourgeoisie means constructing fortresses of tradition or invented tradition, rather than breaking down barriers to embrace people of all creeds. Secularism under today's conditions will require a much higher degree of economic and social equality, with a better distribution of initial assets and a levelling-up of chances of betterment for everybody.

In Europe, the businessmen with the Protestant ethic wanting to create a distance between God and Mammon did not opt for a multicultural democracy. He was forced to do so through several centuries of popular struggle and changes in the structure of the economy and society. In India too, if multicultural democracy with equality of rights for everybody is to win through, it will be largely in spite of, rather than because of, the Indian bourgeoisie as they are culturally, socially and politically constituted today.

Non-incriminating thanks are due to Javeed Alam and Jasodhara Bagchi for trenchant comments on an earlier version of the paper.

References

Alam, M., 1996, *Shariat and Language in Medieval India,* S.G. Deuskar Lecture, Centre for Studies in Social Sciences, Calcutta.
Ambedkar, B.R., 1932, 'A Note on the Indian Depressed Classes', in *Report of the Indian Franchise Committee,* Vol. 1, reprinted in K.I. Chanchreek, S. Prasad and R. Kumar (eds), 1991, *Fight for the Right of the Depressed Classes,* H.K. Publishers, Delhi, pp. 249–61.
Ascherson, N., 1995, *Black Sea: The Birth Place of Civilization and Barbarism,* Jonathan Cape, London.
Bagchi, A.K., 1972, *Private Investment in India: 1900–39,* Cambridge University Press, Cambridge.
———, 1985, 'Merchants and Colonialism', in D.N. Panigrahi (ed.), *Economy Society and Politics in Modern India,* Vikas, New Delhi, (also included in this volume).
———, 1990, 'Wealth and Work in Calcutta: 1860–1921', in S. Chaudhuri (ed.), *Calcutta: The Living City,* Vol. 1, *The Past,* Oxford University Press, Calcutta, pp. 212–23 (also included in this volume).
———, 1991, 'Predatory Commercialization and Communalism in India', in S. Gopal (ed.), *Anatomy of a Confrontation: The Babri Masjid–Ramjanmabhoomi Issue,* Viking, Penguin, New Delhi, (also included in this volume), pp. 193–218.
Bagchi, J., 1996, 'Secularism as Identity: The Case of Tagore's Gora', in M. Dutta, F. Agnes and N. Adarkar (eds), *The Nation, the State and Indian Identity,* Samya, Calcutta, pp. 46–47.
Banerjee-Guha, S., 1995, 'Urban Development Process in Bombay: Planning for Whom?', in Patel and Thorner (eds), *Bombay: Metaphor for Modern India.*
Basu, T., P. Dutta, S. Sarkar, T. Sarkar and S. Sen (eds), 1993, *Khaki Shorts and Saffron Flags,* Orient Longman, New Delhi, p. 65.
Baxi, U., 1995, 'Emancipation as Justice: Babasaheb Ambedkar's Legacy', in U. Baxi and B. Parekh (eds), *Crisis and Change in Contemporary India,* Sage, New Delhi, pp. 122–49.
Chandavarkar, R., 1994, *The Origins of Industrial Capitalism in India: Business Strategies and the Working Classes in Bombay, 1900–40,* Cambridge University Press, Cambridge.
Das Gupta, A., 1970, 'The Merchants of Surat: *c.* 1700–5', in E.R. Leach and S.N. Mukherjee (eds), *Elites in South Asia,* Cambridge University Press, Cambridge.
———, 1979, *Indian Merchants and the Decline of Surat, c.* 1700–50, Wiesbaden.
Dayanand, 1978, *Autobiography of Dayanand Saraswati,* K.C. Yadav (ed.), second revised edn, Manohar, Delhi.
Divekar, V.D., 1982, 'The Emergence of an Indigenous Business Class in Maharashtra in Eighteenth Century', *Modern Asian Studies,* Vol. 16, Part 3, July, pp. 427–43.
Dobbin, C., 1992, *Urban Leadership in Western India,* Oxford University Press, Oxford.
Edwardes, S.M., 1909, *The Gazetteer of Bombay City and Island,* Vol. 2, Times Press, Bombay, pp. 150–96.
Gandhi, M.K , 1916, 'Swadeshi as an Active Force', in *Speeches and Writings of*

Mahatma Gandhi, fourth edn, reprinted in Iyer (ed.), 1991.
———, 1920, 'The Vaishnava Ideal', in *Navajivan,* 5 December; translated form Gujrati in Iyer (ed.), *The Essential Writings of Mahatma Gandhi,* Oxford University Press, Delhi, 1991.
———, 1935, 'Religion and Social Service', reprinted in Iyer (ed.), *The Essential Writing;* 1991, pp. 158-9.
———, 1946, 'Action is My Domain', in Harijan, 3 March; reprinted in Raghavan Iyer (ed.), 1991.
GBP, 1901, *Gazetteeer of Bombay Presidency,* Vol. 9, Part 1, *Gujarat Population: Hindus,* Government Central Press, Bombay.
Gordon, A.D.D., 1978, *Businessmen and Politics: Rising Nationalism and a Modernizing Economy in Bombay, 1918-33,* Manohar, Delhi.
Gupta, D., 1982, *Nativism in a Metropolis: The Shiv Sena in Bombay,* Manohar, Delhi.
Hansen, T.B., 1997, *The Saffron Wave: Democratic Revolution and the Growth of Hindu Nationalism in India,* Vols 1-3, International Development Studies, Roskilde University, Roskilde, Denmark.
Herdeck, M. and G. Piramal, 1986, *India's Industrialists,* Vol. 1, Three Continents, Washington D.C.
Heuze, G., 1995, 'Cultural Populism: The Appeal of the Shiv sena', in Patel and Thorner (eds), *Bombay: Metaphor for Modern India,* Oxford University Press, New Delhi.
Hill, C., 1986, 'The First Century of the Church of England', in *The Collected Essays of Chistopher Hill,* Vol. 2, *Religion and Politics in 17th Century England,* Harvester Press, Brighton, Sussex, pp. 19-20.
IPHRC, 1994, *An Inquiry into the December 1992 and January 1993 Riots in Bombay by the Indian People's Human Rights Tribunal Conducted by Justice S.M. Daud and Justice H. Suresh,* second edn, P.A. Sebastian for Indian People's Human Rights Commission, Bombay, pp. 95-116.
Iyer, R. (ed.), 1987, *The Moral and Political Writings of Mahatma Gandhi,* vol. 3, *Non-Violent Resistance and Social Transformation,* Clarendon Press, Oxford.
———, 1991, Iyer, R. (ed.), *The Essential Writings of Mahatma Gandhi,* Oxford University Press, New Delhi.
Jenkins, R., 1827, *Report on the Territories of the Rajah of Nagpur,* Calcutta Gazette Government Press, Calcutta.
Kamath, M.V., 1988, *Gandhi's Coolie: Life and Times of Ramakrishna Bajaj,* Allied Publishers, Ahmedabad, pp. 166-68.
Kolff, D.H.A., 1980, 'A Study of Land Transfers in Mau Tehsil, District Jhansi', in K.N. Chaudhuri and C.J. Dewey (eds), *Economy and Society: Essays in Indian Economic and Social History,* Oxford University Press, New Delhi, pp. 53-85.
Lala, R.M., 1992, *Beyond the Last Blue Mountains: A Life of J.R.D. Tata,* Viking, Penguin, New Delhi.
Lele, J., 1981, *Elite Pluralism and Class Rule: Political Development in Maharashtra, India,* University of Toronto Press, Toronto.
———, 1995, 'Saffronization of the Shiv Sena: The Political Economy of City, State and Nation', in S. Patel and A. Thorner (eds), *Bombay: Metaphor for Modern India,* Oxford University Press, Bombay, pp. 185-212.

Little, J.H., 1967, *House of Jagatseth,* Calcutta Historical Society, Calcutta.
Masselos, 1993, 'The City as Represented in Crowd Action: Bombay, 1893, in *Economic and Political Weekly,* vol. 28, no. 5, January, pp. 182–8.
Moosvi, S., (ed.), 1994, *Episodes in the Life of Akbar: Contemporary Records and Reminiscences,* National Book Trust, New Delhi.
Nanda, B.R., 1990, *In Gandhi's Footsteps: The Life and Times of Mahatma Gandhi,* Oxford University Press, New Delhi.
Nayar, P., 1977, *Lala Lajpat Rai: The Man and His Ideas,* Manohar, Delhi.
Pandey, G., 1990, *The Construction of Communalism in Colonial India,* Oxford University Press, New Delhi.
Prabhu, R.K. and U.R. Rao (eds), 1946, *The Mind of Mahatma Gandhi,* second edn, Oxford University Press, Madras.
Raghavan, Iyer, (ed.), 1987, *The Moral and Political Writings of Mahatma Gandhi,* Vol. 3: *Non-violent Resistance and Social Transformation,* Clarendon Press, Oxford.
Ray, R.K., 1992, 'Introduction', in R.K. Ray (ed.), *Entrepreneurship in Indian Industries, 1800–1947,* Oxford University Press, New Delhi, pp. 1–69.
Russell, R.V. and Hira Lal, 1915, *The Tribes and Castes of the Central Provinces of India,* Vol. 2, reprinted in 1975, Cosmo, Delhi.
Sabine, G.H. and T.L. Thorson, 1973, *A History of Political Thought,* fourth edn, Oxford and IBH, New Delhi.
Sharma, K., 1995, 'Chronicle of a Riot Foretold', in Patel and Thorner (eds), *Bombay: Metaphor for Modern India,* pp. 268–86.
Sharma, R.S., 1972, 'Swami Dayanand: 1825–83', in S.P. Sen (ed.), *Dictionary of National Biography,* Vol. 1, Calcutta Institute of Historical Studies, Calcutta, pp. 406–9.
Subrahmanyam, S., 1990, *The Political Economy of Commerce: Southern India, 1500–1650,* Cambridge University Press, Cambridge.
Tagore, R., 1912, 'Atmaparichay' (Bengali), *Tattabodhini Patrika,* Calcutta, Baishakh; reprinted, Tagore 1361 BS, pp. 452–87.
———, 1912 b, 'Hindu Brahmo' (Bengali), *Tattabodhini Patrika,* Calcutta, Jaistha, reprinted, Tagore, 1361 BD, pp. 580–9.
Tawney, R.H., *Religion and the Rise of Capitalism,* Penguin, Harmondsworth, Middlesex, pp. 89–1100.
Timberg, T.A., 1972, *The Rise of the Marwari Merchants as Industrial Entrepreneurs,* Ph. D. thesis, Harvard University, Cambridge, Mass.
Upadhyay, S.S., 1993, 'Communalism and the Working Class: Riot of 1893 in Bombay City', in *Economic and Political Weekly,* Vol. 28, No. 30, July, 29, pp. PE 69–PE 75.
Vaid, S. and K. Sangari, 1991, 'Institutions, Beliefs, Ideologies: Widow Immolation in Contemporary Rajasthan', in *Economic and Political Weekly,* Vol. 6, No. 17, April, pp. WS 7 to WS 13.
Weber, M., 1925, 'Die protestantische Ethik und Giest des Kapitalismus', in *Archiv fur Sozialwissenschaft and Sozialpolitik Statistik,* Vols. 20 and 21; concluding part translated by E. Mathews and published as 'Protestant Asceticism and the Spirit of Capitalism', in S.G. Runciman (ed.), 1978, *Max Weber: Selections in Translation,* Cambridge University Press, Cambridge, pp. 138–73.
Wolpert, S., 1984, *Jinnah of Pakistan,* Oxford University Press, New York.

Index

Abdul Ghafur, 22
Abirchand, Bansilal, 53, 54
absentee landlordism, and British colonialism, 209; the growth of, 124; *see also* landlordism
accommodating saraf, an image of, 50
accumulation, crises of, 244–48; *see also* capitalist accumulation
Acharya, S., 283
Achcar, G., 253
adjustment, neo-liberal theology of, 245
Advani, L.K., 87
Africa, *Homo sapiens* in, 242; Indian businessmen in, 86
Africa and Asia, population growth, 242
African slavery, 'new systems' of, 223
agents provocateur, 283
agglomeration, economies of, 76
agrarian structure, vulnerability of, 19
agrarian system, highly exploitative, 185
agrestic slavery, 143; the end of, 128; *see also* slavery
agrestic slaves, 226
agriculture, capitalist transformation of, 126, 129; employment in, 276
Ahmad, Muzaffar, 194
Ahmed, A.M., 289
Ahmed, R., 190, 289
Ahmedabad, family of Shantidas at, 22
Akbar, 296
Akerlof, G., 109; and Yellen, J.L., 245
akhai shai, 54
Alam, M., 293
Alexander and Co., 36; *banians* of, 37
Altimir, O., 245

Ambedkar, B.R., 305
American plantations, chattel slavery of, 204; *see also* slavery
Americanized Weberianism, 119
amils, 53, 60–61
Amin, S., 104
Amsden, A.H., 253
Anandamayi Ma, 303
Anderson, M.R., 222, 227
Anglo-Orientalist movement of Sir Syed Ahmad, 270
Anglophile Bengali intelligentsia, 56
animosity, feelings of, 263, 264
ant system, 58
anti-reservation movement, 288
Arbuthnot and Co., 81
Aristotelian (and Thomist) dualism, 201
Aristotle, *Politics*, 3, 201, 204
Arrighi, G., 231
Arrow, Kenneth, 4, 5, 63
artisanal industry, three-fold transition from, 30–31; labour processes in, 129
artisanal method, 104
artisans, *panches* of, 22
Arya and *Dasyu*, 292
Arya Samaj, 288, 303
Arya Samaj movement, 303
ashraf and *ajlaf*, 292
Asian economic crisis, 243, 250
Asian Wall Street Journal, 254
Assam Labour and Emigration Act, (Act VI of 1901), 228
Assamese tea plantation, servile labour process in, 77

Assurance Game, 14
Atarthi, Premankur, 195
Atiyah, Premankur, 179, 220
Atlantic slave trade, 249
'Atmaparichay', 304
authoritarianism, 244–48
authority, monolithic structure of, 194
authority and control, hierarchical structures of, 143
automatic looms, 113
Axelrod, Robert, 13
Ayodhya, Babri Masjid at: demolition of, 306, 313
Azim us-shan, 25

babu–coolie relationship, 180–84
'backwash effects', 78
Bagchi, A.K., 37, 46, 50, 51, 71, 80, 84, 86, 89, 93, 96–97, 104, 106–07, 109, 113, 116, 118, 121, 122, 129, 145, 146, 150, 151, 179, 185, 186, 188, 190, 191, 197, 207, 213, 215, 218, 222, 227, 231–33, 244, 251, 253, 254, 256, 267, 296, 307, 313, 317
Bagchi, J., 305
Bahl, Vinay, 216
Bairoch, P., 252
Bajaj, Jamunalal, 299, 201, 302, 308
Bajaj, Kamal Nayan, 312
Bajaj, Ramkrishna, 312
Baker, C.J., 112
baladia, 66
Ballhatchet, K., 179, 197
Balloo, Jivraj, 57
Banerjee, A.C., 99, 195
Banerjee, Sibnath, 183, 184
Banerjee-Guha, S., 316
banian, 36; Bengali, 42
banias, 308; Gujarati, 62, 63, 64; Marwari, 308; Multani, 301
Banjaras, 23, 24, 59, 60
bankers and moneylenders, 297
banking capital, 19
banniyals, 227
Baran, P.A., 96
Bartlett, R., 218
Barua, S.K. and V. Raghunathan, 89

Barui, B.C., 33, 34
Basu, 120
Basu, Amritalal, *Babu,* 181
Basu, Pramathanath, 171
Basu, T. et al., 306
Baxi, U., 305
Bayly, C.A., 22, 93
Bedaux system, 120
Begg, Sutherland and Co., 107
belief systems, 303; a complex of, 305; the specificities of, 191
Bengal, Bengali capitalists in, 81; Faraizi and Taiyuni movements in, 289; handicraft exports from: collapse of, 98; handloom exports of: collapse of, 37; jute industry in: evolution of, 184; jute-mill workers in: consciousness of, 179, condition of, 177; peasant uprisings in, 100; *see also* Faraizi, Taiyuni movements
Bengal Chamber of Commerce, 186
Bengal National Chamber of Commerce, 311
Bengal Regulation III of 1820, 222
Bengal Regulation IV, 227
Bengal Tenancy Act (1885), 171
Benjamin, N., 38
Bentham, 179
Berar districts, acquisition of, 39
Bhadra, G., 22, 24, 26, 33, 35
bhadralok, and *chasa,* 292
Bhaduri, Satinath, *Dhorai Charit Manas,* 298
Bhagalpur riots, 271
Bhalla, S., 124
Bharadwaj, K., 121, 129, 140
Bharat Chamber of Commerce, 311
Bharatiya Janata Party (BJP), 288, 312; and Vishwa Hindu Parishad, 87
Bhatias, 309
Bhats, 26
Bhattacharya, N., 122, 123, 124, 227
Bhattacharya, S., 213
Bhavsars, 78
Bhogendranath, N.C., 112
Birdwood, George, 171
Birla, G.D., 299, 201, 302, 306, 308, 315

Index

Blyn, G., 122
Bohras, 80; Dawoode, 309
Bombay, Indian merchants in, 39, 94; parallel economy of, 312; Parsi capitalists in, 81; Parsi or Gujarati collaborators of: Europeans in, 37–38; *saheb* collaborators of, 41–42; *see also* merchants
Bombay riots of 1992–93, 294, 314, 316
Bombay Shareholders' Association, 120
Bombay's Indian Capitalists, 307–14
Bombay's major manufacturing industry, decline of, 316
bondage, casual, 147; not-so-casual, 148
Bose, N.S., 218; *see also* Basu
Botwinick, H., 233
bourgeois–democratic, organization, 183; revolution, 31
bourgeois, freedom, 180; laws, 80; legality, 182; philosophers, 179
Bowles, S. and R. Boyer, 245
Boxer, C.R., 27, 218
Brahmachari, Dhirendra, 306
brahmacharya, 300
Brahmanical Hinduism, 287
Brass, Paul, 270, 271
Brass, T., 244
Braudel, Fernand, 127, 241
Braverman, H., 207
Breman, J., 88, 148, 181, 182, 244, 282
Brenner, R., 125, 128
Britain, feudalism in, 218; usury in: abolition of, 145
British Caribbean, three major slave revolts in, 206
British India, merchants turning landlords in, 48–50; 'mixed occupations' in, 149; *see also* merchants
British laws, apparent failure of, 7
British or Dutch-style colonialism, 95
British Paramountcy, 18
British policy, intended and unintended consequences of, 145
British rule, apparatus of, 197
British-style capitalist colonialism, predatory commerialization, 266
Buchanan, D.H., 101, 211, 230, 232; *Development of Capitalistic Enterprise in India,* 97
Buchanan, Francis, 43–44; reports of, 31
Budri Dass, 65
Bugotee Ram, ten descendants of, 58
Burawoy, M., 130, 193, 207
Burke, Edmond, 189; *Ninth Report,* 32
Burrals, 37
business, new economics of, 4
business associates, trust in, 4
business communities, separate existence of, 301; *see also* Indian business communities
business environment, British inves-tors in, 185; stability of, 186

Cain, P.J. and A.G. Hopkins, 221
Calcutta, *babu* collaborators of, 41; Birla group in, 88; commercial and financial world of, 157; Indian business communities in, 311; Industry: ownership and management of, 168–72; Living space in, 164–68; managing agency houses of, 185; Population and occupational structure of, 157–64; Talla riots of (1897), 264; wage earners in, 172–75
Calcutta municipal administration, constitution of, 166
Camargo, J.M. et al., 244
capital, demands of, 177; internationalization of, 256; licentiousness of, 249, 257; mobility of, 77
capital–labour relationship, 178, 203, 221
capital stock, greater share of, 10
capital with immobile labour, increased mobility of, 256
capitalism, 3, 18; and colonialism, 78; contradictions of, 242; evolution of, 244; forces of, 82; gender ethnicity and class under, 251–54; logic of, 75; nature of, 79; structure of, 96; theoretical model of, 71; uneven development under, 241; unfolding of, 72
capitalism *à la* Polanyi and Wallerstein, 118

capitalist accumulation, 121
capitalist class, behaviour of, 71; nature of, 79; operation of, 76
capitalist colonialism, 125, 266, 272, 273; formative ideology of, 84; free labour under, 216; spread of, 203; working of, 101
capitalist competition, 256; forces of, 248; theory of, 233
capitalist farming, 82
capitalist growth, 86
capitalist labour process, 118
capitalist–landlord stratum, 78
capitalist production, 88
capitalist regulation, modes of, 96
capitalist reproduction, Marx's macro-economic theory of, 233
capitalist society, inequality in, 177
capitalist-style plantations, 205
capitalist transformation, Protestant ethic in, 298
capitalist unfreedom, and nominal freedom, 207; problems of, 208
capitalists, 13, 74, 206; innovative role of, 17; political authority of, 207
capitalist or bourgeois ideologies, 72
Caribbean, slavery in: abolition of, 222
Carnoy, M., 229
cartazes, 27
caste, consciousness, 150; hierarchies, 113; system, 140, 141, 142, 143, 288
casteism, communalism and collaborationism, 89
casteist, 89; and communalist, 87
casual and not-so-casual bondage, 148
Catholic Emancipation Act (1829), 217
Central Provinces, immigrant Marwari community in, 300
Chakrabarty, Dipesh, 71, 151, 212, 215–17, 233, 251; reductionist methodology of, 197; *Rethinking Working Class History: Bengal, 1890–1940*, 176
Channaiwa, D., 223
Chandavarkar, R., 109, 113, 212, 230–31, 314
Chandraswamy, 306
char land, gradual exhaustion of, 100

Charans, 26
chassars, 33
Chatterjee, P., 267
Chattopadhyay, Bankimchandra, 181
Chattopadhyay, Basudev, 197
Chaudharis, 57
Chaudhuri, K.N., 28, 29, 30
Chaudhuri, S., 23, 29, 30, 89
Chavan, Y.B., 312
Chettiars, 61, 62, 63, 301; Nattukottai, 61–63, 80
Chinmayananda (Swami), 306
Chowdhury, B., 99
civil freedom, ideas of, 217
civil law, importance of, 285
civil peace, preservation of, 308
Civil Rights Act (1964), 229
class and community, Chakrabarty's treatment of, 187–93
class society, 79
classical political economy, 177; *see also* political economy
Clive's Society of Trade, 32
closure, rules of, 79, 80, 84
Coase, R.H., 207
coercion, apparatus of, 117; different degrees of, 117
Cohn, B.S., 60, 102
collaborationist, 89
colonial capital, Chakrabarty's conceptualization of, 178; specificities of, 187
colonial control, 30
colonial exploitation, as a process, 121
colonial India, bourgeois–democratic trade unions in, 183; social change in, 129; working-class Indian man/woman in, 177
colonial land-revenue system, 190
colonial productive forces, retardation of, 96; *see also* productive forces
colonial state, Chakrabarty's conceptualization of, 178; the broader arrangements of, 185
colonial workers, historiography of, 216
colonialism, 190; and landlordism, 113; and racism, 221; Chakrabarty's formulation of, 180; differential impact of, 42; general system of,

Index

145; influence of, 109; legacy of, 197, operation of, 31; revenue extraction under, 267; *see also* capitalist colonialism
Colonialism, Ideology and Society, 116–25
commercialization process, 128, 145, 146, 149, 266, 267, 286
commodity production, 75
communal and caste violence, 281
communal riots, predisposing conditions of, 273
communal violence, 284, 290; flaring of, 288; ideological and political aspects of, 283; tide of, 287
communalism, and casteism, 265, 280
communists, Nehru's apparent fraternization with, 311
community, affiliation, 216; consciousness, 150
competition and regulation, capitalist-style of, 242
conceptualization, framework of, 209; Polanyi-like, 117
Conklin, A.L., 224
Conrad, J., 223
consciousness, aetiology of, 196; chronological characterization of, 196; secrets of, 193
contact and contract, 117
contraband trade, infantry of, 286
Conquery-Vidrovitch, C., 223
corporatism, 244–48
Corrigan, P. and D. Sayer, 218
Cotton, H.E.A., 157
cotton cloth, mill-production of, 46
Cotton Frauds Act (1863), 109–10
cotton textiles, manufacture of, 108–16
cotton trade, 40
Court of Wards, 272
cow protection movement, 269, 270
cow-protection society, agitation of, 314
cow-slaughter, allowance of, 308
Cowasjee, Framjee, 42
craft industry, wage-earners in, 46
craft production, 46; loss of, 267
Craton, M., 205, 206
credit and marketing, conditions of, 107
Creole ruling classes, 251

Croft, Sir Frederick Leigh, 310
Crooke, W., 60
cultivators, exploitation of, 20
cultural barriers, 273
culture and consciousness, 176
Cumings, B., 254
customer–supplier relationship, 8
Cutch, Lohanes of, 60

Daily Status (DS), 276, 278
dalal merchants, 32
dalali system, 24
Dalmia, R.K., 301, 308
Darity, W.A. and P.L. Mason, 229
Das, Rajani Kanta, 210, 222, 230
Das, R.R., 227
Das, S., 267
Dasgupta, Ashin, 22, 26, 296
Dasgupta, Prabhabati, 195
Dasgupta, Ranjit, 152, 212, 215, 227
Dasnami Gossains, 60
Davar, Cowasjee, 108
Dawood, Adamji Haji, 172
Dayabhaga, 55–56
Dayanand Sarswati (Swami), 303; followers of, 304
de Albuquerque, Afonso, 27
de Las Casas, Bartolome, 204
de Soto, Hernan, 230, 245
de Tocqueville, A., 219
de Victoria, Francisco, 204
Deb, Satyasundar, 171
debt, bondage, 34, 127, 145, 146; crisis, 256; slavery, 44; *see also* bondage
dehat lands, 100
de-industrialization, 35, 46, 128, 231
democratic society, foundation of, 198
'denatured' capital and labour, 203; *see also* capital
Deoband, the Dar-ul-Ulum, 190
Descarte, Rene, 201
dialectical process, working of, 203
Dickens, Theodore, 180, 218
differentiation, process of, 124
Dighton, 53
discrimination, stigmata of, 232
Divekar, V.D., 297
Dobb, Maurice, 125, 241
Dobbin, C., 38, 309

Douglas, James, 38, 57, 58
Dualism, Formal and the Informal/Primary and Peripheral sectors, 229–33; kinds of, 202–03
dualistic growth, Lewis-type models of, 202
Dumont, L., 141; followers of, 119
Dunn, J., 205, 220
Dutch East India Company, 28
Dutt, R.C., 181
Dutt, R.P., 83
Dwarkanath's knowledge of the law, 37

East India Company, 28–35, 36, 37, 42, 43
eastern Europe, so-called 'second serfdom' in, 127
eastern India, opium production and trade in, 38
economics and property relations, 144
educational system, changes in, 144
Edwardes, S.M., 314
efficiency wages, theory of, 245
Elbaum, B.W., 207; and F. Wilkinson, 207
Elbawm, B.W. et al., 251
employer–worker relationship, 117
employment, alternative avenues of, 244; strong positive growth of, 290; relationship, 118
endogenous technical development, 95
Engels, Frederick, 208, 209, 241
Engineer, A.A., 281
England, anti-slavery agitation in, 222; Puritan Revolution in, 189
entrepreneurship, Indian cases of, 80
environmental protection, 252
equality, bourgeois notion of, 179
escape routes, three types of, 33–35
ethnic exclusion, 244
Europe, and America: *homo equalis* in, 142; feudal lords in, 79; feudalism in, 79; merchants in: guilds or associations of, 79
European Agency Houses, nominal partners of, 37
European Enlightenment and non-European superstitions, 203
European feudalism, 141

European private enterprise, patron of, 122
European trading companies, 30; records of, 28
exploitation, and ideology: modes of, 197; methods of, 141; peculiar amalgam of, 51–52
export trade, 29, 38

family behaviour, conservative codes for, 317
family groups, control of business vested in, 6–7
Faraizi movement, 190, 289; *see also* Bengal
Farruckabad coins, *toras* of, 58
Fateh Singh, 22
female emancipation, 309
Ferrier, R.W., 23
feudal system, economic theory of, 127
feudalism to capitalism, 88, 125
fiefs or rights, reciprocal grant of, 141
financial crisis (1865–67), 39
financial institutions, spread of, 40
Finley, M.I., 204
Fisher, C.H., 99
foreign capital, 94; movement and behaviour of, 250
foreign enterprises, touts of, 88
foreign expertise, unprincipled import of, 83
formal, and informal sectors, 248; sector, 245, 246
formal guild, emphasis on, 21
Foucault, 177
Fox, R.G., 122, 123, 227
France, parliamentary democracy in, 73
free peasants, 18
free social system, final flowering of, 72
free trade, 87
freedom, enlightenment philosophy of, 178
Freedom and Bondage, dualism and dialectics of, 216–29
freedom and unfreedom, duality of, 227, 228; under capitalism, 206–08
French East India Company, 28
Freund, B., 223, 231
Friedman, Milton, 87

Index

Friedmann, A., 193, 207
Friend of India, 169

G-7 countries, capitalists of, 256
Gadgil, D.R., 22; *Origins of the Modern Indian Business Class: An Interim Report*, 19
game theory, a cue from, 13
Gandhabaniks, 26
Gandhi, Indira, 306
Gandhi, Mahatma, 293, 298, 299, 300, 303, 304, 305; and the Bania practice of multiculturalism, 297–301
Gazetteer of the Bombay City and Island, 314
Gazetteer of the Bombay Presidency (1877), 40; (1884), 58; (1880), 61, 63; (1883), 52; (1901), 47
Gazetteer of the Rampur State (1911), 60
gender development index (GDI), 253
gender discrimination, 251
Genovese, E.D., 205
German idealism and *fin-de-siecle* aestheticism, 118
Germany, capitalist class in, 73
Ghosh, Jogendra Chandra, 171
Ghosh, Parimal, 89, 192, 197, 264; evidence garnered by, 185
goalas, semi-nomadic, 190
Goldie, George, 225
gomastahs, 58, 59
Gopal, 42, 44
Gopalrao Mairal, house of, 52
Gordon, A.D.D., 311
Gorky's *Mother*, 209
governance, imperatives of, 224
Gramsci, 183
Grant, John Peter, 97
Grant's Minute in Buckland, 99
Guha, Amalendu, 38, 93, 212, 227
Guha, R., 151
Gujarat, activitists in, 282; Hindu *banias* of, 300; Meshri and Shravak *banias* of, 303; *see also banias*
Gujarati, Hindus, 309; Muslims, 309; shipowning merchants, 24
Gupta, D., 312

Hadi, S.M., 107
Hamid, N., 123
handloom industry, 44; failure of, 108
Hansen, T.B., 312
Hardy, P., 267
Hari Bhakti, house of, 52
Hart, Keith, 230
Hatton, T.J. and J.G. Williamson, 249
Havell, E.B., 171
Hawthorn, G., 177
Hazari, R.K., 120
Herdeck, M. and G. Piramal, 307, 311
Heuze, G., 316
Hicks, J., 231, 246
hierarchial order, Brahmin–Kshatriya-centred, 293; code of, 292
hierarchical society, ideological basis of, 118
hierarchical subjection, relation of, 117
hierarchy and segmentation, 141
high wages, economy of, 9
Hill, Christopher, 210, 308
Hindu business communities, conservativeness of, 309; *see also* business communities
Hindu Mahasabha, 190
Hindu undivided family, ownership and inheritance within, 302; Indian Law of, 315
Hinduism as multiculturalism; evolution of, 304; Gandhi and Tagore as exponents of, 301–07
Hirschman, O., 247
Hobbes, Thomas, 179, 189
Hobsbawm, E.J., 117, 210, 244
Hobson-Jobson, 180, 181
Holmstrom, M., 212, 231
Homi, Maneck, 216
Homo equalis, ideology of, 198
Hossain, H., 108
House, Humphry, 197
human and labour rights, international surveillance of, 256
human development index (HDI), 253
Human Development Report (1998), 253
Human Rights Watch, 256
Hume, David, 189
hundis, of great bankers, 57

Hunter, W.W., 102
Hyslop, J., 233

identity politics, overt espousal of, 294
ideological apparatus, 117
ideology, substantive issues of, 289
Ignatiev, N., 221
immigrant-exclusion laws, 250
immigrant workers, plight of, 250
Imperial Gazetter of India, 54
indenture, 232
indentured labour, 222
independent merchants and artisans, fate of, 30–40
India, British business practices in, 301; British ruling class in, 197; business communities of, 20; capitalism in, 71, 84; capitalist colonialism in, 77; economic crime of, 316; finance capital and landlords in, 89; government-backed apex banking in, 113; handloom weavers in, 108; *homo hierarchicus* in, 142; indigenous banking in, 57; industrial capitalism in, 88; labour in, 227; mercantile communities in, 46–47; mercantile groups in, 19–27; nationalism in, 304; pre-British mercantile groups in, 19; pre-British social formation in, 18; pre-capitalist and capitalist production relations and ideologies, 75; private network of trust in, 11; private research and development expenditures, 12; private sector in, 16; wage labour in, 74; workers' consciousness in, 179
Indian agriculture, 88
Indian *banias,* religiosity of, 303; *see also* banias
Indian bourgeoisie, in a multicultural setting, 292–97
Indian business, exporting record of, 15
Indian business communities, 293, 294; non-competitive non-entrepreneurial characteristics of, 302; *see also* business communities
Indian businessmen, self-definition, 301

Indian capitalism, 74–77; major cradles of, 299; *see also* capitalism
Indian capitalist classes, behaviour of, 79–88; *see also* capitalist class
Indian capitalist groups, 88; exclusivist attitude of, 86
Indian capitalist-turned-collaborationists, 86
Indian Central Cotton Commitee (1921), 110
Indian cotton mill industry, 108
Indian economy, perepheralization, 127
Indian exports, growth of, 314
Indian Factory Labour Commission, 188
Indian glass industry, 94
Indian Hindu bourgeoisie, 302
Indian home market, growth of, 83
Indian industry, capitalist system of, 120
Indian Iron and Steel Co., 85
Indian labour, Marxist historians: Chakrabarty's accusation of, 178–79; socio-anthropological studies of, 212
Indian mercantile community, history of, 56
Indian merchants, and artisans, 27–30; and bankers, 298; sanctuaries of, 52–56; operations of, 19; *see also* merchants
Indian private capital, 86
Indian ruling classes, 88
Indian social system, 140
Indian society, 140, 141, 143
Indian upper-class groups, 85
indigenous development process, 96
indigenous merchants, behaviour of, 94
indigo industry, labour process in, 99
indigo manufacture, European enterprise in, 103
indigo production, as capitalist enterprise, 97–103
indigo trade, crisis in, 37
industrial capitalism, 73, 75, 89
industrial capitalists, 45, 46
industrial growth, high rate of, 83; two paths to, 78
industrial licensing, 15
industrial relations, 247

Index

industrialization, nodes of, 273; slow pace of, 125
industries, new types of, 82
inequality, aspects of, 178; origins of, 177; particular system of, 120; pre-existing systems of, 244
infant and adult mortality, 255
informal sector, 245, 246
institutional, innovations, 120; structures, 286
intermediary rights, 285
international capital, favoured destination of, 255
international capitalism, 125; spread of, 197; *see also* capitalism
International Confederation of Free Trade Unions (ICFTU), 250
International Labour Organization (ILO), 230
International Monetary Fund and the World Bank, 249
international trade, ebb and flow of, 105
'international domestic capital', 86
intra-Asian trade, 24, 29
intra-caste and intra-clan networks, 286
Ireland, British colonialism in, 217
Islam, S., 34, 37
Islamic theocracy, principles of, 190
Ismaili Khojas, 309
investment, movements of, 16
Iyengar, S., and S. Patel, 281
Iyer, R., 299

izaradars, 52
jajmani system, 143
Jajodia, Girdharilal, daughter of, 301
jakhmi hundis, 57; *see also hundis*
Jamaat-e-Islami, 305
James, C.I.R., 205
James Finlay and Co., 112
Jamshedpur Labour Association, 216
Jain, L.C., 57
Jankidevi, 301
Jejeebhoy, Jamsetji, 42
Jewish firms, 84, 85
Jinah, Mohammad Ali, 310
Jinkins, R., 297
jizyah, reimposition of, 296
jointly coercive system, 101, 102

jolahas, 191
Jomo, K.S. and V. Kanapathy, 250
Joshi, A., 65
Joshi, C., 114
jute, emergence of, 100

kabuliyats, 148
Kalathil, M., 282
Kamath, M.V., 312
Kamatis, 61, 62
Kamias, 227
Kareem, 44
Karim, A., 25
karkhanas, 27; labour processes in, 131
Kautilya, *Arthashastra*, 3
Kaye, J.W., 53
Keynes, John Maynard, 10
Khan, Ali Muhammad, 22, 25
khudkasht, ideology, 124; tenure, 268
kinship, business vested in, 6–7
Kirloskar, S.L., 315
Kiyokawa, Y., 109, 114, 115
Kling, B.B., 36, 37, 42, 120
Kolff, D.H.A., 50, 300
Kozlowski, G.C., 227
Kray, Geoffrey, 96
Kripalani, J.B., 312
Krishna Menon, V.K., 312
Kuczynski, Jurgen, 'Condition of Workers, 1880–1950', 211
Kula, Witold, 127

labour, and land control, 224; behaviour of 113; historiography of, 233; casualization of, 256; reproduction of, 233, 243;
labour control, a model of, 223; coercive methods of, 113–14, 224
labour force, so-called feminization of, 255
labour market, dualistic phenomena in, 203; passive function of, 185; rigidities, 245; regulations, 247
labour power, as a commodity, 246; increase in, 255
labour processes, nature of, 93
labour productivity, 76
labour resistance, role of, 113
labour-saving innovations, 77

Laitin, David, 189
Lala, R.M., 315
Lambert, R.D., 212
land, alienation of, 145; and the Indian Mercantile Community, 47–51; peasant proprietorship of, 83; private property in, 144
land reform, pro-peasant, 284, 290
land revenue, prompt payment of, 268
landless labourers, 18, 124
landlord, and moneylenders, 109, 272; intransigence, 15; lineages, 285; power: abolition of, 302; rent-enhancing powers of, 171
landlordism, 51, 83, 284, 285; coercive apparatus of, 113
landownership, 268
Landon, James, 108
Lardinois, Ronald, 80
large business houses, controllers of, 46
large-scale western-style plantation slavery, abolition of, 205
law of inheritance, pre-bourgeois, 55–56
Lawrence, Sir John, 157
Lazonick, W., 193, 207
Lee, E., 243, 246
Leibenstein, H., 245
Lele, J., 312, 316
Lenin, 73
lifestyles, occasional splurges in, 303
Lindauer, D.L., et al., 254
Lipietz, A., 96
literacy, lack of, 95
Little, J.H., 24, 29, 297
Littler, C., 120
L'Onverture, Toussaint, 205
'local indigo seigniories', creation of, 97
Locke, 179
Lohanas, 59, 60, 61
Lokanathan, 120
Long, D., 179
Lovejoy, P.E. and J.S. Hogendorn, 225, 226
Lugard, Frederick, 225
Lustig, N., 250

'ma-bap' relationship, 194
Macallister, Richard, 185
Mackintosh and Co., 36
Macpherson, C.B., 179, 220
Madras, demographic disasters in, 81; indigenous capitalist growth in, 82; internal structure of, 82
Madras Chamber of Commerce, 81
Mafatlal, Arvind, 307
mahajan panchayats, 21
mahajans, 57, 297
Maharashtra, Employment Guarantee Scheme in, 282–83; rural–male unemployment rates in, 282; urban unemployed males in, 283
Mahatab Chand, Jagat Seth, 22; families of, 296
Maine, Henry, 130
majoritarian despotism, 294
Malwa opium, 38, 40
'man in nature', Rousseau's view, 177–78
management–labour relations, 11
managerial economics, 3, 16
managing agency system, 120, 186
Manchester Chamber of Commerce, 80
manorial system, 127
Mao Tse-tung, 289
Maratha-Kunbi chauvinism and communalism, 312
Maratha-supremacist ideology, 312
Maratha territory, Patwardhan lordship in, 78
Marglins and Schor, 243
markets, interlocking of, 147–48
Marwaris, 54, 59, 61, 62, 63, 66, 80–82, 301
Marx, Karl, 30, 77, 78, 88, 124, 128, 177, 193, 241; and Engels, 72, 242, *Communist Manifesto*, 208; *Capital*, 17; *Grundrisse*, 207; *Theories of Surplus Value*, 17
Marxian political economy, 176
Marxist historiography, and Mind–Body dialectics, 208–10
Mason, P.L., 233
Masselos, 314
Massey, D.S., 249, 252
Mathooramohan Sein & Co., 37
McCarthy, Mary, *Groves of Academe*, 3

Index

McLane, J.R., 190, 267
medicine, *Tibbia* system of, 192
medieval India, multicuturalism and governance in, 293
Meerut Conspiracy Case, 183, 216
Mehta, M.J., 22
Mehta, Narasimha, poem by, 300
Meller, 245
Memons, 80
Mendels, F., 126
mercantile capital, 18, 93, 128
mercantile communities, behaviour and modes of, 22; enforced disarmament of, 48; internal organization of, 59
mercantile firms, initial bases for, 54
merchant capital, 89; three-fold transition from 30–31; and pre-capitalist social formations, 17–19
merchants, 74, 75, 78; and artisans, 21; behaviour of, 24–25; inter-group and intragroup cohesion: the survival value of, 57–64; life cycles of, 31; *mahajans* of, 22
Metcalf, Barbara D., 190, 192
Metcalfe, Charles, 53
Metcalfe, T.R., 65
metropolitan, capital, 94; capitalists, 93, 94, 95, 112
migrant workers, 190, 191
militant, Hinduism, 286; Hindutva, 289, 316; Islam, 289
mill barracks, wage labourers in, 46
Mill, James, 220; *Representative Government*, 220
mind and body, dualism of: and slave workers, 203–06
Mind-Body dualism and Indian historiography of Labour, 210–16
Mir Jumla, 25
mirasidars, 82, 297
Mishra, S.C., 101, 123, 126
Misra, B., 187
Mitakshara, 55–56; law, 88; system, 39, 47, 145, 284
Mitra, D.B., 33; *Neel Bidroha* or Indigo Revolt, 97
Mitra, M., 197
mobile capital and (im)mobile labour,
the web of: workers in, 249–50
modern capitalism, ideological and structural foundation of, 202
modern capitalist firms, hierarchy in, 142
modern factory system, 75
modern industry, growth of, 82
molungees, 33
moneylender and landlord, 106
monotheistic faiths, believers in, 305
Moosvi, S., 296
Mosley, P., 224
Mukerji, K., 232; *Levels of Living of Industrial Workers,* 211
Mukherjee, R.K., 211, 214, 230, 232
Mukherji, Trailokyanath, 171
multiculturalism, as belief system, 295; as private and social practice, 295; as public policy, 295; choice of stance on, 314; Gandhi and Tagore on, 305–06; gradations of, 294
multilateral investment guarantee agreement (MIGA), 250
Muslim businessmen, 311
Muslim landlords, 285; *see also* landlord
Muslim League, 190
Muslim workers, consciousness of, 189
Muslims, urbanization of, 273
Musson, 46
mutual forbearance, unwritten code of, 25–26
mutual non-cooperation, 13, 14
mutual reassurance, 14
Myrdal, Gunnar, terminology of, 78–79
Mysore, iron-smelting enterprise in, 43

nagarseths, 57; institution of, 23
Nair, J., 215, 216
Nair, T.M., Minute of the Dissent to the Report of Indian Factory Labour Commission (1908), 213
Namier, Sir Lewis, formulation of, 308
Nanda, B.R., 301
Nandi, Manindra Chandra, 171
narwadars, 144
nation-building, 241, 244
national states, 257

Native States, as sanctuaries of Indian merchants, 52–56
natural slavery, 204, 205; *see also* slavery
Neale, 47
Nehru, Jawaharlal, 293, 307
neoimperialist neo-Marxist School, 96
'new man', emergence of, 209
Nigeria, Yorubas of, 189
Nightingale, 38
nij or *zerat* cultivation, 99, 100
non-exemption debate of the 1950s, 180
'non-individualistic prebourgeois nature of identity', evidence of, 188
nonviolence, necessity of, 300
North American Free Trade Agreement (NAFTA), 250

Om Kanwar, the case of, 303
Om Prakash, 28
'one-way-free-trade', 83, 108, 185
ordinary workers, rigorous immobilization of, 249; *see also* workers
organizational patterns, diversity of, 23
Oriental Chamber of Commerce, 311
Owen, Robert, labour welfare practices of, 246

Pachhal, 194
Pagden, A., 204
Paine, Tom, *Rights of Man*, 178
Palat, R. et al., 127
Palit, C., 100
Palmer and Co., 36
panchayats, 57, 62
Pandey, G., 35, 190, 267, 293, 308
parakudis/puliyas, 227
Park, C.B., 248; and Cho, N.H., 254
Park, Y., 250
Parry, J.H., 218
Parsi, guarantee brokers, 42; merchants, 66
Parsis, 309
Pastor (Jr.), 250
Patel, S., 281
Patel, Vallabhabhai (Sardar), 311
patidars, 26, 144, 268
Patnaik, 127
patriarchy, 244; tentacles of, 208

patron–client relations, 244
patronage system, 244
Patroni, V., 248
pattas, 148
pauperization, 266, 273
Pavlov, V.I., 24; *Indian Capitalist Class*, 19–21
Pawar, Sharad, 312
Pearse, Arno, 110, 114
Pearson, M.N., 22, 25, 28
peasant differentiation, 126
peasant–*mirasidar* relations, 78
peasant revolts, potent causes of, 145
peasant–*zamindar* relations, 78
peasants and graziers, clashes between, 269
peonage, 244
'peripheral fordism', 96
Perlin, F., 126, 149
Petit, Dinshaw Manockjee, 310
Petrusewics, M., 128
photedars, 58
Pocock, J.G.A., 189, 220
Polanyi, Karal, 116
Polish feudalism, structure of, 127
political economy, 3, 4, 79, 193
political obligation, Hobbes' or Locke's theory of, 220
political patronage, importance of, 20
politics, communalization of, 287
popular culture, changes in, 144
Porter, R., 218
Portes, A. and R. Schaffler, 230, 248
potedari system, 52
poverty, incidence of, 281
power-subordination nexus, 119
Prabhu, R.K. and U.R. Rao, 300
Prakash, G., 227
Prasad, P.H., 121, 245
pre-British and colonial India, social changes in, 142
precapitalist, bonded labour, 216; culture, 196; features, 180; merchants in, 17; production relations, 74; social formations, 75, 178; social structure, 197; society: inequality in, 177
precolonial labour and society, precapitalist values of, 217

Index

precolonial slavery, formal abolition of, 128; *see also* slavery
predatory commercialization, operation of, 271–72; *see also* commercialization
predator–prey relationship, 8–9
prestations, 224
principal–sub-contractor relationship, 8
private faith, sphere of, 294–95
private goods, 4; profit-making, 266
'probabilistic discrimination', 109
procurement (*dadan*), system of, 24
production, forces of: retardation, 92; modes of, 152; techniques of, 17, 76
productive forces, retardation of, 96; underdevelopment of, 83
productive sectors, high rate of investment in, 9
productivity, growth of, 77
productivity-raising innovations, 76; *see also* innovation
profit-driven market, 208
profit-earners, separation of, 301
property, sequestration of, 25; capitalist 'trustees' of, 305; possession of, 80
property holding, Hindu joint family system of, 56
property laws, 'progressive' system of, 47
property rights, unequal disposition of, 117
protest, typical modes of, 26–27
Protestant, the role of: Weber–Sombart–Tawney problematic of, 298
'protestant ethic', statement of, 299
proto-industrialization, 149; and rural industrialization, 126
Psacharapoulos, G. and H.A. Patrinos, 251
Punekar, S.D. and R. Varickayil, 215
putting-out system, 75
pykars or *byaparis,* 23, 33, 34, 35

quasi-monopolistic structure, 186
quick money mentality, 184

racialism, 80

racially-governed system, 203
racism, 244
Radhakrishnan, Sarvepalli, 299
radical republicanism, 220
railway network, development of, 105
Rajasthan, Marwari Vaishnava *banias* of, 301; Charans or Bhats of, 59
Rajputs and Brahmins, ideology of, 102
Ralli Brothers, 39
Ramaswamy, E.A., 212
ramshila, first puja of, 87
Ranger, T.O., 223
Rao, Narasimha, 306
Rashtriya Swayamsevak Sangh (RSS), 288, 305, 316
rational management methods, 116
raw cotton, peasant production of, 108
Ray, A.K., *A Short History of Calcutta,* 164
Ray, R., 34, 48
Ray, R.K., 317
Ray, Rammohun, on the rights of Hindu over ancestral property, 55
reactionary ideology, fostering of, 89
redress, legal mechanisms of, 244
reform movements, series of, 190
regressive labour processes, 96
religion, sectarian use of, 307; simple duality of, 294
religious belief, nature of, 304; plurality of, 295
religious domination, organizational apparatus of, 307
religious practices, materiality of, 192
religious sectarianism, 304
Report of the Indigo Commission (1861), 97, 98
Report of the Royal Commission on Labour in India (1931), 191, 210
revenue farming, 48, 82, 83
revenue farming rights, 38
Ricardo, David, 77
Richards, E.P., 160, 166
Robinson, F., 190, 270*n*
Roediger, D.R., 221
Roop Kanwar, 87, 303
Rousseau, Jean Jacques, 177, 220
Roxborough, I., 244, 248
Royal Commission on Labour, 210

Roy Chowdhury, K.C., 195
Rungta, R.S., 120
Russell, Bertrand, 201
Russell, R.V. and Hiralal, 64, 300
Russia, capitalism in, 73
ryotwari land, 50
ryotwari system, 82

Sabine, G.H. and T.L. Thorson, 204, 308
Sabol, C. and J. Zeittin, 128
sahukars, 53, 297
salt production, 33
sanatana dharma, 190, 293, 303
Sandberg, L.G., 114
Sandhya, 304
Santipur, handloom weavers of, 35
Sanyal, H., 26
Sargeson, S., 256
Sarkar, J., 60
Sarkar, S., 213
Sarkar, T., 227, 267
Sassoon, Elias David, 84; firm, 84, 85
satta, a regular income form, 65
Saunders, C.B., 60
Schama, S., 218
Schatz, S.P., 109
scientific management system, 120
sea-lands, Portuguese control of, 27
secular authority, effective voice of, 303
secularism, 290, 293, 317
semi-feudal, relations, 88; social formation, 127
Sen, A., 125, 193; and B. Williams, 193
Sen, A.K., 220
Sen, Amartya, 14
Sen, S., 208
Sen, Samita, 228
Seoul Women's Trade Union, 254
Seth, Bachhraj (Wardha), 301
Seth, M.J., 23
Seth, N.R., 212
Shah Bano case, 88
sharecropping, 123, 124
Sharma, K., 316
Sharma, R.S., 303
Shepstone, Theophilus, 223
Shivaji, the cult of, 316
Shiv Sena, 312, 316

Shklar, Judith N., 177, 198
Shroff's insurance, 57
Shulman, S., 233, 251
silk production, 33
Simeon, Dileep, 216
Simon, H.A., 142, 207
Singh, D., 26
Singh, S. et al., 151
Singh, V.B., 211; 'Trade Union Movement', 211
Sinha, N.K., 33, 35, 37
Skidmore, T.E. and P.H. Smith, 244
slave-holding landlord group, 73
slave-owning family, 3
slave revolts, 205, 206
slavery, 225, 226, 227, 229
Smith, Adam, 3, 183
Smith, M.G., 204
so-called 'outsiders', 213, 214, 215, 216
social Darwinism, 282
social hierarchies, 116, 152; *see also* hierarchy
social imperialist party, 73
social inequality, evidence of, 312; *see also* inequality
social organization, coercive methods of, 95
social relation, reproduction of, 89
social security system, 285
socialism, as a system, 4
South Korean women, education of, 254
Sparks, A., 223
speculation, the role of, 64
speculative capital market, 89
speculative trade, 19
Sreenivasan, M.A., 215
state, existence of, 178; mercantilist role of, 122; nature of, 177; notion of, 179
state apparatus, 293, 295, 296, 307; connivance and collusion of, 282; post-colonial mimetic, 272; pre-capitalist and colonial, 298;
state protection, withdrawal of, 255
Statesman (The), 172
Stengers, J., 223
Stokes, E., 60, 65
structural transformation, 92
Subarnabaniks, 26

Index

Subrahmanyam, S., 296
Subramanian Swamy, 306
subordination, different degrees of, 129
Sugar Manufacture, 103–07
Sullivan, R.J.E., 38
Surat, leading Muslim merchants, 296
surplus, limited domestic investment of, 122; one-way flow of, 20; colonial extraction of, 146
surplus extraction, methods of, 141
surplus labour, proportion of, 76
Swatantra Party, 311
Sweezy, Paul, 125
syncretic religious belief-system, 305; see also religious belief, belief systems
Szreter, S., 249, 252

Tabb, W.K. and L. Sawers, 233
Tagore, Dwarkanath, 42
Tagore, Rabindranath, 304; *Gora*, 305
Taiyuni movements, 190
Taknet, D.B., 315
talukdars, 49, 51, 297
Tamil Nadu, Nadars of, 80
tariqah movement, 190
Tata, J.R.D., 315
Tata Iron and Steel Company, workers of, 216
Tawney, R.H., 308
tax farmers, 24
Taylorism, 120
technical change, 92, 93–94, 95, 113, 114
techniques, choice of, 113
technology, imports of, 11–12
Teetabadli, makers of *tanjeebs* at, 35
Telis, 26
Temple, R., 60
thika and *mukarrai* tenure, 101
Third World, fortunes of labour in, 244–48
Thompson, E.P., 53, 189, 213, 218, 231; influence of, 212; *The Making of the English Working Class*, 210
Thomson and Myline, 107
Thorner, Daniel, 141
Thurston, E. and K. Rangachari, 62
Tilly, C. and R. Tilly, 126

Timberg, T.A., 50, 54, 64, 308
Times of India Directory and Almanac, 84
Tinker, H., 182, 222, 227
Tipu versus capitalist colonialism, 41–46
Tipu's trade policies, 42
Tod, J., 59, 140
Todd, J.A., 109
town planning regulations, 160
trade-related investment measures (TRIMS), 250
Trade Union Act (1926), 183
trade union movements, 183
trade unionism, 286, 316
trader and cultivator, nexus between, 109
trader lineages, 285
transition, unequal development and underdevelopment, 125–31
transnational capital, dominance of, 83
transnational corporations, rise of, 256
transoceanic trade, European aggrandizement of, 296; see also trade
tribute, transaction costs of, 146
tribute-extraction, 266
Trivedi, P.K., 64
trust, 4, 5, 13; network of, 6–9
Tully, J., 189

ulama, communalist ideology of, 270
ulmas' movement, 270
umma, 289
underemployment, endemic, 244
unemployment, seasonal, 244; urban, 281
uneven development, 243, 251
unfreedom, structures of, 221; precapitalist forms of, 208; constraints of, 232
Union Bank, fall of, 37
universal adult suffrage, basis of, 117
universal literacy, 290
UNRISD, 252, 256
unskilled labour, wages of, 232; see also labour
untouchability, practices of, 229
untouchables, 287
Upadhyay, Brahmabandhab, 304

Upadhyay, S.B., 213
Upadhyay, S.S., 314
urban India, tensions in 313
urban–rural distribution of populations, the data on, 273
urbanization, 20, 252, 276
Urry, J., 120
Usual Principal Status (UPS) criterion, 276, 279
usury, 51, 127; capital, 19

Vagrancy Act, 226
Vaid, S. and K. Sangari, 303
Vaishnava sect, Vallabhacharya of, 300
Vaishyas, 84
Vallabhacharya sect, 303
value, labour theory of, 202
Van Leur, J.C., formulation of, 20–21
varnasrama dharma, 142, 143; Mahatma Gandhi's espousal of, 301
Vasco Da Gama, 296
Veeraghavan, D. and T. Thankappan, 215
village economy, monetization in, 268
Vishwa Hindu Parishad (VHP), 288, 305, 306
Volkart Brothers, 39
Vora, Virjee, 22

Wade (Col.), 58–59
Wadia, Ardeseer Cursetjee, 42
Wadia, Neville, 310
wage-labour, 124, 143
Walchand Brothers, 311
Walker (Col.), 52
Wallerstein, Immanuel, 127
Warren, Bill, 96
Washbrook, D., 119, 122
Watson, I.B., 28
Watt, G., 105
weavers, the case of, 266–67
Weber, Max, 298, 299
Weekly Status (WS), 276
welfare economics, 193
Welsh, D., 223
West African Frontier Force, 225
western capitalism, impulsive forces of, 299; *see also* capitalism
western India, Indian merchants in 38–39; *see also* Indian merchants
Whitcombe, E., 100
white sugar, production of, 106
Wilkinson, F., 207
William Palmer and Co., 53
Williamson, O., 118, 142
Wilson, H.H., 60
Wollstonecroft, Mary, 178
Wolpert, S., 310
women, in the maelstrom of competition, 252–54; special position of, 284
Woo-Cumings, M.J., 254
Wood, A., 256
Woodruff, W., 249
Worden, N., 223
worker, and employer: binary relations of, 119; as fancy-free beings, 202; management relations, 118
workers, class of, 206; double disability of, 234; under capitalism, 255–57; white superiority on, 186
workers' consciousness, 189, 211, 212, 216; *see also* consciousness
workforce, casualisation of, 277; female participation rate in, 280
working class, 72, 245; bargaining strength of, 83; history of, 176; ideology of, 71; oversimplified model of, 179; segmentation of, 241;
working class culture, 195
Working Class Differentiation, Social Reproduction of Stigmata of, 251–52
'World-system' school, 96, 127
World Trade Organization (WTO), 250

Yadav, 303
Yang, Anand A., 190, 197

zamindari, rights, 25–26, 49, 50, 51; system, 83
zamindars, 26, 35, 82, 102, 297
zamindars vis-à-vis peasants, 102
zamindars vis-à-vis planters, 102
Zeitlin, J., 207
Zeng Yi et al., 254
Zia-ul-Haq, 265

www.ingramcontent.com/pod-product-compliance
Lightning Source LLC
Chambersburg PA
CBHW052049230426
43671CB00011B/1839